European Language Matters

Why do Greek lorries have *Metaphorés* written on the side? Is it grammatically correct to say 'the best team won' after a football match? What is the difference between *manly*, *male*, *masculine* and *macho*? Bringing together Peter Trudgill's highly popular columns for the *New European*, this fascinating collection explores how English has been influenced, both linguistically and culturally, by its neighbouring languages in Europe. English is very much a European language and Trudgill delves into the rich linguistic legacy that links all European languages. The bite-sized pieces are grouped together in thematically arranged sections, to allow the reader to dip in and out at will, and cover a wide range of topics, from the etymology of words, to illuminating pieces on grammar. Written in an engaging and lively style, and full of intriguing facts about language and languages in Europe, this book will appeal to both language specialists and to general readers with no prior experience.

PETER TRUDGILL is a theoretical dialectologist who is the author of *Dialects in Contact* (1986), *Sociolinguistic Typology* (2011) and *Investigations in Sociohistorical Linguistics* (2010). He has Honorary Doctorates from the Universities of Uppsala, East Anglia, La Trobe, British Colombia and Patras.

European Language Matters

English in Its European Context
Columns from the *New European*

PETER TRUDGILL
University of Fribourg

CAMBRIDGE
UNIVERSITY PRESS

CAMBRIDGE
UNIVERSITY PRESS

University Printing House, Cambridge CB2 8BS, United Kingdom

One Liberty Plaza, 20th Floor, New York, NY 10006, USA

477 Williamstown Road, Port Melbourne, VIC 3207, Australia

314–321, 3rd Floor, Plot 3, Splendor Forum, Jasola District Centre,
New Delhi – 110025, India

103 Penang Road, #05–06/07, Visioncrest Commercial, Singapore 238467

Cambridge University Press is part of the University of Cambridge.

It furthers the University's mission by disseminating knowledge in the pursuit of
education, learning, and research at the highest international levels of excellence.

www.cambridge.org
Information on this title: www.cambridge.org/9781108832960
DOI: 10.1017/9781108966498

© Peter Trudgill 2022

First published 2022

A catalogue record for this publication is available from the British Library.

Library of Congress Cataloging-in-Publication Data
Names: Trudgill, Peter, author.
Title: European language matters : English in its European context : columns from the New
European / Peter Trudgill.
Other titles: New European.
Description: Cambridge, United Kingdom ; New York, NY : Cambridge University Press, 2022. |
Includes bibliographical references and index.
Identifiers: LCCN 2021024827 (print) | LCCN 2021024828 (ebook) | ISBN 9781108832960
(hardback) | ISBN 9781108966498 (ebook)
Subjects: LCSH: English language – Etymology. | Europe – Languages – Influence on English. |
Languages in contact – Europe. | BISAC: LANGUAGE ARTS & DISCIPLINES / Linguistics /
Historical & Comparative | LANGUAGE ARTS & DISCIPLINES / Linguistics / Historical &
Comparative
Classification: LCC PE1574 .T83 2021 (print) | LCC PE1574 (ebook) | DDC 422–dc23
LC record available at https://lccn.loc.gov/2021024827
LC ebook record available at https://lccn.loc.gov/2021024828

ISBN 978-1-108-83296-0 Hardback
ISBN 978-1-108-96592-7 Paperback

Contents

Prologue

English is very much a European language, as the story of its origins shows. These origins lie rather long ago chronologically, but not particularly far away geographically. It was more than 1,500 years ago that boatloads of Germanic people started crossing the North Sea to the eastern shores of Britain. But they had not come from very far away. The Germanic people who arrived were mostly members of the tribal groupings we now refer to as the Jutes, Angles, Saxons and Frisians, who had resided mainly in coastal districts just across the North Sea from Britain.

The Jutes had originally come from the furthest north, from northern and central Jutland, now part of Denmark. The Angles lived in areas to the south of them in southern Jutland and Schleswig-Holstein. The Saxons were located to the west of them, along the North Sea coastal areas of northern Germany in the Elbe–Weser region. And the Frisians came from Friesland, the area of coastline between the homeland of the Saxons and the mouth of the River Rhine in the modern Netherlands. The great estuaries of the English east coast – such as the Humber, the Wash, the estuary of the Stour and the Orwell at Harwich and the Thames Estuary – formed major entry points into Britain for many of these people.

Of these Germanic tribes, it was the Saxons who eventually gave their name to the areas of southern England known as Wessex, Sussex, Middlesex and Essex, the names referring respectively to the West, South, Middle and East Saxons. In these Saxon-dominated areas of England, we find a few toponyms which indicate rather clearly that most people in Wessex were not Angles, such as the settlement of Englefield, now in Berkshire, which meant the 'field of the Angles', and Englebourne, 'stream of the Angles', in Devon.

There were also Frisians around, as we can see from the Suffolk village names Friston and Freston, 'homestead of the Frisians', as well as from the name Frisby in Leicestershire. But most of non-Saxon England and south-eastern Scotland came to be dominated by Angles. In these Anglian zones, there are still to this day village names such as Saxham, 'home of the Saxons', near Bury St Edmunds, and Saxton, 'homestead of the Saxons', in North Yorkshire: these villages were obviously so called because there was something unusual about being a Saxon in Suffolk and Yorkshire.

Although Essex and Middlesex and Sussex were named after the Saxons, it was the Angles who had the honour of eventually giving their name to England, 'the land of the Angles', and to the English language. But why were they called Angles?

We first hear about them from the Roman historian Tacitus (c. AD 56–120) in his work *Germania*, on the Germanic tribes. They seem to have come originally from the area of Germany which is known as Angeln, a peninsula located on the eastern coast of Schleswig-Holstein, on the Baltic Sea. Angeln lies between the Flensburg Firth, which today forms part of the border between Denmark and Germany, and the Schlei Inlet, which leads from the Baltic Sea to the town of Schleswig. Almost everybody from the Angeln area seems to have emigrated to Britain in the fifth century AD.

There are different theories about the origin of the name *Angeln*. It could be derived from the word which has come down into modern German as *eng*, 'narrow', referring perhaps to the narrow waters of the Schlei Inlet. Or it could be related to *angle* 'bend, corner', or to *angling* as in fishing: *angle* in the fishing sense originally referred to the bent or angled implement fishermen use for catching fish on a line. It would be rather amusing to think that, ultimately, the name of our now world-dominating language was derived from a simple word meaning 'fish-hook'.

English, then, is very much a language *from* Europe. But in the modern world it is also very much a language *of* Europe. Over the last millennium and a half, from these origins in a rather small area of Germania, English has become a language of European-wide importance. There are countless examples of this one could cite. When Finnish tourists get off the plane in Athens, they do not expect to find Finnish-speaking Greeks, but they do expect to be able to communicate in English. In official EU meetings in Brussels and Strasbourg, simultaneous translation is used; but when an Estonian MEP has a quiet chat in the corridor with one of their Slovenian counterparts, or a Latvian official wants to buttonhole an Italian, it is almost certain that they will speak English to each other. At the European Football Championships, a Portuguese full back may shout at a Bulgarian referee, but what language is he shouting in? If he wishes the referee to understand what he is saying, it is certainly more likely to be English than anything else. English is the default language for international communication in most parts of Europe.

Of all the European nations, only two – Ireland and the UK – are inhabited mainly by native English speakers; and in only two other countries, Cyprus and Malta, is English an important language of internal communication. There are more native speakers of German than of English in Europe, but German still plays nothing like the same kind of international role.

This has had some effect on the language itself. The EU has published a document called 'Misused English Words and Expressions in EU Publications'. One of the words they cite is *actorness*, which seems to mean 'the quality of being an actor', an actor being a person or organisation involved in doing something.

Even in our everyday lives, English has been influenced by its role in Europe. Although I was studying A-level French in the 1960s, I had no idea what *tranche* meant. If I had looked it up in my dictionary, it would have said 'slice' – as in cake. But now most people know this word: the first instance in English of *tranche* comes from 1963, and since then it has become a normal English term for an instalment of a payment.

It is not surprising that English, in its turn, has influenced European languages. Fascinatingly, some of the English words which continental languages have adopted are not really English at all – like *actorness*. The German for a mobile phone is *ein Handy*. The French for a dinner jacket is *un smoking*. The same sort of thing happens in reverse. If you ask for a *latte* in London, you will get a cup of coffee. If you do the same in Milan, you might get a glass of milk, but there is no guarantee at all that you will be served a coffee.

English is very useful as a European lingua franca – a means of communication which can be used between speakers who have no native language in common. Even though Europe is the least multilingual continent in the world, it is still far from monolingual. The twenty-six countries that make up the EU do not actually have twenty-six major languages between them, because some countries share a language: German in Germany, Austria and Luxembourg; French in France and Belgium; Dutch in Belgium as well as Holland; Greek in Cyprus and Greece. But Europe also has very many minority languages, of varying sizes: at the extremes, Catalan has millions of speakers, while the Pite Sami (Lappish) language of northern Scandinavia has only about twenty; and there is a long list of languages which come demographically in between – North Sami, Romany, Basque, Breton, Welsh, Gaelic, Frisian, Romansh, etc.

People who are keen on European solidarity will be glad to know that, with a few exceptions, all of these languages descend from a single parent language known as Indo-European. The major exceptions are Finnish, Estonian, Sami and Hungarian, which are all related to one another; Turkish; Maltese, which is historically a variety of Arabic; and the pre-Indo-European language Basque, which may well once have been spoken over the whole of Western Europe, in which case there was probably no need for a European lingua franca in 5000 BC. Now there is, and English is fulfilling this role.

This has nothing to do with the qualities of the English language itself. It is a historical accident. English became the world language for economic, military and political – not linguistic – reasons. The situation came about as a result of the British Empire's many decades of economic and political domination of the world from the eighteenth century onwards and, later, the same kind of dominance as exercised by the USA, which had itself become English-speaking as a result of colonisation by the British Empire.

Introduction

In the preparation of these columns, the first of which appeared in print in July 2016, my remit from the *New European* newspaper has been to write about language and languages in Europe. This has not at all meant that I have never written about other parts of the world, but it does mean that each column has at least some connection with at least one language of European origin. Although the focus is very much on Europe, the columns have been written by an Englishman who lives in England and is a native speaker of English; so when I write 'we', I often mean English speakers; and when I write 'in this country', I mean England, or Great Britain, or the United Kingdom.

This book collects together four years' worth of my weekly columns. It can obviously be read, if desired, from beginning to end, but the columns are all free-standing; some facts and figures are repeated from one column and another; and the pieces have been grouped together in thematic sections, which will also make for easier browsing if that is the preferred approach. Many of the pieces are accompanied by a box containing a short discussion of a particular word which occurs in that article.

*

I am very grateful to Jasper Copping and the other Archant staff at the *New European* in Norwich for their original invitation to contribute to the journal, and for their continuing support.

I am also particularly grateful to the very large number of linguistic scientists who have helped me in the writing of these columns by supplying information, examples and corrections. I have been working as an academic linguist for five decades now, and over that period of time I have been fortunate enough to come to know a very large number of experts around the world in the many different areas of linguistics and language study. Since I started writing these columns, I have constantly been plaguing these unfortunate colleagues for confirmation and information; and the wonderful thing has been that if they did not know the answers to my questions themselves, they were almost certain to know somebody who did. Many of the columns in this book I would never have dared to publish without first checking facts with, and obtaining examples from, one or more of these kind contacts, including also personal friends who I have consulted in their capacity as native speakers of a particular language which I needed information on, or as experts on other topics, such as botany. They have all been extremely generous with their time and erudition. I hope they have not minded too much that I have been so irritatingly demanding.

The list of people whose brains I have unscrupulously picked in this way is exceedingly long, and I am most grateful to all of them. They are:

Anders Ahlqvist, Ulrike Altendorf, Enam Al-Wer, Margrethe Heidemann Andersen, Lars-Gunnar Andersson, Eleni Antonopoulou, Peter Arkadiev, Amalia Arvaniti, Peter Bakker, Raphi Berthele, David Britain, Bettina von Bonin, Keith Brown, Ranko Bugarski, Andy Butcher, Juan Manuel Hernández Campoy, Cathy Carmichael, Magdalena Charzyńska-Wójcik, Donna Christian, Jan Chromý, Bernard Comrie, Jeroen Darquennes, Gunther De Vogelaer, Kai Artur Diers, Stefan Dollinger, Yvonne Droeschel, Martin Durrell, Kasia Dziubalska-Kołaczyk, Pinar Elman, Michael Elmentaler, Jan Terje Faarlund, Luna Filipović, Daniele Franceschi, Victor Friedman, Piotr Gąsiorowski, Mike Garman, Elizabeth Gordon, John Hajek, Ian Hancock, Jack Hawkins, Kaisa Rautio Helander, Ray Hickey, Michael Hitchcock, Jan Hognestad, David Hornsby, Arthur Hughes, Ernst Håkon Jahr, Mark Janse, Lars Johanson, Ian Jones, Mari Jones, Mike Jones, Brian Joseph, Jeff Kallen, Kathleen Keeler, Paul Kerswill, Agnieszka Kielkiewicz-Janowiak, David King, Jacob King, Jussi Klemola, Miklós Kontra, Maarten Kossmann, Nils Langer, Roger Lass, Martin Maiden, Anthony Mortimer, Andreas Musolff, Terttu Nevalainen, Johanna Nichols, Hans Frede Nielsen, Andy Pawley, Ralph Penny, Marcel Pouplier, Dennis Preston, Tom Priestley, Andrew Radford, Marianne Rathje, Don Reindl, Gijsbert Rutten, John Sandford, Sue Sandford, Klára Sándor, Peter Schrijver, Maria Sifianou, Patrick Sims-Williams, Malcolm Spencer, Domhnall Uilleam Stiùbhart, Deborah Tannen, Stephen Trudgill, Willy Van Haver, Wim Vandenbussche, Nigel Vincent, Rik Vosters, Alastair Walker, John Wells, Max Wheeler, Henry Widdowson, David Willis, Ilse Wischer and Laura Wright.

It is also rather likely that I have forgotten quite a number of people who I should have thanked, and if so I apologise to them. But there is one person who there is absolutely no danger of me forgetting to thank for her vital contribution to this book, and this is my wife, Jean Hannah, who I am most enormously grateful to for the brilliant way in which she has used her linguistic knowledge, and her first-class editorial skills, to refine and improve every single one of the pieces which now appear in these pages.

1 Words

The origins of English amongst the Germanic peoples of northern Europe, as described in the Prologue, explain why English is classified as a member of the Germanic language family and is, specifically, a West Germanic language. Much of its basic vocabulary is shared with the other West Germanic languages such as Dutch and German, including words for the numbers from *one* to a *thousand*; basic body parts like *hand, arm, foot, finger, toe* and *eye*; and the terms for the primary family relatives, *father, mother, brother, sister, son* and *daughter* – though the words *uncle, aunt, nephew, niece* and *cousin* are French in origin.

But of all the words in the *Shorter Oxford Dictionary*, only 27 per cent are Germanic in origin, and many hundreds of those are not West Germanic but North Germanic – Old Norse. Most of the rest, though by no means all, are from other European languages. Around 28 per cent of our English words come from French, with another 28 per cent derived from Latin; and a total of about 15 per cent are from Ancient Greek, Italian, Dutch and German.

Of course, these numbers apply to words as they appear in the dictionary, not to the vocabulary we actually use in our everyday lives: the majority of our most frequently used words, like *the, and* and *but*, come from West Germanic Old English stock, and most of the other words we utter over the course of a day are English in origin.

Latin vocabulary has been entering the English lexicon for many hundreds of years, starting with words for sophisticated portable items which the Romans had but we lacked, such as *wine* and *tile*. The influence of Latin as the international language of learning then continued for centuries, with English acquiring scores of words ranging from *abdomen* and *arduous*, to *ubiquity* and *ulterior*.

Ancient Greek, as we shall see in this chapter, has also provided us with a great deal of our learned vocabulary – *amnesia, iconoclast, heptagon* and *synergy* are but a few examples – and numerous more ordinary words, such as *athlete, energy* and *helicopter*. As we shall also see, English has a number of Greek–Latin doublets such as *sympathy–compassion, hypodermic–subcutaneous* and *synchronous–contemporary*.

There are more than 1,500 words of Old Norse origin in Modern English (and more than that in the local dialects of the north and east of Britain). These include common everyday items like *angry, egg, flat, gasp, get, guess, hit, ill, knife, leg, lift, low, same, sick, scare, take, tight* and *window* – and, perhaps surprisingly, the pronouns *they, their* and *them*. Many Norse words actually replaced their Old

English equivalents: our original word for 'egg' was *ey* (the Modern Dutch word is *ei*). In some cases, though, we have retained words from both language sources, with a small difference in meaning. Doublets of this kind include Norse *skirt* alongside Old English *shirt*, and Norse *disk* versus English *dish*.

Very many of our French-origin words came into English via Norman French, after 1066. These were typically words having to do with government and war — the word *government* itself, *court*, *crown*, *state*; and *battle*, *enemy*, *lance* and *castle*. The Normans also introduced many religious words such as *faith*, *saint* and *mercy*, as well as vocabulary dealing with art and fashion: *beauty*, *figure*, *dress* and *garment*. Some Norman French words have become very much entrenched in our language as part of our normal way of speaking: *just*, *very*, *people*, *face*, *place*, *piece*, *easy*, *strange*. Sometimes Norman words did not replace English ones but relegated them to a more lowly or informal status, so we have pairs such as Norman *chair* versus English *stool*, *aid* versus *help*, *conceal* versus *hide*. Famously, the upper-class Normans also provided us with vocabulary for food such as *beef*, *pork*, *joint*, *cutlet*, *dinner* and *supper*, while we retained more proletarian English words like *oxtail*, *tongue*, *brains* and *breakfast*.

Sometimes we took a word from Norman French and then, later, also from Parisian French. The English language contains doublets such as Norman *warden* versus Parisian *guardian*, *catch* versus *chase*, *cattle* and *chattel*, *warranty* and *guarantee*, *reward* and *regard*. Parisian *guichet*, a word which came into English in the 1800s, refers to a hatch which tickets are issued through, but in origin it is the same word as the Norman-origin form *wicket*, which arrived in English in the early 1300s. More recent French imports include *brochure*, *baton*, *ballet*, *bizarre*, *brusque* and *beret*.

And we should not forget other less prominent European languages which have also contributed to our lexicon. Romani has given us the words *pal*, *cushy* and *lollipop*, amongst others. And Yiddish, the German-derived language of the East European Jews, has contributed items such as *glitch*, *nosh*, *schmaltz* and *schnozz*.

In this chapter, we look at only a very small selection, albeit hopefully a particularly interesting one, of English vocabulary items, as well as words from many other languages.

1.1 Manly, Male, Masculine, Macho

You sometimes hear it said that English has more words than other languages. But what does it imply for a language to 'have' a word? Is it enough for that word to exist in a dictionary somewhere? If so, English certainly does very well on the lots-of-words front: the *Oxford English Dictionary* contains over 600,000 words. But this is really due more than anything else to the diligence of the Oxford lexico-graphers, the length of time they have been working on the dictionary (over 160 years), and the time-depth of the forms of the English language they have been studying (going back well over 1,000 years).

It is safe to say, too, that very few native speakers of English actually know even a small percentage of that number of the words. Looking at a sequence of forty words beginning with B in the *OED*, I found that I had never heard of fifteen of them, even though I am perhaps professionally obliged to know more about words than most other people. No doubt some readers of the *New European* will know what *baccated* means – 'berried, berry-bearing' – but I most certainly did not.

It is true, though, that English has over the centuries borrowed very many words from other – mainly European – languages, and that as a consequence it seems to have quite a number of sets of near-synonyms which correspond to single words in other languages. The example which is always cited in student textbooks is the triplet formed by *regal, royal* and *kingly*. My German dictionary gives *königlich* as a possible translation for all of these, although there are other possible German words as well; and my French dictionary similarly comes up with *royal* for all three.

The three English words are not totally synonymous, although their meanings are, of course, closely related. *Kingly* is the original Germanic-origin form. It derives from Old English *cyning*, 'king', which has been part of our language ever since there was such a language. *Kingly* corresponds to German *königlich*, Dutch *koninklijk* and Swedish *kunglig*.

Royal came into English from outside the Germanic language family. It was borrowed from the Anglo-Norman tongue which arrived in England in 1066; the word is first attested in English from about 1400. *Royal* is the Old French descendant of the Latin word *regalis*, from *rex*, 'king', altered through processes of sound change over the centuries – the Catalan is *reial* and the Spanish *real*. But Old French also borrowed *regalis* directly from Latin in the form of *regal*, which was in its turn also borrowed into English.

The way the English language has expanded its European-origin vocabulary over the centuries gives us many other similar examples of near-synonyms. *Male* is the relatively neutral English word which does duty as the opposite of *female* – the *OED* has a very nice technical definition of *male*: 'of the sex which can beget, but not bear, offspring'. Like *royal*, this word came originally from Latin (from *masculus*, 'male'), but it was borrowed into English from the Anglo-Norman descendant of this Latin word, *masle*. Our word *masculine*, on the other hand, was taken into English directly from the Latin. It is a more semantically loaded word than *male*: English speakers are very aware of the difference between the meanings of *maleness* and *masculinity*. A perhaps even more loaded term is the word *manly*. This, like *kingly*, comes from our original native stock of Germanic words. German *männlich* simply means 'male', but *manly* means a lot more than just that. A related and even less neutral English word is *macho*, which did not enter into written (originally American) English to any extent until the 1960s, when it was borrowed from

Spanish, where it is simply a word meaning *male*. It, too, has its origin in the Latin word *masculus*.

The fact is that, while some of our compatriots may currently be trying to reject their European Union citizenship, they would find it impossible to reject their European vocabulary.

VIRILE

The original meaning of Old English *man* was 'human being' – which is why we also find this element in *woman*. The ancient word for 'man' was *wer*, with the same origin as Latin *vir*, 'man'. We have now lost *wer*, except in *werewolf*, but we have borrowed the Latin equivalent in words like *virile* and *virility*.

1.2 Boys and Girls

Some categories of words seem to be much more stable over the centuries than others. The Germanic words for female and male offspring, *daughter* and *son*, have hardly changed over two millennia. English *daughter* corresponds to Scots, Frisian and Dutch *dochter*, German *Tochter*, Danish and Norwegian *datter*, Swedish *dotter*, Norwegian *dåtter*, Faroese and Icelandic *dóttir*. Similarly, the equivalents of English *son* are Frisian *soan*, Dutch *zoon*, German *Sohn*, Danish *søn*, Norwegian *sønn*, Swedish *son* and Faroese and Icelandic *sonur*. Philologists agree that these words go back to ancient Germanic *duhter* and *sunuz*; and in fact they go back even further – something like 6,000 years – to ancient Indo-European *dhugheter* and *suhnu*.

Compare this with the numerous changes which have happened to our everyday words for young people generally. In English, the most common word for a young female human being is *girl*. But in the north of Britain *lass* and *lassie* are extremely common; and until relatively recently the East Anglian word was *mawther*, with *maid* and *wench* being normal in different parts of western England. The Frisian word for girl is *famke*, the Norwegian is *jente*, the Danish is *pige*, the Swedish *flicka* and the Icelandic *stelpa*. The Faroese *genta* does show a resemblance to the Norwegian; and we can see a relationship between *maid*, German *Mädchen* and Dutch *meisje*; but the variation is considerable compared to *daughter*.

The English word *girl* itself is rather tricky in other ways, too. It didn't appear in English until about 1300, when it seems to have referred to both males and females. And nobody knows for sure where the word came from. Some experts think there may have been an Old English word *gyrela* meaning 'dress', in which case *girl* may represent a jocular usage, rather like the slang form *skirt* for 'girl'. Others believe it was a late mediaeval borrowing from Low German *gör*, 'small child': there is a Modern German word *Göre* which means 'cheeky little girl'– but then there is the problem of where did the *l* come from?

There has also been some ideological discussion in recent decades in the English-speaking world about the usage of *girl* to refer to adults, the argument being that it is demeaning to refer to people over the age of majority by using a word for a child. In fact, the normal meaning of *girl* in most contexts in Modern English, as the *Oxford English Dictionary* states, is precisely that of 'a young or relatively young woman'. A female child would most normally be referred to as a 'little girl', and a young teenager as a 'young girl'. Most native English speakers, if told that a woman was coming to see them, would be rather surprised if, when she arrived, she turned out to be eighteen.

The English word *boy* shows an almost equally varied set of correspondences: *dreng* in Danish, *gutt* in Norwegian, *pojke* in Swedish, *strákur* in Icelandic – though admittedly Dutch *jongen*, Frisian *jonge* and German *Junge* present a more united front. The word *boy*, too, is mysterious; no one is very sure where it came from. Like *girl*, it arrived in English around 1300. Its original meaning was 'male servant', reminding us of French *garçon* meaning 'boy' but also 'waiter'. Danish *dreng* also used to mean 'servant'. There is a suggestion that *boy* came from Anglo-Norman *emboyé*, 'in chains', from Latin *boia*, 'leg iron', hence 'slave, servant'. But it could have been borrowed from Frisian, Dutch or Low German. Nobody really knows.

So, while we are entirely sure about the origins of words like *daughter* and *son* which are thousands of years old, we are not at all sure about a couple of words which arrived only 600 years ago.

Why is this? Maybe words for boys and girls vary and change more than others because they so often originate in colloquial or humorous nicknames and endearments.

KID

The original meaning of *kid* was 'a young goat'. It came into English from Old Norse. The related German *Kitz* most often means 'fawn, young deer', but can also be 'young goat'. *Kid* started being used as a jocular word for a child in the sixteenth century, and became established as a common and increasingly less informal word during the 1800s.

1.3 Madam

It is often the fate of words and phrases, over the millennia, to get shorter and shorter. The Latin phrase *hoc die*, 'this day' famously became so shortened in French – as *hui* 'today' – that French speakers increased its length again by saying *au-jour-d'hui*, literally 'on the day of this day'. Modern French *août*, 'August', pronounced 'oo', comes from Latin *augustum*. English *going to* is now very often simply *gonna*. There used to be five separate sounds in *knight*: *k*, *n*, *i*, *h* and *t*, but now it only has three. *Or* is a reduced form of *other*, and *but* was originally *be-utan*. In Old English, *forty* was *feowertig*.

In some parts of the USA it is not altogether uncommon – or at least it used not to be – for people to respond to a question, request or instruction on the part of an adult female speaker by responding 'Yes'm!' That *'m* is a short, weakened, unstressed form of *ma'am* – a word which you hear rather more frequently as a polite form of address in the USA than on this side of the Atlantic. (It can be very useful for attracting a woman's attention if, say, you notice she has just dropped something. Over here we might find ourselves using rather more awkward strategies such as calling out 'Excuse me!' or 'Hey!')

Ma'am seems to have first come into use in English in the late 1600s; it is in its turn an abbreviated form of *madam*, which until about 1600 had generally been spelt *madame* and was pronounced with the stress on the second syllable, 'ma-DAHM'. This is what you might expect of a word borrowed from French, where stress, insofar as there is any at all, occurs on the last syllable – Americans still pronounce many French-origin words like *debris*, *ballet*, *garage* and *beret* with the stress at the end. The pronunciation of *madame*, however, was gradually anglicised to MADD'm, with the stress on the first syllable (the letter *e* was also generally dropped from the spelling). *Madam* then acquired the shortened form, *ma'am*, as a term of address.

The original French word which was the source of these forms had originally been two separate words: *ma dame*, meaning 'my lady'. This is parallel to the Italian term *ma donna* > *madonna*. Both the French and the Italian forms are derived from the Latin *mea domina*, which had the same meaning. So in the American address-form *'m*, all that remains of the nine vowels and consonants of the original Latin phrase *mea domina* is the second *m*-sound – a loss of 89 per cent!

The male equivalent of *madam* is, of course, *sir*. This has no connection with *dominus*, the masculine equivalent of *domina*, but is instead derived from Old French *sire*, which came from an earlier form *sieire*, from Late Spoken Latin *seior*. This was a reduced version of the Classical Latin adjective *senior*, 'older, elder', the comparative form of *senex*, 'old'. We have since borrowed the words *senior* and *seniority* into English directly; *senex* is also the source of the words *senile*, *senility*, *senescent*, *senator* and *senate*.

The use of *senior* as a noun has also given us the well-known terms of respectful address used to men in the modern Romance languages, equivalent to *sir* or *Mr*: Portuguese *senhor*, Spanish *señor*, Catalan *senyor*, Italian *signor*. The *-sieur* part of the Modern French word *monsieur* has the same origin.

When I was at my all-male secondary school in the 1950s and '60s, we were expected to address all our teachers as *sir*. We were so well trained in this that any utterance which passed our lips when talking to a schoolmaster ended in this word, pronounced rapidly and in very reduced form. For us, all that was left of the original Latin word *senior* was the very brief syllable *suh*.

SENATE

Deriving its name from the Latin word *senex*, 'old', the original Senate of Ancient Rome was the 'council of old men'. The point was, of course, that age and wisdom went together. These days we can wonder how valid it still is to suppose that the US Senate is truly a 'council of the wise' as opposed to just the old.

1.4 Awesome

'Cash or card?' the boy at the checkout asked me. 'Cash', I said. 'Awesome!', he replied.

Awesome used to mean 'inspiring a feeling of solemn and reverential wonder'. As employed by many English speakers today, however, its most usual meaning has been weakened to the extent that it can now simply mean something like 'very good'. Certainly, most of the connections to the original meaning of *awe* have been lost. Most English speakers today would have to say *awe-inspiring* in order to recapture the original meaning of *awe-some*.

This kind of weakening is a fate which commonly befalls evaluative words: the more they are used, the less impact they make. *Awful* has gone through the same process. And if someone says my handwriting is *terrible*, that just means that they think it is not very legible, not that it inspires terror.

Historically, the *awe-* bit of *awesome* comes from ancient Germanic *agiz*, 'fear'. But what about the *-some* part? This is also a very venerable part of our linguistic heritage: our ancestral Old English language had a suffix *-sum* which was used to form adjectives from nouns, verbs and other adjectives. Twelve hundred years ago, *langsum* meant 'enduring', and *hearsum* signified 'obedient'. Old English *wynsum* still survives in Modern English as *winsome*, but rather few *-some* words in use today date from the Old English period. A number of modern words ending in *-some* have been around for quite a long time though: *loathsome* dates from 1200, and *wholesome* from the 1400s. And we have many other adjectives in Modern English which are formed with this suffix, ranging from *irksome, burdensome, loathsome, fearsome, wearisome, quarrelsome, meddlesome* and *bothersome* to *adventuresome, fulsome* and *cuddlesome*. Large numbers of *-some* words have come and gone over the centuries – *friendsome, brightsome, darksome* and *lustsome* are no longer in use. Many Americans still say *lonesome*, while we normally prefer *lonely*.

Many *-some* words are fairly transparent in terms of their origins and meanings, such as *toothsome*, 'tasty', but a number of others have become somewhat disguised in the modern language. *Lissom* or *lissome* was originally *lithe-some*. *Cumbersome* comes from the mediaeval verb *to cumber*, while these days we usually say *encumber*. *Noisome* is derived from the archaic noun *noy*, 'annoyance, trouble'. The obsolete verb *to grue*, which means 'to dread, to shudder', gave us *gruesome*. *Handsome* is now most usually applied to good-looking men, but originally it meant *hand-some*, 'easy to handle'. *Buxom*, now most often an adjective applied to full-bosomed women, was originally *bucsum*, 'bow-some, flexible, pliant'. It then gradually came to mean 'agreeable, pleasant', later 'lively, cheerful' and then 'healthy, vigorous, well-favoured', ending up as 'plump and comely'. The German word corresponding to buxom is *biegsam*, 'pliant', from *biegen*, 'to bend'.

The other Germanic languages all have a version of our *-some* suffix, but which forms it can be added to is rather unpredictable. English no longer has *langsum*, 'long-some', but the Dutch word *langzaam* means 'slow', and so does the German word *langsam*; the North Frisian version is *lungsoom* and the West Frisian *langsum*.

In English there is no word *helpsome*, but in Swedish we find *hjälpsam* and in Danish *hjælpsom*. English lacks *thanksome*, but Swedish has *tacksam*. West Frisian has the nice adjective *sjongsum*, 'melodious' – it is rather a pity we do not have the English equivalent *songsome*. *Awesome* itself seems not to have come into use until around 1600, and then to have lasted a good three-and-a-half centuries in its literal meaning before semantic weakening set in. The word started appearing in a watered-down sense – having little or nothing to do with *awe*, as in 'she has an awesome memory' – in the USA during the 1960s.

And the current more trivial usage of the word *awesome*, simply indicating enthusiasm or approval, first made an appearance in American English in the late 1970s: the *Oxford English Dictionary* quotes 'Third Grade is awesome' from the *New Yorker* magazine in 1983.

BLEACHING

Semantic bleaching, or weakening of meaning, is a process which commonly affects emotive words. In Modern English, *dreadful* no longer has very much connection with *dread*, and *horrible* has little to do with *horror*. *Wonderful* most often does not refer to experiencing a sense of wonder. And something that is *terrific* does not 'cause terror'.

1.5 Cheap

The Dutch word for 'to buy' is *kopen*. The corresponding word in German is *kaufen*; and the West Frisian equivalent is *keapje*. All the Scandinavian languages also have a related form: Norwegian *kjøpe*, Danish *købe*, Swedish *köpa*, Icelandic *kaupa* and

Faroese *keypa*. So a form of this word is found in all of the languages English is most closely related to – but it is strangely absent from English itself.

Why is it that English so mysteriously lacks a *kopen*-type word? In fact English did have such a word, for many centuries, until it was gradually replaced by *to buy*. In Old English, the related verb-form was *ceapian*, 'to bargain, to buy'. And there were also a number of other Old English words which were derived from it, such as *ceapmann*, later *chapman*, meaning a merchant or trader. We have now lost this word too, except that it does survive as a surname. Dutch has a similar surname, Koopman and German has Kaufmann.

Another related Old English word was *ceping* or *cieping*, which meant 'market town' – a place where one bargained for and bought things. There are still several places in England which have this element in their names: Chipping Ongar, Chipping Norton, Chipping Sodbury, Chipping Camden. There are a number of similar place names in other areas of the Germanic-speaking word, too, with the same origin. The Old Norse equivalent to *cieping* was *kaupangr*, and there was an important Viking Age trading town on the south coast of Norway which was called Kaupang. In modern Sweden there are towns called Linköping, Nyköping and Norrköping which contain this same element. And in Denmark we find Ringkøbing, Nykøbing, Rudkøbing and Sakskøbing. The Nordic word has also been borrowed into Finnish as *kaupunki*, where it signifies 'town'.

Back in this country, we can see the Old English verb cropping up in the name of Cheapside, which was the main shopping street in the old City of London, as well as in Eastcheap, also an ancient London commercial street. And the name of Chipstead in Kent comes from Old English *ceap-stede*, 'buying place'.

By the mediaeval English period, the verb *ceapian* had become *chepen*. In Chaucer's *Wife of Bath's Tale*, we find the sentence 'For as a spanyel she wol on hym lepe, Til that she fynde som man hire to chepe' ('For like a spaniel she will leap on him, Until she finds some man to buy her'). *Chepe(n)*, 'to buy, bargain' continued to be used in the sixteenth and early seventeenth centuries, but then it gradually died out.

Except that it did not really die out at all. The word survives today in the form of our modern adjective *cheap*. The way we use the word nowadays is actually comparatively recent, not becoming current until the 1500s. It was originally an abbreviation of the phrase 'good cheap', where *cheap* was a noun derived from *chepen* meaning 'a bargain, commodity'. If something was 'good cheap', then that meant that it was a good bargain, that you got it at a good price.

So the ancient pan-Germanic word does survive in English, just not as a verb as it does in our sister languages. But we can now ask how long even this adjective is going to survive. It already seems that quite a lot of Americans do not like this word: it is noticeable that there is a strong tendency for many of them to prefer to say *inexpensive* rather than *cheap*. What seems to be going on is that *cheap* has acquired too many negative connotations in American English of the 'cheap-and-nasty' type for speakers to feel comfortable about using it in a neutral way in the original sense 'of good value in proportion to its price'. And there are also other associated negative usages such as *cheap trick* and *cheapskate* which may in the end send the adjective *cheap* along the same road into linguistic oblivion that the verb *to cheap* has already travelled.

ONGAR

Ongar strikes many people as being a rather unusual name, and it does seem to be the only place-name in Britain with a name beginning with *Ong-*. Actually, though, it is a perfectly good English-language name which is derived from the Old English word *angr* which meant 'meadow' or 'grazing land'.

1.6 Time and Tide

In English, when we speak about the approximately twice-a-day rising and falling of the seas along our shores, we talk of *high tides* and *low tides*. Norwegian uses similar terminology: *høgvatn*, 'high water' and *lågvatn*, 'low water', as does Afrikaans: *hoogwater* and *laagwater*.

But German has two entirely different words which can be used for these tidal phenomena: high tide is *Flut*, while low tide is *Ebbe*. These lexical items are instantly recognisable to English speakers as being related to our words *flood* and *ebb*. *Flood* itself is related to *flow* – and of course we do talk about the 'ebb and flow' of the sea, as well as, metaphorically, of human fortunes.

The complex nature of the historical relationships between the different languages of the Germanic family can further be seen in the way that our word *tide* is in origin the same word as German *Zeit*, Dutch *tijd*, West Frisian *tiid* and Norwegian, Swedish and Danish *tid*. However, in all of those languages, these words do not actually mean 'tide', but rather 'time'. This is not particularly mysterious: high and low tides occur at more or less predictable times, even if this involves somewhat complex calculations – tides are dependent on the phases of the moon, and are therefore in principle known in advance indefinitely.

The English word *time*, on the other hand, clearly has the same origin as Norwegian and Danish *time* (pronounced as two syllables, 'teem-uh'), Swedish *timme*, and Faroese *timi*. But in these Scandinavian languages, the words do not mean 'time' but rather 'hour' – a period of 60 minutes – or in an educational context 'lesson', because traditionally lessons lasted for an hour.

If we now look more closely at our English word *hour*, it turns out that it has the same origin as French *heure* and Greek *ora*, 'hour, time', but it also corresponds to German *Uhr* and Scandinavian *ur*. However, these last two words do not mean 'hour' or 'time', but 'clock'. Again, you can see how that came about – we look at clocks in order to see what time or 'hour' it is.

Following the thread along from there, English *clock* is related to the Norwegian word *klokke*, Swedish *klocka* and Faroese *klokka*, with the corresponding German form being *Glocke* – but these words all mean 'bell'. Many people will know that a *glockenspiel* (literally a 'bell-play') is a musical instrument which resembles a xylophone, but with keys that are made of metal rather than wood so that it sounds like bells are being struck. Once again, we can see how this semantic change could have arisen: clocks very often had bells which sounded to mark the hour.

English *clock* was actually originally borrowed either from Dutch *klok*, 'clock, bell' or from French *cloche*, 'bell'. We have also borrowed *cloche* more directly into Modern English in the sense of, originally, a kind of bell-shaped glass jar used for rearing young plants and, more recently, any rigid, translucent cover that protects plants from the cold. We also use the term *cloche hat* to refer to a woman's hat that is close-fitting and shaped like a bell.

The Modern English word *bell* itself comes down to us from Old English *belle*, which was related to mediaeval Dutch and Low German *belle*, with the same meaning. But no related word can be found in German, and Scandinavian forms such as Norwegian *bjelle*, Danish *bjælde* and Icelandic *bjalla* seem to have been borrowed from an older form of English. The origin of *bell* may well lie in the Old English verb *bellan*, 'to roar, make a loud vocal noise', which would provide a link to *bellow*; German *bellen* does mean 'to bark', as of a dog.

It is a very long way, in terms of meaning, from 'ebbing and flowing' to 'barking', but these are the sorts of lengthy journeys that etymological research into words with related meanings can take us on.

BELLOWS

The word *bellows*, referring to a device for blasting air onto a fire, has nothing to do with bellowing in the sense of shouting loudly. It has a closer connection to the word *belly*. Both of these forms appear to be related to the Old English word *belig*, which meant 'bag, sack, container'.

1.7 Feet and Inches

Of the approximately eighty countries in the world which drive on the left-hand side of the road, only four are European: Ireland, Malta, Cyprus and the UK (plus the Isle of Man and the Channel Islands). This is due in some measure to Napoleon, Hitler and other despots.

There is no particular reason why driving on the right or left should be preferred, so we would expect to find something like a 50–50 distribution of driving on the right versus the left in Europe. In fact, there were originally probably more polities travelling on the left than on the right. Napoleon's conquests, however, resulted in French-style driving on the right being imposed in Belgium, Holland, Luxembourg, Switzerland and much of Spain and Italy. Those places which drove on the left and were not conquered by Napoleon, such as the Austro-Hungarian Empire, mostly retained their original system, but Tsar Alexander II of Russia then forced driving on the right in Finland, while later on Hitler did the same thing elsewhere, including in Austria and Czechoslovakia. As time has gone by, other nations that drove on the left, finding themselves in the minority, changed voluntarily, most recently Iceland and Sweden.

Something not totally dissimilar happened with European systems of measurement. Because Britain was not conquered by Napoleon, we could choose to stay with the same natural Germanic measurement system which had served us well for a millennium or two. Our anatomical word *foot* comes from Anglo-Saxon *fot* and is related to Norwegian and Swedish *fot*, Danish *fod*, Dutch *voet*, West Frisian *foet*, North Frisian *fötj*, German *Fuss* and Low German *foot*. But a foot is also, of course, an ancient unit of measurement, based on the length of the foot of a typical adult male. The word first appeared in this usage in written English 1,100 years ago.

An *inch* is often taken to be equivalent to the width of a man's thumb. The French word *pouce*, 'thumb', also means 'inch', as does Italian *pollice*. In Hungarian, *hüvelyk* means both 'inch' and 'thumb', but 'thumb' can also be *hüvelykujj*, 'inch-finger'. Romanian *deget* means both 'finger' and 'inch'.

Another natural unit of measurement is the *fathom*, which was originally the length of the outstretched arms from fingertip to fingertip. A fathom is equivalent to six feet, and these days it is mostly used in measuring the depth of water. It, too, is an old Germanic word and is related to Modern Swedish *famn* and Danish *favn*, which mean 'embrace' as well as 'fathom' – if you are going to embrace somebody, you do start with your arms stretched out.

In Western Europe, natural measurements of this type started disappearing in those countries which had fallen to Napoleon, being officially replaced by the new, more logical French metric system. But even in many of those nations, the foot, inch and fathom still survive as units of measurement today, more than 200 years later. Scandinavian carpenters can still talk in thumbs or inches. In Norway, the length of a boat is always still quoted in feet. And in Sweden, the depth of the sea is often measured in fathoms. Internationally, too, it is still widespread practice to give the flying height of aeroplanes in feet. It is the intuitive naturalness of measurements like inch, foot and fathom which make them hard to get rid of. We like them because we can relate to them.

Some while ago I was in a stationery shop looking for plastic folders. The young assistant showed me what they had and, wanting to know if they were the right size, I asked how many inches across they were. She said: 'I don't know anything about feet and inches' and gave me the dimensions in centimetres. Later on, as I was leaving the shop, I asked her how tall she was. 'Five foot seven', she replied.

ELL

The ell was a traditional measurement of length, originally representing 45 inches. The word has the same linguistic origin as Latin *ulna*, which meant 'forearm'; it was intended to represent the length of a man's arm from the elbow to the wrist. *Elbow* itself is derived from *ell*, plus *bow* in the sense of 'bend'.

1.8 Colours

Some English words for colours are obviously derived from the names of objects and substances. The most obvious case is *orange*, which clearly comes from the name of the fruit. *Orange* is a rather important English colour term nowadays, which is interesting when you consider that oranges do not naturally grow in Britain, and that the first written mention of the fruit in English does not appear until about 1400. In fact, its first recorded use as a colour term dates from 1557 – which raises the interesting question of what the colour we now call *orange* used to be called before that. The answer is: *red* or *yellow* – which must mean that these two words used to cover a wider range of hues than they do now.

English has many other secondary colour words which also originate in the hue of objects: for example, *plum, amber, cream, gold* . . . Modern manufacturers of paints and clothing have become very creative with such terminology. But surely our more commonly used colour terms did not arise in this same way? Well, some of them did. *Purple* (earlier *purpure*) came from Latin *purpura*, from Greek *porphýra*, which was the name of the Mediterranean sea snail which purple dye was originally obtained from. The word may have come originally from Phoenician.

Pink as a colour term is even newer than *orange*, dating from 1669. It too is derived from a word for an object – in this case the flower of the same name. But that raises the question as to the origin of the name of the flower. The disappointing answer is that nobody is very sure about that.

Another possible example is *black*, which is derived from the same source as mediaeval Dutch *blac*, Low German *blak* and Modern Norwegian *blekk* – which all mean 'ink'. But which came first, the name of the colour or the name of the substance? Actually, it seems most likely that the continental words for 'ink' were borrowed from the Old English colour word *blæc*. But where did *blæc* come from? We do not really know, but there is a Dutch word *blaken*, 'to blaze', so *black* might derive from a word meaning 'burnt'. The Modern German, Dutch and Swedish words for 'black' are respectively *schwarz*, *zwart* and *svart*, which are the same word in origin as English *swarthy*, and go back to a root meaning 'dark'.

Interestingly, a number of other colour terms come from ancient verb forms rather than the names of substances. *Yellow* has the same origin as Frisian *giel*, Dutch *geel* and German *gelb*, 'yellow', but the ultimate source seems to be an ancient Indo-European root meaning 'to shine'; our word *gold* comes from the same source.

Green, too, is a shared Germanic word – compare Frisian *grien*, Dutch *groen*, German *grün*, Danish *grøn*. This goes back to the same Germanic root which gave us our verb *grow*; a related word is *grass* – after all, grass is green, and it does grow.

The Germanic languages also derive their words for 'white' from a common root. *White* has the same origin as the word *wheat*, possibly because of the colour of the flour produced from this grain. Words for 'white' and 'wheat' respectively in other Germanic languages which show this relationship include Frisian *wyt* and *weet*, Dutch *wit* and *weit*, German *weiss* and *Weizen*, and Norwegian *hvit* and *hvete*. The ultimate source of *white* is probably an Indo-European root meaning 'to be bright'.

Red is an exception to these patterns. Once again the Germanic languages have a shared word for this colour term: Frisian *read*, Dutch *rood*, German *rot*, Norwegian *rød*. But more interesting is the fact that these derive from the ancient Indo-European form *reudh-* 'red'. This was also the source for our words *ruddy*, *rust*, *rufous* and *ruby*. Surprisingly, it is the only common ancient Indo-European colour word we know of.

PHOENICIAN

Phoenician was a Semitic language which was originally spoken in the area which is modern Lebanon. The colonial dialect of Phoenician which was spoken in ancient Carthage, in North Africa – by Hannibal, for example – was known as Punic. We do not know a great deal about Punic, but we do know that Ancient Hebrew and Phoenician were closely related languages.

1.9 Orangemen

The Democratic Unionist Party are having difficulty coming to terms with the official use in Ulster of Irish Gaelic, the indigenous Celtic language of Ireland.

They also have a predilection for the colour orange. Belfast is a long way from Andhra Pradesh, but the Indian subcontinent is where we need to start if we want to explain the attraction this colour has for certain Irish Protestants.

Oranges seem to have originated in South East Asia. Our Modern English word *orange* probably goes back very many centuries to one of the Dravidian languages of southern India such as Tamil or Telugu: the Modern Telugu word for orange is *narinja*. The ancient Dravidian word for this fruit eventually made its way north into the classical North Indian language Sanskrit as *naranga*. It then was carried across the mountains of the Hindu Kush into Persian as *narang*, and from there it crossed into Arabic in the form of *naranj*.

Oranges were probably first introduced into Europe by Portuguese traders – the Greek word for orange is *portokali* – but English speakers most likely acquired the word for the fruit via the language of the maritime Venetians, who called it *naranza*, or the Spanish, where it was *naranja*. The word then was taken north into France, where it passed into French as *orange*: the initial *n* went missing as a result of *une norange* being re-interpreted by speakers as *une orange*.

Some time around 1400, *orange* came into the English language from French, having of course made the 5,000-mile journey from southern Asia to our island along with the fruit itself.

The first known usage of the word as the name of a colour dates to the 1550s. Prior to the arrival of oranges on these shores, the colour was most often regarded as a kind of red: the 'red' breast of the European robin is often actually closer in hue to what English speakers these days would most likely label 'orange' in other contexts.

Orange is also the name of a town in the Vaucluse, in southern France. The town was the centre of a principality that in the sixteenth century passed into the ownership of a branch of the Dutch aristocratic dynasty, the House of Nassau, which led to this particular branch of the family being known as the House of Orange.

In the following century, the Dutch aristocrat William of Orange married Mary Stuart, the Protestant daughter of James II & VII, the Catholic King of England, Ireland and Scotland. After James was deposed in the Glorious Revolution of 1688, William and Mary became joint monarchs of the three kingdoms. James then attempted to regain his crown by raising an army in Ireland, but the victory of William's army over James's forces at the Battle of the Boyne in northern Ireland in 1690 established William as a champion of the Protestants. This led to the name *Orangemen* being used to refer to members of anti-Catholic groups in the north of Ireland who regarded him as a hero. They also came to adopt the colour orange as a symbol of their group membership; the tricolour flag of modern Ireland has one of its vertical stripes in orange to represent the Protestant section of the island's population.

But it is a complete and utter coincidence that the English-language word for the colour (and the fruit) and the name of the town in southern France just happen to be identical.

And there is also an irony here which anti-Gaelic-language members of the DUP may not be aware of. It is true that the originally Dravidian word for the citrus fruit came into English via French. But the original Latin word which the name of the

French town of Orange descends from, *Arausio*, came into Latin from ancient Celtic, where it was the name of a Celtic water-god.

CHINESE APPLE

The Low German word for 'orange' is *Appelsien*. High German speakers in northern Germany say *Apfelsine* (other German speakers have *Orange*). The Low German word spread into Danish and Norwegian, where it is *applesin*. In Icelandic it appears as *appelsína*, in Faroese *appilsin* and Swedish *apelsin*. These words recognise the Asian origins of the fruit: literally they mean 'apple (from) China'.

1.10 Denim

The sad Iraqi city of Mosul, or what is left of it, has been very much in the news. Thousands of its inhabitants have been killed, wounded or displaced; and there has been much anguish over the preservation of its architectural splendours.

It is not very widely recognised, though – and this will be absolutely no consolation – that the name of the city is preserved in the English language in the shape of our word for the fabric *muslin*. We acquired this word in the seventeenth century from French *mousseline*, which had come into French from Italian *mussolo*, 'muslin', or more accurately from *mussolina*, 'made from muslin'. This term was derived from the name of the city where muslin was originally made, most likely in its Kurdish form Musil, though possibly also Arabic Mawsil.

Many English-language names for fabrics are derived from Middle Eastern or Far Eastern languages. *Taffeta* comes from Persian *taftah*; and the origin of *cotton* lies in Arabic *qutn*. And a number of these fabric names, like *muslin*, come from the names of Eastern cities which were renowned for the manufacture of that particular cloth. *Damask* comes from Damascus. *Satin* may be derived, via Arabic, from Zaitun, the name of an ancient city in southern China. *Calico* is from Calicut, an Indian city on the coast of Kerala (known in Keralese as Kozhikode).

But there are a small number of fabrics whose English names derive from European locations. The most famous of these is perhaps *denim*, which is a kind of serge. (The word *serge* itself supposedly comes from the name of the Seres, an ancient Far Eastern people.) The source of the word *denim* lies in the French city of Nîmes, which the fabric was originally associated with: the material was originally known as *serge de Nîmes*. An edition of the *London Gazette* from 1703 mentions 'a pair of Serge de Nim breeches'.

Another fabric for which we can claim a European place-name origin is *cambric*, named after Cambrai in north-eastern France – its Dutch name is Kamerijk. And *lisle* comes from the name of the nearby French city of Lille, earlier spelt Lisle. The town was originally Dutch speaking, and its Dutch name is Rijsel, from *ter ijsel*, 'at the island'. The French name has the same kind of origin: it comes from *l'isle*, 'the island', hence the earlier spelling.

There is also one well-known fabric name which has a British topographical origin. This is *worsted* (pronounced 'woosted'), named after the Norfolk village of Worstead (pronounced in the same way), which is located to the north-east of Norwich near Aylsham and North Walsham, which were also both associated with the manufacture of this type of cloth.

It is widely believed that the name *nylon*, too, was derived in part from a British place-name. There is a story that the term was created from the initial letters of New York, plus the first syllable of London – but that is not true. The word was invented out of the blue by the Du Pont company, which manufactured the material; they decided to create a name ending in *-on* based on the pattern of *cotton* and *rayon*.

The other fabric which we might want to claim a British place-name origin for – this time Scottish rather than English – is *tweed*. After all, the River Tweed does form the historical boundary between Scotland and England, and tweed fabric is famously associated with Scotland. Once again, however, this explanation is not correct. A clue to this being a misconception is the fact that one of the most famous cloths of this type is Harris Tweed, from the Outer Hebridean islands – which are nowhere near the River Tweed.

The truth of the matter is that the fabric name *tweed* was a mistake, a cross-linguistic misunderstanding. The Scots word corresponding to English *twill* is *tweel*. Some time around 1830, a London-based merchant, not being familiar with the Scots form, misread *tweel* as *tweed*, no doubt influenced by the name of the river, and put in an order for . . . tweed.

1.11 Foxglove

It is not a totally straightforward matter to explain how the flower we call the *foxglove* got its name. We can, however, at least figure out where the *glove* part comes from: the flowers look like the fingers of gloves, and small fingers, as children know, can be inserted into them.

In many languages, there is a more direct link between the plant's name and the word for 'finger'. In Greek, one name for the foxglove is *daktylís*, from *dáchtilo*, 'finger'. The Spanish is *dedalera*, from *dedo*, 'finger' (the Portuguese is *dedaleira*, the Catalan *didalera*). In Albanian the name is *lule gishti*, with *lule* meaning 'flower' and *gisht* 'finger'. The Latin name of the plant is *digitalis* – the Modern Italian is *digitale*. This name is now most frequently used to refer to the important heart drug which is derived from the foxglove, but *digitalis* originally meant 'a finger width', from *digitus*, 'finger'. We have borrowed this word, in the form of *digit*, into Modern

English, where it has come to mean not only 'finger' but 'a whole number less than ten', presumably because of our ten anatomical digits. And of course these days we most often hear the word *digital* – as opposed to *analogue* – in connection with 'the usage of numerical digits in electronics'.

Other languages have been a little more imaginative in developing their words for *Digitalis purpurea* and related flowers. The Polish for foxglove is *naparstnica*, from *naparstek* (*na+parst* is 'on+finger'). Hungarian *gyűszűvirág* also means 'thimble flower'. The Dutch word *vingerhoedskruid* literally means 'finger hat' (= thimble) herb'; and German *Fingerhut*, 'finger hat' signifies both a thimble and a foxglove. The Finnish for foxglove is *sormustinkukkai*, 'thimble flower', and Swedish *fingerborgsblomma* has the same meaning, with *fingerborg* literally meaning 'finger castle'.

These continental thimble terms all relate in a rather transparent way to the covering or protecting of fingers. But English *thimble* – an Old English word, first recorded around AD 1000 – is historically derived from *thumb*, even though people who use thimbles when sewing more often than not put them on their index finger rather than their thumb.

Some other languages' words for foxgloves are enjoyably more whimsical than those relating rather prosaically to fingers and thimbles. For example, another Greek word for foxglove is *chelidonó-horto*, 'swallow plant': there was apparently an ancient belief that the flowers bloomed when the swallows arrived from the south and withered away again when these birds departed for the winter. (It seems, though, that this Greek term is more often used with reference to the flowers we call *celandines* – an English name which is itself ultimately derived from Greek *chelidon*, 'swallow'.)

Even more delightful is the Scottish Gaelic word for foxglove, *lus nam ban-sìth*: *lus* means 'plant' and a *ban-sìth* is 'female fairy', so it means 'the fairy women's plant'. (Many people will know *ban-sìth* in its anglicised form, *banshee*.) Then there is the lovely Welsh flower-name *bysedd y cŵn*, 'dog-fingers'. Dogs do not have fingers, of course, but then neither do foxes.

Which brings us back to the mystery of the origins of the English word. We can understand the 'glove' element in *foxglove*. But why would anybody think that the flower had anything to do with foxes? And we really are talking about foxes here – there is no distortion of some other word involved: our Anglo-Saxon forebears actually did call the flower *foxes glófa*. Did this have something to do with the colour of the flowers, or the fact that foxgloves grew in wooded areas that foxes frequent? Or did our English ancestors fantasise that small foxes went around sticking their paws into digitalis flowers? If so, they seem not to have been alone in being fanciful about foxes. Some of our Scandinavian cousins must have had the same kind of flights of fancy: the Norwegian word for foxglove is *revebjelle*, 'fox bell'.

> **DACTYL**
>
> *Pterodactyl* comes from classical Greek *pterón*, 'wing', and *dáktylos*, 'finger'. Humans are *pentadactylous* (five-fingered). *Dactyloscopy* is the study of fingerprints. In poetry, a *dactyl* is a metrical foot consisting of an accented syllable followed by two unaccented ones (fingers have one long joint and two shorter ones!); an example is the word *strawberry*.

1.12 Passengers

The word *passenger* has been part of our normal English vocabulary for 700 years or so, and it has been the usual term for 'a person in or on a conveyance, other than its driver, pilot, or crew' for at least five centuries. Now this word is under attack. In many parts of the anglophone world, nobody is any longer officially a passenger, unless perhaps when on a ferry. British railway companies these days have 'customers', as do many airlines (although the Virgin Australia airline now addresses its passengers as 'guests', which is rather galling when you have paid them large sums of money for your ticket).

Of course, everybody still normally *says* 'passengers'. Anybody who has grown up speaking English knows very well that people travelling on trains and buses are not customers but passengers. It is a fact about the English language that *customer* does not mean 'a person in or on a conveyance other than its driver, pilot, or crew'. This knowledge is naturally also shared by railway and airline company employees: if you overhear them talking to each other, or if they are chatting informally to you, they also always quite naturally use the word *passenger*. But they have clearly had strict instructions from their bosses to avoid this word, and nearly all airline and rail notices, printed materials and public announcements eschew it.

There are several disadvantages resulting from the fact that the United Kingdom is a predominantly English-speaking nation. One of them is that we are much more open to cultural and linguistic influences from the USA than most other European countries. (I would not be at all surprised if there were rather few high-school proms in Kazakhstan; and I suspect that Halloween, American style, may not be too big in Azerbaijan.) The attempted extermination of *passenger* on the part of airline and railway companies is part of this picture: American business-school-speak does not like the word. Business-school ideology holds that the capitalist free market solves all problems, and that everything which can be marketised therefore should be marketised. Even some patients these days are being referred to as 'customers', which sounds especially bad to those of us who are used to healthcare being free at the point of delivery.

Non-anglophone European countries seem to be linguistically less exposed to American marketisation ideology. France and French-speaking Switzerland continue to have *passagers*. In Athens, metro users are still addressed as *agapití epivátes*, 'dear passengers'; in Serbia, railway travellers are referred to as *putnici*, 'passengers'; and in Poland you are a *pasażer* or a *podróżny*, 'traveller', not a *klient*, 'customer'. Hungarian is also totally resistant to US business-school-speak in this context: the home page of the Hungarian airline WizzAir has over thirty instances of the word *utas*, 'passenger' and none at all of the equivalent of *customer*. The Danish railway company DSB still normally uses *passager* rather than *kunde*, 'customer'; and *Kunde*, 'customer', is not used by German or Austrian railways to refer to people who are actually travelling, although there is a venerable German word *Fahrgast*, 'travel guest'.

English-speaking travellers, however, are not totally alone in suffering from this attack by business-speak. In Spain, the word *clientes*, 'customers', is now found alongside *pasageros*; and in Italian, while *passeggeri* is more common than *clienti*, the latter can now be encountered.

A Finnish traveller may now also be called *asiakas*, 'customer', but the word for 'passenger', *matkustaja*, is still alive and well in Finland. It comes from the verb *matkustaa*, 'to travel', and will therefore be difficult for free-market-oriented corporations to abolish, not least because of other words related to it: *matkustus* means 'journey', and the word for 'cabin' is *matkustamo*, literally 'place for travelling'. A business-speak translation of 'cabin' as a 'place for being a customer' will hopefully seem a step too far even for avid business-school-speak devotees.

CUSTOM

Custom and *costume* were in origin the same word, both deriving from Latin *consuetudo*, 'habit'. *Costume* referred to clothing which it was customary to wear. The same kind of semantic link can be seen in the case of *habit*, which means both 'clothing, dress', and 'tendency to act in a certain way'.

1.13 Manure

English speakers know very well what the word *opera* means: an opera is a dramatic, classical-music composition involving singing – Bizet's *Carmen*, Mozart's *The Marriage of Figaro*, Puccini's *Madame Butterfly*. The word *opera* was borrowed into English from Italian, but if we go back far enough in time we can see that the word was originally Latin, and that it was originally plural. Latin *opus* meant 'work', and so its plural, *opera*, meant 'works'. It came to have its seventeenth-century Italian meaning of 'musical drama' through a series of semantic shifts, starting with significations such as 'works produced' and continuing on to meanings such as 'musical work produced'.

The original Latin singular, *opus*, is used in Modern English to refer to a musical composition which is numbered according to a catalogue which has been compiled of a composer's works. It is also used to mean a book or some other artistic or scientific work, particularly if it is considered to be important. A magnum opus is a great work or, to use the French term, a *chef-d'œuvre*.

But Latin *opera* has also found its way into English in ways which are rather less obvious. The word *manoeuvre*, for instance, was borrowed into English from French. (In American English it is most often spelt *maneuver*.) It derives from Late Latin *manuopera*, and so ultimately from classical Latin *manus*, 'hand', and *opera*, 'works' — so it actually meant 'manual labour'. The word later acquired various other meanings, including 'control with the hands', as in the manoeuvring of a boat, which may be how it came to apply to naval exercises, and hence perhaps to military exercises in general. The modern military usage of the term *manoeuvre* did not become current in English until the 1700s. The word has also found its way into many other languages — in Spanish it is *maniobra*, the Portuguese version is *manovra*, the Italian is *manovra*, in Polish it is *manewr* and in Croatian *manevar*.

It is a bit of a surprise, however, to discover that *manoeuvre* has a twin in the form of *manure* — the two words have exactly the same origin. Admittedly, *manoeuvre* and *manure* look rather alike on the page, and the older pronunciation of *manoeuvre*, 'man-yoover', made them sound more alike than they do today for most speakers. But how can a word meaning 'the planned movement of troops and military vehicles' have the same origin as a word meaning 'dung, excrement, or compost spread over soil in order to fertilise it'?

The answer is partly connected to the fact that while Late Latin *opera* came to be *oeuvre* in the mediaeval French of Paris, in the Anglo-Norman French of mediaeval England it became *eure*, with the loss of the *v*-sound. This version survived in English until the eighteenth century in the form of *ure*. The sixteenth-century poet Thomas Wyatt wrote: 'Truth is trayed [betrayed] where craft is in ure', that is, '... where guile is at work'. Correspondingly, Late Latin *manuopera* became *maneure* in Anglo-Norman.

By the fifteenth century, Anglo-Norman *maneure* 'work with the hands' had become an English word signifying 'cultivation of the land'. It can be seen in this sense in Milton, who used the word figuratively with the meaning 'to cultivate the mind', as in 'it is the inward calling of God that makes a Minister, and it is his own painful study and diligence that manures and improves his ministerial gifts' (and not, the Puritan Milton implies, the laying on of hands by some bishop).

The literal sense of 'cultivating the earth' then gradually came to mean 'putting dung on soil to fertilise it'. And then, later on, the label *manure* was transferred to the dung itself, so long as it was being used as a fertiliser. Today, no one would consider *manoeuvre* and *manure* to be the same word, but the fact is that they do come from one and the same Latin phrase.

NUPTIALS

The Italian title of Mozart's comic opera is *Le nozze di Figaro*. It might seem strange to English speakers that *nozze*, 'marriage', is plural. But Italian *nozze* and French *noces*, which is also plural, both come from the plural Latin noun *nuptiae*, 'marriage'– which reminds us that English, too, has a plural word for this: *nuptials*.

1.14 *Apothec*

In Britain we normally say that we are going to take our doctors' prescriptions to the *chemists*. We are also perfectly familiar with the word which most Americans and Canadians would use, *pharmacy*. Some form of this latter word is also used in most of the languages of southern Europe: *pharmacie* in French, *farmacia* in Spanish and Portuguese, *farmaci* in Albanian, *pharmakeio* in Greek.

The older English word for a chemist was *apothecary*. Chaucer wrote of his character the Doctor: 'Ful redy hadde he his apothecaries to send him drogges and his letuaries [medicines]'. There are still people in Britain whose family name is Potticary, derived from the name of this occupation with the first syllable missing. In mediaeval England, the apothecary was the person who ran the chemist's establishment, while the shop itself was known as an *apothec*, meaning 'store house', but especially one for keeping medicines.

We have since lost this word ourselves, but some form of *apothec* is still the normal term for a chemist's shop in most of northern Europe. In Danish, Norwegian and Swedish, it's *apotek*, and in Dutch *apotheek*. Polish has *apteka*, Estonian *apteek*, Finnish has *apteekki* and in Latvian it is *aptieka*.

In fact, in one form or another, *apothec* is an extremely European word. It came into English from Old French *apotheque*, meaning 'shop' or 'magazine'. This had in turn come down from Latin *apotheca*, which had been borrowed into Latin from the Greek word *apothiki*, which is still the Modern Greek word for a 'warehouse'. The source was the Ancient Greek verb *apo-theto*, where *apo* meant 'from' and *theto* meant 'to put' or 'place' – so, 'to put away, to place in storage'.

But there is another chapter in the story of *apothiki*. Italians use the word *farmacia* for chemist, like other southern European languages, but they do also have a word which descends directly from Greek/Latin *apotheca*. This is *bottega*, 'shop', where the first syllable of the original word has been dropped. A similar process has produced the Catalan word for shop, *botiga*. The Spanish form *bodega* refers to a cellar, but particularly a wine cellar; the Danes have borrowed the Spanish word to signify a wine bar. In Portuguese the first syllable still survives: their word *abdega*, 'wine-shop', derives from an older Portuguese version *abodega*.

Over the centuries the Italian form *bottega* eventually made its way north into the Provençal language of southern France in the form of *botica*. This then spread up into northern France, where it became *boutique* in French. I first heard the word *boutique* when I started learning French at secondary school – we were taught it was the word for 'shop'. But recently it has become very much an English word: these days we have boutique hotels, boutique rooms, even boutique bars.

We can understand how this development came about if we note that *boutique* first came into English from French in the late 1700s with the meaning of 'shop', but that even then it most usually referred to a small shop. In 1950s America, *boutique* then started acquiring the more specialised meaning of an establishment – especially a clothes shop – which was not just small but was also specialised, trend-setting and fashionable. (In Dartmouth, Nova Scotia, there is even a clothes shop which calls itself *Bodega Boutique*). By the 1960s, *boutique* had begun to be used as an adjective referring to the sort of items which are offered for sale in these small, would-be-exclusive businesses – a boutique dress, boutique shoes, a boutique handbag. And since the 1980s it has increasingly been employed to describe small businesses – especially hotels – which provide services for a limited, exclusive, sophisticated clientele.

So there we have it. The Greek word for a warehouse; the Latvian word for a chemist's store; the Danish word for a wine bar; the Catalan word for a shop; and the English word for something small, exclusive and expensive – they all come from the same Ancient Greek word for a place where you put something away in order to store it. Over the last 2,000 years, this word has travelled all over Europe leaving various versions of itself behind with different meanings in different places.

1.15 Compassion and Sympathy

The Modern Greek word for the number 6 is *exi*. From the point of view of an English speaker, it seems as if there is something missing from the beginning of this word – and in a way, there is. The Ancient Greek form was *hex*, but the *h* (which came from an earlier *s*) has been dropped in the modern language. This earlier *s* is still preserved in the corresponding Latin word for 6, *sex*, as well as in English *six*, German *sechs* and Gaelic *sia*. The pre-Ancient Greek change of *s* to *h* is also reflected in Latin *super* versus Greek *hyper*, 'over'; and in Latin *sub* versus Greek *hypo*, 'under'.

The parallel forms *sub* and *hypo* both occur as prefixes in Modern English in words like *subcutaneous* and *hypodermic*. These two words actually have more or less the same meaning: *subcutaneous* comes from Latin *sub* plus *cutis*, 'skin', while *hypodermic* is from Ancient Greek *hypo* plus *derma*, 'skin', so both versions mean 'under the skin'. English has frequently borrowed pairs of equivalent words like this from the two classical languages and then assigned them different – sometimes only subtly different – meanings. In Modern English, we have sorted this particular pair out in such a way that *hypodermic* refers mostly to needles, and *subcutaneous* most often to medical conditions and procedures.

Similarly, *sympathy* and *compassion* do not mean exactly the same thing in English, but the words have the same origins in terms of classical elements. *Sympathy* comes from Ancient Greek *sympatheia*, composed of *syn*, 'with', plus *pathos*, 'suffering'; and *compassion* is from Late Latin *compassionem*, from *com*, 'with', plus *passionem* 'suffering'. So these two words are simply Greek- and Latin-origin versions of the same term which we have given slightly different meanings to.

Another *syn-* and *con-* pair is *synchronous* and *contemporary*. Ancient Greek *chronos* and Latin *tempus* both mean 'time'. Once again, this pair are by no means totally synonymous in English: *contemporary* means 'at the same time' in the sense of 'at the same period of history', while *synchronous* tends to be used more often to mean 'at the same (brief) point of time'.

Synthesis and *composition* also bear the same kind of relationship to each other. The second parts of these two words both carry the same meaning – 'putting, placing' – and come from, respectively, Ancient Greek *thesis* and Latin *positio*. Both words therefore have the sense of 'placing together'.

There is yet another English word-pair which is constructed from two sets of parallel elements, *hypo-sub* and *thesis-positio*. This is *hypothesis* and *supposition*. The basic senses of both terms – 'under' plus 'placing' – to give us the meaning 'foundation, basis, basis for an argument'. In Modern English, although the two terms do not denote exactly the same concept, they are clearly linked: a hypothesis really is something which you suppose.

Another Greek–Latin meaning pair is *periphery* and *circumference*. *Peri* and *circum* are respectively the (unrelated) Greek and Latin words for 'around'. But the second elements of the two words – from Ancient Greek *pherein*, 'to carry, bear', and Latin *ferre*, 'to carry, bear' – do have the same origin.

This same second element also appears in another Latin–Greek pair, again with unrelated first elements: *transfer* and *metaphor*. Latin *trans*, 'across, on the farther side of, beyond, over', plus *ferre* combine to give us *transfer*; and Greek *meta*, also indicating some kind of movement from one place to another, plus *phora*, 'carrying' – derived from *pherein*, 'to carry' – gives us *metaphor*. Tourists in Greece are often amused by the sight of lorries driving around with the word *metaphorés* written on the side in large letters. While in English *metaphor* is a word which is – appropriately enough – only used metaphorically, in Modern Greek it is also used literally to mean 'transport, haulage'.

SUPPOSITORY

One way to say 'I suppose' in Modern Greek is *hypothéto* – except that the *h* has been lost, so it is actually *ypothéto*. But if you are trying to speak Greek, be sure to put the stress in the right place: *ypótheto* means 'suppository'. The Latin-derived English words *suppose* and *suppository* are, of course, also related in the same way.

1.16 Apocalypse

In English we do not really have a true equivalent of the French expression *bon appétit* to wish people who are about to start a meal a 'good appetite'. But most other European languages do seem to have some kind of similar formula: German speakers say *Guten Appetit!*, Polish has *Smacznego!* and in Greek the corresponding phrase is *Kalí órexi!*

In Greek *kalí* means 'good'. And the Greek term *órexi*, 'appetite', will not be totally unknown to English speakers these days because of the much discussed eating disorder, anorexia nervosa. The *an-* prefix in *anorexia* signifies 'absence of' (as also in *anaerobic*, 'without air'). So *anorexia* – also *anorexy* in older English usage – indicates 'absence of appetite'. A much more recent coinage is *orthorexia* 'a pathological fixation on eating proper food', with the *ortho-* part meaning 'straight, upright, correct, proper', as in *orthodox, orthography* and so on. And there is another medical term, *polyorexia*, which means 'having excessive appetite' – in other words, eating too much.

The English language itself seems to have had a very healthy appetite for borrowing Greek words for undesirable conditions, unfortunate events and other unpleasant phenomena (*phenomenon* is also a Greek word, from the verb *phenein*, 'to appear'). The name of the eating disorder *bulimia* comes from Ancient Greek *boulimía*, 'ravenous hunger', originally composed of *bous*, 'ox' and *limós*, 'hunger'. *Xenophobia* is put together from Greek *xénos*, 'stranger, foreigner, guest', followed by *phóbos*, 'fear'. And *misogyny* consists of the Ancient Greek word for 'hatred', *mísos*, also seen in *misanthropy*, and the word for 'woman', *gyné*, which also occurs in *gynaecology*.

We would, in fact, have a hard time talking and writing about disasters in English if it were not for the Ancient Greeks. Our Greek-origin vocabulary for various types of crisis is very extensive. The word *crisis* itself has its origins in the Ancient Greek word *krísis*, from the verb *krinein*, 'to decide'. In Modern Greek, *kríno* means 'I judge'. So a crisis was originally some kind of decisive turning point.

Much worse than a crisis, of course, is an *apocalypse* – from Ancient Greek *apokálypsis*, where *apo-* meant 'off, from' and *kálypsis* meant 'cover', so the whole word meant 'uncovering, disclosure'. The original meaning in English was 'revelation'; but because of the events described in the Revelation of St John – the destruction of the world after the Second Coming of Christ – it came to signify a disaster resulting in drastic, irreversible and possibly worldwide damage to human societies – some kind of major cataclysm, in other words.

Cataclysm is also a Greek-origin word. In Modern Greek the most usual meaning of *kataklysmós* is 'flood', which was its earliest meaning in English too, particularly with reference to the biblical flood. But then it acquired the more figurative meaning of a political or social upheaval which sweeps away the established order. The ultimate origin of the word lies in Greek *kata*, 'down' and *klýzo*, 'to clean with water, wash down, wash out'.

And of course a cataclysm can lead to *chaos* – which is also a Greek word. Ancient Greek *kháos* meant 'a gulf or chasm of emptiness'. Needless to say, *chasm*, too, is a word we borrowed from the Ancient Greeks. And the *cha-* at the beginning of *chaos* and *chasm* comes from the Greek root *kha-*, 'gape'. In Modern Greek, *khásima* means 'yawn'.

Cataclysms, apocalypses and crises can all end in *tragedy*, a word which comes from the Ancient Greek *tragodía*, 'tragic play, tragic drama'. The second element of the word is from *ódé*, 'ode'. Rather surprisingly, it is thought that the first part probably derives from *trágos*, 'billy-goat'. One possible explanation for this etymology is that a goat was awarded as a prize to the winner of early Athenian tragedy-writing contests.

CHAOS AND GAS

The Flemish scientist J. B. van Helmont invented the word *gas*, which he derived from Ancient Greek *kháos*, 'total emptiness'. To understand how he arrived at this neologism, it helps to know that the *g* at the beginning of *gas* in Dutch is pronounced like the *kh* at the beginning of Greek *kháos* – that is, rather like the *ch* in German *Nacht* or Scots *loch*.

1.17 Patron

Many people who have visited Crete as tourists will have walked down the Samariá Gorge, the longest and deepest ravine in Europe. The strenuous but beautiful 10-mile hike, which ends on the shores of the Libyan Sea on the south coast of the island, starts at a height of about 3,500 feet, in the heart of the famous White Mountains of Crete, on the beautiful mountain-ringed Omalós Plateau.

The name of this high plain famously features in one of the best-known of all Greek songs. Sometimes called 'The Rebel', it is a traditional song of the Cretans' resistance in their struggle against the occupying powers of, first, the Venetians and then the Ottoman Turks.

The song, in Cretan Greek, starts: *Pótes tha kámi ksasteriá?* 'When will there be clear skies?' It continues with lines which can be translated into English as: 'When will February come, so I can take my rifle, and my beautiful *patróna*, and go up to Omalós?' As sung by the renowned Cretan musician Nikos Ksylouris, the song became a rallying cry for the resistance movement against the military junta which ruled Greece from 1967 to 1974. The memory of this fascist dictatorship, and the strong desire that nothing of the sort should ever be allowed to happen in Greece again, was one of the reasons why the Greek people were so keen to join the democratic bulwark of the European Union, which they did in 1981.

The Greek word *patróna* which occurs in this revolutionary song is sometimes translated as 'cartridge belt' or 'cartridge case'; but it has been argued that the original meaning of the word – as borrowed from Venetian – was 'cartridge pouch'. One thing that is certain is that, unlikely as this may seem, *patróna* has the same origin as the English words *patron* and *pattern* – which were originally simply two different pronunciations and spellings of the same word.

Patron, which comes from Latin *patronus*, 'protector, defender' – in some cases via the French word *patron*, 'chief, boss' – is ultimately derived from Latin *pater*, 'father', in much the same way that *matron* is derived from *mater*, 'mother'.

The word *patron* has many different meanings in English. It can denote the host or landlord of an inn or restaurant; and, confusingly, it can also refer to someone who is a loyal and regular customer of the same restaurant – or even just a one-time customer. It can also refer to a donor or supporter – as in a 'patron of the arts' – and to the patron saint of a church or nation. And while *patronising* a restaurant is a good thing for that establishment, *patronising* a person is, these days, mostly a bad thing – as accusations that someone is being 'patronising' reveal.

But what does any of this have to do with Cretan rebels waiting for spring to come so that they can assemble up on the mountain fastness of the Omalós Plateau?

The answer lies in some of the Modern English meanings of *pattern* which come from the use of *patron* in the sense of 'master copy, original version, exemplar, model to copy from'. (Modern French *patron* can also mean 'pattern'.)

This sense of being a model, or an object with a particular shape, gave rise in English to certain usages in which the spelling *patron* continued to be employed. In some of these, we can see how the Cretan use of the term *patróna* may have arisen. According to the *Oxford English Dictionary*, in sixteenth- and seventeenth-century English, one of the meanings of *patron* was 'a paper container for the charge of a cannon or pistol; a paper cartridge'. And by the nineteenth century, the word had come to have the possible military meaning of a wooden or steel 'box for holding cartridges' – precisely the sort of object that Cretan rebels would want to take with them up into the mountains in the spring.

BOULEVARD

Bulwark is a common Germanic word – in Dutch it is *bolwerk*, in Norwegian *bolverk*. It probably came from the older forms which in Modern English have become *bole*, 'tree-trunk' and *work* – so referring to defences made from tree trunks. The Germanic word was also borrowed into French, where it appears today as *boulevard* – originally a walkway on top of the defences around a town.

1.18 Liturgy

If you are on holiday in Greece or Cyprus, you may be unlucky enough to come across a sign hanging on the door of your hotel lift saying *Ektós liturgías*.

Ektós is not necessarily a totally unfamiliar form to all English speakers since it occurs in a number of technical words, like *ectoparasite*, 'a parasite – such as a flea living outside its host'; *ectothermic*, referring to animals which obtain their heat from external sources, such as by basking in the sun; and the infamous *ectoplasm*, 'a supernatural viscous substance exuded by a spiritual medium during a trance'. In Greek, on the other hand, *ektós* is a perfectly normal everyday word which simply means 'outside, without, except'.

Liturgia looks even more familiar. *Liturgy*, according to the *Oxford English Dictionary*, signifies 'a form of public worship, especially in the Christian Church; a collection of formularies for the conduct of divine service'. For us, it is a specifically religious word referring to a church service. The term first appeared in English in the sixteenth century as a loan from Greek via French.

But in Modern Greek, *liturgía* is an everyday word referring to any kind of service. As in English, it can refer to a religious service. But it can just as well refer to the functioning, operation, running or working of more or less anything. So this Greek-origin word with a rather specific meaning in English has a much more general meaning in Modern Greek itself. The sad fact is that the sign on the lift saying *Ektós liturgías* just means 'out of service' – you are going to have to walk up the stairs.

The same process has happened the other way round. In English, *service* can mean any number of different things. We have the health service, the police service, the probation service, social services and armed services. You can be involved in domestic service, military service or voluntary service. We might eat off and drink from a dinner service and a tea service. Institutions which have borrowed money may have to service a debt. You can perform a service for someone. And engineers service boilers – and even lifts.

But our word *service* has been borrowed into Greek as *sérvis* and, like *liturgy* in English, it has a much more limited range of meanings there. As in English, *sérvis* can be used in connection with having your car or your air-conditioning checked, or informally with reference to service in a restaurant or hotel – some Greek restaurants are *selph-sérvis*. But that's about it.

A similar example of an everyday Greek word having a more restricted and erudite meaning in English can be seen any day of the week along Greek roads, where, as we have seen, you are bound to come across lorries with the word *metaphorés* written on the side, often as part of the phrase *Metaphorés-Metakomísis*.

A *metaphor* in English is a figure of speech in which a word or phrase is transferred to an entity which, according to the *Oxford English Dictionary*, is 'different from but analogous to' what it is literally applicable to – as when Shakespeare wrote 'All the world's a stage, and all the men and women merely players'; or, more prosaically, when we talk of the 'mouth' of a river or the 'foot' of a hill.

Metaphor was also first borrowed from Greek into English in the sixteenth century. It comes from Ancient Greek *meta*, 'across', and *phora*, 'carrying'. In English we use the word – there is no other way of saying this! – metaphorically, to indicate a transfer of meaning from one entity to another. In Modern Greek it can be used in this way, too. But it is also much more frequently used, entirely literally, to refer to the transfer of anything or anybody from one place to another. *Metaphorés-Metakomísis* means 'Transport-Removals': *metaphorá*, plural *metaphorés*, is most often used to mean simply 'transport, haulage'.

SERVE

The Australian Sam Groth holds the record for the fastest tennis serve of all time, 163 mph. After this masterly feat of athletic prowess, Sam might have been surprised to learn that *to serve*, 'to start play by striking the ball into the opposite court', comes originally from the Latin word *servus*, 'slave'.

1.19 Focus

From time to time on our TV screens we are shown events such as royal gala performances, awards ceremonies and film premieres, where cameramen focus their lenses on celebrities as they enter the foyer of the theatre which is hosting the event.

Most of the participants at such events are probably not even slightly interested in the fact that the two words *focus* and *foyer* originally derive from the same source. How on earth could it come about that a verb meaning 'to adjust an optical instrument so as to see a sharply defined image' and a noun meaning 'the entrance lobby of a theatre' come from the same root? The story of the strange journeys these words have taken is a fascinating one, which shows very clearly the extent to which it is natural for languages to change with respect to both their sound systems and word meanings.

In the classical Latin of Ancient Rome, the word *focus* meant 'hearth'. There was also an adjective *focarium*, derived from *focus*, which meant 'having to do with a hearth' as used, for instance, to refer to a kitchen servant – someone whose job it was to work around the fireplace. Over the centuries, as the Vulgar Latin that was spoken in northern France gradually morphed into mediaeval Old French, through natural processes of sound change *focarium* became *foier*, which came to be used as a noun referring specifically to a domestic hearth.

In the fullness of time, this French word *foier* (later spelt *foyer*) acquired the meaning of 'a cosy, friendly place'. It eventually began to be used in the context of theatres to refer to what is known in English as the 'green room', signifying the cosy, friendly place where performers wait in a theatre before going on stage. The meaning of 'a cosy, welcoming lobby of a theatre' developed later; and it was not until the nineteenth century that the word finally made its way into English. The *Oxford English Dictionary* gives 1859 for the earliest usage of *foyer* in this sense, and even then it was printed in italics, indicating that it was still considered to be a word of foreign origin. *Foyer* rapidly made its way into many other languages as well, sometimes with respelling: Swedish *foajé*, Croatian *foaje*, Estonian *fuajee*, Romanian *foaier*, Turkish *fuaye*.

So that was one – very long – route which the Latin word *focus* took on its journey towards becoming a part of English vocabulary. But it also took another, much more straightforward route. Starting in the 1600s, scholars who knew Latin introduced the word *focus* directly into their English writings, without any mediation from French, so that *focus* arrived in English much earlier than *foyer*. For a brief period when *focus* was first used in English, it meant 'hearth' as in the original Latin, though it could also refer to a source of heat. But almost from the very beginning, it also tended to be employed figuratively.

Focus was first used in its modern scientific sense of 'point of convergence' by Johannes Kepler, the German mathematician and astronomer, in his work on optics in the early 1600s. Kepler wrote in Latin, not English, and would have spoken about the topic in German, so the first known usages in English of the word *focus* in the optical sense come later, from the 1650s and 1660s. Its first metaphorical usages, such as *focus of attention*, date from the 1700s.

Kepler probably chose the Latin word *focus* because he was likening a point of optical convergence, where light rays meet, to a source from which light rays emanate, such as a hearth with a fire burning in it. In Modern French, *foyer* can still mean both 'hearth, lobby, fireplace' and 'focus'. And even today, English-speaking people can be heard to remark that their fireplace, or their wood-burning stove, is the focus of their living room.

1.20 Remain or Stay?

On flights coming into London, airline passengers often hear messages from the cabin crew along the lines of 'we are about to commence our descent into Heathrow Airport'. Anybody who knows anything about English will recognise that this is not anything any native English speaker would normally say in the course of their everyday lives. Very few of us, on spotting the Channel coast coming up out of the plane window, would turn to our partner and say: 'Look dear, I think we must be about to commence our descent'.

Commence is not a word that English speakers use on a day-to-day basis . At the beginning of a dinner party, it is not usual for the host(ess) to say, to the assembled company: 'Please commence'. Teachers do not tell pupils about to take an exam that 'you may now commence'. Football fans do not ask 'what time does the match commence tomorrow?'

Commence is a word which people who make public announcements use only because they have been told to do so by their bosses, because the bosses think it sounds more impressive. This is the same phenomenon as railway passengers being told to *alight* from the train rather than *get off*: railway chiefs seem to think it is more important for their announcements to sound impressive than to be understood. And it is the same phenomenon we find in notices reading 'No alcoholic beverages to be consumed on these premises'.

A large proportion of would-be-'impressive' English words come from French. *Alight* is not one of those – it is Old English in origin. But *commence* is from French, and so are *descent, consume* and *beverage*.

The *Oxford English Dictionary* tells us that the word *commence* is 'precisely equivalent to the native *begin*', and that *begin* is 'preferred in ordinary use; *commence* has more formal associations with law and procedure, combat, divine service, and ceremonial'. A plane coming into land has nothing to do with combat, divine service or ceremonial, but for reasons best known to themselves, many airlines prefer to use artificially ceremonial language for such routine events: they may also have mislaid your baggage rather than lost your suitcase.

This point about natural, informal words versus artificially formal vocabulary can be raised in connection with the 2016 EU referendum. The choice we were given on the ballot paper was between *leave* and *remain*.

Leave is an ancient Germanic word which has been part of English ever since it was a language. The Old English form *læfan* was related to Old Frisian *leva*, Old Saxon *levian* and Old High German *leiben*. The word was brought across the North Sea to this island by our Anglo-Saxon linguistic ancestors during the period AD 350–550 and has always been a natural part of our speech.

This is not true of *remain*. This word was not used in English until the fifteenth century, having originally been found only in the Norman French of our post-1066 overlords. It is still relatively formal in tone, and is not much used in daily conversation. We don't command the dog to 'Remain!' – dogs are instructed to 'Stay!' We do not normally ask 'How long are you remaining in Marbella?' It is not usual to say 'Just remain there while I get it for you'. *Remain* is a member of the *commence–consume–beverage* set of formal words which are generally absent from normal, everyday conversation.

Is it totally impossible that the result of the EU referendum could have been different if the ballot paper had asked us, not if we wanted to *remain* in the EU, but if we wanted to *stay*? After all, the wording for the 1975 referendum was: 'Do you think that the United Kingdom should stay in the European Community (the Common Market)?' The result back then was a 67 per cent 'yes' vote.

It would be interesting to know who decided to use *remain* rather than *stay* this time round.

2 Food and Drink

As we noted in the previous chapter, English is full of words which have come from other languages. But we have to be careful in any given case when assessing where a particular word comes from. For English speakers, it is not at all surprising to discover that the Dutch word for coffee is *koffie*. But English *coffee* is not a loan word from Dutch. The familiar 'coffee' word is something which is shared amongst all European languages. Here is a by-no-means-complete list:

Albanian	*kafe*	German	*Kaffee*	Norwegian	*kaffe*
Basque	*kafea*	Greek	*Kafés*	Polish	*kawa*
Croatian	*kava*	Hungarian	*Kávé*	Portuguese	*café*
Czech	*káva*	Icelandic	*Kaffi*	Romanian	*cafea*
Danish	*kaffe*	Irish Gaelic	*Caife*	Scottish Gaelic	*cofaidh*
Estonian	*kohvi*	Latvian	*Kafija*	Spanish	*café*
Finnish	*kahvi*	Lithuanian	*Kafija*	Welsh	*coffi*
French	*café*	Maltese	*Kafè*		

However, this common European word is not any kind of indication of a common European linguistic heritage. This becomes obvious when we see that different variants of the 'coffee' word are used all over the world. Here is a brief sample:

Chichewa	*Khofi*	(Malawi, and neighbouring areas)
Filipino	*Kape*	(Philippines)
Hausa	*Kofi*	(Nigeria, and neighbouring areas)
Hawaiian	*Kope*	
Indonesian	*Kopi*	
Malagasy	*Kofi*	(Madagascar)
Māori	*Kawhe*	(New Zealand)
Samoan	*Kofe*	
Shona	*Kofi*	(Zimbabwe)
Xhosa	*Kofu*	(South Africa)

Languages everywhere use versions of the same word because they have all acquired it from the same source – and very recently, too. In English, the earliest instances of *coffee/cophee* date to the 1660s.

This worldwide spread of the 'coffee' word is easy to understand. Coffee was originally an East African substance unknown in Europe until 400 years ago –

think of a life without espresso, latte or a cappuccino! Then, as knowledge of this stimulating drink spread, European languages needed and acquired a name for it. The word they adopted came from Turkish *kahveh*, which the Turks had themselves acquired, along with the drink itself, from the Arabs, who called it *qahwah*. The Arabs, in their turn, may have borrowed the word from some East African language, but we are not sure.

Many words for foodstuffs and beverages have similar, and indeed sometimes much more complicated, historical stories to tell. In this chapter, I try to relate a few of them.

2.1 Burgundy

The word *burgundy* has a number of different meanings: it can refer to a particular dark red colour; it can apply to certain kinds of wine; or it can signify an area of eastern France. These meanings are, of course, all linked. Burgundy – in French *Bourgogne* – is the area of eastern France where Burgundy wines are made, and the colour is named after the specific red colour of the wines of that region.

The valley of the Saône, the home of red and white burgundies, is a long way from Scandinavia, but amazingly that is where the story of Burgundy begins. The original Burgundians were a Germanic people who lived in southern Sweden. At some point they migrated to the island of Bornholm (now part of Denmark), which lies in the Baltic Sea about 20 miles off the coast of southern Sweden. In Old Norse, the island was known as Burgundarholmr, 'isle of the Burgundians'. The Saga of Torstein Vikingsson (who came from Sogn in western Norway) also mentions an island called 'Burgenda Land'.

The Burgundians later crossed the Baltic Sea to what is now Poland, and it is believed that by the AD 300s they were living by the River Vistula, which flows through Torun, Bydgoszcz and Warsaw. They spoke an East Germanic language which was closely related to the languages of their neighbours to the south of the Baltic Sea, the Goths and the Vandals.

By the early fifth century, at least some of the Burgundians had travelled on from there far to the west, into the territory of the West Germanic-speaking Swabians and Franks, and were occupying land in the Rhine Valley on the borders of the Roman Empire. Later in the 400s, they crossed the Rhine into Roman territory and formed a kingdom at the western end of the Alps.

We know that at some point after that they gradually abandoned their East Germanic tongue and started speaking a language which was descended from the Latin of the Romans. The Burgundian kingdom occupied an area in which Latin subsequently developed, not into French or Italian, but into Franco-Provencal (or Arpitan), and it has been argued that this is not a coincidence. Some linguistic scientists have suggested that Franco-Provencal arose as a result of East-Germanic-speaking Burgundians learning Vulgar Latin, just as French resulted from West-Germanic-speaking Franks learning Vulgar Latin. Until the nineteenth century, Arpitan was spoken throughout the western Swiss Romandie, in the area around Lausanne, Neuchatel and Geneva, as well as in the adjacent regions of eastern France, including Lyon, St Etienne and Grenoble. It now survives most strongly in the Val d'Aosta region of north-western Italy (see also Section 2.5).

This kingdom of the Burgundians was then swallowed up into the kingdom of the Franks in 534. Part of it later re-emerged as an independent entity in the 800s, as the Duchy of Burgundy. The area of modern France now known as Bourgogne or Burgundy coincides fairly well with the area of that Duchy.

Red wines from the vineyards of modern Burgundy – the wines associated with the colour burgundy – are made from grapes which are known to us by the French name Pinot Noir, 'black pinot'. The word *pinot* is derived from the French word *pin*, 'pine', referring to the fact that the grapes typically grow in tightly clustered, pine-cone-shaped bunches.

The German name for the Pinot Noir grape is *Spätburgunder*, 'late burgundy'. The other types of pinot grape are also overtly recognised in the German language as having an association with Burgundy: the *pinot gris* grape (Italian *pinot grigio*) is known as *Grauburgunder*, 'grey burgundy', and *pinot blanc* (*pinot bianco*) is called *Weissburgunder*, 'white burgundy'.

Sweden is not world famous for its wines, but it is where the name of all these Burgundy wines originally came from.

BALCONY

Burgundy used to be stressed on the second syllable – burGUNdy, rhyming with *Lundy*. Nowadays we stress the first syllable and say BURgundy. This change is only one of a number of examples of the stress in English words being shifted backwards from the second syllable to the first. Until the 1930s, *balcony* was pronounced balCONy – Irish people still say that. We also used to say comPENsate, conCENtrate, comTEMplate and reCONcile.

2.2 Champagne and Prosecco

It is rather well known that champagne is called after the wine-growing Champagne area of north-eastern France. The name of the area itself came originally from the Latin word *Campania*, 'field, open country'. Via Italian *campagna* and French *campagne*, *campania* also gave us English *campaign*, which came to refer specifically to a battlefield, and thus by extension to military operations.

Latin *campania* was derived from *campus*, 'field'. The French word *champs*, as in Champs Elysées, 'Elysian Fields', is the Modern French descendant of Latin *campus*. The Italian equivalent *campo* was also borrowed into French as *camp*, and from there it came into English in the early 1500s, originally with the meaning of a military camp.

The originally American term *campus*, 'grounds of a university or college', was borrowed directly from Latin in the late eighteenth century by Princeton University and adapted to the specialised academic meaning we are now familiar with. It was not used in Britain until the late 1950s – the older British universities did not have campuses. I remember not knowing what *campus* meant when I first encountered it in an American novel in 1964.

It is probably less well known that the name of that popular competitor of champagne, the Italian sparkling wine Prosecco, is also derived from a topographical term referring to open land. The name has nothing at all to do with the Italian word *secco*, 'dry'. In fact, *prosecco* was not originally an Italian word at all. It's true that there is a little disagreement about this, but it seems more or less certain that the name originally came from the village of Prosecco, which is now part of Trieste, in north-eastern Italy.

The city of Trieste has a very multilingual history. Its earliest known local language was a form of Friulian, a Latin-descended Romance language related to Italian and, more closely, to the Swiss language Romansch. As the power of Venice grew, Friulian was gradually replaced by Venetian, a language which is more closely related to Italian and which forms the basis of Trieste's current urban dialect. Trieste was also part of the Austrian Empire for over 500 years and was its only major seaport, so the German language established an important presence there, too.

But, crucially, Trieste has for many centuries also been located in the zone where the western Romance languages of Europe meet the South Slavic languages: Slovenian (also called Slovene) and Croat (or Croatian) are their closest neighbours. There are many Slovenian speakers (with their own Trieste dialect) in the city, as well as elsewhere in north-eastern Italy, and a daily newspaper in Slovenian which is called the *Primorski Dnevnik* ('Coastal Journal') is published there (see also Section 4.9). Trieste was only confirmed in its post-World-War-II status as part of Italy in 1954, and its borders with the neighbouring Yugoslav republics of Slovenia and Croatia were not precisely determined until 1975.

The village of Prosecco was originally called Prosek, a Slovenian dialect name. (German speakers from time to time called it Proseck or Prossegg.) *Prosek* is derived from the historic Slavic verb root *sek-* meaning 'cut, slash, hack' and the Slavic prefix *pro-* meaning 'through', so *proseka* meant 'something cut through'. It typically referred to a strip of land cleared in a forest to provide access, or to mark a boundary, or to act as a fire break. The modern Standard Slovenian variant is *preseka*.

Because it was a common practice in earlier times to build settlements in forest clearings, the name is found as a toponym in many different Slavic-speaking areas. There is an area of Prague called Prosek, and there are Russian and Ukrainian villages called Proseka, as well as Polish settlements named Przesieka. So Slovenian Prosek, now Triestine Prosecco, is just one of many such places originally built in a forest clearing. But it is the only one which has achieved global fame, if only indirectly, in the world of alcohol consumption.

DISSECTION

The ancient Slavic form *sek-* which still survives in Prosecco had the same prehistoric origin as the *sec-* in the Latin word *secare*, 'to cut'. We have borrowed this Latin form into English in words like *dissect*, *bisect*, *intersect* and *section*, which all have to do with cutting in some way or other, as does the – originally French – *secateurs*.

2.3 Water

Anyone noticing that the Dutch word for water is *water* and that the German word is *Wasser* might guess that these two languages are closely related to English.

The fact that Spanish *agua*, Catalan *aigua* and Italian *acqua* all mean 'water' would similarly also suggest to us that these three languages are historically related to each other. And we might infer the same from observing that in Czech and Bulgarian the word for water is *voda*, while in Polish it is *woda*.

These would all be correct guesses and inferences.

Of course, it would generally be unwise to draw strong conclusions about linguistic relationships and language family membership just from similarities between individual words. These might be due to chance: the Malay word for 'name' is, totally coincidentally, *nama*. Or they might be due to common borrowings from the same external source: the Azerbaijani word for 'banana' is *banan*, but this language is not even slightly related to English. Azerbaijani is a Turkic language related to languages like Turkish and Kazakh: their common word for water is *su*.

Words for water are a more reliable pointer to relatedness between languages than words for bananas. We can often get a feel for the different degrees of relatedness between European languages by looking carefully at their basic vocabularies for culturally neutral, fundamental terms such as *water, sun, moon, arm, hand*. I do not need to explain what the German words *Sonne, Mond, Arm, Hand* mean, nor the Dutch words *zon, maan, arm, hand*.

English, Dutch and German are all members of the West Germanic language family. So are West Frisian and North Frisian, where the words for water are, respectively, *wetter* and *weeter*. Low German has *water*, and in Luxembourgish it is *waasser*.

The Scandinavian languages are all members of the North Germanic family, which are related to English, though not so closely as Dutch and German. Their words for 'water' are rather similar to the West Germanic words, and extremely similar to each other: in Norwegian, Icelandic and Faroese the word is *vatn*, the Swedish is *vatten* and the Danish is *vand*.

Czech, Polish and Bulgarian are all members of another language family, Slavic. *Voda* is the word for 'water' not only in these languages but also in Slovak, Slovenian, Croatian, Serbian and the other Slavic languages of the Balkans. (*Vodka* means 'little water'.) Philologists know that the similarities between *voda*, *water* and *vatten* are a consequence of a distant historical relationship between the Germanic and Slavic languages.

Spanish, Catalan and Italian are all members of the Romance family of languages, descended from Latin. So are Portuguese and Romanian, where 'water' is rendered as *agua* and *apa* respectively. These words all derive from Latin *aqua*. Even though the Romance languages are related to English, we cannot tell this from their words for 'water' because *aqua* goes back to a totally different source in our parent Indo-European language. *Water*, *vatn* and *voda* came from Indo-European *ud-or*, while the Latin word descends from the root *akwa-*.

Getting a feel for relationships between languages just by looking at individual words can be fun, but it is no substitute for deeper scientific linguistic research. The Welsh word for 'water' is *dwr*, and the Modern Greek word is *neró*, both of which are so different from the other European words for water that we might conclude that Welsh and Greek are not related to English or Czech or French. But this conclusion would be wrong: Welsh and Greek are certainly Indo-European languages. But Welsh *dwr* comes from yet another Indo-European root, *dubros*, which meant 'deep'. And the Greek word *neró* is a testament to the many different types of development which can occur as languages change. The Modern Greek word does in a way come from ancient *wod-or*, but it is a shortening of Ancient Greek *neron hydor*, 'fresh water', where it was *hydor* which descended from *ud-or*. But you can't tell that just by looking.

What we need in order to study historical relationships is a study of systematic correspondences. We can see, for example, that the English word *five* corresponds to the Dutch *fijf*. German *fünf* also has the same origin, though we might wonder where that *n* comes from. And if we look at the Norwegian, Swedish and Danish word *fem*, plus Icelandic *fimm*, we can again see the similarity, though here the final *f* is missing.

The fact is that all these modern words for 'five' come from the original, ancient Germanic word *fimf* which our linguistic ancestors would have used 2,000 years ago. Since then, as the languages have all changed, English has lost the *m* in this word while Scandinavian languages have lost the final *f*.

Of course, arguing for a shared, wider European ancestry on the basis of a single Germanic root really is not good enough. But we can begin to get an idea of how that argument would work on a larger scale if we look at the Welsh word for 'five', *pump*, pronounced 'pimp'. If you change the *p*'s to *f*'s, then this becomes identical to Germanic *fimf*. And that is actually what happened: the original *p* became *f* in Germanic, but stayed unchanged in other European language families. The word for 'five' still begins with *p* in most European languages: Greek *pente*, Slovenian *pet*, Lithuanian *penti*, Albanian *pesë*, Romany *panj*.

This is not a coincidence. All these forms go back to the word *penkwe*, which meant 'five' in the ancient Indo-European tongue that was the parent language of nearly all modern European languages.

There is one major anomaly. In the Romance languages, words for 'five' have no initial *p* or *f*: it is *cinq* in French, *cinco* in Spanish, *cinque* in Italian. These words all descend from the Latin word *quinque* ('kwinkwe'). That *qu* at the beginning is strange, but we do understand how it came about. When numbers are used for counting, they occur in the same sequence, with *four* coming before *five*. The Latin word for 'four' is *quattuor*. The *p* in the word for 'five' in the original pre-Latin sequence *quattuor – pinque* changed to Latin *qu* under the influence of the two *qu* sounds which occurred before and after it.

LOIRE

Many Western European river names are Celtic. The name of the Loire came from Gaulish *liga*, 'silt, sediment', via Latin *liger*. This Gaulish word was also the source of the French word *lie(s)*, which we have borrowed into English as *lees*, 'sediment at the bottom of a bottle of wine' – including, of course, bottles of wine from the Loire valley.

2.4 Cheese

The distribution of words meaning 'cheese' in different European languages has an interesting geographical pattern. These words fall into four rather clearly separate zones.

In the northern zone, the North Germanic languages have a word for cheese which is related to Latin *ius*, 'broth, sauce', and English *juice*, perhaps originally reflecting a soft type of curdled milk product. 'Cheese' is *ost* in Danish, Norwegian and Swedish, and *ostur* in Icelandic and Faroese; these words have come down from ancient Germanic *justaz*. Words for 'cheese' in the non-Germanic neighbours of the Scandinavians are also derived from this borrowed Germanic root, appearing as *juusto* in Finnish, *juust* in Estonian and *vuostá* in Sami (Lappish).

The second zone lies in eastern Europe, where the Slavic language family's 'cheese' word also suggests a simple kind of fermented milk product: Polish *ser*, Slovak *syr* and Slovenian *sir* are related to English *sour*. The Slavic languages share this form with their neighbours, the Baltic languages: Lithuanian has *suris*, and Latvian *siers*.

In contrast, most of the continent's westernmost languages have borrowed or inherited forms of the Latin word *caseus*, 'cheese'. The widespread occurrence of derivatives of *caseus* in this third zone is thought by some historians to be related to the introduction into northern Europe of the practice of making solid cheese with rennet; this was certainly part of a larger Mediterranean cultural package, arriving together with words for wine and oil. Versions of *caseus* turn up in the Celtic languages that lie on the western fringes of Europe – Welsh, Breton and Gaelic – as *caws*, *keuz* and *cais* respectively. In the West Germanic languages, we find German *Käse*, Dutch *kaas*, Frisian *tsiis* and English *cheese*, suggesting that *caseus* was probably borrowed into Germanic from Latin before the departure of the Anglo-Saxons for England. The most westerly Iberian Romance languages – Galician, Portuguese and Spanish – also have 'cheese' words derived from *caseum*: *queixo*, *queijo* and *queso*.

In this respect they differ markedly from their linguistic neighbour immediately to the east, Catalan, where the word for cheese is *formatge*. Catalan is located in a fourth, even more innovating zone which also includes – on the other side of the Pyrenees in southern France – the Occitan language, where the word for cheese is again *formatge*. Similarly, the French word is *fromage* (from mediaeval French *formage*), the Franco-Provencal (Arpitan) language of eastern France and western Switzerland has *fourmazho* and the Corsican version is *furmagliu*. These words come from Late Latin *formaticum*, from *formare*, 'to form', implying a technical innovation involving shaping cheeses using a mould. Italy straddles zones three and four: the Standard Italian word is *formaggio*, but *cacio* also occurs frequently; and the Sardinian word is *casu*.

The remaining languages of eastern and southern Europe do not fall into this zonal patterning of words for cheese. Albanian *djathë* is related to the classical Indian Sanskrit *dadhi*, 'sour milk'. The Hungarian word is *sajt*, which was borrowed from Old Turkic, but may originally have come from Iranian. The Modern Turkish word is *peynir*, which is certainly of Iranian origin. Maltese *gobon* comes from the same Semitic root as Arabic *jubn* and Aramaic *gwbn*, 'cheese'. And Modern Greek *tirí*, Ancient Greek *tyrós*, probably descended from an Indo-European root *tuhro-*, from *teuh-*, 'to be strong, swell', which, rather remarkably, may also be the ultimate source of English 'thigh'. The origins of our word butter lie in Ancient Greek *boútyron*, which is probably derived from Greek *bous*, 'ox, cow', plus *tyrós*, 'cheese'.

Finally, the Romanian word for cheese is a bit of a mystery. Romanian does have the *caseum*-derived term *cas* for a particular type of cheese, but the most common and general modern word is *branza*, which seems most likely to have come from Latin *brandea*, 'linen wrappings'. This is guesswork – but it's intelligent guesswork, because this would be another example, like *fromage*, of cheese being named after the container in which it is made.

RENNET

The word *rennet* is related to the verb *to run*. It originally referred to the inner membrane of a calf's fourth stomach, or curdled milk from that stomach, and was derived from the Old English verb *rennan*, 'to cause to run together', that is, to coagulate, precisely because it makes milk curdle.

2.5 Gruyère and Tilsit

Very few people in Britain will have heard of Grevire, in spite of the fact that the place is known the world over. It is a small town in Switzerland which is called Greyerz in German, and Greierz, Griiertsch or Grüüersch in Swiss German.

Grevire is the town's name in the local language, Arpitan. Other Arpitan place names include Dzenèva, Lojena and Môtroelx. Since the invasion of Switzerland by Napoleon in 1797, Arpitan has gradually been obliterated in most of the western areas of the country, where it was originally spoken, though it does survive rather strongly across the border from Switzerland in north-western Italy, in the Val d'Aosta. Grevire itself is one of the few places where the language still survives in Switzerland – nearly everywhere else it has been replaced by French.

In French, Dzenèva, Lojena and Môtroelx are known respectively as Genève (Geneva in English), Lausanne and Montreux. And Grevire is Gruyères – it is under this name that the town has become world famous as the home of a certain type of cheese.

The name Grevire/Gruyères/Grüüersch comes from the Vulgar Latin language which was spoken all over Switzerland after the original Celtic and other languages disappeared under the Roman Empire. In Latin it called was *Grusaria*, with *grus* being the Latin word for 'crane' (the bird), so the name presumably originally meant 'place where cranes gather'. Experts do not in fact believe that cranes were ever very common in the area, so the name may go back to a single unexpected – and therefore memorable – sighting.

The name of the town, and the cheese, is so famous that at least one other type of cheese has been named after it. This is the Greek cheese *graviera*, which is particularly associated with certain Greek islands, notably Crete, but which in fact does not resemble Gruyère very closely. The word came into Greek from Italian, where the Swiss cheese is called *gruviera* or *groviera*.

Another rather famous place that most people in this country will never have heard of is Sovetsk. This is a town in the Kaliningrad area of Russia, an exclave which is surrounded by Lithuania, Poland and the Baltic Sea and is well over 400 miles by road from the nearest part of the rest of Russia.

The local language in Sovetsk today is Russian, but the original tongue was the now extinct Baltic language Prussian, which was related to Lithuanian. German-speaking colonisation from the west, led by the Teutonic Knights, began in the mediaeval period; and Old Prussian, like Arpitan, was obliterated – though even more thoroughly, since the language died out completely in the 1600s.

Until World War II, Sovetsk was part of the German province of East Prussia; Kaliningrad was called Königsberg at that time. Before 1945, the main languages in the town were Lithuanian, Low German and German. In Lithuanian, Sovetsk was called Tilže, and in Polish it was known as Tylża. The German name – and this is the one you will have heard of – was Tilsit.

People have heard of Tilsit because it, too, is the name of a well-known type of cheese. In a sense it is also a Swiss cheese. Tilsit was originally made by members of a Mennonite Swiss family who had emigrated to German East Prussia from Emmental – which is about 60 miles from Gruyères. The particular type of cheese they manufactured was developed in East Prussia by a Mrs Westphal, née Klunk. In the early twentieth century, a man called August Westphal became famous as the 'Cheese King' of Wisconsin in the USA, because he owned numerous dairies and cheese factories there.

Today there are no German speakers left in Sovetsk; the Russians who took over Kaliningrad in 1945 replaced them with speakers of Russian and Belorussian. But, unlike Grevire, the older name of Tilsit still lives on in the name of a cheese.

CRANE

Cranes are large birds from the Gruidae family (from Latin *grus*). From the fifteenth century, the English word *crane* has also been used to refer to machines – which resemble the bird – used for raising and lowering heavy objects. The same practice of naming the machine after the bird occurs in other languages: in French they're both called *grue* (also from Latin *grus*).

2.6 Quince

Anyone who's ever eaten one will know that a hamburger has nothing to do with ham. But since we now have beefburgers and cheeseburgers, and even just burgers, it is rather obvious that the word *hamburger* has lost all the connections it used to have with the city of Hamburg. This food item was originally called a 'Hamburger steak' and represented a way of cooking and serving minced beef which was typical of Hamburg. A frankfurter was, similarly, a type of sausage associated with Frankfurt.

Different types of fruit, too, are named after specific places. It is fairly obvious that *tangerines* are named after the Moroccan city of Tangiers. And it is not too surprising to learn that the word *damson* comes from Damascus: the original English name was *damascene*, 'from Damascus', and the Latin name for the fruit was *prunum damascenum*, 'plum of Damascus'. It is possible that damsons were first cultivated in Syria and introduced into Britain by the Romans.

But it is not immediately obvious that the word *currant* is also derived from a place-name. The place in question is the town of Corinth – Kórinthos, in Greek – which must have been one of the areas which currants were originally exported from. They were known in the mediaeval Anglo-Norman French of England as *raisins de Corauntz*, 'grapes of Corinth' (from French *raisins de Corinthe*), and then during the 1400s this started being reduced to simply *corauntz*, *corantes* and then *currants*. It is easier to see the Greek geographical origin of the word in the German name for the dried fruit, *Korinthe*, as well as in Swedish *korint* and Finnish *korintti*. Dutch *krent*, though, is much harder to unravel.

The way in which the word *quince* derives from the name of another Greek town is even more convoluted. The town in question is Canea (in Greek, Chaniá) in Crete. The modern name Chaniá probably comes from Arabic *hani*, 'hostel, inn' – much of Crete was under Arab control from AD 824 to 961. But the original name of the town, which had been built on the site of a Minoan settlement, was Kydonía. The Modern Greek name for quince is *kydóni*, and the Ancient Greek name for the fruit was *melon Kydonion*, 'apple of Kydonía'.

Mediaeval English *quinse* or *quyns* was originally the plural of a form derived from Old French *cooin* (the Modern French is *coing*). *Cooin* came from Latin *cotoneum*, an abbreviation of *malum cotoneum* (the Modern Italian is still *mela cotogna*). The Latin phrase had originally been *malum Cydonium*, a borrowing from the Ancient Greek.

The Estonian word *küdoonia* and the Latvian *cidonija* still show the supposed origin of the name of the fruit in the town of Kydonía rather clearly. It is a little harder to see the connection in the Slovenian version *kutine*. And the German word *Quitte* and Norwegian word *kvede* make it even harder for us to detect the link – but these words do ultimately go back to Kydonía, too.

Whether quinces really had anything to do with Kydonía/Chaniá in the first place is another matter, however. The very earliest Ancient Greek form of the name of the fruit was *kodýmalon*, and it is possible that this was a word borrowed into Greek from some other language – possibly an ancient tongue of Asia Minor, if that is where the fruit originated. The transformation of *kodýmalon* into *Kydonion milon* would then have been a case of folk etymology: Ancient Greek speakers tried to make sense of what, to them, was a nonsensical non-Greek word by turning it into

Greek, much as some English speakers from the 1600s onwards took to changing the meaningless (to them) Latin term *asparagus* into the more meaningful *sparrow grass*, even though many of them must have known that sparrows do not normally eat grass.

PEACH

The English word *peach* came from Old French *pesche*. This had descended from mediaeval Latin *persica*, from classical Latin *persicum malum*, which meant 'Persian apple'. The German name for peach, *Pfirsich*, shows this belief about the geographical origin of peaches more directly. In actual fact, though, botanists believe that peaches originally came from China.

2.7 Bergamot

Many Scandinavians of my acquaintance seem to think that one of the finest things ever to come out of England is Earl Grey tea. They are surprised when I do not share their enthusiasm – it has never been clear to me why anyone would want to ruin a perfectly good cup of tea by putting essence of bergamot in it.

The essence comes from bergamot oranges: a bergamot orange is a citrus fruit, *Citrus bergamia*, first referred to in print in English around 1700. Its name is said by the *Oxford English Dictionary* to be 'apparently from Bergamo, the Italian town'. But this origin is rather hard to credit, since Bergamo lies in the foothills of the Alps, and according to the American botanist Professor Kathleen Keeler, oranges cannot grow there. Most bergamot essence is made from the fruit of trees grown in Calabria in southern Italy, about 600 miles south of Bergamo.

The issue is further confused by the fact that bergamot is not only a term for a citrus fruit, but is also the name of at least two different herbs. In North America, the name generally refers to *Monarda fistulosa*, an indigenous mint, while in Britain it more often refers to *Monarda didyma*, another American plant. Both of these herbs are also known as bee balm. The first recorded use of *bergamot* referring to a herb comes from 1843. As to where the name comes from in this case, we can simply suppose that the herbs' aroma reminded the first Europeans in America of the scent of bergamot oranges.

It is disconcerting, then, to note that a bergamot is not only a herb and a type of orange, but also a kind of pear: there is a particularly juicy and delicious fruit known as a bergamot pear. Scientifically, it is a variety of *Pyrus communis*. The name of the bergamot pear made its first appearance in written English around 1600. Interestingly, the *OED* gives a different etymology for this meaning than it does for the citrus fruit and herb. The dictionary states that the name of the pear came into English from French *bergamotte*, which was from Italian *bergamotta*, which came from Ottoman Turkish *beg armudi*, 'prince's pear' – in Modern Turkish, *bey armudu*.

There may also have been a link somewhere along the line with the name of the Turkish town of Bergama, which in Ancient Greek was Pergamon or Pergamos. (The Greek word for bergamot orange is *pergamonto*.) In 1885, the *New York Times* claimed that bergamot pears were first introduced into Europe by the Crusaders – which was 'no doubt the reason why in some parts of southern Europe they are still known by the name of Syrian pears'. The *Times* also wrote that the word *bergamot* was believed to be derived from the name of a village in Cyprus called Pergama or Pergamos, which may or may not have been named after classical Pergamon. In the 1950s, the Turkish-speaking inhabitants of this Cypriot village gave it the name of Beyarmudu.

The 'prince's pear' etymology actually makes rather good sense; and we can suppose that *beg armudi* became Italian *bergamotta* through the well-known process of folk etymology: Italian speakers made sense of what, to them, was a new and meaningless Turkish form by making an (unwarranted) link from it to their own town of Bergamo, which had had in fact nothing to do with it.

Happily, there is no need to restrict this etymological explanation solely to the word for the pear. The first bergamots were indeed pears; but Professor Keeler suggests that the name was then later transferred to the citrus fruit (about a hundred years later, in the case of English) because it looked very similar to the (very round) bergamot pear. And then, because of the scent, to the herbs.

Interestingly, *beg armudi* has made its way back to its original homeland. Unlike in English, there is no linguistic confusion in Modern Turkish between the bergamot pear and the citrus bergamot: the pear is called *bey armudu*, while the citrus fruit is called . . . *bergamot*.

CITRUS

Citrus was a Latin word which originally referred to a scented conifer native to North Africa. Etymologists are not agreed about the word's origin, but it may be related to Greek *kedros*, 'cedar'. Or it may be of Etruscan origin: one place where Etruscan was probably spoken around 600 BC was Bergamo.

2.8 Mayonnaise

The popular name of the French national anthem, the Marseillaise, is the feminine form of the adjective meaning 'from Marseilles' (*Marseille* in French). The French suffix *-ais* (masculine) and *-aise* (feminine) is generally used to indicate that a person or entity comes from a particular place, as with *anglais*, 'from England, English', *francais*, 'French', *irlandais*, 'Irish'.

This *-ais(e)* suffix had two sources: the Latin ending *-ensis*; and the Frankish ending *-isk*, from the ancient Germanic *-iskaz* meaning 'pertaining to', which also produced English *-ish*, Danish *-isk* and German *-isch*. Both endings turned into *-ais* through processes of linguistic change in French.

While French is not a Germanic language – it is a Romance language descended from Latin – France is named after the Franks, the Germanic people who, from the fourth century AD onwards, moved westwards across the Rhine into the Roman territory of northern Gaul – now southern Belgium and northern France. So the Germanic source of the *-ais* suffix is no surprise.

The Franks who stayed outside the Roman Empire remain Germanic speaking to this day. Modern Dutch is classified by linguists as a Low Frankish or Low Franconian dialect. Luxembourgish is also Franconian, and so are the dialects of the whole of central Germany, from Cologne to Frankfurt, Heidelberg and across to Nuremburg.

But the Franks who moved into Roman territory gradually became more and more Romanised, and changed from using Germanic Frankish as their language to Vulgar Latin. In shifting to speaking what was to them originally a foreign language, they influenced the local Vulgar Latin considerably (see also Section 2.1), rather as Modern Caribbean English has been influenced by the majority of its first speakers shifting to English from West African languages. We can say that early French was essentially a Germanicised version of the Vulgar Latin of northern Gaul.

Given this French naturalisation of the originally Germanic *-isk* as *-ais(e)*, it is now amusing to see that *-ais(e)* has made its way back again into our own Germanic language, English, and become somewhat naturalised here. English-speaking cooks talk readily of Hollandaise sauce, using the originally French word meaning 'from Holland, Dutch'. We also have Bordelaise sauce, which we are not too surprised to learn is named after the Bordeaux area of south-western France; though it is perhaps not quite so obvious that Béarnaise sauce derives its name from the neighbouring Bearn area of Gascony.

But what about *mayonnaise*? Mayonnaise is more of a dressing than a sauce, but we can see that once again it has this *-aise* suffix, indicating that it too is associated with a particular place. But which place? No one has ever claimed that it comes from County Mayo in Ireland. But where is it from?

In a desperate attempt to credit the origins of yet another culinary preparation to south-western France, some French philologists have argued that *mayonnaise* was a spelling mistake and the name should really be *bayonnaise*, 'from Bayonne'. Others have argued that the word does not have its origins in a place name at all and that it is really *moyeunaise*, derived from an Old French word *moyeu* meaning 'egg yolk'.

But the most likely explanation is that this is one culinary success that cannot be claimed by the French at all, and that the word has its origins further south. The name of the capital of the Balearic island of Menorca (often Minorca in English) is most often written Mahon in English; its Spanish name is Mahón. But Minorca is Catalan speaking, with the local variant of the language being known as Menorquín. In Catalan, the name of the capital of the island is Maó: mayonnaise most likely means 'from Mahon'.

MAHON

The next time you open a jar of mayonnaise, you might like to think that the name of the Minorcan capital Maó, from which *mayonnaise* derives, is believed to be taken from the name of the Carthaginian military leader Mago Barca. This general is thought to have taken refuge on the island of Minorca after a defeat by the Romans, and possibly to have even founded the city. Mago was the brother of that other Carthaginian general Hannibal, who famously crossed the Alps with his elephants.

2.9 Stew

If you have been up in the Greek mountains, you may have encountered the word *somba*. This is an important Greek word in the wintertime, as it means 'stove' – in mountainous country most often referring to a wood-burning heater.

Somba is a much-travelled word. It came into Greek from Turkish: the Modern Turkish word for 'stove' is *soba*. Most Greek speakers were under the suzerainty of the Ottoman empire for several centuries, and during that time many words of Turkish origin made their way into Modern Greek. This was also true of Romanian speakers – one of their modern words for 'stove' is *soba* – and of Albanian speakers – the corresponding word in Albanian is *sobe*.

But *soba* was not originally a Turkish word. The Turks had borrowed it from Hungarian. In Modern Hungarian the word *szoba* means 'room', though this originally referred to a heated room – as it did in German, which is where the Hungarians, in their turn, got the word from. In Old High German, which is what the language of southern Germany up until about AD 1000 is known as, the corresponding word was *stuba*.

But it turns out that *stuba* was not originally a German word either. The details are not totally clear, but it seems that it came into German from the Late Latin form *stufa*, from the verb *stufare*, which was originally *extufare* in Vulgar Latin, where it meant 'to take a steam bath'. Amazingly, though, this was not even originally a Latin word. The *ex-* part of *extufare* certainly was Latin, but the *-tufare* part came from *tupha*, which had been borrowed into Latin from another language: *tupha* meant 'steam' or 'smoke' in Ancient Greek, first recorded in the writings of Hippocrates in the 400s BC! So over the course of several centuries, the word went full circle, from Greek to Latin to German to Hungarian to Turkish and back to Greek again.

This word also made its way into many other languages. The Modern German descendant of ancient *stuba* is *Stube*, which refers to a (heated) sitting-room. In the Plattdeutsch or Low German of northern Germany, the corresponding word is *stuuv*. From there, it made its way north into the Scandinavian languages: in Icelandic it's *stofu*, in Norwegian *stove* or *stue*, in Danish *stue*; and in Swedish, *stuga* means 'a cabin'.

Remarkably, English has borrowed the *stufa* word no fewer than three times. Old English had a rare word *stofa*, meaning a room for taking a steam- or hot-air bath in; the form *stuf-bæþ* also occurred, meaning 'hot-air bath'. Then the word seems to have disappeared from the language, not coming back into English again until around 1450 as *stove*, a borrowing from Low German meaning 'heated room'. Gradually, from about 1600 onwards, the meaning of the word started being transferred from referring to a heated room to the device used to do the heating. During the 1700s it then also came to refer to a device used for cooking as well as heating.

But during the fifteenth century, English not only borrowed *stove* from Low German, it also borrowed the word *estuve* from mediaeval French. This, too, had originally descended from Late Latin *stufa*: Modern French *étuve* means 'steam room'. *Estuve* became *stuwe* or *stewe* in English, where it meant one of two things. First, it could, like *stove*, mean a heated room – and by the 1300s it was also being used to mean 'brothel', presumably because of the frequent use of bathhouses for prostitution. Secondly, it also referred to a vessel used for cooking by means of steaming or boiling, so 'cauldron'. During the 1700s there was then another transfer of meaning, with the result that *stew* gradually came to refer to the food cooked in a cauldron rather than to the vessel itself.

It was a long journey from Hippocrates to Irish stew.

METONYMY

Metonymy is the substitution of one word by another which has an association with it of some kind: *suit* for 'business executive' is an example. Changes in the meanings of words can involve metonymic processes, as with *stove*, 'heated room', becoming 'heater'; and *stew*, 'cauldron', becoming 'food cooked in a cauldron'.

2.10 Danish

The term *Danish pastry* first hit the English-speaking world when these pastries were served in Washington, DC at the wedding of President Woodrow Wilson in 1915. It was his second marriage, to a younger woman; it took place rather soon after his first wife had died; and he was the incumbent president. This event was always going to attract lots of attention.

But people did not just notice the wedding – they noticed the pastries too, which subsequently went on to take New York society by storm, and then spread from there to the rest of America. Today, Danish pastries have become so common in the USA that Americans when ordering one generally just ask for 'a Danish'. There is no need to specify any further.

In this country, we lagged a couple of decades behind. The term *Danish pastry* did not arrive in Britain until the 1930s, when it turned up in London along with the pastries themselves.

But why were they called Danish? That is a rather easy question to answer. To hunt for the origins of this name we just have to go back from New York City to Copenhagen, which was where the bakers who first brought the pastries to the USA had come from, and where these treats had been being produced since the 1850s.

But this raises the interesting linguistic question of what these pastries are called in Denmark. It made sense to refer to them as 'Danish' in the USA but, very obviously, it would not be any good asking for a Danish pastry in Denmark because all pastries in Denmark are Danish … And the fact is that if you want a Danish pastry in Copenhagen or Odense or Aarhus, you have to ask for a *wienerbrød* – which means 'Viennese bread'.

That then sets us another lexical puzzle: what did Vienna have to do with it? Why did the Danes think of these pastries as being Viennese? It turns out that Danish pastries were first made in Copenhagen by bakers from the Austrian capital who had come to Denmark by invitation because the Danish bakers were on strike.

But then one can't help wondering what *wienerbrød* are called in Vienna, where everything is Viennese. According to native Austrian informants, there is no single word in Vienna for *wienerbrød* – there are so many sub-types of this kind of pastry there that the usual practice is to ask for a particular sort by name. But it also seems that the Viennese pastry which originally found its way to Copenhagen and became the prototype of what we now think of as 'a Danish' was of the particular type which Viennese people call a *golatsche*.

But that is not the end of the story, because it emerges that *golatsche* – which actually doesn't sound at all like a German-language word – was not originally an Austrian term. The Viennese took this name from the Czech language of Bohemia, which in the nineteenth century was part of the Austro-Hungarian Empire, of which Vienna was the capital; Bohemia is now on the other side of the Austrian border with Czechia. So we should really be calling Danish pastries and *wienerbrød*, 'Bohemian pastries'.

The Czech word which *golatsche* derives from is *koláč*, and there is a suggestion that this comes from the Slavic word for 'wheel' – *kolo* in Czech – because a Bohemian *koláč* is typically round. If so, this circularity is rather appropriate because, according to native Czech informants, if you are in Prague and want a Danish pastry, the most usual thing is, as in Vienna, to specify the particular type you want. A *koláč* would be just one possibility.

But there is now also a rather new Czech term you can use if you want to ask for a *wienerbrød* without specifying a particular type: *dánské pečivo*. It is not too hard to guess what that means. *Dánské* is the Czech word for 'Danish'. And *pečivo* means pastry . . .

2.11 Loaf

It is a common enough process in linguistic change for two words to end up coalescing into one. It is really rather obvious that *afternoon* was originally two words, even if it is clearly a single word now. And, although this is not so obvious from the pronunciation, we can see from the spelling that *cupboard* started out as the two words, *cup board*. But there are plenty of other instances of 'univerbation' – as this two-words-into-one coalescing process is called – which are much less obvious than these. For example, *but* comes from Old English *butan*, 'outside, except', which had formerly been two words, *bi*, 'by', and *utan*, 'from outside'.

The English word *lord* has a similar history. In late Old English, the form of the word was *hlaford*, from an earlier two-part compound, *hlaf-weard*. The Modern English forms corresponding to *hlaf* and *weard* are respectively *loaf* and *ward*, but Old English *hlaf* seems to have meant 'bread' rather than 'loaf', and *weard* is probably best translated as 'guardian'. So a *lord* was originally a 'bread guardian' – the person responsible for the provision of bread. The centrality of the role of providing bread in an Anglo-Saxon household can be surmised from the fact that *lady* also originally came from two words, *hlaf dige*, 'bread kneader', where *dige* is related to our contemporary word *dough*. There was also another Old English form *hlaf-æta*, 'household servant', which literally meant 'loaf-eater' – so someone who ate the bread provided by their master.

The word *hlaf*, Modern English *loaf*, descended from an ancient Proto-Germanic root *hlaibaz*. We do not really know if *hlaibaz* originally meant 'bread' as a substance or 'loaf (of bread)' as an object. The Modern German word *Laib* means 'loaf', and so do the Scots word *laif* and the North Frisian form *liaf*. The corresponding Norwegian word *leiv* signifies 'slice (of bread)'. (Norwegian, incidentally, has also borrowed our Modern English word *loaf* in the form of *loff* meaning 'white bread'.) There is probably not too much point in worrying about this, though, because in many languages there is no real distinction between 'loaf' and 'bread' anyway: in Danish, the phrase *tre brød* is literally 'three breads' but has to be translated into English as 'three loaves (of bread)'.

Interestingly, the old Germanic word *hlaibaz* also seems to have been borrowed into a number of other neighbouring languages with the meaning of 'bread'. Finnish *leipä* means 'bread', and so do Estonian *leib* and Sami (Lappish) *láibi*. The ancient Slavic language also borrowed this word from Germanic: the Modern Polish word for bread is *chleb*, and Czech, Slovak and Russian have *chléb*, *chlieb* and *khleb* respectively.

It is interesting to wonder why the speakers of these languages borrowed this word from their Germanic-speaking neighbours. The Slavic-speaking ancestors of the Poles, Czechs, Russians and Slovaks certainly knew how to make bread, so surely they must have had their own words for this foodstuff as well? Could it be that Germanic speakers introduced some kind of improved bread-making technology which resulted in a somewhat different and perhaps better product? Well, maybe, but to confuse the issue further there is also a theory that *hlaibaz* originally referred to unleavened flatbread, while Germanic *braudoz*, the ancestor of the word *bread*, meant leavened bread. The *Oxford English Dictionary*, though, believes that while *hlaibaz* meant 'bread', *braudoz* originally meant 'piece, bit' or 'fragment'. This came to be interpreted as 'piece of bread', 'broken bread', and then ultimately simply as 'bread as a substance'.

People in Scotland and the North of England may accept this particular account readily enough since, in those parts of Britain, our Modern English word *piece* can be used to refer specifically to a slice of bread: in Scotland, a *jelly-piece* or *jeely-piece* is a slice of bread and jam, especially as given to children.

JELLY

Jelly was originally the French word *gelée*, meaning 'frost'. This had come from the Latin *gelata*, 'frozen, congealed', from the verb *gelare*, 'to freeze'. *Jam* is more mysterious in terms of its origins, but it seems to have come from the verb *to jam* meaning 'to crush something into a confined space'.

2.12 Pizza

When I was at school, we had no idea what a pizza was. We did not know the word – we had never seen a pizza, and we had certainly never tasted one. I do not remember ever eating pizza until 1968, and even that was in Germany. The dish is said to have arrived in Britain in the 1960s; friends who were in London at the time recall the years around 1967 and 1968 as the period when they had their first UK pizza experience. So the English word *pizza* is really very recent.

Nowadays people in most parts of the world know that the word *pizza* means, as the *Oxford English Dictionary* describes it, 'a savoury dish of Italian origin, consisting of a flat, usually round base of dough, baked with a topping of tomatoes, cheese, and any of various other ingredients, such as meat, anchovies, or olives'. So it is interesting to discover that the origins of the word itself are actually a bit obscure, even if it seems rather certain, for all that its arrival in English is very recent, that its source is very ancient.

It will be no surprise to anyone if I say that the word *pizza* came into English from Italian; but beyond that, its beginnings are somewhat mysterious. For a start, it was not a Standard Italian word but came from some regional dialect: it was associated especially with Naples, though there is a suggestion that the word originally came from the Abruzzo region, on the Adriatic coast of Italy to the east of Rome.

After that, the professional etymologists seem rather stumped. One possibility is that *pizza* was originally a (West) Germanic word, going back to the word *bizzo* which meant 'bite, piece bitten off' in Old High German, the ancestor of Modern German. The origin of our English word *bit* – which I used just a few sentences back – is the same: the original meaning was 'a piece of food bitten off', or 'a mouthful'.

If the Modern Italian word is of Germanic origin, then it would probably have come from the language of the Lombards. They were a Germanic tribe who invaded Italy during the sixth century A D and formed a kingdom which survived until 774, when they were conquered by the (also Germanic) Frankish leader Charlemagne. The kingdom of the Lombards included the area of Abruzzo.

There is also the possibility that *pizza* is related to the word *pitta* or *pita* meaning 'flatbread'. This word, too, is relatively new in English, dating from the 1930s, and seems rather clearly to have been borrowed from Greek, though in Greece today *pitta* also means a pie made with filo pastry, as in *tirópitta*, 'cheese pie'. *Pitta* may well be of mediaeval Greek origin. If so, it might just be the source of Italian *pizza*. It is certainly the source of the Serbian and Bulgarian word for flatbread, *pita*, as well as Albanian *pite* and Ladino (Judeo-Spanish) *pita*.

But where did the Greek word come from? There is a strong possibility that a Germanic language was once again involved somewhere along the line. There is a suggestion that the Greek word came from Gothic *bita*, also meaning 'bite'. Gothic was the (East) Germanic language that was spoken by the Ostrogothic tribe who started migrating down into the Balkans from north of the Danube in the late 300s A D. Like English *bite* and *bit*, Old High German *bizzo* and Modern German *Bisschen*, 'a bit', the Gothic word ultimately goes back to the form *bheid*, which 6,000 years ago meant 'to split' or 'to crack' in our ancestral language, Proto-Indo-European.

So nobody really knows for sure what the linguistic origin of the word is, but next time you take a bite of pizza, you might consider that it is perfectly possible that *bite* and *pizza* were originally the same word.

3 People

As we have already seen, English is the most important lingua franca in modern Europe, if not in the world. But that has not always been the case. And there are still many situations where English does not necessarily function very well.

Some of the biggest issues of our day are intimately tied up with using language, and yet we rarely stop to think about the problems this might entail. The British Prime Minister and Angela Merkel have a telephone conversation about important European issues – but how does that work? Did the Prime Minister's expensive education buy him fluency in German? How good is Merkel's English? Do they use interpreters? How do you organise a telephone conversation using interpreters?

The individual linguistic competence of prominent people is not often a subject of interest or inquiry, but it can sometimes be of considerable importance. The vitally important Yalta conference, held in February 1945, consisted of top-level discussions and negotiations involving the Soviet Union, the United Kingdom and the United States. It was very easy for the UK's Churchill and the USA's Roosevelt to chat to each other informally there, in the Crimea, in English, their shared mother tongue. But Stalin could not join in: his native tongue was Georgian, and he was also a fluent speaker of Russian, although he spoke it with a very noticeable Georgian accent. But he could not speak English.

In many other cases, the subject of which languages prominent people may be able to speak is not of any great importance, but it can still be of considerable interest. The famous Czech composer Antonin Dvorak conducted orchestras in England and became the director of the National Conservatory of Music of America in New York. But how good was his English? And how did he learn it? In this chapter, we examine the linguistic histories and abilities of a number of prominent figures, both historical and not so historical.

3.1 Gaius Julius Caesar

Every year, the Greeks celebrate Ochi Day. *Ochi* is the Greek word for 'no', and 28 October is the national holiday when the whole country commemorates saying No! The man who actually said 'ochi' on the nation's behalf, in 1940, was the Greek fascist dictator, Ioánnis Metaxás, and the man he said it to was the fascist dictator of Italy, Benito Mussolini. He did not say 'no' to him face to face, but to the Italian ambassador to Athens, Emanuele Grazzi, who had been tasked by Mussolini to deliver an ultimatum. Mussolini was demanding that his Italian troops, who had already invaded southern Albania, should be allowed to enter northern Greece and occupy strategic sites. The ultimatum was: either you allow us to occupy these sites, or we invade. As every Greek schoolchild knows, Metaxás rejected the ultimatum by proudly replying 'Ochi'.

Except that he almost certainly didn't. Crowds were, for sure, out in the streets of Athens later that day shouting 'Ochi!' But we can very seriously doubt that Metaxás himself uttered this word.

There are many linguistic details we are not sure about as far as the meeting between the ambassador and the dictator is concerned, but we do know that Metaxás was a native speaker of Greek and Grazzi was an Italian speaker. Were interpreters present? It appears not. Did Grazzi speak Greek? That seems unlikely. How was Metaxás's Italian? Probably non-existent. Metaxás had studied in Germany, so if Grazzi also knew German, it is possible that they conversed in that language.

But in fact, the most likely scenario is that Metaxás replied to the ultimatum by using, not the Greek word *ochi*, nor the German word *nein*, nor the Italian word *no*, but the French word *non*. Ochi Day might really have been Non Day. There are reports that what Metaxás actually said was 'Alors, c'est la guerre' ('OK, so it's war, then'). The point is that, up until 1918, the undisputed lingua franca – a language of wider communication between peoples who have no native language in common – was French as far as international diplomacy was concerned. It had been the major language of communication at the 1814–15 Congress of Vienna which followed the defeat of Napoleon, and by 1940 French was still maintaining this role rather strongly, at least in Europe. It was probably the only language Metaxás and Grazzi had in common, so they were very probably both using French.

Another similar language-based 'fact' that most people seem to know is that, as Julius Caesar was being stabbed to death, he turned to his friend Brutus, who was one of the assassins, and said 'Et tu, Brute?', the Latin for 'And you too, Brutus?' People know that because those were the words put into Caesar's mouth by Shakespeare in his play *The Tragedy of Julius Caesar*.

But that, too, is probably wrong. We do not in fact know if Caesar said anything at all when he was stabbed – there are no eyewitness reports from 44 BC. But we do know that if he did say something, it very probably was not in Latin – it is much more likely that his dying words were uttered in Greek. The Roman historian Suetonius – it is true that he was not an eyewitness, since he was writing about the event well over a century after it happened – claimed that what Caesar said was 'Kai su, teknon?', which is the Ancient Greek for 'And you, my son?'

The main language of Ancient Rome was Latin, but we can be rather certain that Caesar would have been speaking Greek rather than Latin at that moment. The reason for this is rather similar to the reason why Metaxás, 2,000 years later, was speaking French. Caesar's native language was undoubtedly Latin; but the patricians of Ancient Rome, the members of the elite upper classes like Julius Caesar, were bilingual in Latin and Greek, and they tended to speak Greek to each other.

At the time when Caesar was murdered, Alexander 'the Great' of Macedon had been dead for nearly three centuries, but his conquests had taken the Greek language, with his armies, across the Middle East and Iran into the places which we today call Turkmenistan, Tajikistan, Uzbekistan, Afghanistan and Pakistan, as well as into north-western India and parts of Kyrgyzstan and Kazakhstan.

As a result of his conquests, Greek became vitally important as a lingua franca over a very large area of the eastern Mediterranean; and later on, even under the Roman Empire, Greek remained the official language of the Roman provinces of Libya, Egypt, Arabia, Judea, Syria and Persia, as well as of Greece and Asia Minor. This widespread knowledge of Greek led to it being used as the language of the New Testament, which greatly aided the rapid spread of Christianity. In Ancient Rome itself, Greek became the prestigious language of learning and cultivation to such an extent that the upper classes spoke it amongst themselves, much as Russian aristocrats in the nineteenth century took to speaking French to each other.

There was one other thing it aided too. The fifty-five-year-old Julius Caesar had for some years been having a love affair with the twenty-four-year-old Queen of Egypt, Cleopatra, who was actually in Rome when he was assassinated. She might never have been able to seduce him, as she is said to have done in Alexandria, if Greek had not been her mother tongue, and if it had not also been Caesar's second language.

3.2 King Knutr

England has a very long tradition of monarchs who could not speak English, or who were at least not native speakers of it. These ranged from the French-speaking William I of 1066 fame and the Provençal-speaking Richard the Lionheart (king from 1189), via the Dutch-speaking William III of 1689, to the German-speaking George I, who became king in 1714, and on to the bilingual germanophone King Edward VII from 1901 (see Section 3.3).

But it is surprising to learn that there is also a distinct possibility that England once had a monarch who was a native speaker of the Slavic language Polish. This is very much speculation, but if it has any basis in fact, then the royal personage concerned was the famous King Canute, who is well known for demonstrating that he was not omnipotent by proving how even he was unable to prevent the tide from coming in – a good story, even if it isn't true.

Canute was known by the name of Cnut in Old English, and Knutr in Old Norse. (In Modern Norwegian and Swedish he is Knut, in Danish Knud.) At the height of his powers he was King of England, which he ruled for nearly twenty years, as well as King of Denmark (from 1018) and Norway (from 1028). He had become England's ruler by invading the country in 1015 and finally taking control of the entire kingdom, through military might and political negotiation, in 1016. Widely known as Cnut the Great, he was a European figure of some considerable consequence: in 1027, he actually travelled all the way to Rome to attend the coronation of the Holy Roman Emperor, Conrad IV.

Cnut seems to have grown up in Denmark, and it is certain that he spoke Old Danish, which was his father's language. He also wrote letters in Old English – though of course he might have had them written and/or translated for him. In one of these missives, he stated: 'Cnut cyning gret his arcebiscopas ond ealle his eorlas ond ealne his þeodscype on Englalande freondlice' ('King Cnut greets his archbishops and all his earls and all his people in England friendly-ly').

But what about the Polish connection? Cnut – Kanut in Polish – was the son of the Danish royal Sweyn Forkbeard, whose wife was reportedly the daughter of King Mieszko I of Poland. She is known as Gunhild in Scandinavian sources, but her Slavic name might actually have been Świętosława. She may not even have been the daughter of the Polish king, but if not, then she was very probably Polabian instead. The Polabians, or Wends, were a West Slavic people who spoke a language closely related to Polish. Their homeland lay in what is now northeastern Germany in the area around Rostock, where the coastline at its closest point is not much more than twenty miles across the Baltic Sea from the Danish island of Falster.

Interestingly, the mother of Sweyn Forkbeard was herself Polabian, which could make Cnut a maximum of three-quarters Slavic! On the other hand, if Cnut's mother really was the daughter of King Mieszko of Poland, whose wife was German, that would make Cnut a quarter German, a quarter Polish, a quarter Polabian and a quarter Danish, so only 50 per cent Slavic. One thing that is certain, though, is that he was precisely 0 per cent English.

There is a story that at some stage Cnut's father Sweyn sent his wife Gunhild/Świętosława back to Poland. But it seems that when Sweyn died, Cnut and his brother Harald travelled to Poland, quite possibly to Poznan, to bring her back to Denmark again. Mothers normally talk to their infants in their native language and, although it does not necessarily follow that Cnut grew up speaking Polish or Polabian, it is really entertaining to suppose that our Germano-Celtic nation might once have had a Slavic-speaking king.

3.3 Richard Quor de Lion

When I was at junior school in the 1950s, one of the most romantic stories we learnt in our history lessons was the heroic tale of the crusading King Richard I, 'The Lionheart'. From 1189 to 1199, he was the king of our country, England – in those days, we never considered we might live in a place called 'Britain', let alone 'the UK'. And he was a Good King – unlike his brother, King John, who was a Bad King.

We also knew that Richard was known not just as The Lionheart, but also by the equivalent French name, Coeur de Lion. But we would have been extremely surprised if anybody had told us – nobody did – that it was really rather probable that this great King of England was not able to speak English.

Richard may perhaps have had some competence in the language: he was born in England. But like all the early kings of England from William the Conqueror onwards, he grew up surrounded by the Norman aristocracy of England, whose everyday language was Anglo-Norman (Norman French), in which the name *Lionheart* would have been rendered as *Quor de Lion*. After he became king, Richard spent a total of only about six months in England, which would have done nothing to improve any English-language skills he might have had.

But there was something rather more unusual about Richard linguistically: his dominant native language was not even Norman French but Occitan, the language of southern France, spoken then and now in different regional varieties such as Provençal, Gascon and Languedocien. Richard's mother was Eleanor of Aquitaine – her actual Occitan name seems to have been Aliénor – and Richard himself became Duke of Aquitaine, the area of south-western France where Bordeaux, Pau and Bayonne are situated. Richard not only spoke Occitan but also wrote poetry in the language.

It was not for another 200 years after Richard that England acquired an English-speaking monarch. The first king since 1066 to have English as his mother tongue was Henry IV, king from 1399 to 1413. And even after that, it was by no means a foregone conclusion that our monarchs were going to be anglophone. Henry VII, who became king in 1485, seems to have spoken Welsh, though possibly only as a second language. James I was certainly a native speaker of Scots. William III, who ruled from 1689 to 1702, was a native speaker of Dutch. The Hanoverian George I, king from 1714, was a German speaker. George II grew up speaking French, but also spoke Low German (Plattdeutsch), the language of northern Germany; he spoke German, too, though reluctantly, and spoke English with a foreign accent. Even George III, who ruled until 1820, was somewhat bilingual in English and German.

George III's granddaughter Queen Victoria had both a mother and a husband, Prince Albert, who were German speakers, and she certainly spoke German herself. Victoria's son, Edward VII, who died in 1910, spoke both German and English from childhood.

But then, seven centuries after Richard the Lionheart, the linguistic tables turned. King George V – Edward's son – and Kaiser Wilhelm II of Germany were both grandsons of Queen Victoria: and Wilhelm happily spoke English to his monolingual cousin George. Wilhelm was also a third cousin of Tsar Nikolas of Russia, whose wife, the Empress Alexandra, was another grandchild of Victoria and spoke English natively. Whenever the Russian Tsar, the German Kaiser and the English king met, their common language was English. Before World War I, the Tsar and the Kaiser frequently corresponded with one another in English, addressing each other as 'Willy' and 'Nicky'.

Of Victoria's other grandchildren, Princess Maud became Queen of Norway, Princess Sophie was Queen of Greece, Princess Marie became Queen of Romania, Princess Margaret was Queen of Sweden and Princess Victoria Eugenie was Queen of Spain.

From having been a language not spoken even by the King of England, it was now English, rather than French, Occitan, Scots, Dutch or German, which had become the common language of the European monarchy.

3.4 Napolione di Buonaparte

Hitler and Napoleon both became rulers of countries they had not been born in. Adolphus Hitler was born in 1889 in the Austro-Hungarian Empire in the town of Braunau am Inn, which is now in Austria. But that did not stop him from becoming Chancellor of Germany in 1933.

Napolione di Buonaparte was born in 1769 in Ajaccio, Corsica. But that did not stop him from becoming the First Consul of France in 1799, and Emperor in 1804. It is true that by the time Napoleon became ruler, the formerly independent Republic of Corsica had become French as a result of invasion and military conquest, but Corsica did not officially become part of France until 1796.

Napoleon's birthplace presented him with a difficulty that Hitler did not experience. Both Austria and Germany were, and are, German speaking. In his informal speaking style, Hitler did retain much of the accent of the area where he grew up, on the borders of Upper Austria and German Bavaria. But on formal occasions he spoke a Standard German which gave away relatively few clues as to his southern origins.

On the other hand, while in 1769 much of France was French speaking, Corsica was not francophone. Napoleon's mother tongue was *Corsu*, which in English is known as Corsican. It is spoken all over the island of Corsica and also, in the form of the Gallurese dialect, in the northern part of neighbouring Sardinia, where it has official recognition.

Like French, Corsican is a Romance linguistic variety descended from Latin, but it is much more closely related to the Romance languages of the Italian peninsula than to French. It would not be at all illegitimate to regard Corsu as a language in its own right, as many Corsicans do. But if you would prefer to consider it a dialect, then you would definitely have to say that it was a dialect of Italian. Its closest linguistic relatives are generally agreed to be the dialects of Tuscany. Corsica is about 55 miles from the coast of Tuscany, and only seven miles from the Italian island of Sardinia, but it lies more than 110 miles off the coast of mainland southern France.

At the time Napoleon was born, Italian was the official language of Corsica, so those Corsicans who were literate learnt to read and write in Italian, even if they usually spoke Corsican. More than two centuries of unsympathetic French rule, however, have considerably weakened the position of Corsican today, and many people on the island no longer speak it. In February this year, Emmanuel Macron infamously made a speech in Bastia, Corsica, in which he stated that he was totally in favour of the *esprit du bilinguisme*, 'the spirit of bilingualism', but at the same time he refused to consider granting Corsu official status on the island alongside French, something which some Corsican language activists believe is as good as sentencing Corsican to death – the language is already described by some linguists as being endangered.

In the eighteenth century, however, everybody in Corsica spoke Corsican – and many of them spoke only Corsican. When Napoleon moved with his family to mainland France as a nine-year-old, he could not speak French and did not start learning it at school until he attended the Royal Military Academy at the age of ten. At some point along the way, he also changed his name to Napoléon Bonaparte, which looked and sounded much less Italian. He did eventually become fluent in French, but spoke it all his life with something of a Corsican accent, which he was teased about when he was a boy. He also reportedly never learnt how to spell French entirely correctly.

It is interesting to consider that all of Napoleon's proclamations, as well as the famously inspirational speeches which he made to his troops, were delivered in what for him was essentially a foreign language.

AUSTRIA, AUSTRALIA

The English name of the country Austria comes from the German label for the region, *Oesterreich*, which means 'eastern realm'. The English name of the country Australia, on the other hand, comes ultimately from the Latin phrase *terra australis*, which means 'southern land'.

3.5 Wolfgang Theophilus Mozart

Wolfgang Amadeus Mozart (1756–1791) was a composer of sublime music which is still very much loved 250 years after it was written. He was undoubtedly an extraordinary and perhaps uniquely gifted musical genius. His compositions are often described as elegant and sophisticated; but it is also rather well known to musicologists that he once wrote in the margin of a musical exercise paper which had been handed in to him by one of his pupils with the words 'You are an ass!' Mozart had a lively and at times rather crude sense of humour, but the point about this scathing comment – even if it was no doubt somewhat humorously intended – is that those were Mozart's own words: he actually wrote this insulting critique in English. The student in question was called Thomas Attwood (1765–1838), who came from Pimlico in London. He had the good fortune to be financed in his studies by a grant from the Prince of Wales, who later became King George IV.

We know that as a boy Mozart had been taught Latin, Italian, French and English by his father, Leopold – who was from Augsburg, now in Germany. Wolfgang himself was a mother-tongue speaker of the dialect of German spoken in his native town of Salzburg, now in Austria.

Mozart had spent fifteen months living, composing and performing in London, from the spring of 1764 till the summer of 1765, when he was a boy prodigy aged eight and nine. At that age, it is likely that he would have learnt quite a lot of colloquial English rather quickly, and the language seems to have stayed with him into adulthood – writing 'you are an ass' probably came to him rather naturally and spontaneously.

Wolfgang must have also been rather good at Latin, because at the age of eleven he wrote an opera in Latin titled *Apollo et Hyacinthus*. It is interesting to note that his middle name was registered at his birth as *Theophilus*, which is Greek for 'loved by God' or 'loving God'. The German equivalent would have been *Gottlieb* (the famous German automotive engineer Daimler went by that name), and Mozart's father also sometimes used this name for him. But Wolfgang himself seems to have preferred the Latin version of his middle name, Amadeus.

Mozart travelled extensively in his childhood and youth as his father showed off Wolfgang's almost superhuman skills as a performer and composer. He visited Italy a number of times and spoke the language rather well. In a letter from Italy to Wolfgang's mother, Leopold wrote that 'the Cardinal appeared to be delighted, and remarked that Wolfgang spoke Italian very well'. A number of operas Wolfgang wrote also had librettos (or *libretti*, if you prefer) in Italian: *Le Nozze di Figaro*, 'The marriage of Figaro', *Idomeneo Re di Creta*, 'Idomeneus, King of Crete', *Don Giovanni*, 'Don Juan', *Così fan tutte*, 'All women behave like that' and *La clemenza di Tito*, 'The mercy of Tito' are the best known. Since Thomas Attwood was studying with Mozart in Vienna at the time *Le Nozze di Figaro* was being composed, it is also perhaps not surprising that Mozart sometimes wrote comments in Italian on work that Attwood submitted to him: 'non è cantabile' ('it is not singable') was one of them.

As a boy, Mozart also spent time in Paris, and he was rather fluent in French. In one of his letters to his father, written when he was a young man, he wrote (in German): 'Countess Salern is a Frenchwoman, and scarcely knows a word of

German; so I have always been in the habit of talking French to her. I do so quite boldly, and she says that I do not speak at all badly.'

Wolfgang Amadeus Mozart was a musical genius. But he was not at all bad at languages either.

COSÌ FAN TUTTE

A good translation of the title of this Mozart opera is not easy to come up with. *Così* means 'thus, so'. *Fare* is 'to make, do, act', and *fan* is its third-person plural, so 'they act'. *Tutte* is the feminine plural of *tutto*, 'all'. Literally, then, 'thus act all (females)'. But that doesn't exactly trip off the tongue in English.

3.6 Janne Sibelius

Music is sometimes said to be the universal language, and it is certainly true that the music of the great classical composers is as well known these days in China, South Korea and Japan as it is in its original European homeland.

But the natural languages which the composers themselves actually spoke are not often thought of as being an interesting or important topic. Surely it is all pretty straightforward? Tchaikovsky was a Russian, so he must have been a Russian speaker; Grieg was Norwegian and therefore, obviously, his mother tongue was Norwegian.

Often, however, the facts are actually not so mundane. Anyone with an interest in symphonic music knows that Sibelius was Finnish. In fact, he is one of Finland's great national heroes. But it would be a mistake to suppose that because of that his native language was Finnish. Jean Sibelius, as he chose to be known, was originally named Johan Julius Christian Sibelius and was born into a Swedish-speaking family who called him Janne.

Finland is officially a bilingual country, with both Finnish and Swedish as official languages. Ninety per cent of the population are Finnish speakers, but there are two major areas of Finland which have been predominantly Swedish speaking for many centuries, one on the south coast, and one on the west coast. Also, the autonomous Åland Islands off the south-west coast of Finland are almost entirely Swedish speaking. From the age of nine, though, Sibelius went to a Finnish-medium school, so his Finnish did become fluent, even if he was not always too confident about it.

Fryderyk Szopen was also bilingual, in his case in Polish and French. He is more usually known by the French version of his name, Frédéric Chopin, but he was born in Żelazowa Wola, in Poland, and lived there until he was twenty. He grew up speaking French as well as Polish because, although his mother was Polish, his father was French. Fryderyk/Frédéric was proficient in both languages, and could write both well. When he died at the young age of thirty-nine, he was buried in Paris, where he had spent most of his adult life and risen to international fame; but his heart was taken back to Poland, where it is still interred at the Bazylika Świętego Krzyża (Church of the Holy Cross) in Warsaw.

In contrast, the Norwegian composer Edvard Grieg was a bit disappointing on the bilingualism front. His great-grandfather was Alexander Greig, who came from Aberdeen. (Norwegians pronounce the re-spelt version of the name as 'Grigg'.) The family maintained their links to Britain for several generations – Grieg's godmother was Mary Stirling from Stirling, and his father, also called Alexander, made frequent business trips to London. Grieg himself, however, did not speak English at all well, although this is said to have improved in later life after a number of visits to England.

Johannes Brahms was a much more accomplished bilingual. We might suppose that, as a German, his native language was German. But he grew up in Hamburg speaking the local variant of the language known in German as Plattdeutsch or Niederdeutsch and in English as Low German. Brahms came from a fairly well-to-do family and was also perfectly comfortable speaking German, which would have been the language he spoke in Vienna, where he spent much of his life. But the depth of his feeling for the language of his native city can be gauged from a conversation he is reported to have had with the Low German poet Klaus Groth, who asked him why he did not set any verses in his native language to music, only poems in German. Brahms replied: 'It doesn't work. I just can't. Low German is too close to me, it's something more than just language to me. I have tried, but it doesn't work.' For Brahms, Plattdeutsch was 'something that comes straight from the heart'.

SYMPHONY

The word *symphony* comes from Ancient Greek *symphonía*, consisting of *syn-*, 'with' and *phone*, 'sound', so the meaning was 'concord, harmony, concert of music'. After 2,000 years, the word still survives with a very everyday meaning in Greece: in Modern Greek, if you want to say 'I agree', you say *symphonó*.

3.7 Sir William Jones

About 230 years ago, Sir William Jones made an amazing intellectual break-through. Jones had been born in London of a Welsh father and an English mother, and some reports suggest that he grew up bilingual in Welsh and English, though this seems unlikely since his father – who actually was a native Welsh speaker, from Anglesey – died when William was three.

Whatever the truth of the matter, William really was a very gifted learner of languages, and by an early age he had mastered Greek, Latin, Hebrew and Arabic. At one stage, he even translated Persian into French, and he wrote a grammar of the Persian language.

In his mid-twenties, Jones started studying law; and in 1783, he arrived in Calcutta to take up an appointment as a judge. Once in India, he began to learn Sanskrit, the classical language of northern India – and it seems that he was one of the very first British people to do so.

Jones was very surprised by what his studies revealed. Sanskrit had ceased to be a living language over 2,000 years before, but in its heyday it had been spoken in the north-west of the Indian subcontinent. How did it come about, then – as Jones now discovered – that the ancient Sanskrit language was in many respects so very similar to Ancient Greek and Latin? Could it just be a coincidence that the Latin word *pater*, Greek *patér* and Sanskrit *pitár* all meant 'father'; and that Latin *frater*, Ancient Greek *phrater* and Sanskrit *bhratar* all meant 'brother'? Latin *mater*, 'mother', also corresponded to Greek *meter* and Sanskrit *matár*.

On the face of it, it seemed unlikely that there could be a connection between these languages. The homeland of Sanskrit was about 2,800 miles from Athens and 3,500 miles from Rome. And yet the similarities between the three ancient languages were undeniable, especially in their grammars. Latin *est*, 'it is' was *asti* in Sanskrit; *sumus*, 'we are' was *smas*; and *sunt*, 'they are' was *santi*.

Jones came up with an explanation for these correspondences. In a famous lecture, he argued that there was 'a stronger affinity' between Sanskrit, Latin and Greek 'than could possibly have been produced by accident'. A few others had noticed this before him, but Jones' breakthrough consisted in the insight that this affinity between the languages was so strong that no linguist could examine the three languages 'without believing them to have sprung from some common source, which, perhaps, no longer exists'.

Which no longer exists – that was his major new idea. Jones suggested that there had been an earlier parent language which had given rise to these ancient languages – as well as to the Persian, Celtic and Germanic languages – which had since disappeared. Previously, scholars had misguidedly wondered which of the world's existing languages might have been the 'first' – Hebrew was often mentioned as a candidate. But Jones argued that the only way to explain these linguistic affinities over such a large geographical area was through positing that there had once been a language which had gradually evolved into Latin, Greek and Sanskrit – also Celtic, Iranian and Germanic – just as Latin had later changed into the Romance languages Italian, Spanish, Romanian and French, and Sanskrit had morphed into the vernacular North Indian languages such as Hindi, Punjabi, Gujarati and Bengali.

From Icelandic and Irish in the west to Tajik and Bengali in the east, and from Russian and Norwegian in the Arctic north to the language of the Maldive Islands in the Indian Ocean in the south, most European languages – and many of those of west and south

Asia – developed over the centuries out of the same single source which went out of existence 5,000 years ago. Today we call that source language Indo-European.

Sir William Jones died in 1794, aged only forty-one. But he revolutionised our way of thinking about language history.

THE ROHINGYA

It is perhaps surprising to learn that the language of the unfortunate Rohingya people of Burma is distantly related to Welsh and English. Rohingyalish is very similar to Chittagonian, which is a subvariety of Bengali spoken in south-east Bangladesh. So the Rohingya language descended from ancient Sanskrit and is, like Welsh and English, an Indo-European language.

3.8 Herbert Huwer

It is said that more Americans are descended from German speakers than from English speakers. English is the main language of the United States today simply because the English-speaking colonists got there first. German speakers came along later, and then only gradually: as each small group arrived, they adapted – or their children did – to English, the majority tongue which they heard all around them.

It is true that German was one of the official languages of Texas when it was briefly an independent republic (1836–46). There is also a well-known story that German was once almost voted into being the official language of the whole of the United States – but that is not true.

Nowadays, modern European Americans are descended from very many different language backgrounds, as can be seen from their surnames, from Brzezinski to Bogart, Jones to Johansson and Pacino to Poitier. But you will find very little trace of this linguistic variety in the family names of American presidents. Only one president has not borne a European-language name: Obama. All the early presidents of the USA had typical English-language names: Washington, Adams, Jefferson, Madison, Jackson, Harrison, Tyler, Taylor . . .

Other languages did quite soon start appearing on the roll of presidential surnames, but there have been surprisingly few of them. The first president without an English-language name was James Monroe, who became president in 1817, but even this surname was British: it comes from Gaelic. Originally the language of Ireland, Gaelic has been a British language for as long as English has, both of them having arrived – in western Scotland and eastern England respectively – from around A D 400 onwards. The original form of Monroe was Bun-Rotha or Mun-Rotha, 'man from Ro', referring to the River Roe in northern Ireland.

Gaelic was also the source of the surnames of four other presidents. The surname of James Buchanan (president 1857–61) comes from the name of a parish in

Stirlingshire, Scotland; in Gaelic it is Both a' Chanain, 'the church of a canon'. The surname of William McKinley (1897–1901) was originally Macfionnlaigh, 'son of Finley'. Kennedy comes from Ó Cinneide or Mac Cinneide, 'descendant of Ceannéidigh'; and Reagan is from Ó Riagáin, 'descendant of Riagan'.

The first language from outside the British Isles to feature on the list of US presidential surnames was Dutch – and that did occur rather early on. The ancestors of Martin Van Buren (1837–41) came from near the town of Buren in the centre of the Netherlands. There have since been two presidents called Roosevelt, which is the Dutch for 'rose field': Theodore (1901–9) and Franklin (1933–45).

So until 1929, only two languages other than English had supplied American presidential surnames: the Celtic language Gaelic, and that close West Germanic relative of English, Dutch.

Then – and surprisingly only then, with the 31st president – did a name of German-language origin finally appear. The first president with a German-origin name was Herbert Hoover (1929–33). His great-great-great-great-grandfather, Gregor Huber, was born in 1668 in Oberkulm, in Aargau, Switzerland. Huber derives from the German word *Hube*, which means 'hide' – an area of land sufficient to support a single household. Gregor emigrated to Germany, and his son, Andreas Huber, was born there in 1723, in Ellerstadt in the Palatinate. There the family name changed from Huber to Huwer because of the local dialect, in which *haben*, 'to have' is *hawwe* and *Nebel*, 'fog' is *Newel* (the German letter *w* represents the same sound as English *v*). Andreas later emigrated to the USA, where he died as Andrew Hoover, the *w* changing to *v* and the *u* to *oo* in accordance with English spelling norms. When you next use your Hoover, you might like to consider that its name is an American re-spelt version of a German-dialect variant of a Swiss name.

The second president with a German surname was Dwight Eisenhower: the German word *Eisenhauer* means 'iron hewer'.

And then there came a third German-language surname into the White House. The grandfather of Donald Trump originally came from Kallstadt in the Mannheim area of Germany, where he was born into a family whose name – which may be derived from a word meaning 'drum' – was Trump (pronounced 'troomp'), Trumpf, or – possibly – Drumpf.

Coincidentally, Kallstadt is only about six miles from Ellerstadt.

3.9 Otlile Mabuse

Advocates of nativism, as well as anti-immigration nationalists, might like to consider the debt which England sports teams owe to inward migration. Of the current cricket test-match squad, Jofra Archer was originally from Barbados, Sam Curran from Zimbabwe and Ben Stokes from New Zealand. The England football squad owes even more to immigration: Ben Chilwell's father came from New

Zealand, Fikayo Tomori was born in Canada, Harry Winks has Spanish ancestry, Tammy Abraham's father came from Nigeria and the fathers of Callum Huson-Odoi and Trent Alexander Arnold were also of African origin. James Maddison, Declan Rice and Harry Kane could have played for Ireland because of their ancestry. Danny Rose's parents and Alex Oxlade-Chamberlain's grandparents emigrated from Jamaica, and Raheem Sterling was born there; Jado Sancho's parents are from Trinidad, and Marcus Rashford's family from St Kitts – where would we be without the *Windrush* generation?

Advocates of an English-only language policy for England might also like to consider the role of multilingual people in one of the most popular programmes on British television. The BBC's *Strictly Come Dancing* averages something like 10 million viewers per episode, and the part played by participants who are not monolingual English speakers or are not English in origin is enormous. One of the three professional dancers in the 2019 *Strictly* final, Otlile 'Oti' Mabuse, comes from South Africa. She speaks extremely fluent English, but her mother tongue is Xhosa, a Bantu language with about 8 million native speakers which is also widely spoken as a second language in the Republic. Oti also speaks five other South African languages, including Afrikaans, which was originally a colonial form of Dutch; she claims that this helped her to learn German when she first started working in Germany, as Dutch and German are very closely related.

Of the other two professional dancers in the 2019 final, Amy Dowden is Welsh, and Anton du Beke has a very interesting linguistic background. He was born Anthony Beke, and both his parents came from EU countries – his father was Hungarian and his mother is Spanish. Anton grew up speaking their native languages in addition to English, but says that he is now no longer able to do so.

The parents of one of the three celebrity finalists, Karim Zeroual, are of Moroccan origin. We tend to think of Morocco as being an Arabic-speaking country, but Zeroual is a name borne by a number of Berber-speaking families there. Arabic is not native to North Africa; the indigenous languages of the region are all varieties of Berber (also known as Amazigh), and more than half the population of Morocco today speak a Berber language.

When it comes to the *Strictly* judges, Shirley Ballas is English, but she has a Greek-language surname from her ex-husband, who was the grandson of Greek emigrants to the USA. Craig Horwood is Australian. And Motsi Mabuse, the sister of Oti, has the same linguistic background as Oti but lives in Germany with her Ukrainian husband and speaks German fluently. The fourth judge is Bruno Tonioli, a native Italian speaker. He has lived in England for over forty years and, in addition to speaking extremely fluent and expressive English, apparently manages rather well in French, Spanish and Portuguese. And one of the two presenters, Claudia Winkleman, had grandparents and great-grandparents who were variously speakers of German, Hungarian, Yiddish and Russian.

And this is just sport and entertainment. The roles which incomers from other countries, and multilingual people generally, have played in the fields of medicine, science, culture, business and industry are incalculable.

If everybody had stayed where they were, if England had been only for the English, if there had been no emigration or immigration, and if everyone had been monolingual in English, then England would be a very much poorer and more dreary place. Whatever you think about *Strictly*, it certainly isn't dreary.

XHOSA

Xhosa is well known to be one of the few languages in the world – all of them in Africa – which use click sounds as consonants. The letter combination *xh* in Xhosa represents a click sound which is not totally unlike the clicking noises it was traditionally supposed that Englishmen made to horses.

4 Geography

The Indo-European language family which nearly all the languages of Europe belong to, as we have already noted, is impressive in its geographical scope. The original homeland of the Indo-European language itself probably lay north of the Black and Caspian Seas on the Pontic–Caspian steppe, the vast treeless plain which stretches from Moldova and Ukraine to Kazakhstan. But the Indo-European dialects, which started to disperse outwards from this homeland in about 4000 BC and eventually became the different Indo-European languages, had by the mediaeval period spread out to cover a more or less contiguous area with an enormous reach in all directions of the compass.

The extent of this premodern east–west spread of these languages was considerable. The homeland of the easternmost Indo-European language lies in South Asia: Assamese, an Indo-Aryan language related to Hindi and Bengali, is spoken by 15 million people in the far north-east of India. Its nearest neighbours are mostly Tibeto-Burman languages, plus Austroasiatic languages distantly related to Cambodian and Vietnamese. Assam is situated at around 92 degrees longitude east.

The westernmost homeland of any Indo-European language is around 5,000 miles from Assam at about 22 degrees west, in Iceland. At one time, Icelandic was even spoken 900 miles further west than it is today, on the western coast of Greenland, at about 52 degrees west. Greenland was settled by Nordic-language speakers from Iceland during the late 900s AD, but by 1450 the Nordic-speaking community had disappeared. The reasons for this are not fully understood, as is discussed further below in this chapter.

The north–south range of the Indo-European language family is equally impressive. Its northernmost homeland also comprises lands occupied by Nordic speakers. Western coastal areas of northern Scandinavia had been settled by Norwegian speakers by AD 900. Tromsø in northern Norway is around 70 degrees north of the equator.

The Indo-European language whose homeland lies furthest to the south even lies partly in the Southern Hemisphere. This is Dhivehi, the language of the Maldive Islands, which lie far out into the Indian Ocean, south of Sri Lanka. Fuvahmulah, the southernmost island in the chain, lies just to the south of the equator, about 800 miles below India. The nearest linguistic relative of Dhivehi is Sinhalese, the major language of Sri Lanka. Dhivehi and Sinhalese are both related to the Indo-Aryan languages of northern India such as Bengali, not to the Dravidian languages of southern India like Tamil, indicating an ancient migration from the northern South Asian subcontinent south into the Indian Ocean. Fuvahmulah is about 6,500 miles from Reykjavik in Iceland, and both are a very long way indeed from the Eurasian steppe.

Geographical and linguistic factors are intimately connected with one another. In this chapter, we shall be examining some of these fascinating geolinguistic issues.

4.1 Colonial Languages

Three Western European colonial languages are notable for having more mother-tongue speakers outside Europe than in their own native continent. The language with the biggest difference between the number of speakers in its homeland and those overseas is Portuguese: this language has about 10 million speakers in Portugal, but there are about twenty times that, over 200 million, in Brazil. Portuguese is also the mother tongue of the Atlantic island of Madeira and, further out into the Atlantic, of the Azores. It is widely spoken, too, in Angola and Mozambique, as well as on the Cape Verde islands, in Guinea-Bissau and in the West African island state of São Tomé and Príncipe.

Spanish provides the next largest mismatch between European and diaspora speakers. There are around 35 million native speakers of Spanish in Spain – as well as some millions of speakers of other languages such as Basque, Catalan and Galician there. But the Americas have around 420 million speakers of Spanish, so about twelve times more than in its European homeland. Spanish is the major language in Argentina, Paraguay, Uruguay, Chile, Peru, Bolivia, Ecuador, Colombia, Venezuela, Panama, Costa Rica, Nicaragua, Honduras, El Salvador, Guatemala, Cuba, the Dominican Republic and Mexico. There are also about 40 million native Spanish speakers in the USA. Spanish has actually been spoken in North America for longer than English: Santa Fe, New Mexico was settled by Spanish speakers in 1598, while Jamestown, Virginia was settled by English speakers only in 1607. And while Spanish is a minority language in the USA/North America, it still has more native speakers there than in Spain.

English also comes into the category of languages whose European speakers are heavily outnumbered by those elsewhere. It has around 60 million native speakers in its homeland, Britain, while overseas there are about five times more than that – 300 million or so – in the USA, Canada, the Bahamas, Bermuda, the Caribbean, Australia, New Zealand, South Africa, Kenya, Zimbabwe, Tristan da Cunha and the Falkland Islands. English has also become the native language for many people in India and Singapore. It is also so widely used as a second language that it is in the unusual position of having more non-native speakers than native speakers.

There are, of course, a number of other major European colonial languages, but a majority of their speakers still live on their native continent. French has about

65 million native speakers in Europe – in France, Belgium and Switzerland – while there are about 16 million elsewhere, including about 7 million mother-tongue French speakers in Canada, and 70,000 in New Caledonia in the Pacific, plus some thousands in Guyane (French Guyana) in South America. French is also widely spoken as a second language over large areas of Africa and in the South Pacific.

Similarly, there are 21 million Dutch speakers in Holland, Belgium and the Dunkirk area of France. But there are another million in Surinam, a few thousand in the Dutch Caribbean – the islands of Aruba, Bonaire, Curaçao and Saint Maarten – plus more than 7 million native speakers of Afrikaans (historically a variety of Dutch) in South Africa, Botswana, Namibia and Zimbabwe.

The Russian language is also interesting in this context. There are something like 144 million Russian native speakers in Russia and neighbouring European countries such as Latvia and Ukraine, but around 30 million of those native speakers are to be found in areas of Russia which are situated in Asia. Russian, like English, French, Spanish and Portuguese, was entirely a language of Europe until the sixteenth century. But then Russian colonial expansion took off, not overseas as with the Western European languages, but overland, both northwards to the shores of the Arctic Ocean and eastwards to Siberia and the Pacific Far East. By 1650, the Russian language had reached Vladivostok on the Pacific Ocean, 4,000 miles east of Moscow. By comparison, Jamestown, Virginia is only about 3,700 miles from London.

DIASPORA

The Greek word *diaspora*, 'dispersion' came into English around 1700. In Ancient Greek *dia*- meant 'through, across' and *spora* meant 'seed': the verb *diaspeirein* meant 'to scatter'. *Disperse* came into English around 1500, via French, from *dispergere*, the Latin equivalent of *diaspeirein*. In the nineteenth century, we also borrowed *spora*, via French, as *spore*.

4.2 Languages on the Edge

Most of the languages from the central part of Europe have found their way to other parts of the world over the last few centuries. It is especially easy to hear them in those countries which experienced large-scale European immigration, such as Canada, the USA, Brazil and Australia.

There are communities of Finnish speakers in Michigan, and Ukrainians who speak their own language on the Canadian prairies. Melbourne has been said to be the third-largest Greek-speaking community in the world after Athens and Salonika. Italian and Maltese are big in Melbourne too. Serbian speakers abound in Sydney. In Brazil there are 4 million German speakers. There are Polish-speaking communities in Chicago, and Slovaks in Cleveland, Ohio. You can hear Croatian in Chile, and Czech in Argentina. But these language communities are small in number compared to those in their homelands, and many of their speakers gradually assimilate to the majority language of the country they live in.

When it comes to the languages from the edges of our continent, however, it is a different story: they have taken over the world. The major languages from the far western seaboard of Europe have spread westwards across the Atlantic and down into the Southern Hemisphere. And they are more widely spoken outside Europe than within it (see Section 4.1).

Portuguese arrived in Madeira in the 1420s, the Azores in the 1430s and Brazil in the 1530s. There are around 200 million speakers of Portuguese in Brazil, compared to only 10 million in Portugal. Spanish arrived in the Canary Islands in the 1400s and reached the Caribbean and the Americas during the 1500s. There are about 420 million Spanish speakers in the New World, as compared to only around 35 million back in Spain.

English first crossed the Atlantic in the 1600s. The Jamestown settlement in Virginia, the first anglophone community on the continent, was founded in 1607. The second followed soon after on Bermuda in 1609, when English speakers were shipwrecked en route for Jamestown; and the third settlement was established in Newfoundland in 1610. Australia, New Zealand and South Africa were mostly settled in the 1800s. Of the 300-plus million native speakers of English in the world today, only one-sixth are located in Britain and Ireland.

French, too, expanded across the Atlantic, notably to Canada, where it has more than 7 million speakers, and to the South Pacific, where it is spoken natively in New Caledonia and to an extent in French Polynesia.

The eastern edge of Europe saw a similar kind of spread at a similar time. From the 1550s onwards, there was extensive expansion of the Russian language out of the Russian homeland, north towards the Arctic Ocean, and east to Siberia and on to the Far East, where Russian colonisation had reached Vladivostok on the Pacific by 1650.

All of these expansions had tragic consequences for indigenous peoples and their languages. Most of the native languages of the Russian far north and Siberia are currently in danger. In Canada and the USA, there were about 300 native languages at the time of European contact, but well over 100 of these have disappeared, and the rest will probably disappear by the end of the twenty-first century, with the exception of Navaho, which still has 100,000 speakers. Australia had 250 languages at the time of British colonisation, but more than half of these have died out already, and only 20 or so are being learnt by children. In the Pacific, some of the approximately forty Polynesian and fifty Micronesian languages are threatened by a shift to English and French, with Hawaiian and Maori being especially endangered.

A few of the languages of Europe, on the other hand, have been content never to leave the continent. The Sami languages, spoken in northern Scandinavia and neighbouring areas of Russia, have not strayed outside these countries. And Romansh seems pretty much to have remained quietly at home in the valleys of eastern Switzerland.

It might have been better for the indigenous peoples and languages of the other continents of the world if the languages of the eastern and western margins of Europe had followed their example.

ISLANDS

Polynesian, Micronesian and Melanesian languages are all Pacific Island members of the large Austronesian language family. These names are all derived from the Ancient Greek word *nesos*, 'island', with *poly*- being Greek for 'many', *micro*- 'small' and *melano*-'black'. *Austro*- derives comes from the Latin *auster*, 'south wind'. Indonesia means 'islands of the Indies'.

4.3 Mount Ofen

There is a mountain in the centre of our continent which forms an interesting feature not only in the natural landscape but also in the European linguistic landscape. Its summit is one of the peaks of the Karavank range in the eastern Alps. The mountain has several names – Ofen, Peč, Mont Fuar, Monte Forno – but these all translate into English as 'oven'.

The name of the Karavank range might be derived from the Celtic root *karv* meaning 'deer' – the Modern Welsh word is *carw* – but no Celtic language has been spoken anywhere near the Karavanks for many centuries. The languages which belong to the Celtic language family are now all confined, as living community speech forms, to the far western edge of Europe: Breton in Brittany, Welsh in Wales, Irish Gaelic in western Ireland and Scottish Gaelic in western Scotland. There are perhaps a million Celtic-language speakers in the world.

Along the far northern edges of Europe we find the Finno-Samic languages – Finnish, Estonian and Sami – and the Baltic languages – Lithuanian and Latvian. And on the south-eastern periphery of Europe are Albanian and Greek. But the rest of the continental mainland is almost entirely covered by languages which belong to just three major language families, each them occupying a vast area of the European mainland and spoken by tens of millions of people. The westernmost of these is the Romance family of the languages that descend from Latin, which stretches eastwards from Portugal's Atlantic coast and southwards from the centre of Belgium to the toe of Italy and Sicily. The major Romance languages are

Portuguese, Spanish, Catalan, French and Italian. The dialects of these languages form a continuum, merging into one another as you travel from east to west or north to south, so that it sometimes is not possible to specify where, for instance, Portuguese stops and Spanish starts.

The easternmost of the three major families consists of the Slavic languages, which form a continuum extending southwards from the Arctic Ocean to the Adriatic Sea, and eastwards to the Urals and beyond. Its major members are Russian, Belarussian, Ukrainian, Polish, Slovak, Czech and Bulgarian, plus Slovenian, Serbian and the other Slavic languages of the former Yugoslavia. (Hungarian, which is distantly related to Finnish, and Romanian, a Romance language, form isolated islands in the middle of this Slavic sea.)

The third and northernmost family consists of the Germanic languages – Norwegian, Swedish, Danish, German, Dutch and Frisian – which cover the continent from the north of Norway to the Alps, and from the shores of the North Sea to the River Oder.

Since 1945, the Germanic and Slavic continua of dialects have met each other along a lengthy border which corresponds roughly to the German–Polish frontier: the borders of Germany and Austria with Czechia, and the Austrian borders with Slovakia and Slovenia.

The Romance and Germanic languages rub up against one another along an extensive frontier which stretches from the North Sea coast around Dunkirk – where French meets Dutch – on through Belgium, down through eastern France and across Switzerland. It then continues southwards and cuts over into Italy, where German is the indigenous language in the South Tyrol.

But there is one special place where all three of these giant language families come together. The national boundaries of Slovenia (Slavic-speaking), Austria (Germanic-speaking) and Italy (Romance-speaking) all meet at a tripoint on the summit of Mount Peč (the Slovenian name), aka Ofen (in German), Monte Forno (in Italian) and Mont Fuar in Friulian.

This is not quite the same thing as saying that the three language families meet there too. Obviously, nobody actually lives on the mountain top, and in the areas at lower altitudes where people do live, there are lots of linguistically mixed communities and many bilingual individuals. The history of this area is also complicated.

The nearest major settlement to the summit on the Austrian side is Arnoldstein, where the local language is an Austro-Bavarian (Germanic) dialect. But there used to be a large Slovenian minority here – 40 per cent in 1880 – and it is still home to a community of Slovenian speakers. On the Slovenian side of the border, the closest main community to the tripoint is Kranjska Gora, where they speak an Upper Carniolian dialect of Slovenian (Slavic). And the nearest location in Italy is Tarvisio. The majority of people there today speak Italian (Romance) and/or Friulian, a Romance language related to the Swiss language Romansh (Fuar is the mountain's name in Friulian,). But until 1918, when this area was transferred from Austria to

Italy, nearly everybody spoke Slovenian and/or German. In other words, up until World War I, the three language families met not in the area immediately around this mountain, but further to the south and west.

Whatever happened in the past, however, we can be inspired by the knowledge that in the streets of modern Tarvisio/Trbiž/Tarvis, signs are displayed in Italian, Friulian, Slovenian and German, publicly stating that all of the inhabitants are entitled to use their own language, whatever it is.

GAELIC

Gaelic has donated rather few words to English despite sharing this island with it for centuries. One is *trousers*, which entered English no more than 400 years ago, from Gaelic *triubhas*. The slang word *gob*, 'mouth' comes from Gaelic *gob*, 'beak'. But many would say our most important borrowing from Gaelic is *whisky*, from Gaelic *uisge-beatha*, 'water of life'.

4.4 Language Islands

Europe is full of language islands. These are places where people who speak one language are entirely surrounded by an area where a different language is spoken. The German term *Sprachinseln* is often used to refer to such places.

A good example is Brussels, which is predominantly French-speaking but is completely surrounded by areas of Belgium where Dutch is the everyday language. As most people know, Belgium is bisected by a line which divides the country into the Flemish (Dutch)-speaking north, where cities like Ghent and Antwerp are located, and the French-speaking south, which includes Liège and Charleroi. But this line passes some way to the south of Brussels, leaving the city as a francophone island in a sea of Flemish.

This situation came about because Brussels was a Dutch-speaking place for a millennium and a half until it became the capital of the new nation-state of Belgium, founded in 1830. The city's new status as the national capital led to a large influx of speakers of French, which was at that time the prestige language as well as the only language of officialdom.

Some language islands are much larger than Brussels. It is perhaps not too well known that Hungarian is spoken in a very extensive area of southern Slovakia, as well as in eastern Austria, eastern Slovenia, northern Croatia, northern Serbia, north-western Romania and eastern Ukraine. These are all areas bordering on Hungary which the country was forced to cede as a result of the 1920 Treaty of Trianon in the aftermath of World War I. Hungary was penalised by this redrawing of its borders, which left 30 per cent of its pre-war population as linguistic minorities in foreign countries. But there is also a large Hungarian language island which is not immediately adjacent to Hungary. This is located in the centre of Romania in the area known as Transylvania, where over a million Hungarian speakers live surrounded by regions which are mainly Romanian speaking.

Further south in the Balkans, the Arumanian language, which is related to Romanian, forms a whole series of *Sprachinseln* – a kind of linguistic archipelago of speech islands encircled by South Slavic languages like Serbian and Bulgarian, as well as by Albanian and Greek. The language is also widely known as Vlach and, like Romanian, it is descended from the variety of Latin which came to be spoken all over the northern and central part of the Balkan peninsula under the Roman Empire. The pre-Roman languages in these areas died out – apart from Albanian in the mountains of the west – while the southern part of the Balkans remained Greek speaking.

The Transylvanian Hungarians and the *Bruxellois* francophones inhabit linguistic islands because their ancestors created the islands themselves. They moved into new territories and settled amongst peoples who were already very well established there. It was the other way round for the Arumanians in Bulgaria and the former Yugoslavia: people speaking an alien language – the Slavs – started moving into the Balkans from the north around AD 600, invading the area where the Vlachs were already located. The newcomers surrounded the Vlachs, dividing them into smaller, separate groups cut off from one another, so that eventually the Romance-speaking Vlachs became marooned in an ocean of Slavic speakers.

If you want to be sure of hearing people speaking Vlach these days, you can go to a particular speech island, the town of Metsovo in the Pindus mountains of central Greece. There are many theories as to how the Vlachs came to be there. Perhaps they are the descendants of a Roman garrison which got left behind. Maybe their ancestors were itinerant Vlach-speaking shepherds who moved south to escape the encroaching Slavs. Whatever the answer, as you walk around the streets of Metsovo you can feel that you are strolling around a linguistic island where the local language, derived from the Latin left behind by the Romans, is surrounded by the modern descendant of that other major classical European language, Ancient Greek.

4.5 Little England beyond Wales

If you look at a map of Wales, you will see that the majority of the places in the country bear unmistakably Welsh-language names: Aberystwyth, Caernarfon, Ffestiniog, Llanelli, Machynlleth, Pwllheli, Ystradgynlais. Certainly no one would ever suppose that Llanrhaeadr-ym-Mochnant was somewhere in Hertfordshire, or that Cwmamman was a place in West Sussex. Welsh names like this are often transparent to native speakers, as they actually mean something in

Modern Welsh: Aberystwyth signifies 'mouth of the River Ystwyth', and Pwllheli means 'briny pool'.

The fact that Wales is full of Welsh-language names can hardly be a surprise, of course. All of Wales was Welsh speaking until relatively recently, and a great deal of it still is, with the language now experiencing a real renaissance and returning in strength to areas from which it had partly or totally disappeared.

But there is one exception to this 'all of Wales' statement. If you look at the names of the towns and villages in the far south-west of the country, you will find a rather different picture. Here we can see place-names, such as Tenby, Milford, Upton, Templeton and Wiston, which do not look very Welsh at all. On the contrary, there are dozens of places in England called Upton, and there are scores of place-names in England ending in *by*, *ford* and *ton*.

This is because there something genuinely rather special, linguistically and culturally, about this south-western area of Wales, which is often known as 'Little England beyond Wales'. The region is demarcated by the so-called Landsker Line, which runs through the old county of Pembrokeshire; areas to the north of the line are mainly Welsh speaking to this day, while the rather sharply delineated area to the south is English speaking. Not only are people of this part of south Pembrokeshire English speaking, however – they have actually been anglophone for very many centuries.

The local English accent of the area also bears a rather close resemblance to the accents of the English West Country rather than to other accents of Welsh English, even though Little England beyond Wales is a long way from England: from Pembroke to Bristol is about 140 miles, or 230 kilometres. Speakers roll their r's in words like *girl* and *farm*. And, unlike any other accent in southern Wales, they pronounce words like *butter* and *up* with the vowel of *foot*, just like people from the North of England.

Experts are not totally sure how this situation came about, but the most usual explanation is to blame it all on King Henry I of England, the fourth son of William the Conqueror. In the wake of the 1066 invasion of England, the Normans began incursions into Wales, and by 1094 they had gained control of large areas of the country. They found it difficult to maintain this control, however, and by 1101 had lost much of it again. Their efforts continued, though, and as part of his anti-Welsh campaign King Henry established a Flemish settlement in southern Pembrokeshire in 1108. The course of the Landsker Line which still delineates the anglophone region does not follow any obvious physical or topographical features, so we can suppose that it was probably imposed by the Anglo-Norman monarchy politically and militarily, with any original inhabitants being expelled.

Twelfth-century Flemish/Dutch and English would have been somewhat similar language varieties, but it is probable that the real reason why the area in the end became totally English speaking was because the 'Flemish' colony from the very beginning had actually contained large numbers of people who had come from

England – which would also explain why there are still settlements there with names such as Picton, Upton and Wiston.

It is remarkable to consider that events which happened more than 900 years ago can still be detected in the linguistic landscape of the Principality.

4.6 The Fens

My late mother-in-law came from the American Midwest, a predominantly flat land of enormously fertile and productive soils. She was not very impressed by the Rocky Mountains, observing that you could not grow much there. For her, the most beautiful part of the British Isles was not the rugged coast of the west of Ireland, nor the mountains of Snowdonia, nor the English Lake District, nor the Scottish Highlands. The area which most impressed her with its beauty was the low-lying English Fenland region of northern Cambridgeshire and adjacent areas of Lincolnshire and Norfolk, together with bits of Suffolk, Huntingdonshire and Northamptonshire. She loved those thousands of acres of rich black soil stretching from horizon to horizon, with no mountains or forests in the way to spoil the view.

Her opinion, however, was not one that has been very widely shared by many British visitors to the Fens. Samuel Pepys, writing in the seventeenth century, describes his travels 'over most sad fenns, all the way observing the sad life which the people of the place do live, sometimes rowing from one spot to another and then wading'. Sad it may have seemed to him, but the few people who inhabited the Fens seem rather to have liked it like that. There were frequent acts of sabotage and rioting throughout the 1700s as local people, whose fishing and wild-fowling lifestyle was being threatened, tried to block the large-scale drainage programmes that were then beginning to be carried out.

Until this drainage began, the Fens had been more or less uninhabitable for the whole of recorded history. The area between Cambridge and the Wash was mostly marshland which was subject to very frequent flooding; and up until the seventeenth century the northern coastline lay 12 miles or so further south than it does at present. Most of the sparse Fenland population lived on a few islands of higher ground and in small communities on this northern coastline.

Because of the impassability of the area, and its undesirability as far as most people were concerned as a place of habitation, the Fens constituted a serious barrier to communication; and it is no accident that one of the most important dialect boundaries in the English-speaking world – the one that runs between East Anglia and the East Midlands – developed there and still remains in place to this day.

The dialect border is very clear-cut in the north of the Fens between Lincolnshire to the west and Norfolk to the east, running from south to north along the River

Nene until it debouches into the Wash. On the west bank of the river, people in Lincolnshire say *butter*, *up* and *cup* in the north-country way with the same vowel as *foot*: so 'booter'; they pronounce *path* with the short vowel of *pat*; and they sometimes drop their *h*'s. If you cross the Nene into Norfolk, the countryside is more or less uninhabited for a while, but when you do encounter settlements again as you travel east, people can suddenly be heard to be saying *butter* in the southern way, pronouncing *path* with the same long vowel as *palm* and not dropping their *h*'s.

Dialect boundaries are often located at points where linguistic changes which were spreading outwards from some centre have come to a halt. Probably the biggest dialect boundary in the English-speaking world developed centuries ago along the line of the physical barrier posed by the Humber Estuary. North of that line, speakers of traditional dialects still pronounce words like *town* and *house* as Chaucer would have done: 'toon' and 'hoose'. The new 'town' and 'howse' pronunciations developed in London and gradually spread north, from person to person and place to place, until they were halted by the break in communication caused by the broad estuary downstream from the confluence of the River Ouse and River Trent.

NENE

Local people along the upper reaches of the Nene mostly know it as the 'Nenn' rather than 'Neen', as it is called lower down. The Old English name was Nen. The most likely origin of the name lies in the form *neigusn-*, which meant 'to wash' in the early Celtic language which was the precursor to Welsh.

4.7 The Baltic Shore

The territory along the southern shore of the Baltic Sea today is shared by Denmark, Germany, Poland, Russia (the Kaliningrad exclave) and Lithuania. It is obvious, if you go to Møn, Rostock, Gdansk, Kaliningrad or Klaipeda, that the official languages in these places are Danish, German, Polish, Russian and Lithuanian respectively.

But if you had travelled to these locations a thousand years ago, the picture would have been very different. It is true that you would have found Old Danish along the coastline of Denmark and Old Lithuanian at the other end, but in between, there would have been no German, no Polish and no Russian. There was no Russian language on the south Baltic coast because Russian speakers did not move into Kaliningrad until 1945. And there was no German because, up until about AD 900, the border between the Germanic and Slavic-speaking areas of

Europe lay much further west than today: it began on the south-western shore of the Baltic near Kiel and ran along the river Elbe.

If you had set out on an eastward journey along the Baltic coast back then, to the immediate east of the Danish-speaking area you would have met people using varieties of West Slavic. Today the major languages in the West Slavic language family are Polish, Czech and Slovak, but you would not have found any of them on the Baltic coast at that time. Instead, you would have encountered people speaking Polabian, Pomeranian and other related West Slavic varieties which have now died out. Very many modern eastern German place-names are of Slavic origin: Rostock was West Slavic Roztok, Leipzig was Lipsk, Chemnitz was Kamjenica, Meissen Mishnia and Dresden Drezhdyany. Berlin and Potsdam were also originally Slavic names.

To the east of these Slavic languages, starting around the mouth of the river Vistula (Polish Wisla, German Weichsel) which flows through Warsaw and empties into the Baltic to the east of Gdansk (Danzig), you would have come across the Baltic language family. The only Baltic languages left today are Lithuanian and Latvian, but there were formerly several more. The one that we know most about (though that is not very much) is Old Prussian, which was spoken along what is now the Polish coastline from the Vistula up into Kaliningrad.

Between about 900 and 1350, there was a large-scale eastward migration of German-speaking peoples into the relatively less-populated Slavic- and Baltic-speaking areas. This expansion gradually pushed the Germanic language boundary into what is now eastern Germany, modern-day Poland, and Lithuania. An often violent conquest by the crusading Christianising Teutonic Knights was part of this picture too.

The Baltic-coast Germans were mostly native speakers of Low German (Plattdeutsch). Coastal dialects of Low German, which had originally been spoken in the areas around Hamburg and Bremen, replaced Pomeranian, Old Prussian and the other now lost Slavic and Baltic languages which had been spoken along the shore.

Until the end of World War II, the now Russian-speaking town of Kaliningrad was German-speaking Königsberg, with the German Memel region lying to the north of that. Memel (now Klaipeda) was transferred to Lithuania in 1923, though its German speakers stayed where they were. Then, as a consequence of the Potsdam Treaty of 1945, the western frontiers of the Soviet Union and Poland were both moved two or three hundred kilometres westwards. Something like 8 million Germans were expelled, and the German/Slavic language boundary moved westwards again. German speakers on the Baltic are now just found along the coastline between Denmark and Poland.

The Polish language, too, only reached the coastline of the Baltic Sea to any significant degree in relatively modern times. However, as a reminder of earlier days, there is an area of the Polish coast to the west of Gdansk which is still home to

Kashubian, a proud survivor of the original pre-German West Slavic coastal languages. We can only hope that it does not go the way of Pomeranian and Old Prussian.

4.8 A Conversation in Three Languages

Some time after the initial break-up of Yugoslavia, I was at a linguistics conference in the Netherlands. One evening, three older professors who I knew called me over to join them at the bar. They came from universities in Sarajevo, Zagreb and Belgrade, and because of the Yugoslav wars, they had not been able to see each other for several years. This was a joyful reunion. 'Look at us', they said cheerfully if rather ruefully, 'aren't we clever – we're having a conversation in three languages!' Their shared language, Serbo-Croat, had now officially been reclassified by their respective governments as Bosnian, Croatian and Serbian (see more in Section 7.12).

There is some truth in the statement that 'a language is a dialect with an army and a navy': most European languages are regarded as distinct entities because of political, cultural and historical factors as well as for linguistic reasons.

Many of these languages have to depend on social factors for their independent language status because they are part of a continuum of dialects. If you travel from Ostend across Belgium, Holland, Germany and Austria to Vienna listening to local dialects as you go, you will find the dialects changing gradually as you travel. The differences between the dialects accumulate along your route, so that people speaking the Ostend Dutch dialect and the Viennese German dialect cannot understand one another. But there is nowhere on your journey where locals cannot understand their neighbours from the next village. The dialects spoken on either side of the Netherlands–Germany border are totally intelligible to one another: we call some of them 'Dutch' and others 'German' for reasons that have nothing to do with the dialects themselves.

Polish, Slovak and Czech form a dialect continuum. Slovaks understand Poles without much difficulty, and Czechs converse with Slovaks easily enough. But we think of them as being three separate languages because there are three distinct standardised varieties with their own writing systems, literatures, dictionaries, grammar books – and names.

The entities we normally call 'languages' have a kind of culturally based independence from one another. This is reflected in the fact that, although a Slovak and a Pole from opposite sides of the border can talk to one another, one will go home and read newspapers in Slovak while the other will go back and write emails in Polish.

This kind of independence may be fragile, and can be won or lost. Languages can become dialects; and dialects can become languages. After 1814, when Norway gained independence from Denmark, moves were made which eventually led to Norwegian becoming an independent language – the dialects of Norway had previously been widely regarded as dialects of Danish.

In 1938, Romansh was declared to be a national language of Switzerland. This was partly in response to nationalistic sentiments being expressed by Mussolini's government over the border in fascist Italy, which claimed that the dialects of Davos and St Moritz were actually Italian.

On 2 August 1944, the government of Yugoslavia formally created Macedonian as a new Slavic language by declaring it to be the official language of Yugoslavian Macedonia. This was partly in response to territorial claims to that area of Yugoslavia by neighbouring Bulgaria. To this day, many Bulgarians claim that Macedonian is a dialect of Bulgarian.

And one Friday quite a while ago now – 24 February 1984 – the government of Luxembourg officially granted Luxembourgish the status of a national language: the day before, it had been a dialect of German.

Sometimes, a dialect can be made into a language against its speakers' will. In the 1940s, after annexing parts of Romania, the Soviet Union declared that the new Soviet Republic of Moldova now had a language of its own, Moldavian, which was distinct from Romanian. They made Moldavians write their language in the Cyrillic alphabet so that it looked different from Romanian.

And, sometimes, speakers do not seem to mind very much one way or the other. The indigenous Albanian-speaking minority in Greece have been there since mediaeval times (see also Section 5.5). The biggest concentration of these speakers is in Attica, Boeotia and the Peloponnese; many of the suburbs of Athens were Albanian speaking until recently. Linguistically, there is little doubt that the language they speak is a variety of Albanian, but all Greeks have adopted the practice of referring to this minority speech form, not as Alvaniká ('Albanian'), but as Arvanítika. This terminology implies that the people who speak it are not Albanians, and that Arvanítika is an independent language rather than a dialect of the language of a neighbouring state. So, while this language is obviously not Greek, it can be thought of as a 'language of Greece'.

Meanwhile, back in ex-Yugoslavia, Serbo-Croat became four languages. On 22 October 2007, the government of Montenegro declared that its national language was henceforth to be known as Montenegrin. On Sunday, the 21st, it had not been a language. On the Monday, it was.

4.9 And Next Year in the City

Macedonia is a geographical term which refers to a region of the southern Balkans. For some centuries, the area was part of the Ottoman Empire and was ruled by the Turks from Constantinople. It contained a mixed population of Orthodox Christians, Muslims and Jews. There were also many different languages spoken in the region: South Slavic varieties variously referred to as Serbian, Bulgarian, Macedonian and Slavo-Macedonian; Greek; Turkish; Albanian; and the Romani of the Gypsies. There were also two groups who spoke Romance languages descended from Latin. The first group, often known as Vlachs, spoke a Balkan language which linguists call Arumanian. The second group, consisting of Jews who had arrived in the Ottoman Empire after being expelled from Spain and Portugal in 1492, used a language known as Ladino or Judeo-Spanish.

In 1912 the armies of the by-now-independent states neighbouring Macedonia – Greece, Bulgaria and Serbia – combined to attack the Ottoman forces, and the Ottomans eventually withdrew. There was further fighting, but in the end the Macedonia region was partitioned between the victorious states, with Albania also becoming an independent nation. Borders in the area were not fully drawn until after World War I, and these were decided in part militarily – on the basis of who had managed to seize and hold which areas by when. Little consideration was given to human factors, such as language background.

The largest portion of the region (about 50 per cent), called Aegean Macedonia, went to Greece; the next largest, Vardar Macedonia, was allotted to Serbia (and thence subsequently to Yugoslavia); a smaller area, Pirin Macedonia, went to Bulgaria; and a tiny portion was awarded to Albania.

Today, Vardar Macedonia is a small independent nation of 2 million known as North Macedonia. About a quarter of its inhabitants are native Albanian speakers, but the majority, about two-thirds of the population, speak the South Slavic language most of us call Macedonian. Some Bulgarians do not like this name – they regard the language as a dialect of Bulgarian; and some Greeks do not like it either – for them the term 'Macedonian' means the Greek spoken in Aegean Macedonia. In 1912, however, fewer than half the people living in Aegean Macedonia were Greek speakers, and most of those lived in the coastal areas, while the rest of the population were predominantly Slavic speakers.

The capital city of Aegean Macedonia is today called Thessaloniki in Greek. It was formerly a very important centre of Sephardic Jewish culture: the largest single linguistic group in 1912 were the Ladino-speaking Jews, who called the city Salonika. Its name in the South Slavic languages is Solun, and it was formerly also an important centre of South Slavic culture. Indeed, many other northern Greek towns also still have many Slavic speakers, and have Slavic as well as Greek names – Flórina is Lerin, Kastoriá is Kostur.

Some South Slavs these days have a drinking toast: *Solun e nash!*, 'Salonica is ours!' In the northern Balkans, the Slovenes have a similar toast: *Trst e naš*, 'Trieste is ours' – in 1910 a quarter of Trieste's population were Slovene speakers (see Section 2.2). The Greeks, too, have a similar saying: *Kai tou chrónou stin Póli!*, 'And next year in the City!' – where 'the City' means Istanbul. For very many centuries, there was no more important centre of Greek language and culture than Constantinople; and even in 1914, around a quarter of the population were Greeks.

The Slovene toast about Trieste is one of those jokes which is not entirely a joke, but in the context of the European Union, the Italians are not going to worry very much about it. The toasts about Salonica and Istanbul have also lost much of their bite in recent decades, but we must hope for further progress. What would help would be a Europe which was increasingly less national; and increasingly more rational.

POLIS

The Ancient Greek word *pólis* meant 'city' or 'city-state'. The Modern Greek word is *póli*. *Metropolis* originally meant 'mother city', from Ancient Greek *méter*, 'mother'. *Megalopolis* comes from Greek *megálo*, 'big', while Acropolis contains the Greek form *ácro-*, 'highest'. The word *politics* comes ultimately from *polítis*, 'citizen, city dweller'.

5 Cities

We have already mentioned several different European cities in this book; and widely travelled readers may have some degree of familiarity with the cities of Bécs, Kodaň, Mediolan and Kelnas. But they will probably not know them by those names. The local names of these places are, respectively, Wien, København, Milano and Köln, but none of these are the names normally used by English speakers: Bécs is Hungarian for Vienna, Kodaň is Slovak and Czech for Copenhagen, Mediolan is Milan in Polish, and Kelnas is Cologne in Lithuanian.

Place-names, not least the names of cities, are of considerable historical interest. There is a common tendency all over our continent for places which have played a significant role in European history to have different names in different languages. French-speaking people do not call the English capital London, but Londres. The Greeks call it Londino, the Italians Londra and the Poles Londyn; in Albanian it is Londer, in Finnish Lontoo, in Lithuanian Londonas and in Welsh Llundain. This plethora of names tells us that London must have been an important city in the European context for many centuries. Europeans wanted and needed to talk about London, so they naturally talked about it in their own languages, and they thereby developed names for the city in those languages. For a place to possess a range of different names in other languages is a sign of fame and distinction: this is not a privilege granted to humbler, lesser-known settlements.

How many names a particular city has, and in which languages, can tell us many things. Some of the stories which city names can tell us are narrated in this chapter.

5.1 Mnichov, Monachium, Mynih

Have you ever been to Mnichov? No? Are you sure? How about Monachium? Or Mynih? It is rather likely in fact that, as readers of the *New European*, you have visited this major European city. Mnichov is the Czech name for Munich, Monachium is the name for the same place in Polish and Mynih is what the city is called in Albanian. The Italians call it Monaco, the Greeks say Mónacho, the Estonian name is Munkeno, in Latvian it is called Minhene and in Lithuanian it is Miunchenas. The people who actually live in Munich naturally use the German-language name and call it München.

Having different names in other languages is a sign of fame and distinction. It is not like that for humbler, lesser-known settlements. A village like Great Snoring in Norfolk is not going to be called anything other than that in any language. If no one in Lithuania has ever heard of Great Snoring, then there is not going to be a special Lithuanian name for this village.

We have very many English-language names for historically important European centres which are different – sometimes very different – from their local names. Rome, Athens, Venice, Naples, Gothenburg, Florence, Belgrade, Prague, Lisbon, Cologne, Copenhagen, Turin and Vienna are just a few of our peculiar English-language names. Vienna is called Wien by the people who live there. Prague is Praha; Florence is Firenze; Venice is called Venezia in Italian; Cologne is Köln in German; Torino is the Italian for Turin; Naples is known as Napoli in Italian; and Belgrade is Beograd in Serbian.

Some exonyms – names used by outsiders – may seem rather improbable to us. We have seen that Bécs is the Hungarian for Vienna, and Kelnas is the Lithuanian for Cologne. Other difficulties include the fact that Tergesti is the Greek for Trieste; and Pozsony is Hungarian for Bratislava (see Section 5.2).

Some of the English-language names we have for important foreign places currently seem to be in the process of being forgotten. The real English name for Basel is Basle, pronounced 'Bahl', but Ryanair, at least, do not know that. They do not seem to know, either, that the second largest city in Greece, Thessaloniki, is called Salonica in English. When it comes to French place-names, it is probably becoming more common these days to write Lyon than Lyons, and Marseille than Marseilles. You can also see Reims rather than Rheims. Some English-speaking people are even beginning to call Seville in Spain by its Spanish name Sevilla.

Other names have been forgotten by nearly all of us. The German city of Trier used to be Treves in English. We originally called Leipzig as Leipsic, but most people do not know that anymore. And who now remembers that Calais – which was actually part of England for a couple of centuries – was called Callis in English and that Boulogne used to have the English-language name Bullen?

It is not only in English that this is happening: in the Netherlands and Flemish-speaking Belgium, Norwich used to be called Noordwijk, but now they just say Norwich. And Yarmouth in Norfolk was formerly called Jarmuiden in Dutch/Flemish but no longer is.

There even seems to be a view these days that we actually OUGHT to use local names rather than exonyms – that it would be polite and respectful to use the names that the local people use rather than our own labels for places. But this would be a great mistake. That would be to demote the most famous and historically important of European cities to the status of – begging its pardon, because it is a very fine village – Great Snoring.

5.2 From Istropolis to Bratislava

The Ancient Greek name for Bratislava was Istropolis, from Istros, the Greek name for the River Danube which runs through the city. Five hundred years ago, Bratislava was the capital of Hungary; today it is the capital of Slovakia. The border with Austria is nearby – the city is about 35 miles from Vienna; and the frontier with Hungary is not much more than 10 miles away.

Bratislava today has a population of just under half a million people, with about 90 per cent of them being native speakers of Slovak. A hundred years ago, just before the end of World War I, things were very different. There was no such country as Slovakia – the area was part of the Austro-Hungarian empire. Bratislava had a population which was only about 15 per cent Slovak speaking; a little more than 40 per cent were native German speakers and 40 per cent were Hungarian speakers (though most people tended to be rather bilingual or even trilingual). And the city was not even called Bratislava.

What it was actually called depended on which language people were speaking. The majority of the inhabitants, the German speakers, called it Pressburg, which was also what it was mostly called in English (in French, it was Presbourg). Hungarian speakers referred to it – as they still do today – as Pozsony: this seems to be derived from a personal name, something like Poson. And the Slovak name was Prešporok, which was simply the Slavic form of Pressburg.

Then, a century ago, after the cessation of the hostilities of World War I, a new country called Czechoslovakia was carved out of the Austro-Hungarian Empire. It was conceived as a homeland for the speakers of the West Slavic languages Czech and Slovak, who had been struggling for decades for cultural and political independence – and many of them had fought on the Allied side during the war. But the town of Pressburg, in spite of its German and Hungarian majorities, also found itself in Czechoslovakia.

In fact, the borders of the new country were generally drawn in such a way that many speakers of languages other than Czech and Slovak were incorporated into the population. The Czech speakers were surrounded on their north, west and south by German speakers; and to the south of the Slovaks was a large area inhabited by Hungarian speakers. Also, the far eastern end of the new country was populated mainly by speakers of East Slavic dialects which were officially deemed to be Ukrainian.

In fact, there were more German speakers in Czechoslovakia than Slovak speakers, but this fact was concealed by deeming Czech and Slovak to be a single language called Czechoslovak – the languages are rather similar. And there were also many speakers of Romani, Polish, Romanian and other languages in the new country.

Most of the German-speaking population were ejected from Czechoslovakia in the aftermath of World War II, in 1945. The far eastern end of the country was then split off and handed over to the Soviet Union: those East Slavic speakers still remaining on the Czechoslovak side of the border were then often deemed to be speakers of a language or dialect called Rusyn.

In 1993, Czechoslovakia became two separate countries: Czechia, which was mostly Czech speaking; and Slovakia, which now had a Hungarian-speaking minority of around 10 per cent. The capital of the newly independent nation of Slovakia was Pressburg-Pozsony. But by then it had long since stopped being called Pressburg or Pozsony, or even Prešporok.

In 1919, there had been a proposal to call this city Wilsonovo Mesto, 'Wilson City', after the American President Woodrow Wilson, who had been very influential in the formation of an independent Czechoslovkia. But in the end it was officially renamed Bratislava. This name was totally invented, and it seems that it may have been based on a mistake. It was supposedly based on the name of a medieval Slavic nobleman and military leader called Bratislav. The problem is that his name was quite possibly not Bratislav at all, but Braslav.

TRIANON

The post–World War I Trianon Treaty dramatically redrew the boundaries of Hungary. From 1920, over 30 per cent of all Hungarian speakers in Europe found themselves, not in Hungary as before, but in Romania, Yugoslavia (today Slovenia and Serbia) and Czechoslovakia (now Slovakia), as well as in the USSR (now Ukraine) and Austria.

5.3 Welsh Glasgow

Dunkirk is a place forever etched in the British memory because of the evacuation of the nation's forces from its beaches in 1940. For the French who actually live there, it is Dunkerque. But whichever name is used, neither of them seems particularly French. And the reason for this becomes clear when you drive six miles along the coast from Dunkirk to the north-east and come to the France–Belgium border: when you cross that border, you find yourself in the part of Belgium where people speak Dutch.

The truth is that the name doesn't sound very French because it isn't – it is Dutch. In Flemish, as Dutch is often called in Belgium, the town is called Duinkerke. This name is meaningless to French speakers, but it is totally transparent in Flemish and means, literally, 'dune-church' – that is, a church in the dunes. If you look at a map of the area of France around Dunkirk, you will see that there are other names there which are obviously also Dutch in origin: Hazebrouck (Dutch Hazebroek), Hondeghem, Morbecque, Steenvoorde . . .

The fact is that this area of France is Dutch speaking – or was until recently. You will perhaps not hear too much Dutch on the streets of Dunkirk these days, but it is still spoken out in the countryside and used in some of the schools. The language border between the Dutch- and French-speaking areas does not coincide with the national frontier; and at earlier periods, it ran even further south than it does today: Calais was formerly a Dutch-speaking town called Kales.

European place-names can tell us a lot about our ethnographic and cultural history. Look at some of the names of places in eastern France: Strasbourg and Colmar, not to mention Schiltigheim and Natzwiller, tell us that this area was – and indeed still is – German speaking. History tells us that Alsace and Lorraine have changed hands several times over the last several centuries between France and Germany.

In eastern Germany, Chemnitz looks suspiciously non-German. And, yes, it was originally the Slavic name Kamjenica – in Czech the city is still often called Kamenice. The name means nothing to Germans, but to most Czechs it will be clear that it has something to do with their word *kamenný*, 'stony'.

If you look at a map of the north-western Karelia area of Russia, you will notice names such as Lahkolampi and Naistenjärvi – which tell us that this area is historically Finnish speaking. Bozen, Brixen, Bruneck and Latsch show us that the South Tyrol area of north-eastern Italy is German speaking rather than Italian. From the name Mariupol, we can see that this southern Ukrainian town has a Greek-speaking history. And Karasjok in Norway indicates that the far north of that country has for millennia been Sami (Lappish) speaking.

To this day, where language borders meet – and especially where they have shifted over the centuries and territorial possession has been disputed – cities may have a number of different names all in current use. In Belgium, the town that is known in French as Liège is called Luik in Dutch and Lüttich in German. Perhaps confusingly for travellers looking at road signs, Mons and Bergen refer to the same Belgian city (in French and Dutch respectively).

Inhabitants may call the multicultural western Ukrainian city Uzhgorod, Uzhhorod, Ungvár, Užhorod or Ujgorod depending on whether they are Russian, Ukrainian, Hungarian, Slovak or Romanian speakers.

Even in Britain, we can tell some rather surprising things about the cultural history of our island from our place-names. The name of our famous Scottish city of Glasgow is not Gaelic, or Scots, or English. It's Welsh. Even in Modern Welsh, *glas* can mean 'green', and *cau* is an archaic word for 'hollow'.

5.4 Stamboul and Micklegarth

I know for a fact that in the 1950s small English boys thought it was very funny to try and trick other small boys by posing the question: 'Constantinople is a long word – how do you spell it?' The correct answer, of course, was 'I T'.

In those days, we still called the city in question by that long name – it was some while before Istanbul began to take over in general vernacular usage. But Constantinople has borne very many different names over the centuries, and still does. Greeks colonised the area during the years after 700 BC, so the first recorded name of the city was in Greek – Byzantion. This form of the name is still familiar to us from its Latin form, Byzantium, and from the Constantinople-based Byzantine Empire. But we are not at all sure about the origin of the name Byzantion or what it meant, or even what language it came from. One scholarly guess is that this was its name in the Thracian language, one of the ancient and now extinct Indo-European languages of the Balkans.

Thracian was spoken in the eastern Balkans, with Illyrian to the west of it and Dacian to the north. It has been extinct for probably 1,000 years, but it was spoken in the area which is still known to us as Thrace (Thraki in Greek, Trakiya in Turkish and Bulgarian): today the area is divided up between Greece, Bulgaria and Turkey. One hypothesis is that the name of the city may perhaps have been derived from the Thracian personal name Byzas.

In the 300s AD, the Roman Emperor Constantinus (Constantine the Great) moved the capital of the Roman Empire from Rome to Byzantium, and because of this it was often known as Nea Romi, 'New Rome'. But by 324, the city was being called Konstantinoupolis – a Greek compound formed from *Konstantinou*, 'of Constantine' and *polis*, 'city' – *poli* in Modern Greek. It was often pronounced without the first *n*, and the spelling Kostantinoupoli occurs early on: frequent visitors to Greece will surely have met men called Kostas, which is the everyday form of Konstantinos.

Greek speakers, however, were quite soon referring to the city simply as *i Polis* 'the City', though it is not known whether this was thought of as being an abbreviation for Konstantinoupolis or not. Modern Greeks certainly refer to it as *i Poli* – for them it is *the* city.

For several hundred years, Constantinople was the largest, richest and most famous city in the whole of Europe. In Icelandic, it was called Mikligarður, 'Great Court' – the English version of this was Micklegarth. In the South Slavic languages, it went by the name of Carigrad, *cari* meaning 'tsar, emperor' and *grad*, 'city'. Its Arabic name was Kostantiniyye.

From the 1400s onwards, however, another name for the city began to appear. English-speaking people are familiar with this name from the title of Graham Greene's famous 1932 novel *Stamboul Train*, which is set on the Orient Express as it travels from Ostend to Constantinople. Stamboul became a traditional English name for the city; Stambuł is still its official Polish name, and Albanian has Stamboll. But where did that name come from?

The answer is that *Stamboul* has Greek origins. In the local Greek dialect of the region, *stan Póli*, pronounced 'stambóli', meant 'in the City' (Standard Modern Greek has *stin Póli*). Turkish speakers adopted this phrase as the name of the city, especially after its capture by the Ottoman Empire in 1453 (although the Arabic

Konstatiniyye was often still used by the Ottomans in formal documents). However, they typically added an *i*-sound at the beginning of the word, giving Istanbul, to fit in with the norms of Turkish pronunciation (like Spanish, Turkish has no native words beginning with *st-*). The same thing can be seen in the Turkish word for 'station', *istasyon*. And the name of the Turkish city of Izmir, originally Smyrni in Greek, shows the same process.

MICKLE

Mickle is an old English word meaning 'big, much', related to Icelandic *mikkil*. The word is no longer much used in southern Britain, but it survives in place-names, such as Michelmersh (Hampshire) 'large marsh', and Mickfield (Suffolk) 'large field'. Mickleover (Derbyshire) 'large place by a ridge' is next door to Littleover.

5.5 Marathónas

The men's race at the Athens marathon (*marathónios* in Greek) was won this year [2018] by the Kenyan athlete Misoi Brimin Kipkorir of Kenya, in 2 hours 10 minutes and 56 seconds; the women's race was also won by a Kenyan, Muriuki Shelmith Nyawira.

The Athens marathon advertises itself as 'The Authentic', on the grounds that it is run along the route of the 'original marathon'. In 490 BC, the Greeks defeated the Persians on the Plain of Marathon, against enormous odds; and the messenger Philippides was sent immediately to cover the distance of approximately 40 kilometres between there and Athens to bring the news of this great and unexpected victory to the Athenian assembly. He supposedly ran the entire distance without stopping, and burst in on the Assembly crying *Nenikekamen*, 'We have been victorious!' A Modern Greek equivalent to this might be *Nikísame*; and in both these verb-forms, you can see the Ancient Greek root *níke* (Modern Greek *níki*) 'victory' – a word which has now been appropriated by an American multinational sporting goods corporation which you may have heard of. To the Ancient Greeks, Nike was the Greek goddess who personified victory.

When the Olympic Games were revived in Greece in 1896, someone had the brilliant idea of including a long-distance race along the route that had so famously been followed by Philippides nearly 2,400 years before. That turned out to be an extremely popular decision – hundreds of marathon races are now run in different parts of the world every year.

The modern Athens marathon is 'authentic' in that it is run along the same route that was followed by the original Olympic marathon in 1896. But whether it is authentic in any other sense is not at all certain. There is no contemporary fifth-century BC documentary evidence of anyone having run non-stop to Athens from the battlefield at Marathon. And even if someone did accomplish this feat, it is far from certain that his name was Philippides. The Greek historian Herodotus made no mention of this deed; and the earliest surviving written mention of the event comes from the work of Plutarch, who was writing about it 600 years later. Modern historians tend to be rather sceptical about the historical validity of the story. Its status is, perhaps, rather that of a legend.

There is no doubting the authenticity, however, of the battle of Marathon itself. The coastal Plain of Marathon, where the battle was certainly fought, seems to have taken its name from the fennel which grew in abundance in the area: in Modern Greek, the word *márathos* means 'fennel'. The modern-day town itself is called Marathónas.

Ironically, for a place so closely associated with the glories of Ancient Greece, Marathónas was, for many hundreds of years until rather recently, more or less entirely Albanian speaking. This is true of most of the villages in a large arc around Athens and Thebes (Greek Thiva), stretching down into the Peloponnese peninsula and out to some of the islands such as Hydra. The migration of large numbers of Albanian speakers into these areas began around 1300 and continued for two or three centuries. In some cases it seems that they were invited to settle in areas which had become underpopulated because of plague or warfare.

When I investigated the linguistic situation in Marathónas in the 1970s, a good half of the population spoke Albanian in their everyday lives, although all except the very elderly were bilingual. Today, Arvanítika – as the language is referred to in that part of Greece (see Section 4.8) – still has many thousands of speakers in the Athens area, but it has become endangered as younger people shift to the national language and villagers migrate to towns. Unlike the Persians, the Albanians have not been defeated. But today they certainly think of themselves as Greek, and their language is gradually disappearing from the Plain of Marathon.

FENNEL

Greek etymologists seem not to know where their word *márathos*, 'fennel', comes from, suggesting simply that it was borrowed from some other unknown language. At least we know that the English word comes from Latin *faeniculum*, the diminutive of *faenum*, 'hay', perhaps because of fennel's feathery leaves. Italian *finocchio* comes from the same source.

5.6 From Knossós to Paisley

Mycenaean Greek is the most ancient form of the Greek language known to us; it was spoken in Greece until about 1200 BC. Most of what we know about the language comes from texts which were written on clay tablets using the Linear

B syllabary. This writing system was not deciphered until the 1950s, when two Englishmen, Michael Ventris and John Chadwick, cracked the code. Linear B tablets have been found on the island of Crete in the remains of the Royal Palace at Cnossos (Greek *Knossós*), and on the Greek mainland, notably at Mycenae, with the oldest texts dating from about 1450 BC.

One of the 3500-year-old words we find in these texts is the item *gwasileus*, which seems to have meant something like 'lower-ranking dignitary'. Specialists in the history of the Greek language do not know much about the origins of this word – there do not appear to be any related items in other Indo-European languages – and the most influential etymological dictionary of Modern Greek gives the verdict of 'etymology unknown'. The general assumption has to be that this word was probably borrowed from some other eastern Mediterranean language, with one very likely candidate being the (unknown) language of the ancient Minoan civilisation which preceded the Greek invasion and settlement of Crete.

Written records from very much later, around 600 BC – by then using the Greek alphabet – show that this word had become *basileus* in the Ancient Greek of the time, and its meaning had changed to something like 'king'. The adjective derived from *basileus* was *basilikos*, 'royal'. The feminine form was *basilike*; and in ancient Athens, the *stoa basilike* was the 'royal portal' of the *archon basileus*, 'the magistrate sovereign', the official who meted out justice.

This word was later borrowed into Latin. In Rome, the feminine form of the adjective, *basilica*, came to refer to large oblong buildings used for dispensation of justice, and subsequently to any similar building used as place of assembly. After the arrival of Christianity, *basilica* continued to be used to refer to such buildings even after they had been appropriated for Christian worship, and so it eventually came to mean any large ecclesiastical building of the appropriate shape.

In the sense of 'church' – and especially (but not only) a large church of this particular design – the word was borrowed into many other languages, including Welsh: there is a place in South Wales called Basaleg, 'place with a church'. Another of the languages which acquired the word was Gaelic: in medieval Irish, the form was *baislec*. As parts of south-western Scotland became Gaelic speakers in the Middle Ages, *baislec* came to be used as the name of one particular settlement in Renfrewshire which was also a place with a church; the first recorded version of the name is Passelek, but the modern form is Paisley.

One does not automatically make a mental connection between the modern town of Paisley, just down the road from Glasgow Airport, and the ruined Ancient Minoan capital of Knossos, a couple of miles inland from the shores of the Aegean Sea. But they probably are linked linguistically.

The name Paisley is now known all over the world – but not in connection with churches. Its fame comes from the Paisley teardrop pattern, originally associated with Persia and north-western India, which became renowned in the nineteenth century through the enormous popularity of shawls featuring this motif. These shawls acquired the epithet 'Paisley' because, from the early 1800s onwards, advances in production techniques introduced by manufacturers in Paisley gradually enabled the producers there to dominate the world market in these textiles and put their competitors out of business.

It is important to point out, however, that the very first British 'Paisley' shawls were actually made in England in the late 1700s and that they were, like the distinguished newspaper which you are currently reading, produced in Norwich.

BASIL

The herb which was called *basilikon*, 'royal', in Ancient Greek is known today by the Latin name of *basilicum*, and in English as *basil*. No one seems to be very sure what is or was kingly about it, but one suggestion is that the herb may perhaps have been used for making perfumes for royalty.

5.7 No Bears

It is a very interesting coincidence that Berlin and Berne, the capitals of Germany and Switzerland respectively, are both named after bears. This can easily be confirmed by noting that these cities' coats of arms both display a heraldic representation of a bear.

The name Berne (Bern in German) came about because at some time during the twelfth century, Duke Berthold V, who founded the city, promised to name his new town after the first animal he came across when he was out hunting – and that just happened to be a bear.

As far as Berlin is concerned, the city is not actually named for a bear as such but after Albert, the first Margrave of Brandenburg, who was nicknamed 'the Bear', presumably because he was thought to have ursine qualities. (It was also during the twelfth century that Albert founded the Margravate – Margraves were military governors of border provinces.)

Except that this is all complete nonsense: neither of these explanations is true. They have been widely believed, but they simply bear (sorry) testimony to the tendency of human beings to try and make sense of words which don't have obvious meanings. We invent stories about words in order to fit them into scenarios which are comprehensible to us; or we just quite simply change the forms of the words themselves to get them to make more sense. Is the English word *belfry* so called because a belfry is where bells are located? Actually, no, it isn't. The original form of the word, which we borrowed from Old French, was *berfrei*. English speakers changed the *ber-* part to *bel-* because that made more sense of the word.

Similarly, the English word *bridegroom* was originally *brydguma*, but as knowledge of the Anglo-Saxon word *guma*, 'man' weakened, so speakers increasingly altered it to *groom* – because *groom* was a word they still knew. This process is known to linguistic scientists as 'folk etymology'.

In German, the syllable *Ber-* which begins the names of both these capital cities can be pronounced the same as *Bär*, 'bear'. The underlying meaning of these two city names was opaque to German speakers, so the folk-etymological supposition that both names began with the German word for 'bear' helped to make sense of them.

In fact, the reason German speakers could not figure out what Berlin and Berne meant was that these were not originally German-language names at all. Berlin is actually a Slavic name in origin. Until the Middle Ages, the whole of Germany east of the River Elbe was occupied by people who spoke West Slavic languages, now extinct, which were related to Modern Polish, Czech and Slovak. It is not certain what the *berl-* part of the name meant in the local West Slavic Polabian language, but the *-in* ending is common in place-names in formerly Slavic-speaking eastern Germany – Schwerin, Templin, Pessin, Lehnin, Wollin, Eutin, Genthin, Passentin, Penzlin; in modern Poland – Lublin, Koszalin (its German name is Köslin) and Szczecin (German Stettin); and in other Slavic-speaking places.

Etymologists and onomasticians are not entirely certain about the origins of the name Berne, but it seems that it, too, is a remnant of the language of the previous inhabitants. In the case of Switzerland, these would have been Celts. People speaking Celtic languages in modern times have been found only on the western edges of Europe – in Brittany, Cornwall, Wales, Ireland, the Isle of Man and western Scotland. But until about 500 BC, before the Germanic peoples began to arrive from the north, the Celts were the dominant ethnolinguistic group across very large areas of central and Western Europe. One suggestion is that the name Bern was in origin an ancient Celtic word *berna* meaning 'cleft' – the River Aare does run through a deep gorge by Berne.

But there is no doubt at all that neither Berlin nor Berne ever had anything to do with bears.

5.8 Paris and Hull

The capital of France has many names. In the Gaelic of Ireland it is known as Páras; the Finnish name is Pariisi; it is called Parijs in Dutch; and in Lithuanian it is known as Paryžius. Our English-language name is, of course, the same as the French name – except that it isn't, because we pronounce it in a completely different way, with the stress on the first syllable and the *s* at the end of the name actually being pronounced.

Many other languages also use the same spelling for Paris as in French but then pronounce the name in their own way: this is true of German, Swedish, Turkish and Portuguese. But elsewhere on the continent, there are many other non-French versions of the name of the city: there is Bosnian Pariz, Estonian Pariis, Hungarian Párizs, Latvian Parīze and Greek Parisi. The Spanish form París looks the same as the French, until you notice that there is an accent above the *i* in the last syllable.

The earliest known name of Paris was the Latin word used by the Romans, Lutetia. This name was probably derived from the Celtic language of the pre-Roman inhabitants of northern France – a Celtic language which was closely related to the language of the ancient Britons on the other side of the English Channel, which survives into modern times as Welsh.

Crucially, though, the Roman town was also known more specifically as Lutetia Parisiorum, signifying 'Lutetia of the Parisii', the point being that the Parisii were the Gaulish Celtic tribe who inhabited this area. They had been living on the banks of the Seine in the area of modern Paris from around 250 BC. In his dictionary of the Gaulish language, the historical linguist and lexicographer Xavier Delamarre has suggested that the name of the tribe came from the Celtic root *pario-*, 'cauldron', indicating that they might have taken their name after a type of Iron Age Celtic cooking vessel. The well-known American linguist Professor Eric Hamp, on the other hand, has suggested that the name of the tribe came from a Celtic root which would have been something like *peri-* meaning 'to command' or 'to cause to have something done'. Their name, then, may have been equivalent to 'the commanders'. It is certainly true that in Modern Welsh *peri* means 'to cause', but otherwise we cannot be exactly sure.

What is certain is that there is no connection, as has sometimes been fancifully suggested, with Páris, the figure from ancient Greek history who was the son of King Priam and Queen Hecuba of Troy and who famously carried off Helen, the Queen of Sparta, supposedly causing the Trojan War. His name was certainly not Celtic, and probably came from one of the languages of ancient Asia Minor, such as Luwian.

Interestingly, there was also a small Celtic tribe known as the Parisii in northern England. It is possible that they were linked to the Gaulish Parisii in some way, and they may at some stage have been one people: the same etymologies have been proposed for their tribal name as for the Gaulish Parisii.

These British Parisii are known to have lived in the coastal area of eastern Yorkshire. If things had worked out differently, Hull might have been called Paris.

SWAMP

The first part of the Latin name for Paris, Lutetia Parisii, may as well be derived from *luto-*, an old Celtic root meaning 'marsh' or 'swamp'. Berlin, too, may originally have been a settlement by a bog: one suggestion is that the first part of the name comes from an ancient Slavic root *birl-* meaning 'marsh' or 'swamp'.

5.9 Toponymic Subjugation

We are used to the fact that towns can be called by different names in different languages. Most often this does not cause any difficulty. Even if British people do not know French, they are generally able to work out which place francophones are talking about when they say 'Édimbourg'. The Dutch-language place-name Parijs similarly does not cause us any problems.

Sometimes, though, deciphering foreign place-names is not so easy. The French town of Lille is called Rijsel in Dutch. Dutch-speaking Mechelen in Belgium is known as Malines in French. As we have already seen, Francophone Liège goes by Luik in Dutch and Lüttich in German and appears under these names on motorway signs. Helsinki, the capital of Finland, is called Helsingfors in the Scandinavian languages including Swedish, which is an official language of Finland.

The usage of different place-names is not necessarily just innocent. The Spanish cities San Sebastian, Bilbao and Pamplona are called Donostia, Bilbo and Iruña in Basque, the indigenous language of the area where they are located, but the fascist nationalist government of General Franco did not want anybody to know that.

The current Polish government is rather keen that English speakers should refer to the city on their Baltic coast by the name of Gdansk rather than by the name we always used to use and which many of us find it easier to pronounce, Danzig, which also just happens to be its German-language name. (The city, by the way, was part of Germany till World War I). And the Italians really want people to call their northern city Bolzano rather than Bozen, which is the German-language name (the city, incidentally, belonged to Austria till World War I, and many of its inhabitants are still German speakers).

In most areas of northern Norway, the indigenous language is Sami (Lappish), and many places have Sami-language names. Kautokeino is Guovdageaidnu, and Kirkenes is Girkonjárga. You will be rather lucky, however, if you spot very many Sami place-names on signs as you travel around Norway. You will certainly see some; but even in highly democratic and human-rights-conscious Norway, all is not entirely well on this front.

As the North-Norway-based linguist Professor Kaisa Rautio Helander has explained, the addition of Sami village names to road signs is perceived as a symbol of Sami rights. This did, sadly, arouse opposition – which of course was opposition not just to the road signs, but to Sami linguistic and historical settlement rights in general.

The official use of Sami names was an attack on the earlier monolingual, monocultural ideology which was Norwegian policy until well into the twentieth century. This has happily long since been abandoned. But the infrequent use of Sami place-names by local councils has represented a form of 'toponymic subjugation' through 'toponymic silence', continuing the historic subjugation of Sami culture by the incoming Norwegian one. This fact has recently been officially recognised, and central government plans have been announced to add Sami names to signs countrywide.

Here, we can be just a little bit satisfied that in recent decades we have got used to seeing road signs in Wales with place-names on them such as Caerdydd, Cas-gwent and Abertawe, and town signs in Scotland with names like An t-Òban, Inbhir Nis and Steòrnabhagh. The addition of these non-English names to road signs is, of course, largely symbolic, but it is symbolic of something extremely important. It is an acknowledgement that Welsh and Scottish Gaelic are the indigenous languages of the areas in question; that they were spoken there long before English – in the case of Welsh, several thousand years earlier; that the speakers of these language have rights; and that their languages, like all human languages, deserve respect.

This is a point worth emphasising, not least because there are quite possibly some British people reading this piece who are still not totally clear about the fact that the English-language names of the above places are Cardiff, Chepstow, Swansea, Oban, Inverness and Stornoway.

TOPONYMS

Toponym is another word for place-name – from Ancient Greek *toponymía*, consisting of *tópos*, 'place', and *ónoma*, 'name'. An exonym (Greek *éxo*, 'out') is a non-local toponym, a name local people don't use. Llundain and Lunnainn are (the Welsh and Gaelic) exonyms for London, which is the city's endonym, the local name (from Greek *éndon*, 'in').

---

6 Countries

We now move up a geographical level, from cities to countries. One historical aspect of the complexity of the relationship between nations and languages that we deal with in this chapter is illustrated by the fact that many countries bear names derived from those of peoples who spoke a language which was not the same as the one we now associate with the nation in question. Bulgaria was named after Turks, and Russia takes its name from a gang of Swedes. England is called after a tribe of Germans, and so is France. And which particular assemblage of Germanic people Germany itself is named after depends, as we discuss below, on who is doing the naming.

Many similar tales can be told of mismatched languages, peoples and labels. A group of Irish people gave their name to Scotland: the original Scots were Gaelic-speaking immigrants to the West Highlands and islands who started arriving from across the Irish Sea at about the same time as the Angles were settling in eastern England. *Scotti* was a Latin word for the Irish people; the earliest use of *Scotland* in English is with reference to Ireland, not Scotland.

Modern Belgium, which straddles the dividing line between Germanic and Romance (Latin-derived) languages, is named after speakers of a language which was neither Germanic nor Romance but Celtic – the Belgae – who are described by Julius Caesar as inhabiting the area north of Gaul.

And when it comes to the complexity of the contemporary relationship between nations and languages, this can be appreciated from the fact that, while it is easy to think of languages and countries as if they simply match up, this is by no means always so. Most people in England do speak English; the citizens of France mainly speak French; the language of Germany is German; people in Spain speak Spanish; and in Italy they use Italian.

But this is a great simplification, and as is so often the case, things are much more complicated than that. English is by no means spoken only in England. French is spoken in Belgium and Switzerland as well as France, and the other indigenous languages of France include Breton, Dutch, German, Basque, Provencal and Catalan. German is also spoken natively in Denmark, Belgium and Switzerland, and it is the language of the vast majority of Austrians. Many Spanish people are mother-tongue speakers of Galician, Catalan and Basque rather than Spanish. Italian is one of the three major languages of Switzerland; and there are many Italians who have other languages as their mother tongue, notably German, Slovenian, Albanian and Greek.

In this chapter we address some of the issues arising from these complexities.

6.1 Just Couldn't Stay at Home

There was a time during the first millennium AD when some of the Germanic peoples of Europe just could not stay at home. As a result of their wanderings, their tribal names are now scattered over much of our continent as labels for various countries and smaller regions.

We are familiar in the British Isles with the story of the westward-travelling Danish Vikings who ended up in England, and of the Norwegian Vikings who made it to Scotland, Ireland, Iceland, Greenland and Canada. We tend to be less familiar with the Swedish Vikings, who travelled eastwards across the Baltic and down the rivers of Russia as far as Constantinople. Some of these Swedes were known as the Rus, and they became the ruling class of an area which at various times included Novgorod and Kiev; hence the name Russia. It is possible that *rus* has etymological links with the ancient Germanic word which in Modern English has become 'row', as in rowing a boat. After all, those Rus would have had to do plenty of rowing.

The Germanic tribe who gave their name to England were the Angles (see the Prologue). Their original German homeland was in Angeln, now part of north-eastern Schleswig-Holstein, just south of the German–Danish border on the coast of the Baltic Sea. It was their migrations across the North Sea to Britain and their eventual occupation of northern and central England (the south was mostly taken by their cousins the Saxons) which led to the development and usage of names such as Ængleland and Englalond, later England – 'the land of the Angles'. *Angeln* might originally have meant 'narrow' or 'bend': topographical justification can be found for both of those labels in the landscape of Schleswig.

The Germanic tribe who gave their name to France were the Franks. The original German homeland of these people lay along banks of the middle Rhine, around Koblenz, Bonn, Cologne and Dusseldorf. A number of them eventually moved across the Rhine into Romanised Celtic territory and gradually came to dominate, militarily and politically, large areas of what is now northern France. As a minority ruling elite, they eventually abandoned their native language and starting speaking the Latin-derived language of the locals which today bears their name – French. In their original non-Romanised homeland beyond the Rhine, their Germanic tongue continued to be spoken; and today the varieties of Dutch and German spoken in Belgium and Holland, and across west central Germany as far as Nuremburg, are still called Franconian by linguists and dialectologists. It is widely believed that the name Frank came from an old Germanic root *frankon* which meant 'javelin', supposedly their weapon of choice.

Normandy, like Russia, is named after Vikings – the 'North men', Danish Vikings who settled there. And Lombardy is so called because of the Germanic Lombards (or Langobards, 'long-beards') who gained control of much of northern Italy from the AD 500s onwards. Like the Franks, the Lombards and Normans had abandoned their Germanic languages by about AD 1000.

And it was not just Germanic people who were wandering around all over the place back then. Modern Slavic-speaking Christian Bulgaria is named after a bunch of migrant pagan Turks. The Bulgars were a semi-nomadic people from the steppes of southern Kazakhstan, Russia and Ukraine who took control of parts of the eastern Balkans and gradually became sedentary. Like the Norman, Rus, Frankish and Lombard minority elites, they also gradually assimilated culturally and linguistically to the local – in this case Slavic – population.

And as for Germany, which holds a central geographical position in Europe, it is not surprising that the country has many different names in various languages. In French, Germany is Allemagne, in Spanish Alemania, in Turkish Almanya; and in English we used to have Almain meaning 'German'. This name comes from the ancient Germanic tribe known as the Alemanni, who lived in the south-west of Germany. Modern German dialects spoken in Alsace, Swabia and Switzerland are still known as Alemannic.

In Finland, Germany is known as Saksa, and it is Saksamaa in Estonian. These names are derived from the North German Saxon tribe, which is also the source of the Irish Gaelic name for England – Sasana – as well as the Scottish label for the English – Sassenachs. The weapon of choice of the Saxons was supposedly the *sahso*, the knife.

The English name Germany, and related forms such as Germania in other languages, come from the classical Latin name Germani, which first appears in the writings of Julius Caesar. It was not used by the Germanic peoples themselves, and it may be derived from some Celtic term – but the truth is that we don't know. We also do not know why Germany is called Vokietija in Lithuanian or Vācija in Latvian.

But we do have a good idea about the origin of the German appellation Deutschland and the related Scandinavian Tyskland. There was an Old English word *theod* which meant 'people': the town of Thetford in Norfolk was originally Theodford, 'the people's ford'. *Theod* went back to an ancient Germanic word *thiud*, with the related form *thiudiskaz* meaning 'of the people', which came down into Old English as *theodisc*. This word no longer exists in our modern language, but the corresponding Old High German word was *diutisc*. This term was often used to refer to the Germanic 'language of the people' – as opposed to Latin – and gradually also came to refer to the people who spoke the German language themselves. In Modern German, *diutisc* has become Deutsch, hence Deutschland.

In English we have the same word, though in the form of Dutch, but we use it with reference to the closely related language of Holland and Belgium and to the people of the Netherlands, although we do not call their country Dutchland. The situation in Italian is similar: Germany is called Germania, but the adjective 'German' is *tedesco*, which has the same root as Deutsch.

It is also clear where the names referring to Germany in the Slavic languages come from. Forms such as Slovak Nemecko and Polish Niemcy are derived from the Slavic word for 'dumb': the Polish word for 'mute' is *niemy*. As far as the Slavs were concerned, the Germans – even if they were good at wandering around and giving their names to other people's countries – were the people who could not speak.

VIKING

The word *Viking* is generally considered to come from the Norse word *vik*, 'bay, inlet', so a Viking was someone who came from the fiords. But it might also come from Old English *wic*, 'settlement', which could also mean 'camp', so a Viking or Wicing was one who, during raids from across the sea, lived in encampments.

6.2 The Baltic States

The Baltic States are, from north to south along the eastern shores of the Baltic Sea, Estonia, Latvia and Lithuania. We often refer to them by this collective name as if they formed some kind of unity – and in some ways, of course, they do. They were all under Russian control for over a century until after World War I, when they became separate independent countries. During World War II, all of them were invaded by the Germans and then were swallowed up by the Soviet Union, becoming independent nations again in 1991. They all contain sizeable Russian-speaking minorities because of in-migration during the period of Soviet control. All three of them are quite small in terms of population, none comprising more than 3 million citizens. They also have a number of cultural affinities with each other.

But there are two major factors which help to distinguish between these three nations. The first is religion. Historically, Estonia and Latvia were predominantly Protestant, like nearby Finland and Sweden, while Lithuania was mainly Catholic, like neighbouring Poland.

The second is language, which divides them in a different way. The Lithuanian and Latvian languages are historically related to one another, but not to Estonian.

Estonian is a Finno-Ugric language, very distantly related to Hungarian, and less distantly to the Sami or Lappish languages of northern Scandinavia. More specifically, Estonian is a Balto-Finnic language, very closely related to Finnish. There is some degree of mutual intelligibility between the two languages – Finnish *yksi kaksi kolme*, 'one two three' is *üks kaks kolm* in Estonian – and Estonians in particular became adept at understanding Finnish as a result of watching Finnish TV during the Soviet era. Specialist academic conferences take place today involving the two countries, at which each linguistic group speaks their own language; participants report that, with good will on both sides and the help of PowerPoint presentations, this works well enough.

In the south of Estonia, a language variety called Voro is spoken which is regarded by its proponents as a language in its own right, related to but different from Estonian. Modern Standard Estonian is certainly based on dialects from the north of the country.

Another (now-extinct) Finnic language of the Baltic States which was closely related to Estonian is Livonian. This was spoken in areas of northern Latvia not far from Estonia, but tragically the person who is thought to have been the last native speaker of this language died in 2013. Place-name evidence shows that at one time Finnic was spoken over substantial areas of what is now Latvia.

Latvian and Lithuanian, on the other hand, are both Indo-European Baltic languages. They are the only two survivors of a bigger Baltic language family which was once spoken over a much larger geographical area, including what is now north-eastern Poland. The best known of the other now-extinct Baltic languages was Prussian, which often today goes by the name of Old Prussian to distinguish it from Prussian varieties of German: Old Prussian died out in the 1600s as speakers of different varieties of German invaded and colonised the area.

The Baltic languages are thought by some scholars to have a historical relationship with Slavic languages such as Polish, and they therefore talk of a Balto-Slavic language family.

Unlike Finnish and Estonian, Latvian and Lithuanian are not mutually intelligible. It has been suggested that the degree of relationship between the two might be rather like English and Dutch: English speakers are not surprised to learn that the Dutch word *water* means 'water', or that *goed* is 'good' or that *een twee drie* means 'one two three' — but we are still not able to understand what Dutch speakers are saying unless we have studied the language. Similarly, Lithuanian *vienas du trys*, 'one two three', is *viens divi tris* in Latvian, but that does not necessarily help either side very much with general comprehension of the other language.

TALLINN

The second part of the name of the capital of Estonia – Tallinn – is the Estonian word *linn*, 'town'. The first part of the name may be derived from the Estonian word *taani*, 'Danish': the northern region of Estonia was under the control of the Kingdom of Denmark from 1219 till 1346.

6.3 Crimea

After the military annexation by Russia of the Ukrainian area of Crimea in 2014, the French politician Marine Le Pen announced that Crimea had 'always been Russian'.

That is not true. But it would not have been true either to claim that Crimea had always been Ukrainian. Linguistic evidence is clear on this point: Russian and Ukrainian, which are closely related East Slavic languages, are both recent arrivals in Crimea.

The Crimean peninsula occupies an area bigger than Wales on the northern shores of the Black Sea; and for most of its recorded history it has been multilingual. From around 500 BC, the coastal areas of Crimea were home to speakers of Ancient Greek, and the Greek language survived in Crimea until modern times: there are still Greek speakers in Mariupol, on the coast of the Sea of Azov, about 150 miles from Crimea.

Inland from these Ancient Greek speakers, in the mountains and plains of the Crimean interior, there were speakers of another Indo-European language, Scythian, which belonged to the Iranian language family. Crimea also came briefly under partial Roman rule, so there would have been some presence of Latin.

Then, in the 3rd century AD, Crimea was invaded by the Goths, who were speakers of yet another Indo-European language, Gothic, which was a member of the eastern branch of the Germanic language family. Their language is important historically because the earliest surviving records we have of any of the Germanic languages consist of parts of a fourth-century Gothic Bible, originally translated somewhere in the Balkans by Bishop Wulfila.

The Goths were heavily involved in the fall of the Roman Empire, and they came to control large areas of eastern and southern Europe, where they gradually assimilated linguistically to the peoples they were living amongst. As a result, there are no East Germanic languages left today – though Crimean Gothic did survive into the seventeenth century.

From about the fifth century onwards, the Indo-European languages of Crimea began to give way to languages from the Turkic family, especially in the north of the peninsula. We are not sure about the language of the Huns, though it was probably a Turkic language that they spoke. The language of the Bulgars was certainly Turkic, although when they later moved on into the Balkans, they abandoned their language for Slavic. They were followed into Crimea by further Turkic peoples, such as the Kipchaks and Khazars; their descendants developed a variety of Turkic which we now call Crimean Tatar. Up until the eighteenth century, this remained the predominant language of Crimea, something which was perhaps helped by the fact that the peninsula came under Ottoman Turkish protection.

The linguistic pendulum in Crimea did eventually swing back in favour of Indo-European languages, but this was not until 1783, when Crimea was invaded and annexed by the Russians, who brought their Slavic language with them. Since then, the Tatar language has been in gradual decline. By 1900, Tatar speakers represented only about one-third of the population of Crimea, though they were still the largest single language group.

The biggest blow to their language occurred during World War II, when Stalin brutally exiled all the Crimean Tatars to Uzbekistan, an atrocity which many of them did not survive. For decades they were not allowed back to their homeland, and they currently constitute only about 12 per cent of the Crimean population, with very many of them no longer able to speak their ancestral language. There are thousands of Tatars left behind in Uzbekistan, as well as groups in Turkey and Romania, but the language is now everywhere considered to be in danger of extinction. And its situation in Crimea, where it did receive some support under the Ukrainians, seems to have worsened since Russia's second annexation of the peninsula in 2014.

If it can be said of any group of people that Crimea has 'always' belonged to them, then it must be the Tatars – unless you want to vote for the Greeks. But it most certainly is not the Russians.

6.4 Jabal Tariq: Gibraltar

Gibraltar is an extraordinarily interesting multicultural country, and it has an extraordinary multilingual history – and multilingual present. The name of Gibraltar itself is Arabic. It comes from Jabal Tariq, 'Mount Tariq', named after the North African Berber leader Tariq ibn Ziyad who took control of the peninsula in AD 711. From then on, and for over 700 years, most people in Gibraltar spoke Arabic and/or Berber. Then in 1462 the territory was conquered by the Kingdom of Spain, and the Spanish language gradually took over.

Spanish-language domination did not last long, however, and other languages started arriving as a result of maritime trade and immigration. Most notable was Genoese, which first made its appearance in the 1500s. Genoa was one of the great Mediterranean maritime powers, and its language was probably the native tongue of Christopher Columbus. Genoese is closely related to Italian and French, and its home lies in Liguria, the coastal area of Italy between Monaco and La Spezia, centring on the city of Genoa.

In 1704, during the War of Spanish Succession, Gibraltar was captured for the Habsburg contender to the throne, Charles VI of Austria, by a joint Dutch–British fleet. It was then ceded to Britain through the Treaty of Utrecht in 1713 in return for the British recognising Philip V, rather than Charles, as the King of Spain. Most of the Spanish speakers left Gibraltar, and by the mid-1700s Genoese speakers were the largest single linguistic group in the colony. A number of Maltese-speaking people also arrived after 1704, encouraged by the British – who had been using Malta as a base – to help fill the gap left by the departing hispanophones. This meant that, after a break of 250 years, Arabic had, in a way, now found its way back into Gibraltar, since the Maltese language was itself originally derived from a dialect of North African Arabic.

There was also a large community of Jews in Gibraltar, the majority of them arriving from Morocco, just across the Straits of Gibraltar. Most of them were descendants of the Jews who had been expelled from Spain in 1492, so they were probably speakers of Haketia. This language is sometimes also known as Western Ladino, to distinguish it from the Eastern Ladino spoken in the Balkans. Both of these languages are derived from Spanish and Portuguese – hence the alternative name, Judeo-Spanish; so a form of Spanish, too, had now rather quickly found its way back onto the peninsula. Both Ladino varieties include liturgical vocabulary from Hebrew, but Haketia also shows considerable influence from Arabic.

Today there are three main languages you can hear being spoken in Gibraltar by its native inhabitants – most Gibraltarians are trilingual. The first, unsurprisingly, is English. But it is an English which over the years has taken on a specifically Gibraltarian form, just as we now have distinctive varieties of English in very many other places in the world. Some of its distinctiveness is due to influence from Spanish.

The second language is Spanish itself, but it is specifically Western Andalusian Spanish which shows significant differences from the Spanish of Madrid. Western Andalusian is the dialect of Seville and Cadiz, and of the area of Spain immediately adjacent to Gibraltar. This dialect played a large role in the formation of the varieties of Spanish spoken in the Canary Islands and in the Americas.

The third tongue is the most interesting. It is a specifically Gibraltarian language which very much symbolises the separate identity of the people on *the Rock*. It is known as Llanito or Yanito, and it arose out of interactions between Gibraltarian English and Western Andalusian. Its grammatical base is more Spanish than English, but it also contains a great deal of vocabulary which is neither Spanish nor English. Unsurprisingly, much of this vocabulary is Genoan, Maltese and Hebrew in origin. So don't think that just because you know English and Spanish you will be able to understand Yanito. You won't.

6.5 Heptanesia

Great Britain started decolonising its imperial possessions in a significant way in 1947, when British India became the two independent states of India and Pakistan. But there is a very interesting example of British decolonisation which comes from well before that time.

In 1864, the Ionian Islands were voluntarily transferred out of British control into the hands of the new Greek state, which had been founded in 1830. The islands which were transferred in this way were Kérkyra (Corfu in English), Paxí (sometimes Paxos in English), Lefkáda (Lefkas), Itháki (Ithaca), Kefaloniá (Cephalonia or Kefallinia), Zákynthos (Zante) and Kýthira (Cythera). Kýthira lies off the south coast of the Peloponnese between the Greek mainland and Crete, but the other islands are all situated off the west coast of Greece in the Ionian Sea, between Greece and Italy. These seven islands are also sometimes known collectively as the Heptanese or Heptanesian Islands, from the Ancient Greek *heptá*, 'seven', and *nesos*, 'island'.

Unlike the rest of Greece, the different Ionian Islands spent very little time – or none at all – as part of the Turkish Ottoman Empire, and instead were mostly under the control of the Venetian Republic until the end of the eighteenth century, when Venice was overrun by Napoleon and the Ionian Islands became French possessions. With the defeat of Bonaparte in 1815, the Treaty of Paris placed the islands under the protection of Great Britain. The period during which the Ionian Islands constituted a kind of British colony thus lasted for nearly fifty years – which was long enough for the game of cricket to establish something of a foothold on Corfu.

These islands, then, have had a rather different history from most other areas of Greece, with considerable Italian influence and a traditionally much greater cultural orientation towards Western Europe. In the struggle for Greek independence from the Ottoman Empire, the quasi-independence of the Ionian Islands under Britain was very influential in showing that Greeks could in principle be free, and that Greeks were very capable of governing themselves.

The linguistic relevance of these islands has to do with the role they played in the development of the modern Greek language. In Greece, under the rule of the Turks starting in the 1400s, contemporary Greek rapidly lost its status and came to be confined almost entirely to its spoken form. In all types of writing, either Turkish was used or else an archaic, elitist and limited mediaeval type of Greek which had little connection to the everyday spoken language of ordinary people.

In the run-up to independence, however, activists started looking for ways to develop written Modern Greek so that the newly independent nation could have its own standard language like the nation-states of Western Europe. There were all sorts of crackpot ideas about this, such as the suggestion that people should go back to writing Ancient Greek (imagine if someone had suggested that English speakers should start writing in Anglo-Saxon)!

The only sensible proposal was that the language question should be solved by simply using a written version of the everyday spoken language, as in Western European countries. This is what eventually happened, although it took until the 1970s to get the issue sorted out properly. But the movement in favour of this proposal was greatly strengthened by the fact that poets in the Ionian Islands of western Greece, which had remained out of Turkish control, had already been writing in their own modern Greek dialect for a considerable time.

The first attempt at developing a vernacular-based Greek standard language came in 1814, proposed by the scholar Yannis Vilaras from Ioannina on the Greek mainland not far from Corfu, who wrote a *Romaic* (Greek) *Grammar* in which he suggested norms for spelling and grammar based on the spoken dialects. This was the forerunner of what was later called Demotic Greek, which is the basis of today's Modern Standard Greek.

QUASI

Pronounced 'kway-zye' or 'kwah-zee', this was originally Latin for 'as if', from *quam*, 'as' plus *si*, 'if'. Since the 1600s it has been used in English as a prefix with the rather complex meaning of 'resembling but not really the same as'. *Quasi-independence* means 'having some but not all the properties of independence'.

6.6 Macedonia

As a topographical term, Macedonia refers to an area which has no official status — rather like East Anglia or the Midwest. But it is generally agreed that Macedonia is the region of the Balkans which includes a large area of northern Greece, a smaller area of southwestern Bulgaria, even smaller areas of southern Serbia, southern Kosovo and eastern Albania and, in the middle, the entirety of what was officially known for some years as FYROM and is now called North Macedonia.

That acronym stands for 'the Former Yugoslav Republic of Macedonia' (see also Section 4.9), a name for the country which English-speaking people usually simply call Macedonia. This strange acronymic name came into being because of the sensibilities of some Greeks. They were not concerned when a constituent republic of Yugoslavia was called Macedonia, but when that same republic became an independent nation, some Greeks then started worrying that this presaged territorial claims by FYROM over parts of Greek Macedonia.

These fears are easy to understand if we recall that the borders of northern Greece were only fixed as recently as 1924, and that there were significant areas of what is now Greek Macedonia which had very few Greek-speaking inhabitants at that time. The 1924 boundaries were also changed — temporarily as it turned out — by the Axis powers during World War II.

One Greek nationalist response to the establishment of FYROM as a new nation was the mantra 'Macedonia is Greece'. That was quite true of course — it is. But it ignored that fact that Macedonia was not only Greece, but also Bulgaria, Albania and ex-Yugoslavia.

The Former-Yugoslav Macedonians did not help their cause by, initially, adopting a national flag based on the Vergina Sun. Vergina is an important archaeological site in northern Greece, located at the site of the original capital of the ancient Kingdom of Macedon. By co-opting an important symbol associated with this ancient kingdom, the Former-Yugoslav Macedonians were seen by Greeks to be claiming descent from the realm of Alexander the Great.

The fact is that the dominant population group in modern North Macedonia are Slavs – in the sense that they speak a Slavic language. And Slavic speakers did not start appearing in that part of the Balkans until the sixth century AD, nearly a millennium after the ascendancy of Alexander. Most people these days use the term 'Macedonian' for the South Slavic language spoken in North Macedonia. Nationalist Greeks do not like this and think it should be called something else, although they do not much mind what. Greeks themselves often call it Slavomakedonika, 'Slavo-Macedonian', which makes good enough sense to them since 'Macedonian' would most usually refer to the Greek dialect of Macedonia. Nationalist Bulgarians also think the language should go by some other name, but they actually do care what that is: they specifically think it should be called 'Bulgarian'.

Modern Slavo-Macedonians are certainly not linguistic descendants of the Ancient Macedonians. Macedon was the home of the civilisation which produced King Philip and his son Alexander, called 'the Great', who went on to conquer territory from North Africa to India, and from Asia Minor to Central Asia. But the widespread assumption that Alexander himself was actually Greek is also hard to defend on linguistic grounds. Alexander could speak Ancient Greek, and his armies did take the language to Libya, Palestine, Central Asia and India; but for Alexander, it was a second language.

His native tongue was Ancient Macedonian. But what kind of language was that? Nationalist Greeks tend to claim that it was a dialect of Greek. But the problem for linguistic scientists is that our knowledge of Ancient Macedonian is extremely limited. The fifth-century AD writings of Hesychius of Alexandria cite several words as being Macedonian; and we have information about a number of place-names and personal names in this language. According to a leading linguistics scholar, Professor Brian Joseph of the Ohio State University, this limited material makes it probable that Ancient Macedonian was either a language related to Greek, or a separate Indo-European language altogether. But it wasn't Greek.

6.7 Norf'k

The legendary mutiny on the Royal Navy ship *Bounty* took place in 1789, one week before the start of the French Revolution. During a voyage from the Polynesian island of Tahiti to the Caribbean, Captain Bligh and eighteen of his loyal crew members were put into a small boat by the mutineers and set adrift in the South Pacific, not far from the Tongan island of Tofua.

The *Bounty*, under the command of Fletcher Christian, then sailed back to Tahiti, where eventually most of the crew – some still loyal to Bligh – remained. But Christian and eight other mutineers, together with a dozen Polynesian women and a few Polynesian men, sailed on eastwards, arriving in January 1790 at the remote island of Pitcairn, about 350 miles south-east of Mangareva, French Polynesia, and over a thousand miles west of Easter Island. The mutineers then marooned themselves by setting fire to the ship in order to avoid detection by the vengeful Royal Navy – something they managed to do for twenty years.

Some of the descendants of this group of twenty-nine people still live on Pitcairn, but most of them have moved to Norfolk Island, between northern New Zealand and southern New Caledonia. In 1856, when conditions on Pitcairn became difficult because of overpopulation, the entire population of 193 were voluntarily relocated to Norfolk Island, which was granted to them in perpetuity by Queen Victoria (a number of them did return to Pitcairn a few years later). Of the current Norfolk Island population of about 1,700, approximately half are descended from those Pitcairnese settlers, many of them still bearing the surnames of the mutineers Fletcher Christian, John Adams, William McCoy, Matthew Quintal and Ned Young.

It is not too surprising that a new language developed on Pitcairn. A majority of the arrivals, including all of the women, were native speakers of Tahitian or related languages, while the mutineers communicated in English. Christian had grown up on the Isle of Man and may also have spoken some Manx Gaelic. John Williams was from Guernsey and knew Guernsey French. McCoy and John Mills were Scots. Quintal was from Cornwall but probably did not speak Cornish. Isaac Martin seems to have been an American. And Young was from St Kitts in the West Indies – his native language was a form of Caribbean Creole.

By 1808 John Adams, a Londoner, was the only adult male still alive on the island. The other mutineers and the Tahitian men had all died or been murdered. There were nine Polynesian women left, and twenty-plus children. It was amongst these children that a fascinating new language developed out of interaction between the English of the mutineers and the Tahitian of the children's mothers. The modern Pitkern-Norf'k language, as it is called, is the intriguing outcome of the way in which that small group of children combined the resources of the Tahitian language and the English dialects they heard around them to shape their own community language.

A majority of the words in Pitkern-Norf'k come from some form of English, but there are many Tahitian items such as *whawhaha*, 'conceited' and *ama'ula*, 'clumsy', as well as words we are not too sure about like *salan*, 'people' and *aklan*, 'us'.

The language is much in evidence on Norfolk Island today as the islanders fight for the restoration of their self-governing status, which was unilaterally taken from them in 2016 by the Australian government against the wishes of a majority of the islanders – and, presumably, those of Queen Victoria. This was a coup which was not much noticed in Australia, let alone beyond – although their case has been presented to the UN – but it has provoked enormous resentment on Norfolk Island. Signs you can see on the island today read *Auwas hoem, auwas chois!*, 'Our home, our choice', and *Du we giw up we gwen win!*, 'Don't give up, we're going to win!'

These people are not Australians. But they are mutineers, and they are not going to give in without a fight.

MAROON

Marooned comes from French *marron*, 'feral', from Spanish *cimarrón*, 'fugitive', which is probably from *cima*, 'summit', in perhaps the original sense of living wild in the mountains. The colour term *maroon* has a different origin. It comes from French *marron*, 'sweet chestnut'. And *maroon*, 'flare', refers – maybe – to its similarity to an exploding roasting chestnut.

---

7 Languages

Many people in the United Kingdom will not know what the word *Saesneg* means. In fact it is the name of a language which also goes by the names *Pelekani*, *Edegeesi* and *Chirungu*. The language in question is English. These are all names for our language in, respectively, Welsh, Hawaiian, Yoruba (Nigeria) and Shona (Zimbabwe).

Saesneg is the Welsh form of the word *Saxon*. The linguistic ancestors of Modern English speakers were mainly Angles and Saxons, and most names for our language (including *English* itself) derive from *Angle*. But the Celtic languages, including Irish and Scottish Gaelic, Manx and Cornish, have based the name they use for our language on the word *Saxon* instead.

Pelekani comes from fitting the word *Britain* into the patterns of pronunciation found in Hawaiian, via an intermediate form *Peretani*. In *Edegeesi*, *ede* means 'language' in Yoruba and the *geesi* part comes from the Portuguese word *ingles*, 'English' – the Portuguese were the first Europeans to establish a presence on the West African coast. And in the Shona name *Chirungu*, *chi* means 'language', while *rungu* originally meant 'white man'.

Some European language names can also be puzzling. Our word *German* comes from the Latin name *Germani*, which first appeared in the writing of Julius Caesar. But the name was not used by the Germanic peoples themselves, and might be derived from some Celtic term – although we do not really know.

But it is clear, as we have already noted, where the names referring to German in the Slavic languages come from. Slovak Nemčina, Croatian Njemački, Slovenian Nemški and Polish Niemiecki are all derived from the Slavic word for 'dumb': the Modern Polish word for 'mute' is *niemy*. As far as the Slavs were concerned, Germans were people who could not speak. Over time, this Slavic name was also borrowed into some non-Slavic languages: the Hungarian word for German is Német, and the colloquial Romanian label is Neamț. The old Turkish name for Austria was Nemçe – many of the areas of the German-language-dominated Austro-Hungarian Empire which abutted on the Ottoman Empire were Slavic speaking.

Other European language names which English speakers find it difficult to recognise – and which etymologists also find it difficult to account for – include *Shqiptar*, the Albanian name for Albanian; *Suomi*, the Finnish for Finnish; *Hrvatski*, the Croatian for Croatian; and *Elliniká*, the Greek for Greek. *Węgierski* is unrecognisable to us as the Polish word for Hungarian; so is *Włoski*, the Polish name for the Italian language. *Ruotsi* is tricky for us to interpret, too – it is the Finnish word for Swedish. *Saksa*, the Finnish word for German, is also not entirely obvious – but it is no surprise to learn that *Saksa* has the same origin as the Welsh word for English, *Saesneg*.

The English name for the English language has not always been *English*. It has also in its time been called *Ænglis*, *Ænglisc*, *Englisc* and *Englis*. The *eng-* part was originally pronounced like the 'eng' in 'length', but the pronunciation changed to 'ing' in the 1400s. We did not change the spelling to match the pronunciation change, but the Scots did: their name for the language is *Inglis*.

This book is mainly concerned with language and languages in Europe. It also, as readers may have noticed, deals with languages of Europe which are no longer entirely in Europe because they have spread to other parts of the world, such as Canadian French and Chilean Spanish. In this chapter, we shall also mention one language which is half European and half not, Metsif or Michif, as well as a language which used to be European but no longer is, Arabic. We also discuss European languages which are, sadly, no longer spoken, such as Prussian and Ubykh, and other languages which are severely endangered, such as Sorbian and Ladino.

7.1 The Birth of English

There was a lot of fruitless speculation in bygone centuries about what the first language in the world was – was it Hebrew, Latin, Sanskrit, Ancient Greek? These days, on the internet, we can find slightly more sensible questions such as 'what are the oldest languages in the world?' The fact is, though, that the age of a language is something which it is almost impossible to measure, because languages do not just come into being suddenly at 2:30 on a Tuesday afternoon.

English is a language which certainly came into existence rather gradually. If we want to know how old it is, the only sensible way of answering that question is to determine when English started breaking away from the other West Germanic languages, and especially from Frisian, which is its closest relative. The West Frisian language is still spoken today in the north-western-most part of the Netherlands. The related North Frisian language is spoken along the western coastline of Schleswig-Holstein, Germany, immediately to the south of the Danish border, and on the offshore islands – this area was settled from West Friesland in the Middle Ages. And East Frisian still survives as a tiny language island (see Section 4.4) in the Saterland, Lower Saxony, Germany.

The English language began to acquire a separate identity of its own once the West Germanic speakers who had originally crossed the North Sea from mainland Europe – initially as mercenaries during the Roman occupation and subsequently as raiders – first started to overwinter and then settle permanently in eastern Britain.

This eventually led to the West Germanic dialects breaking up into separate languages, and so to the development of the English language.

The settlement started happening in the 300s AD but only gathered significant momentum in the 400s. English and Frisian speakers, as speakers of West Germanic dialects, probably remained reasonably intelligible to one another into the sixth and seventh centuries, and maybe well beyond. But it would not be unreasonable to suggest that English came into being during the fifth century AD.

But if that is *when* English started – then *where* did it start? The two leading contenders for that honour seem to be East Anglia – Norfolk and Suffolk – and Kent and Sussex. These areas lay immediately across the North Sea from the coastline of the original area occupied by the West Germanic people, and were probably the very first British places where these intruders settled on this island.

East Anglia is said to be the area of England with the lowest proportion of surviving pre-English Romano-Celtic place-names, something which can be interpreted as suggesting that there was heavier Germanic immigration to this region than anywhere else in the south-east of England. East Anglia is also the region where the largest concentration of early Old English (pre-AD 650) runic inscriptions has been found, for example at Binham and North Elmham in north Norfolk, and at Lakenheath in north-west Suffolk. (Before Christianisation and the introduction of the Latin alphabet into northern Europe, runes were used for writing in a number of languages such as Old Norse, Old English and Gothic.)

So it is not stretching things too much to suggest that East Anglia was perhaps the earliest place in the world where anybody ever spoke English. Certainly, the oldest piece of written English ever discovered anywhere was found in the Anglo-Saxon graveyard in Caistor St Edmund, just outside Norwich. It consists of a runic inscription on a piece of deer bone. One theory suggests that this bone may have been used as a piece or counter in some kind of game. The inscription dates from the early 400s AD and consists of the single word RAIHAN, 'roe deer'. It is on display today very close to where it was found, in Norwich Castle Museum, in what may well have been the region of the world where the dialect which became English was first spoken.

RUNES

From the first century AD, runic inscriptions were carved on wood, stone or bone, using a pre-Christian Germanic alphabet of between twenty and thirty letters. These were angular, straight-lined symbols, which made for easier engraving. These runic symbols were probably derived from ancient alphabets which had been used to write some of the different languages of the Italian peninsula.

7.2 Irish

English has been spoken in the British Isles for no longer than 1,600 years or so. We know quite a lot about its arrival on these shores, as Anglo-Saxon speakers of the West Germanic dialects which developed into English started landing in eastern England from coastal areas across the North Sea.

We also know that at the time of the arrival of these Germanic dialects, the British Isles were Celtic speaking. In Britain, people spoke Brittonic Celtic, the ancestor of Modern Welsh, while the inhabitants of Ireland spoke Goidelic Celtic, the ancestor of Modern Irish and Scottish Gaelic. But when did these Celtic languages arrive on our islands, and where did they come from?

The archaeologist Colin Renfrew has argued for a Celtic presence in Britain as early as 4000 BC. Other writers reckon that westward-moving Celtic migrants had advanced no further than Poland by 3000 BC. The traditional linguists' view places Celts in the British Isles no earlier than 2000 BC, but more recently some linguists have come to the view that Celtic speakers did not arrive in south-eastern England until some point after 1000 BC. In other words, we really don't know.

Archaeology and genetics are not much help with this problem because archaeological remains cannot tell you what language was spoken by the people who left them; and there is no connection between genes and language – millions of people with originally West African genes are now native English speakers in the USA and elsewhere, for instance.

As far as the 'where' question is concerned, it is obviously rather probable that Celtic speakers crossed over to Britain via the Straits of Dover; during the Roman period, the Celtic dialects spoken in southern England and in northern Gaul (France) were very similar.

But what about Ireland? Did Goidelic Celtic speakers cross the sea from Scotland – after all, Ireland is only about twelve miles from the Mull of Kintyre – or from Wales or England? Or did the language arrive with voyagers travelling north from France, or from Spain, where we know Celtic languages were also spoken?

The distinguished Dutch linguist Peter Schrijver has proposed a rather different theory, namely that Goidelic Celtic was not taken to Ireland at all, but developed there. He suggests that Celtic speakers may not have arrived in Ireland until the first century AD and that they came from Britain, bringing Brittonic Celtic with them. It would be no surprise if these people had left Britain as a result of the Roman conquest, which began in earnest in the first century AD and which involved many decades of violent subjugation of the native population by the Roman invaders.

Once British Celtic speakers had arrived in Ireland, the argument goes, their language came into contact with some pre-Celtic language which was already spoken there. From around 300 AD onwards, the speakers of this original language, who must have formed a majority of the population, gradually switched to Celtic, probably because the Celts were perceived as being dominant in some way – militarily, culturally, technologically. In learning Brittonic as a foreign language in large numbers, they then transformed it considerably, and relatively rapidly, to the extent that it became a rather different language. Welsh and Irish are today no longer mutually intelligible, and yet the historical relationship between them is still clear.

Old Irish written records dating from the 600s AD show that, at that time, Irish was a monolithic language with no regional variation. This supports the thesis that it had not been spoken in Ireland for more than a few centuries – the longer a language is spoken in a particular area, the more dialectal differences it will develop. The fact that all Modern Irish dialects can be traced back to this same monolithic Old Irish also reinforces this interpretation.

This still leaves us with the intriguing question as to what the pre-Celtic language of Ireland was. The answer is that this is something else we simply don't know.

CELTIC

There are two pronunciations of the word *Celtic*, 'Seltic' and 'Keltic'. Both of these are correct, but linguists and anthropologists usually refer to the Celtic languages and peoples as 'Keltic'. This allows us to reserve the pronunciation 'Seltic' for the well-known Glasgow football and Boston basketball teams.

7.3 The Language of the Vikings

We are very familiar with the fact that the English language started life in a rather isolated corner of northern Europe, and subsequently spread to many parts of the globe. But there was another northern European language which, long before English, broke away from its own isolated corner of our continent and travelled way beyond the bounds of its homeland.

Old Norse was the language of the Vikings. A western variety was originally spoken in what is now Norway, and an eastern variety in Sweden and Denmark. The age of Viking expansion, from the late 700s AD onwards, carried this language amazing distances from its homeland.

Old West Norse was transported by Norwegian Vikings into the vastness of the Atlantic Ocean, and is still there – in Iceland and the Faroe Islands. The Modern Icelandic and Faroese languages have changed less than the contemporary continental Scandinavian languages, and even now retain many Old Norse features. They also remain quite similar to one another: a Faroese speaker once told me that when he first arrived in Iceland he could not understand what people were saying – but after four days he could!

It is just under 1,000 miles from the west coast of Norway to Iceland, so it is no surprise that on their westward journey the Vikings settled first on the Faroe Islands, which are about 400 miles from the Norwegian coast. And it also makes good sense that, on their way to the Faroes, they stopped off on the Shetland and Orkney Islands. Shetland is no more than 220 miles from Norway; there is a story that conscripts from Shetland during World War II annoyed British Army bureau-crats by stating that Bergen was their nearest railway station – though the truth is that it wasn't!

A linguistic descendant of Old West Norse called Norn was spoken on Orkney until the early eighteenth century, and it was still alive in Shetland in the late 1700s (see next section, 7.4).

West Norse was also spoken for many generations in Viking settlements in north-east Scotland (surviving in Caithness until the 1400s), the Hebrides, the Isle of Man, north-west England and coastal areas of Ireland. There are still many traces of this language in surviving place-names in these locations. The name Caithness is from Norse *Katanes*, and Sutherland was Norse *Suðrland*, 'south land': if this seems a strange name for a place on the north coast of Britain, we must understand that the Vikings called it that because it lay to the south of the Viking settlements on Orkney. Barra is probably from Old Norse *barr-ey*, 'bare island'. Ramsey, on the Isle of Man, comes from Old West Norse *hrams-á*, 'ramsons (wild garlic) river' – in Modern Norwegian it would be *Ramså*. Ambleside in the English Lake District was West Norse *Ámelrsætr*, which literally translates as 'a summer pasture on a sand-bank by a river'. And Waterford in Ireland comes from *Veðrafjǫrðr*, 'ram (or wether) fjord'.

West Norse was also spoken in Greenland as a result of colonisation from Iceland. The northernmost Greenlandic settlement was *Vestribyggð*, 'western settlement', which was about 1,500 miles from Iceland. More than 50 inscriptions in West Norse have been found in Greenland, where Norse-speaking colonies survived for almost 500 years, dying out in the late 1400s. No one is quite sure what happened to the colonists, but climate change, overgrazing and conflict with the Inuit have all been suggested as reasons for the abandonment of the settlements. There is also a suggestion that people just got fed up and left.

Some time during that 500 years, however, Vikings sailed from Greenland to explore what they called *Vinland* – the eastern shores of Canada – as we know from the Icelandic sagas. Remains of a Viking site have been found on the northern tip of Newfoundland, about 600 miles south-west of Greenland – and a very long way indeed from Norway. No Viking inscriptions have been discovered there, but Old West Norse was certainly the very first European language ever to be spoken in the Americas.

7.4 Shetland Norn

Philologists generally divide the Scandinavian languages into two historical branches: eastern and western. Swedish and Danish fall into the Eastern Scandinavian division, while Norwegian, Faroese and Icelandic form the Western Scandinavian languages, the Faroe Islands and Iceland having been colonised by mainly Norwegian Viking settlers during the 800s AD.

However, there also used to be another Western Scandinavian language which is now extinct, but which probably had communities of native speakers until the 1800s. If you look at a map of the North Atlantic, you may be able to work out where those communities were. If you are sailing from western Norway to Iceland, it would make sense to stop off in the Faroes on the way. But if you are sailing from western Norway to the Faroes, it would also make sense to stop off along the way in Shetland. In fact, the Shetland Islands were probably settled by Norsemen in the late 700s AD, with the Faroe Islands being settled in the early 800s, and Iceland in the mid-800s.

The Nordic language that was spoken in Shetland for over a thousand years is known to us as Norn. It was also spoken in Orkney and on the north-east Scottish mainland in Caithness. However, Norn did not survive as long in these place as it did in Shetland, probably losing its last native speakers in Caithness in the 1400s and in Orkney in the 1700s, though there is considerable controversy about how long the language survived – and how 'Norn' it actually was in the mouths of its last speakers.

One of the last redoubts of the language seems to have been the northernmost Shetland island, Unst – which is in fact the most northerly inhabited territory in the British Isles – where the supposedly last speaker of Norn, Walter Sutherland, died in the hamlet of Skaw, the UK's northernmost settlement, in about 1850. The name Skaw comes from Old Norse *skagi*, 'headland'; the Modern Norwegian word is *skage*. Skagen 'the cape', which is what the northernmost tip of Jutland is called in Danish, is known as the Skaw to English-speaking seamen.

Other sources, though, claim that the Norn language lasted even longer on the remote island of Foula (from Old Norse *fugl-ey*, 'bird-island' – there is also an island called Fugloy in the Faroes). Foula lies twenty miles out into the Atlantic, to the west of the rest of the Shetland archipelago.

Orkney and Shetland – the Northern Isles – were essentially part of Norway until 1468–9, but then the Danish–Norwegian monarchy handed them over to Scotland in lieu of a dowry for Princess Margaret of Denmark on the occasion of her marriage to the Scottish King James III. A process of scotticisation then very gradually set in. Scottish law rather than Scandinavian law started being enforced in 1611; immigration from Scotland increased; and the Scots language began to be used in church – the Society for the Propagation of Christian Knowledge and their schools are often blamed for accelerating the death of Norn. By 1700, there were very few monolingual Norn speakers left.

The modern dialect of Shetland is a dialect of Scots, but large numbers of Norn words have survived in it. Many seabirds, for instance, are still referred to by their Norn names. A *longie* is a guillemot, from Old Norse *langvé* (the Modern Norwegian is *lomvi*); a *maa* is a seagull (the Old Norse was *már*); a *shalder* is an oyster catcher, from Old Norse *tjaldr* (*tjeld* in Modern Norwegian); and a *skarf* is a cormorant, from Old Norse *skarfr* (Modern Norwegian *skarv*). Other everyday Norn words survive: *de haaf* means 'the deep sea', from Old Norse *haf*, 'ocean', Modern Norwegian *hav*; and *bigg* signifies 'to build' (the Modern Icelandic is *byggja*).

It is a tragedy that this British Scandinavian language died. But at least some of it survives in the vocabulary of the modern Shetland Scots dialect.

CORMORANT

A cormorant is not a crow. But the seabird *phalacrocorax carbo* derives its English name from the Latin word *marinus*, 'marine', preceded by the word *corvus*, 'crow'. *Corvus marinus* became Old French *corp-marin*, and then *cormoran*. English speakers then added a *t* to the word, just as we did with French *paysan*, 'peasant', *faisan*, 'pheasant' and *tyran*, 'tyrant'.

7.5 Romani: the Truly European Language

If I had to nominate a language as being the most European of all European languages, one candidate which would certainly have to be considered would be Romani. Romani – also spelt Romany – is the language of the Romani people, also known as Gypsies. It is a truly pan-European language because it has long-standing communities of native speakers in just about every country on our continent – from Portugal to Ukraine, and from Norway to Italy. It is said that as much as 10 per cent of the population of Bulgaria are Romani (Roma), and several other European countries have very sizeable Romani minorities, especially North Macedonia, Hungary, Slovakia, Romania, Serbia and Kosovo.

It is true that Romani was not a European language in origin. It arose in north-western India, and its closest linguistic relatives are languages such as Hindi, Punjabi and Gujarati. Like them, it is a member of the Indo-Aryan sub-family of Indo-European languages.

It is also true that the language is one of the most recent linguistic arrivals in Europe, having reached the continent some time in the Middle Ages. The people who came to be called Romani did not leave India until some time after AD 1000, so the language arrived after Hungarian, whose speakers turned up in Europe around AD 900; and after Maltese, originally an Arabic dialect brought across from North

Africa in about the year 1000; but before Turkish, which started penetrating into the Balkans from the east from about 1300 onwards.

Language scientists have been able to deduce which routes the Romani travelled into Europe. Words incorporated into Romani from other languages indicate that, on their journeys westwards, they passed through Afghanistan, Iran, Armenia, Asia Minor and Greece; Romani was especially heavily influenced by the vocabulary of Byzantine Greek.

Dispersed, as its speakers are, all over Europe, it is no surprise to discover that the language has branched into a number of different, sometimes very different, dialects. Major varieties include Vlax (Vlach) Romani in Bosnia, Romania and elsewhere in Eastern Europe; Balkan Romani in Albania, Kosovo, Greece and Turkey; and Sinte Romani, found especially in Germany.

Because of their traditionally migratory way of life, the number of speakers of the Romani language in Europe is difficult to determine, but there are probably something like 5 million. Whatever the total, it is certainly considerably less than it was before World War II, when the Romani suffered from the same kind of appalling extermination programme as the Jews at the hands of the Nazis and their collaborators. The London-born linguistic scientist Ian Hancock, who is a professor at the University of Texas at Austin and the author of an autobiographical book titled *Danger! Educated Gypsy*, calculates that a million and a half Gypsies died in German concentration camps during the Holocaust. This terrible human tragedy had linguistic as well as cultural consequences: the Lithuanian dialect of Romani vanished forever, because all its speakers were exterminated.

These days there are many Roma, particularly in Western Europe, who sadly no longer speak Romani, which is very much an endangered language in many regions. But many of them can speak in-group language varieties known to linguists as Para-Romani. In England, we have Angloromani, whose speakers use English pronunciation and grammar, but with a high proportion of originally Romani words.

A number of Angloromani words have made their way into Modern English, including *pal*, 'friend'; *lolly*, the Australian and New Zealand word for 'sweet' or 'candy'; *cosh*; *nark*, meaning 'informer'; and *rum*, in the sense of 'strange'. This fact is not always recognised by professional etymologists, whose training means that they are much less familiar with Romani than they are with Sanskrit, Latin, Ancient Greek, Old Church Slavonic and Old High German.

But Romani deserves their attention. And it deserves our protection. It is, after all, the most truly European of languages.

7.6 Basque

I have suggested that Romani might be the most European of all European languages because it is spoken natively over a larger geographical area of our continent than any other language. But there is another very strong candidate for the label of 'most European language', though this candidacy is based on a very different argument. This second nomination for the label of 'most European language' is Basque, which is spoken in south-western France and the adjoining area of northern Spain.

Unlike the very widely distributed Romani speakers, native Basque speakers occupy an area of Europe of only about 4,000 square miles, which is about half the size of Wales. The coastline of the Basque language area runs along the Bay of Biscay from Biarritz in France southwards to St Jean de Luz, and then across the border between France and Spain and around to San Sebastian and Bilbao, so it straddles the western edge of the Pyrenees, reaching inland as far as Pamplona.

Basque is currently said to have approximately 750,000 mother-tongue speakers, which makes it one of the smallest languages of Europe. But there is actually something else which makes it very special.

Nearly all of the languages of modern Europe are members of the Indo-European language family. There are exceptions, such as the Finnic languages of the north – Sami, Finnish, Estonian – and a few other languages which are relative newcomers like Maltese, Hungarian and Turkish. But, compared to Basque, even the Indo-European languages are very much newcomers.

The Celtic languages may well have been the earliest of the Indo-European languages to arrive in our continent from the east. They certainly seem to have been the languages which penetrated furthest to the west. But it is extremely difficult to determine exactly when the Indo-Europeans turned up in Europe. Estimates for when Celtic speakers first came to the British Isles, for instance, vary enormously: disappointingly, experts seem able to agree only on the fact that it was very definitely some time between 4500 and 1000 BC.

But of all the indigenous languages spoken in Europe today, Basque has most certainly been here the longest. It was spoken in Europe long before – maybe very many millennia before – Celtic, Latin, Greek, Old Norse, Old High German and Old Church Slavonic.

Basque is the only language in Europe which is an 'isolate' – a language which has no known relatives. There have been attempts over the years to link it to other languages in Europe, North Africa and elsewhere. One of the less outlandish suggestions is that Basque might be historically connected to some of the languages of the Caucasus, like Georgian, which are also not Indo-European languages. But any relationship would lie so far back in history that this could never be anything other than speculation.

Whatever its linguistic relationships, we can be rather sure that the Basque language is descended from a prehistoric language which was spoken in the area of the western Pyrenees 5,000 years or more ago. Professor Theo Vennemann of the University of Munich has suggested that, from as long ago as 8000 BC, much of Western Europe was occupied by people who spoke languages which were members of the Vasconic language family, of which Basque is the only modern survivor. We do know that a language variety called Aquitanian, which was either a dialect of Basque or a language closely related to Basque, was spoken as far north as Bordeaux as late as the time of the Roman occupation of what is now France. So of course it is perfectly possible that, before peoples speaking Celtic and other Indo-European dialects arrived at the Atlantic seaboard, languages ancestral to Basque were spoken over a very wide area. And it is not at all too far-fetched to suppose that Basque is the last remnant of a language which was spoken in Western Europe as far back as the end of the last ice age.

7.7 Guanche

The Canary Islands are a long way from mainland Europe, but the Romans knew they were there. Pliny the Elder (AD 23–79) referred to them as the *Canaria*, supposedly because of the large numbers of big dogs (Latin *canes*) which were reported to live on the archipelago.

The islands' human inhabitants, however, were pretty much left on their own for many centuries, apart from some visits by Arab traders, until inquisitive Europeans began nosing around in the 1200s. Navigators started arriving from Portugal, Majorca and Genoa; and in 1402 an expedition led by two adventurers, Gadifer de la Salle and Jean de Béthencourt, invaded the islands. De la Salle was from Aquitaine in western France, which had been under the control of the monarchy of England when he was born; and de Béthencourt came from Normandy.

They initially conquered Lanzarote, and by 1406 had also taken control of Fuerteventura and El Hierro, ultimately in the name of the Spanish Kingdom of Castile, whose monarch Henry III had supplied the expedition with reinforcements. The king was known as Enrique el Doliente 'Henry the Sufferer', but it was actually the native inhabitants of the Canaries who ended up doing the suffering. During the fifteenth century very many of them, if they were not enslaved or deported, were slaughtered in battle or killed by imported diseases. While a proportion of the current inhabitants of the Canaries do retain some aboriginal genetic material, their culture and language are gone.

Who were these unfortunate people? The aboriginal inhabitants of the islands are known to us as the Guanche, though originally that term was applied only to the inhabitants of Tenerife. They reportedly had brown skin, fair hair, and blue-grey eyes. Their culture was monotheistic and organised into kingdoms. The Guanche also demonstrated a rather advanced military capability: Spain did not succeed in conquering the last independent island, Tenerife, until 1496, and Spanish soldiers suffered several significant defeats at their hands.

But what language did they speak? We do not have very much evidence about this: their language died out in the 1600s. There is, though, something of a consensus amongst linguists that the language, generally referred to as Guanche, has some connection with the Berber language family.

The Berber languages are indigenous to North Africa, including the Barbary Coast. In spite of the seventh-century Arab invasions, these languages are still spoken by many millions of people in an area which stretches from Morocco across Algeria and Libya as far as the Siwa oasis in western Egypt, as well as southwards into Mali and Niger. Probably about a third of the population of Morocco and Algeria speak Berber languages – about 25 million speakers. Tuareg, a Berber language, is spoken over a vast area of the Sahara Desert covering large parts of Mali, Niger, Algeria and Libya.

Maarten Kossmann, who is Professor of Berber Studies at Leiden University in the Netherlands, says that from what little Guanche we know there is no doubt that the language does genuinely contain Berber elements: many words show a clear link to Berber, such as *ilfe*, 'pig', which is related to the northern Berber form *ilef*, 'pig'. But there are also many Guanche words which do not seem to bear any resemblance to Berber. Professor Kossmann points out that it may be significant that many of the Guanche words which do show some relationship to Berber are agricultural terms connected to topics such as livestock and crops.

At their closest, the Canaries lie 58 nautical miles off the west coast of Morocco, where the Berber language Tashelhiyt is today spoken by around 7 million people. The Guanche language may well have been historically related to Berber but, even if it was not, it is rather clear that it was at the very least influenced by contact with speakers of some language ancestral to Tashelhiyt.

MOROCCO

Turkish speakers call Morocco *Fas* – the word is derived from the name of the Moroccan city of Fez. We should not be too surprised about this because the English, French and Spanish names for the country – Morocco, Maroc and Marruecos – are also derived from the name of a Moroccan city, Marrakesh – which was formerly the nation's capital.

7.8 Ladino

The city of Thessaloniki is known as Salonika in English, Solun in Bulgarian and Salonik in Turkish. It is the second-largest urban centre in Greece: the metropolitan area of Athens has more than $3\frac{1}{2}$ million inhabitants, while metropolitan Thessaloniki numbers about 1 million.

The remarkable thing about this seven-figure population figure, however, is that in 1900 – when the city was still part of the Ottoman Empire – there were really rather few Greek people living in Salonika, probably no more than about 17,000, or

15 per cent of the city's population. Getting on for 10 per cent of the inhabitants at that time were Bulgarian speaking, with another 15 per cent being Turkish. Another 10 per cent of the population spoke languages such as Armenian and Romany. But a massive 50 per cent of Salonika's population spoke another language altogether, and one that did not have its origins in the Balkans. If you are not familiar with the history of the city, you will have difficulty guessing what it was. The fact is that, a little more than a 100 years ago, the language which was spoken by more than half of the population of what is now Greece's second city was . . . Spanish.

The people who spoke this language in Salonika tended, unsurprisingly, to call it *Espanyol*, 'Spanish'; but these days we often refer to it – in the particular form in which it was spoken in Salonika – by other names. It is very often called *Ladino* or *Judesmo*; many academics use the label *Jud(a)eo-Spanish* as well or instead.

As the name Judeo-Spanish suggests, the people who spoke this version of the Spanish language, in Salonika and elsewhere, were Jewish. Sephardic Jews had arrived in the eastern Mediterranean after being expelled from Spain and Portugal en masse in 1492 and finding a welcome in the much more tolerant Turkish-controlled Ottoman Empire. There were eventually large communities of these speakers not only in Thessaloniki but also elsewhere in the Balkans, notably in Sarajevo, as well as in North Africa, Palestine and Turkey itself. Judeo-Spanish eventually became an important trading lingua franca in the Adriatic, and produced a rich body of literature.

Linguistically, Ladino owes something to Portuguese as well as Spanish, and contains also a certain amount of learned and religious vocabulary borrowed from Hebrew. It has also over the centuries acquired elements of Aramaic, Arabic, Bulgarian, French, Greek and Turkish. The language was traditionally written in the Hebrew script, but the Latin alphabet is now very often employed.

In 1912, Thessaloniki ceased to be an Ottoman city. The Greek army invaded and took control of the city, and it has belonged to Greece since then. But in 1928, Ladino was still the third largest minority language in Greece after Turkish and Slavic – the official census at the time suggested it had about 65,000 speakers – and there were thriving communities of Ladino speakers in other urban areas of Greece besides Thessaloniki. Appallingly, most of the language's speakers in the Balkans were then deported and exterminated by the Nazis during World War II: the 1951 census tragically showed only about 1,300 speakers of 'Spanish' left in Greece as a whole.

A sizeable community of Jewish Ladino speakers did remain in Istanbul, however, since they were not exposed there to the horrors of the Nazi extermination campaign. However, this community is now being gradually eroded as a result of emigration to Israel where, regrettably, the language has received rather little official support. The Istanbul community continues to enjoy a cultural and literary life focussed on the Ladino language, but in spite of a revival of scholarly interest in the language in the

USA, and enthusiasm for Judeo-Spanish music and songs in many parts of the world today, the future of Ladino does not look particularly secure.

OTTOMAN

The Ottoman Empire derived its name from the dynasty founded by the Turkic ruler Osman or Othman (from Arabic Uthman) in northern Turkey in the late 1200s. An *ottoman* is a kind of settee with no back or arms – a style of furniture originally associated by Europeans with the Ottoman Empire.

7.9 Catalan

The men's final at the Australia Open tennis championships last week [in 2017] was played out between two Europeans, Roger Federer from Switzerland and Rafael Nadal from Spain. After Federer's win, both players gave on-court interviews. These were conducted in English, which is what you would expect in Australia. But it is also what you would expect in most international sports competitions, since English is these days very much the language of transnational communication. If you watch tennis on TV, you can often hear Bulgarian or Czech players, for example, using English to talk to Belgian or German competitors.

Federer speaks brilliant English – his mother is a South African English speaker – amazingly good French and perfect German. But his primary language is Swiss-German, which is more of a language in its own right than it is a variety of the language of Germany. Nadal is not nearly as good at speaking English as Federer is, but it is his third language. Though he speaks Spanish very fluently, his native language is Majorcan (Mallorquín), which is a variety of Catalan (Català).

In the UK, we do not seem to know very much about the Catalan language. It is difficult to find a good English–Catalan dictionary, and it is not particularly easy to study Catalan as a foreign language here. Many tourists who travel to Spain fly off to Barcelona or Minorca completely ignorant of the fact that Spanish is not the indigenous language in these places. It is true that Spanish works well in both of these destinations, but it is a bit disappointing to find that northern Europeans can be so relatively uninformed about one of our continent's major languages.

Because Catalan really is a major language. It may be a minority language in the context of the Spanish state, but it has 9 million speakers. That is many more than several of the better known national European languages. Danish, Finnish and Slovak have only around $5\frac{1}{2}$ million speakers each, and Norwegian has about $4\frac{1}{2}$ million. Slovenian is spoken by about $2\frac{1}{2}$ million people, and Latvian rather fewer than that. There are 2 million Lithuanian speakers, and not many more than 1 million Estonian speakers.

Catalan is the indigenous language not just in Catalonia (Catalunya in Catalan), the area of Spain centred on Barcelona. It is also spoken in the autonomous Spanish region of Valencia, where it spreads over the border a little into the region of Murcia; on the Balearic islands of Majorca (Mallorca in Catalan), Minorca (Menorca) and Ibiza (Eivissa); in Andorra; and in the area of southern France around Roussillon (Rosselló). The Catalan language has speakers in the Alghero region of northern Sardinia as well.

In addition to Rafa Nadal, many other well-known figures have Catalan as their mother tongue. The artists Joan Miró and Salvador Dali were Catalan speakers – and so was Picasso, though he learnt the language later in life, having moved to Barcelona when he was fourteen. The world-famous cellist and conductor Pau Casals, also known by the Spanish first name of Pablo, was a Catalan speaker, as are the opera singers Montserrat Caballé and Josep Carreras (the latter better known internationally by the Spanish-language version of his name, José). The footballer Cesc Fàbregas and the Manchester City manager Pep Guardiola speak this language. And Nadal is not the only famous Catalan-speaking tennis star: Arantxa Sánchez Vicario and David Ferrer are also Catalans.

One reason why Catalan is not so well known as might be expected of a language with many millions of speakers is its tragic experience of political oppression and suppression. After the end of the Spanish Civil War in 1939, the fascist military dictator General Franco attempted to ban the use of Catalan and reduce it to the status of a dialect.

But that is a story for another time – and one which does have a happy ending.

7.10 The Rebirth of Catalan

The First International Congress of the Catalan Congress took place in 1906. The Second International Congress was in 1986, and I was asked to go and speak at it. The invitation was something of a surprise to me, as I did not know anything more about the Catalan language than the average linguist. But I gladly accepted: it would be a good opportunity to learn more about Catalan and, besides, the invitation was to go to Palma, Majorca, in the early spring.

It turned out that the Congress was taking place simultaneously in seven different Catalan-speaking locations: Perpignan in France, Andorra, and five places in Spain – Lleida, Girona, Valencia, Tarragona and Majorca.

In Palma, I met a large number of prominent linguists who were as puzzled as I was about why we had all been invited to this Congress. But it soon became clear why we were there.

The story which explained our presence had begun in 1939. After coming to power in Spain through a military coup against the Spanish government, and after the civil war which followed it, the fascist dictator General Francisco Franco also carried out a coup against the Catalan language, which had until then been the official language of the Spanish province of Catalonia. He banned the publication of books and newspapers in Catalan and abolished the Professorships of Catalan Language and Catalan Literature at the University of Barcelona. The use of Catalan was not allowed in schools or on the radio. The sports team FC (Futbol Club) Barcelona was forced to change its name to the Spanish equivalent, CF (Club de Fútbol) Barcelona. And infants were no longer allowed to be registered with anything other than Spanish-language names. The fact that the famous Catalan tenor Josep Carreras, born in 1946, is more widely known by the Spanish-language version of his first name – José – is poignant testimony to this fact.

Documents written in a form of the Catalan language date from the early Middle Ages, and in mediaeval times it was one of the great languages of the Mediterranean world. But Franco attempted to destroy it by trying to force everyone to speak Spanish, and by bullying those who did speak Catalan into believing it was not a language in its own right, but just a dialect of Spanish. He could do this without appearing too absurd because the two languages are related, both being modern descendants of Latin. But Catalan is linguistically much closer to the Occitan language of southern France, and no linguistic scientist would accept that it is a variety of Spanish.

In the late 1970s, after forty years of despotism, democracy was eventually restored to Spain – and linguistic democracy returned with it. Catalan gradually became a public and official language again, and it started reappearing in print, on radio and television and in education. But there was still the problem that, after four decades of brainwashing, not everyone in the Catalan-speaking area of eastern Spain was entirely persuaded about the status of Catalan as a major, independent language.

That was why we were there. We were a group of language experts from all over the world who were talking about Catalan as a language.

We were able to make our presentations in any language we liked – except Spanish! The most popular participants were those foreigners who could actually speak Catalan – they were much in demand for radio and TV interviews. 'Look', the Congress was in effect saying to Catalan people, 'here are some distinguished foreign academics who study and teach and speak our language. If they can do it, so should you.' It was a propaganda exercise in the best sense of the word.

And it worked. Catalan is now for the most part back where it belongs, respected by its speakers, and serving a strong role in the media, politics, culture and education – and to an extent in the European Union.

7.11 Sorbian

The boundary in northern Europe between the areas where Germanic languages are spoken and those which are occupied by Slavic-language speakers has been shifting backwards and forwards on an east–west axis for at least a millennium and a half. By the 500s AD, Slavic speakers were inhabiting the area which lies between the rivers Oder and Elbe in what is now Germany. At their point of furthest expansion, Slavic dialects crossed the Elbe and were spoken as far west as the Luneburg Heath in northern Germany, where place-names like Luchow and Wüstrow indicate a Slavic-speaking past. But then, by the late Middle Ages, Germanic dialects, at their furthest point of expansion, had reached as far east as what is now Lithuania. As the centuries passed, this to-ing and fro-ing of the boundary between the two language families covered a distance of at least 600 miles.

For the last 70 years, since national frontiers were redrawn in the aftermath of World War II, the Slavic–Germanic language boundary has been situated in between those two extreme points, at the Poland–Germany border, more than 150 miles to the east of the Luneburg Heath. But, as these tides of history have washed backwards and forwards across the northern part of our continent, some groups of speakers have unsurprisingly been left behind, stranded on the 'wrong' side of the border.

There are still many pockets of German speakers in Poland, Ukraine and Russia. And even today there are groups of Slavic speakers left in Germany. These people speak Sorbian, a West Slavic language related to Polish, Czech and Slovak, which is spoken as a mother tongue by some tens of thousands of people in an area of eastern Germany, starting around 50 miles south of Berlin.

The language comes in two major variants. Lower Sorbian, which is closer to Polish, is spoken in Brandenburg, in the predominantly Lutheran area around the town of Cottbus (Chóśebuz in Lower Sorbian, Chociebuż in Polish). Upper Sorbian, which is closer to Czech, is spoken a little further to the south, in Saxony, in the area around the town of Bautzen (Upper Sorbian Budyšin, Czech Budyšín), where a majority of Sorbs are historically Catholics. The language is sometimes called Lusatian, after the area of Germany where it is spoken – Lausitz in German. Wendish has also been used as a name for the language: the Slavic peoples living immediately to the east of the Germans were historically known as Wends.

As a minority Slavic people surrounded by Germans, the Sorbs have not always fared too well. Lusatia was subjected to ruthless Germanisation in the twelfth century. In the nineteenth century, the Lower Sorbs were persecuted by the Prussians, who banned the use of their language in public spheres. And then under the Nazis, publications in both forms of Sorbian were banned, libraries were destroyed and Sorbian-speaking intellectuals were arrested, some of them perishing in concentration camps.

Things started looking up for the language and its speakers under the German Democratic Republic (East Germany) from 1949 to 1990, when the cultural rights of the Sorbians became guaranteed in the constitution, something which continues in contemporary Germany. The language can now be used in schools, and currently one daily newspaper and some radio and TV broadcasts are produced in Sorbian. There are theatrical productions in the language, and bilingual public signs are also in evidence.

The University of Leipzig has a Department of Sorbian which offers degrees in Sorbian language and culture, as well as providing teacher-training courses. Nevertheless, representatives of the Sorbian people remain far from satisfied with the support they are getting, and they look to the European Union for assistance. Lower Sorbian in particular is an endangered language, having many more older speakers than younger ones.

Sorbian speakers have resisted the influence of the German language for 1,000 years, but it is not clear how much longer they will be able to hold out.

RUTHLESS

Just as *hopeless* means 'without hope', so *ruthless* means 'without ruth'. But *ruth* is not a word most of us would ever use these days. It was formerly used to mean 'compassion, pity', and was derived – just as *truth* is derived from *true* – from the verb *to rue*, meaning 'to feel sorrow, regret'.

7.12 A Common Language

In a bookshop some years ago I came across a Croatian phrasebook, published by a reputable British publisher. Then, on a higher shelf, I also noticed a Bosnian phrasebook from the same company. A few minutes perusal of the two volumes, holding them side by side, showed that the books were exactly the same in every respect – except for the covers and title pages.

The major language of Yugoslavia used to be known as Serbo-Croat(ian). It was spoken in the Yugoslav republics of Bosnia, Croatia, Montenegro and Serbia. Serbs most often wrote it using the Cyrillic alphabet, while Croats employed the Latin alphabet. The language was also used everywhere else in the country – for example, in Slovenia – as the lingua franca of wider communication.

Then, as Yugoslavia gradually split up into separate republics, the Croats declared that they no longer spoke Serbo-Croat but rather Croatian, whereupon the Serbs began referring to the language they used as Serbian. The Bosniaks then had little choice but to declare that the language they spoke was Bosnian. And when in 2007 Montenegro became an independent country after departing from a short-lived Serbia–Montenegro federation, it too promptly declared that its language was called Montenegrin. One language had become four (as also mentioned in Section 4.8).

This was all rather silly. The four varieties – Bosnian, Croatian, Montenegrin and Serbian – are all totally mutually comprehensible, and the written forms of the languages are almost exactly the same. It is true that, as one would expect, there are considerable regional dialect differences within the former Serbo-Croatian-speaking territories, but the boundaries between the dialects do not coincide at all with the boundaries between the states.

People who favour linguistic common sense will therefore be pleased to learn that, on 30 March 2017, a rather remarkable event happened in the four countries. A declaration was published in Zagreb (Croatia), Belgrade (Serbia), Podgorica (Montenegro) and Sarajevo (Bosnia and Hercegovina) which was signed by hundreds of intellectuals and other influential people; initially around 200 linguists, writers, scientists and other public figures added their signatures. The declaration was intended to counter 'the negative social, cultural, and economic consequences of political manipulations of language in the current language policies' of the four countries. It asserts that the use of four different language names – Bosnian, Croatian, Montenegrin, Serbian – does not imply that there are four different languages. What there is a common, polycentric standard language – just like, say, French, which has Belgian, Swiss, French and Canadian variants but is definitely not four different languages.

Pretending that BCSM, as some linguists now call it, is four separate languages has particularly serious consequences in Bosnia, where Orthodox Serbs, Catholic Croats and Muslim Bosniaks are deemed by politicians to use different languages, even though the way they speak in any given town or village is exactly the same. Children are taught in separate streams at school, with separate curricula, on the grounds that they speak different languages. All public documents have to be 'translated' and published in three versions. And there is even a story that a Bosniak being prosecuted in Serbia for some offence had to be released because no 'interpreter' could be found for him.

Some nationalists are doing their best to make the four varieties more distinct from one another by artificially introducing differences where none existed. Writers in Croatia have had their work censored through the removal of supposedly 'Serbian' words, which are replaced with 'Croatian' words, some of them recent inventions.

This is all seriously at odds with common sense, and it is no surprise that the declaration now [2017] has almost 9,000 signatures. Linguistic scientists are agreed that BCSM is essentially a single language with four different standard variants bearing different names; it is unsurprising that linguists are well represented on the list of signatories. I have signed it myself. And I wish the defenders of linguistic common sense every success in their struggle against the linguistic unreason of the nationalists.

POLYCENTRIC

Polycentric –'many-centred' – languages have two or more different standard variants. Standard German differs as between Austria, Switzerland and Germany. Latin American Spanish is not the same as the Spanish of Spain. Portuguese and Brazilian Portuguese are quite divergent. And of course English comes in many versions around the world.

7.13 Arabic

We do not generally think of Arabic as a being a European language, but for many centuries it was very much a language *of* Europe.

Arabic-speaking Muslims expanded out of the Arabian peninsula during the 600s AD and reached the shores of southern Europe via North Africa in AD 711, when Islamic forces crossed the Straits of Gibraltar and began taking control of southern Iberia. These forces obviously brought the Arabic language with them, but they were also accompanied by large numbers of speakers of the indigenous Berber languages of North Africa from areas which are now Libya, Tunisia, Algeria and Morocco.

These invading Muslims of Arabic and Berber ancestry came to be known as the Moors – from the Latin name of the North African Berber kingdom Mauretania, which was overrun by the Arabs in the seventh century. The modern – and mostly non-Berber – nation of Mauritania today lies much further to the south.

Andalusia, in southern Spain (Spanish *Andalucía*), derives its name from Arabic *al-Andalus*, the name which the Moorish conquerors gave to the large area – eventually covering much of modern Portugal and Spain – which had come under their domination by AD 1000. The origin of this Arabic name is disputed: some say it came from the name of the East Germanic tribe, the Vandals, who had passed through Iberia on their way to establishing their fifth-century kingdom in North Africa.

Under the Moors of al-Andalus, much of the population of southern Iberia continued to speak the Romance dialects which they had inherited from the Latin-speaking overlords of the Roman Empire. These dialects are often referred to as Mozarabic, from the Arabic word *mustarib*, 'those who have adopted Arabic ways' – even though the dialects were also spoken by Jews and Christians. A better name is Andalusi Romance. Andalusi Romance was not generally used as a written language, and the few records we have of it are mostly written in the Arabic script, though there are also some which use the Hebrew writing system. These records show that the language was rather different from Spanish, which had its origins in Castile in northern-central Iberia.

After centuries of conflict between the Christian north of Iberia and Moslem al-Andalus, the Moorish rulers were eventually driven out. They finally evacuated the city of Granada in 1492.

The Berber languages of the Moors did not survive anywhere in Europe, and their Arabic now survives only in the form of the language which we today call Maltese, historically a variety of Arabic much influenced by Sicilian and Italian. Some recent linguistic research has shown that speakers of Tunisian Arabic and the Libyan Arabic of Benghazi are able to understand about 40 per cent of what is said to them in Maltese. It does not work quite so well the other way round, but Maltese speakers do best when listening to the Arabic of Tunisia.

Although the Arabic language itself did eventually vanish from mainland Europe, very many Arabic words still survive in Modern Spanish and Portuguese as remnants of the seven centuries of Arabic domination. Most European languages borrowed many, often scientific, words from Arabic, ranging from *alcohol*, *algebra* and *alcove* – the *al-* part is the Arabic definite article 'the' – to *zenith* and *zero*: Arabic-speaking scholars and scientists were for very many generations far ahead of Europeans in terms of scientific thinking, research and knowledge.

But Modern Portuguese and Spanish have very many more Arabic words than other European languages, including such everyday terms as Spanish *almohada*, Portuguese *almofada*, 'pillow', which come from Arabic *al-mahadda* (Modern Maltese has *mhadda*); Spanish and Portuguese *alicate*, 'pliers', which originates in Arabic *al-qati'a*; and Spanish *alforja*, Portuguese *alforje*, 'saddle-bag', which are from Arabic *al-khurj*.

These humble domestic items bespeak a long-term, intimate bilingual co-existence between the Romance- and Arabic-speaking communities of the Iberian peninsula.

TRAFALGAR

Trafalgar Square is named for the British naval victory which took place in 1805 off the coast of southern Spain in the vicinity of Cape Trafalgar – the Spanish name is *Cabo Trafalgar*. This was originally Arabic *Taraf-al-gharb*, where *taraf* meant 'cape' and *gharb* 'west'.

7.14 Maltese

'Anti-Semitic' is a term which is used to apply to people who demonstrate prejudice against or hostility to Jews as an entire ethnic or religious group.

For a linguist, though, the widespread use of *anti-Semitic* to mean 'anti-Jewish' is a rather unsatisfactory practice, because *Semitic* does not actually mean 'Jewish'. It is true that in deeply racist Victorian England, the term *Semite* did come to be used as a kind of distorted euphemism for *Jew* – a word which was considered to be 'not very nice' in polite society, very much as we used to say *Negro* instead of *Black* (see also Section 11.9). But the term Semitic actually refers to many more peoples than just the Jews.

In linguistics, Semitic refers to the family of languages which descend from Proto-Semitic, a language that was spoken somewhere in the Middle East – we are not sure exactly where – in the fourth millennium BC. The Jewish language Hebrew, which most of the Old Testament was written in, was one of many ancient Semitic languages, which also included Aramaic, Akkadian, Phoenician and Ugaritic. Aramaic eventually became the most powerful language in the Middle East. Some books of the Bible were written in Aramaic, and it was a major lingua franca in the Middle East for nearly a thousand years. In fact, by the first century BC, the widespread adoption of Aramaic by peoples who had formerly spoken other languages had led to the death of Hebrew and other local languages such as Phoenician. Jesus and his disciples were mother-tongue speakers of Aramaic.

Hebrew did survive, though, as the religious language of the Jews; and after many centuries it was artificially resurrected as the national language of modern Israel. A number of linguists have argued that Modern Hebrew – they prefer to call it Israeli – is actually as much a European language as it is Semitic, since many of its structures are actually Slavic or Germanic in origin. This is because many of the early founders of Israel were Eastern European Jews who had grown up speaking Yiddish, which is a form of German which over the centuries has been influenced in its structure by Slavic languages such as Polish and Ukrainian, though it does also contain many words derived from liturgical Hebrew. These founders were not mother-tongue speakers of Hebrew – there had not been any of those for two millennia; and the way they spoke this language, which they were doing their best to turn into a living tongue, was naturally very much influenced by their native languages (see also Section 7.15).

Aramaic survives to this day and is still spoken by mostly small and often endangered groups of Syriac Christians, as well as Moslems and Jews, in parts of Iran, Iraq, Syria and Turkey; but its future in some of these places is rather uncertain because of the current traumatic upheavals going on in the area. The major Semitic languages in the world today are Amharic, which is the official language of Ethiopia; the Tigre and Tigrinya languages of Eritrea; and Arabic, which is probably better regarded as a group of related languages.

One of the official languages of the European Union is also Semitic. This is Maltese, which was originally a form of North African Arabic that was brought to Sicily and Malta by Arab conquerors, starting in the seventh century. It is now regarded as a language distinct from Arabic, and is written in the Latin alphabet by speakers who have a Christian rather than Muslim heritage. Although Maltese has been heavily influenced by the Romance language Sicilian – to the extent that perhaps 40 per cent of its vocabulary is Sicilian in origin – and, in more recent centuries, by Italian and English, the basic grammar and vocabulary of Maltese remain genuinely Semitic.

But, of course, if you ever feel like criticising Malta or the Maltese, for whatever reason, no one is going to call you anti-Semitic.

7.15 Hebrew

It is generally agreed by linguistic scientists who are experts on the Semitic language family that Jesus and his disciples were not native speakers of Hebrew but of Aramaic – a related Semitic language. Hebrew had certainly totally disappeared as a spoken native language by AD 300 or so. For the next 1,700 years, Hebrew had no mother-tongue speakers at all, although it did survive as a religious and literary language, rather as Latin survived in the same way for many centuries in Western Europe.

As is well known, over the last 130 years or so Hebrew has been revived as a spoken language. It once again has mother-tongue speakers – currently perhaps around 5 million of them. Hebrew is one of the official languages of Israel: it is spoken natively by about half the population, and non-natively by most of the rest. After many centuries as a dead language, Hebrew has, rather remarkably – and probably uniquely – been successfully revived.

But what exactly is it that has been revived? The lack of continuous language transmission through families from one generation to another means that the results of the revival of Hebrew are not those that were intended by the original revivalists. The language spoken in Israel today is not the language of the Hebrew Bible which was used as the basis of the revival. One Israeli linguist has called it 'a semi-engineered Semito-European hybrid language'.

The fact is that Modern Israeli is a very different language from Old Testament Hebrew. The sound system of contemporary Israeli Hebrew is basically very similar to that of Yiddish, the Eastern European Ashkenazi Jewish variety of German. This is obviously because most of the early Zionists in Palestine, who gave themselves the very difficult task of converting a dead biblical tongue into a living modern language, were themselves native speakers of Yiddish. Modern Hebrew's sentence grammar has also been very strongly influenced by Yiddish and German, as well as by Slavic languages such as Polish and Ukrainian, because many of the revivalists had come from Slavic-speaking areas of Eastern Europe, including Poland, Belarus and Ukraine. Another Jewish linguist has referred to Israeli Hebrew as 'a Slavic language in search of a Semitic past'.

Revivalists of any language who are active today will similarly have to assume that the mother-tongue background of the speakers who are being tasked with the revival will inevitably play a role in determining what the revived language will be like. This is because, while small children are brilliant language learners, adolescents and adults are not. The number of adults who can learn to speak a foreign language in exactly the same way as a native speaker, without a foreign accent and using the same grammar and vocabulary as mother-tongue speakers without error, is near enough zero as makes no difference.

One current example of a language revival in progress is provided in the United Kingdom by the (mostly) English speakers who are currently attempting to resurrect Cornish – a language historically closely related to Welsh and Breton whose last native speakers died out in south-western Cornwall in the late eighteenth century or soon after. The less-than-wonderful language-learning abilities of human adults means that any natively spoken revived twenty-first-century Cornish is bound to have been influenced by English, and is very unlikely to be exactly what Cornish would have been like today if the modern language had evolved as the natural continuation of mother-tongue language learning with no break in transmission.

But of course, this is absolutely not a reason not to support current revival attempts. It is extremely pleasing to see that since 2002, Cornish has been recognised as a minority language under the European Charter for Regional or Minority Languages, the European treaty which was adopted by the Council of Europe in 1992 for the protection and promotion of such European languages.

HYBRID

The most recent meaning of *hybrid* is 'a vehicle powered by an engine which uses both petrol and electricity'. The word is of Latin origin, and in that classical language it had a very different meaning. To the Romans, a *hybrida* was the offspring of a wild boar and a domestic sow.

7.16 Hawaiian

It is very quick and easy for English people to travel the twenty-odd miles across the English Channel between Dover and Calais: the ferry does not take more than an hour and a half. And you do not even need a visa – yet.

As everybody knows, when you arrive on the other side of the Channel you find that the people who live there speak a language which is so different from English that you cannot understand it unless you have studied French. This is the way things have been linguistically for something like 1,500 years, in spite of the invasion of England by French speakers in 1066.

In the Pacific Ocean, the situation is quite different. The sea journey from Tahiti to New Zealand is not at all quick and easy – it is an enormous 2,500 miles, and even today powered sailing vessels take many days to complete the journey. But any native speaker of the indigenous Polynesian language Tahitian arriving in New Zealand will find that they can understand the language of the New Zealand Maori reasonably well. The Yorkshireman Captain James Cook explored parts of the Pacific in the second half of the 1700s with the aid of a Tahitian navigator called Tupaia, who was invaluable not only because of his navigational skills but also because, when Cook and his men arrived in New Zealand, Tupaia was able to act as an interpreter.

We do not know when the ancestors of the modern Maori first arrived in New Zealand, but it was probably some time between AD 800 and 1400. What we do know, however, is that they arrived from the east; and we know this on linguistic grounds, amongst other evidence. The closest linguistic relative of New Zealand Maori is the language of the Cook Islands, notably the major island of Rarotonga. This language is also called (Cook Islands) Maori. The Cook Islands are about 2,000 miles north-east of New Zealand. The Tahitians, from even further east, can understand this language pretty well, too.

It is a remarkable fact that languages spoken so very far apart, with nothing between them except thousands of miles of more or less empty ocean, are so similar and so mutually intelligible. This is due to the well-known but remarkable seafaring abilities of the Polynesian peoples. Over the centuries, they settled on islands as far apart as Easter Island, lying 2,300 miles off Chile's west coast, and Norfolk Island, located between New Caledonia, New Zealand and Australia (though the Polynesians had left Norfolk Island by the time Europeans first arrived). These two islands are 5,000 miles apart, not much less than the distance from London to Calcutta.

The Polynesians also appear to have travelled far enough south in the Pacific towards Antarctica to have seen icebergs. And they certainly made it as far into the northern hemisphere as Hawaii. The contemporary Hawaiian language is also a very close linguistic relative of Tahitian and Maori, in spite of the fact that Hawaii is 2,700 miles from Tahiti, and over 4,000 miles from New Zealand. In fact, Hawaii is about a thousand miles from *anywhere* else.

Professor David Adger of Queen Mary College, London University, has entertainingly observed that, while the *Star Wars* character Yoda speaks English (like most other beings of the universe in science fiction films), it is clearly not his native language. David argues that the order of words Yoda typically uses in sentences, such as *The greatest teacher failure is*, 'The greatest teacher is failure', suggests that Yoda's native language is Hawaiian, because that is the word order you would find in a typical Hawaiian sentence. This is absolutely true, but in fact Yoda might just as well have a been a native speaker of Maori or Tahitian. We will probably never know.

AUSTRONESIAN

The Austronesian language family is very remarkable in many ways. These languages stretch halfway across the globe, from the Malagasy language of Madagascar to Rapanui, the Polynesian language of Easter Island, in the far eastern Pacific. At the northern and southern extremities of the language family's range, we find two other Polynesian languages: Hawaiian and New Zealand Maori, spoken 7,000 kilometres apart.

7.17 Metsif

From time to time we hear about 'mixed languages'. Maltese, for example, is sometimes said to be a mixture of the European language Italian with the North African variety of Arabic. But it isn't really: its grammatical structures show that Maltese is basically still a Semitic language.

Similarly, English can be said to be a mixture of Anglo-Saxon and French – we do have a very large number (about 40 per cent) of French-origin words in our language (including *origin* and *language*, for instance – and *instance*). But when we look at its grammatical words and structures, we can see that English is still fundamentally a Germanic language.

In the same kind of way, about 60 per cent of Albanian vocabulary is derived from Latin, but its grammatical structures are nothing like those of Italian or Spanish, which are truly descended from Latin, and we would not want to consider it to be a Romance language.

However, a fascinating language which really is a genuine mixture in more or less equal parts of two languages, one European and one non-European, goes by the name of Michif (also Metsif – there are various spellings). It is a remarkable combination of French and the indigenous Canadian Algonquian language Cree. It is spoken by some of the peoples known in Canada by the French name of Métis, earlier Métif, meaning 'of mixed ancestry, *mestizo*'. The language has its origins in Canada, and there are still speakers of it in Manitoba and Saskatchewan, though most of them nowadays live in North Dakota in the USA.

The language arose around the turn of the nineteenth century as a result of intermarriage between male European-origin – mostly French-Canadian – fur traders, who had ventured west across the plains from Quebec and the Canadian Maritime Provinces, and indigenous women, mostly Plains Cree. Although the community was mixed in origin, by 1820 or so a distinctive culture had emerged, and it had a distinctive language to go with it: its speakers today mostly do not know any French or Cree as such.

One of the most remarkable things about Metsif linguistically is that most of its nouns are French, complete with French-style grammatical gender and grammatical agreement between nouns and adjectives, while its verbs – which can be highly complex – are Cree.

For example, *la fam miciminêw li pci* means 'The woman is holding the child'. The way that sentence works is this. *La fam* is in origin French *la femme*, 'the woman', complete with the feminine form of the definite article *la*, 'the'. *Li pci* is French *le petit* 'the small (one)', with the masculine definite article *le* and the masculine form of *petit* (the feminine would be *petite*). *Micimin-êw* is Cree and means literally 'holds she-him'.

Verbs in Algonquian languages have a very interesting structure. We can compare them with, for instance, Italian verbs, where you can omit the subject pronoun if you like because the verb already has a suffix at the end which tells you if the subject is first, second or third person: *(io) parl-o*, 'I speak', *(tu) parl-I*, 'you speak', *(noi) parl-iamo*, 'we speak'. Cree goes one better, because the verb suffix – and I am simplifying here – tells you both what the person of the subject is *and* what the person of the object is. The suffix *-êw* in *micimin-êw* marks the fact that the subject of the verb is in the third person (so *he/she*) and that the object is also in the third person (so *him/her*).

The leading authority on Michif, the linguistic scientist Peter Bakker, says that genuinely mixed languages like this are generally spoken by people with dual ancestry, where all the original fathers spoke one language and all the mothers spoke another, with their bilingual offspring being responsible, as children or adolescents, for the creation, deliberate or not, of the mixed language.

MESTIZO

French *métis*, Portuguese *mestiço* and Spanish *mestizo* all come from Latin *mixtus*, 'mixed', from *miscere*, 'to mix'. The originally Spanish word has been borrowed into (particularly American) English, where the *z* is pronounced as in English. In Spanish, the word is pronounced 'mess-teess-o' or 'mess-teeth-o'.

8   Peoples

No one really knows when the peoples who spoke Indo-European languages first arrived in Europe. Some linguists and archaeologists believe that our linguistic ancestors first arrived on our continent around 4500 BC. Others place the date much later. But the fact is that nearly all the languages of the continent are related to each other. They descend from a single common ancestor which was spoken somewhere further east – probably between the Black Sea and the Caspian Sea – in about 4000 BC, and which then gradually spread westwards with the peoples who spoke it. So we are nearly all linguistic brothers and sisters. This includes the Gypsies, who did not start arriving in Europe until the mediaeval period but whose language, Romani, has its origins in northern India and is also Indo-European (see Section 7.5).

The European languages which are not part of our large Indo-European linguistic family are mostly spoken by peoples who settled here after us. Maltese, as we have already seen, is in origin a form of Arabic which came from north Africa after AD 800. Speakers of Hungarian started to arrive from the east around AD 900. And Turkish, originally a Central Asian language, made its first appearance in Asia Minor about 1,000 years ago. But the people who speak Finno-Samic languages (which are distantly related to Hungarian), such as Finnish, Estonian and the Sami (Lappish) languages of northern Scandinavia, are not newcomers and may have arrived from their homeland in northern Eurasia at around the same time as Indo-European speakers.

Of course, our linguistic ancestors were certainly not the first human beings to inhabit the European continent. Other languages were spoken here for very many millennia before we arrived – and we have a major clue as to what some of them might have been. As we saw earlier, Basque, now spoken in northern Spain and south-western France, is not related to any other language in the world, as far as we know; and when Indo-European-speaking peoples first arrived in Western Europe, Basque speakers were already here. In fact, large areas of Western Europe may have been inhabited by speakers of languages and dialects related to Modern Basque. Some linguists today refer to these hypothetical dialects as Vasconic. But today, everywhere except in the modern Basque Country, these languages have disappeared.

The stories of the peoples of Europe and their languages are the subject matter of this chapter.

8.1 Minoans

The ancient Minoan culture of Crete grew out of a peaceful, matriarchal society where women enjoyed a privileged position and a mother-goddess played an important role. The apogee of this first great European civilisation was reached between 2000 and 1500 BC.

We do not know what language the Minoans spoke, but we do have Minoan clay tablets dating from that period with writing on them in a syllabary known as Linear A. (A syllabary has a symbol for each possible syllable, so 'pa' and 'ka', 'te' and 'to', each have a single different symbol.) If we could tell what language these tablets were written in, we might have a better idea of where the Minoans came from originally. But, unfortunately, Linear A has not yet been deciphered, despite many attempts by many different scholars to do so.

We are rather certain that the Minoans' language was not Greek. But did they speak a Semitic language connected to Phoenician; or something like Ancient Egyptian, which was related to the Berber languages of north Africa? The Oxford philologist L. R. Palmer argued that Minoan was likely to have been an Indo-European language related to Luwian, a member of the now extinct Anatolian language sub-family of Indo-European which also included Hittite. Luwian was spoken across much of southern Asia Minor – modern Turkey – including the south-western coastal districts, which were a relatively easy sea journey away from Crete.

Our best understanding of what happened to Minoan civilisation is that there were two large series of earthquakes in the area, followed by a truly colossal volcanic eruption in about 1500 BC on the island of Thera (Santorini), about 70 miles to the north of Crete. Massive tidal waves bore down on the Cretan north coast, and earthquakes caused widespread destruction in Crete itself.

Then, around 1400 BC, the archaeological record shows signs of a major upheaval on Crete with widespread destruction of cities and palaces, often by fire, accom-panied by signs that another group of people had arrived from elsewhere, bearing a different culture. Clay tablets have been found from this period employing a writing system and a language different from the Minoans'. The Minoan people, probably weakened by the series of natural disasters, were overrun by these invaders, who appear to have systematically destroyed all the major Minoan cities of central and eastern Crete, although the main centre at Knossos seems to have been spared, perhaps because they wanted to preserve it for their own use.

But who were these invaders? Their identity was not established until the 1950s, when it was discovered by one of the most impressive intellectual feats of all time. The invaders' new writing system, known as Linear B, had defied all earlier efforts at decipherment. However, in 1951 a brilliant young English amateur linguist, Michael Ventris, succeeded in decoding the script, and in 1953 he published a paper together with the Cambridge classical philologist John Chadwick – who had worked at Bletchley Park as a cryptographer during World War II – showing that the language of Linear B was a very early form of Greek.

From about 2000 BC onwards, people speaking a language ancestral to Greek had begun arriving in the southern Balkans from the north, and had established a civilisation in what is now mainland Greece. Their culture was very different from the Minoans': patriarchal, militaristic, hierarchical and authoritarian. The invasion of Crete showed that these Greeks had now continued their southward migration from the mainland across the Aegean sea.

Linguistic evidence suggests that Minoan and Greek populations coexisted on the island for many generations, as the Minoan language seems to have had some influence on Greek. The Archaic Greek words *basileus*, 'king', *woinos*, 'wine', and *wrodon*, 'rose' are of pre-Greek origin; and one Minoan word, *labyrinth*, has even made its way into English.

But it is ironic, given the importance of Crete to modern Greece, that linguistic research suggests that the people who destroyed Minoan Crete were actually Greeks.

LABYRINTH

Our word *labyrinth* was borrowed from Latin *labyrinthus*, 'maze', originally the mythical maze of Minoan Crete, but it was not originally a Latin word – Latin had no *th* sound. It came from Ancient Greek *labyrinthos*. The origin of this word is not known for certain, but it is very likely that it came from the ancient pre-Greek language of the Minoans – whatever that was.

8.2 Norse Gaels

During the first millennium AD, Britain was home to four major languages, each of which had arrived from a different point of the compass. The first was Britonnic Celtic, the ancestor of Breton and Cornish, which had come to the south coast of this island from across the English Channel, perhaps as long as 4,000 years ago.

The next two languages to arrive were Old English and Goidelic Celtic. Old English developed from Germanic dialects which were brought to our eastern shores from across the North Sea starting about 1,600 years ago. At about the same time, speakers of Goidelic Celtic, the ancestor of Irish Gaelic and Manx, began to arrive from the west across the Irish Sea.

Finally, starting about 1,200 years ago, Old Norse, the language ancestral to the modern Scandinavian languages, turned up with the Vikings who sailed here on their longships from the north.

Three of these ancient languages are still alive and in various degrees of good health in Britain today. Modern English, the descendant of Old English, is our dominant language. But Britonnic also survives, after very many millennia, in the form of Modern Welsh, a language with considerable official recognition in Wales and several hundreds of thousands of speakers. Goidelic, too, lives on as Scottish Gaelic, with its greatest concentration of speakers in the Western Highlands and Hebridean Islands, as well as in Glasgow.

However Old Norse, even though it was spoken in Shetland until the eighteenth century, now has no British descendants . . . except that it has left so much of itself behind in English grammar and vocabulary that some linguists have been moved to say that English is as much a descendant of Old Norse as of Old English. There was so much long-term intimate contact between speakers of Old Norse and Old English in the areas known as the Danelaw that we can regard what happened linguistically as much a coalescence of the two languages as a replacement of the one by the other.

But Old Norse can also be said to live on to an extent in Modern Gaelic in the same kind of way. After the arrival of the Old Norse-speaking Scandinavians on the coasts of Scotland and Ireland, a group of people who are often described as the Norse Gaels emerged after Scandinavian settlers in Scotland and Ireland intermarried with Gaelic-speaking people and gradually adopted very many aspects of Gaelic culture. There was once again long-term intimate contact, this time between speakers of Old Norse and Gaelic.

These Norse Gaels, part-descendants of the seafaring Vikings, came to control large areas of the Irish Sea, including the Isle of Man, as well as the seas off the coast of western Scotland, from about AD 800 until perhaps as late as the 1200s. The Kingdom of the Isles, which included the Hebrides, the Kintyre Peninsula, the Isle of Arran and the Isle of Man, was essentially a political entity founded by mixed bilingual groups of Gaels and Norsemen. The same was true of the Kingdom of Galloway on the far south-western mainland of Scotland: the name Galloway derives from the Gaelic *Gall Ghaidheil* 'stranger Gaels'.

Scottish Gaelic has a number of words derived from Norse, such as *acair*, 'anchor' from Norse *akkeri*; *bideadh*, 'to bite' from *bita*; *dorgh*, 'fishing line' from *dorg*; *nabaidh*, 'neighbour' from *nabua*; *sgarbh*, 'cormorant' from *skarf*; and *trosg*, 'cod' from *thorsk*. Some Gaelic personal names have Norse origins, such as Ruairidh (Rory) from *Hrodrik*, and Tormod from *Thormund*. It is also possible that the Gaelic word *far*, 'where', derives from Old Norse *hvar* (Modern Norwegian *kvar*), 'where'.

And most experts suppose that one special feature of Scottish Gaelic pronunciation is the result of intense, centuries-long Old Norse influence. This is the phenomenon which linguistic scientists refer to as 'pre-aspiration', as when, for example, the word *Mac*, 'son', is pronounced with an *h* sound before the *c*, so 'mahhc' − all thanks to those Norse Gaels.

MULL

All fans of Paul McCartney are familiar with the Mull of Kintyre, the south-westernmost tip of the Scottish Kintyre Peninsula, just across the sea from northern Ireland. *Mull* is the English-language version of the Gaelic word *maol*, which means 'bald' and, by extension, 'a rounded cape or promontory'.

8.3 Galloway

A senior advisor to Donald Trump once accused a journalist of 'cosmopolitan bias'. The Nazis under Hitler also opposed 'cosmopolitan internationalism'. And even in this country, there are people who use *cosmopolitan* as a derogatory term. Many of them seem to be the same British people who can from time to time be heard to say 'we want our country back'. They appear to be harking back to a vision of some monocultural, monolingual utopia of Britain long ago.

But there never was any such Britain, at least not in the last 2,000 years. Perhaps before that there may have been something like monolingualism in Britain for a while. The oldest known language of our island is Brittonic Celtic, the ancestor of Modern Welsh, Cornish and Breton, which was probably spoken all over the island, from Sussex to Sutherland, and Colchester to Caernarvon. If Brittonic monolingualism ever did exist on the entire island, then we might actually have to allow the Welsh to complain that 'we want our country back'; but the rest of us have absolutely no linguistic basis for saying any such thing.

There are clear signs of our multicultural, multilingual long-ago past even in what one might think of as being the remotest parts of this island. In Galloway, south-western Scotland, the very earliest surviving stratum of place-names is clearly Welsh. The westward spread of English, in the wake of the invasions of eastern Britain by Anglo-Saxons from continental Europe, gradually led to Brittonic speakers being split into three separate western zones. Philologists write of the Celts, after they were cut off from one another, as speaking Cornish in Devon and Cornwall, Welsh in Wales and Cumbric in the Lake District and the south-west of Scotland – though these were initially just three different dialects of the same language.

Welsh/Cumbric place-names still survive in Galloway, including Terregles, which meant 'farmstead by the church' – in Modern Welsh *tre* means 'town' and *eglwys* is 'church'; and Troqueer, where the first element is the same as *tre*, and the second comes from a root meaning 'bend (in the river)' – *gwyro* is 'to bend' in Modern Welsh.

Then the Northumbrian dialect of Anglo-Saxon also found its way into Galloway, in the 700s AD, with its speakers, too, leaving place-names behind them. Whithorn is Old English *whit*, 'white' plus *ærn*, 'building'. Nearby Wigtown is the *tun*, 'farmstead' of an Old-English-speaking man called *Wicga*.

But Welsh–English bilingualism was not the whole story. Just as English was spreading into Galloway from the east, so Gaelic had already started arriving from the west, from Ireland. During the 800s AD, there was then a further influx of Gaelic speakers from the Hebrides and the Western Highlands, and English came to be dominated by Gaelic as the main language of the area. Since the mid-1700s, Gaelic is no longer spoken in Galloway, but Gaelic place-names are still numerous. Drummore comes from the Gaelic word for 'ridge', Modern Scottish Gaelic *druim*, plus the word for 'big', Modern Gaelic *mòr*. Stranraer corresponds to Modern Gaelic *sròn*, 'promontory' and *reamhar*, 'thick'.

But the mediaeval linguistic situation was even more complex than that, because many of the newcomers from the Hebrides were descendants of the Vikings and spoke Old Norse as well as Gaelic. These Scandinavians also left place-names behind in Galloway. Sorbie comes from Old Norse *saurr*, 'mud' – the Modern Norwegian is *saur* – and *by*, 'settlement', which is the Modern Norwegian word for 'town'. The place-name Borgue derives from Old Norse *borg*, 'stronghold': as devotees of the Scandinavian noir TV series will know, *Borgen* means 'the castle' in Modern Danish.

So Galloway in the twelfth century was a very quadrilingual place, home to people who spoke Welsh, English, Gaelic and Norse. And there was also a role for Latin as the language of religion and scholarship. Like many other parts of Britain long ago, south-western Scotland was a highly cosmopolitan place.

GOIDELIC

Irish, Scottish Gaelic and Manx are Goidelic languages. In the 1200s, Gaelic was spoken all over Scotland, except for the Scots-speaking south-east and the Norse-speaking Western and Northern Isles. Gaelic was also spoken on the Isle of Man and in Ireland, its original homeland. A continuum of related dialects stretched all the way from the south-west of Ireland to the north-east of Scotland.

8.4 The Welsch

Fribourg University in Switzerland is a bilingual institution: French and German are both used for teaching and administration. Fribourg itself is a bilingual town: the language frontier between Romance-speaking and Germanic-speaking Europe runs right through the middle – rather more than half of the locals are native speakers of French, and the others are mother-tongue Swiss-German speakers. (German and Swiss-German are best regarded as two separate languages – though of course they are closely related, rather like German and Dutch – but Swiss-German speakers are all educated in German as well and use it for official purposes.)

When I first took up my post as Professor of English at Fribourg University in the late 1990s, one of the Swiss-German administrators asked my young assistant a question about me: 'Spricht er Welsch?' – 'Does he speak Welsch?'

It is no big surprise to learn that the German word *Welsch* is in origin the same word as the English word Welsh. But the colleague was not asking if I spoke Celtic; she wanted to know if I spoke French. Welsch is what the Swiss-Germans call Swiss French; and Welschland is their name for the French-speaking part of Switzerland.

The word *Welsch* has a history of being rather widely used throughout the German-speaking world to refer to speakers of Romance languages, notably French and Italian. The Dutch variant of the word has given us the word Walloon for people from the French-speaking part of Belgium.

Wales, Welsh, Welsch, Walloon – and the *-wall* part of Cornwall – are all variants of an ancient Germanic word meaning 'foreigner'. In early England, the Anglo-Saxon variant of the word, *Wealh* or *Walh*, soon came to have a more specialised meaning, referring to those foreigners who Old English speakers most often came into contact with, namely the Celtic-speaking people who had been living on the island of Britain for very many centuries before the Anglo-Saxons arrived. It also for a while acquired the meaning of 'slave' – which tells us something rather unpleasant about race relations in sixth-century England. Place-names in central and eastern England, such as Walbrook, Walburn, Walcot, Walden, Walford, Wallington, Walmer, Walshford, Walton and Walworth, tell us that people speaking the Brittonic Celtic language which was the ancestor of Modern Welsh and Cornish, lived amongst the descendants of the Germanic invaders for many generations.

The Germanic word Welsch/Welsh is thought to have come originally from the name of a powerful Celtic tribe, the Volcae, who were the western neighbours of the Germanic people in central Europe. Over time, this name acquired a generic sense, applying to any group who did not speak Germanic. But it was used especially of Celts and, later on, after the Romanisation of the Celts under the Roman Empire, to any group of people speaking Romance languages descended from Latin.

The Slavs, who were the eastern neighbours of the Germanic people, then also borrowed this word from them and used it in a similar way to refer to any Romance-speaking people they encountered. The Modern Polish word for Italy is Wlochy. Wallachia was an earlier name for what is now southern Romania (Vlad the Impaler, or Vlad Dracula, was a fifteenth-century prince of Wallachia). And the name Vlach or Vlah has been used by Serbs, Bulgarians and other South Slavs to refer to scattered groups of originally semi-nomadic Romanian-speaking people who are still found today over much of the southern Balkans. The Albanians call them

Vlleh. (Some people claim that the father of Mother Teresa – who was born in Skopje and was an Albanian speaker – was a Vlach.) The Greeks also call them Vlachs: there is a Vlach-speaking town called Metsovo with about 5,000 inhabitants in the Pindus mountains of central Greece.

Remarkably, the first part the word *walnut* also comes from the same linguistic source – these nuts were first obtained by our Germanic ancestors from the southern Romance-speaking areas of Europe.

8.5 The People of the Vorarlberg

On 11 May 1919, a *Volksabstimmung* took place in the mountainous region that is now the Austrian province of Vorarlberg. *Vorarlberg* means 'before Arlberg', the Arlberg being the mountain massif which contains the steep pass that separates the province from the rest of Austria to its east.

The German term *Volksabstimmung* literally means 'people's vote' – the dictionary translation is 'referendum' or 'plebiscite'. The *Volksabstimmung* was held in the aftermath of World War I, when the Austro-Hungarian Empire of the Habsburgs, which Vorarlberg had long been part of, was being broken up and reorganised into separate, new ethnolinguistically based nations such as Hungary and Czechoslovakia. The question which the referendum posed was: 'Is it the wish of the people of the Vorarlberg that the National Council of the Swiss Federal Government should announce the intention of the people of the Vorarlberg to join the Swiss Confederation and enter into negotiations with the Federal Government?'

When the results of the referendum were announced on 14 May, they showed that 81 per cent of the electors had voted in favour of beginning negotiations to become part of neighbouring Switzerland, with 19 per cent voting against. The small minority who voted not to join Switzerland were said to be mainly elite capitalists and big industrialists, plus politicians and the clergy – some of these people would have preferred to join Germany.

The overwhelming majority who did vote to join Switzerland – and in this case the majority truly was overwhelming, unlike in certain other referendums we might be familiar with – were motivated by many factors: the uncertain future of Austria after the military defeat of Austria–Hungary; severe economic problems; the large distance between Vorarlberg and the Austrian capital Vienna; and the historical neglect of the Vorarlberg region by the Viennese government.

Vienna was over 500 kilometres or 300 miles from Feldkirch in Vorarlberg. The quickest journey by road today is about 7 hours, on a route which takes you out of Austria into Germany and back into Austria again – it would, of course, have taken much longer in 1919. By rail, the trip today also takes more than 7 hours, with the route going over the Arlberg pass.

But, crucially, the pro-Switzerland voters were undoubtedly also motivated, in that era of ethnolinguistic reorganisation, by a feeling of solidarity and kinship with their neighbours in Switzerland. Like the citizens of neighbouring Liechtenstein, the people of Vorarlberg spoke, and still speak, Swiss-German, not the Austrian German of the Austrians on the other side of the Arlberg pass. The geographical barrier of the Arlberg marks a very strong and clear dialect boundary between the High Alemannic German dialects of Switzerland, Liechtenstein and the Vorarlberg, on the one hand, and the Austro-Bavarian dialects of the Tyrol and the rest of Austria on the other.

In the end, the residents of the Vorarlberg did not join the Swiss Confederation. Swiss Protestants were uneasy about adding more Catholics to their population. French-speaking and Italian-speaking Swiss citizens were not very happy about enlarging the German-speaking population of the Confederation. The Austrian government was opposed to the transfer, as were the Allies who had defeated Austria–Hungary. The Swiss Federal Council eventually voted against it.

According to the Treaty of Saint-Germain between Austria and the Allies, which was signed near Paris in September 1919, the independence of Czechoslovakia, Poland, Hungary and Yugoslavia were recognised, with certain border issues being settled by plebiscites. A vote in 1920 in southern Carinthia determined the location of the border between Austria and Yugoslavia in that region; and in 1921 the town of Sopron (German Ödenburg) voted to be incorporated into Hungary rather than Austria.

But the referendum in the Vorarlberg, which had taken place before the Treaty was signed, had no effect. The Vorarlberg today remains a Swiss-speaking enclave of 400,000 High Alemannic speakers at the far western end of the otherwise Austro-Bavarian-speaking Republic of Austria.

PLEBISCITE

Referendum is a Latin word meaning 'thing to be referred'. *Plebiscite* comes from the Latin word *plebiscitum*, from an original *plebis*, 'of the plebs', plus *scitum*, ordinance – thus, 'an ordinance passed by the plebs', where the *plebs* were the ordinary people of Rome, the so-called plebeian class or common people.

8.6 The Csángós

Hungarian is a language which is generally considered to have no close linguistic relatives, in any sense of the word 'close'. Its nearest linguistic relations seem to be the Mansi and Khanty languages, which are linguistically rather distant from Hungarian, and are certainly geographically very distant – their speakers are located about 3,000 miles from Hungary, in the western part of Siberia.

But there is another candidate for the label 'linguistic relative of Hungarian'. The fact that there is a very large Hungarian-speaking minority in Romanian Transylvania is rather well known. What is much less widely known, at least in Western Europe, is that there is also another Hungarian-speaking minority in the east of Romania on the other side of the Carpathian mountains, towards the border with Moldova, in Romanian Moldavia. These are the Csángós, who are an ignored and oppressed linguistic minority whose language is dying out as younger people shift to Romanian. They are distinguished from their Romanian-speaking neighbours by their poverty, isolation and Catholicism (most Romanians are Orthodox). Romanian governments have denied that they form a distinct ethnolinguistic group, and denied that they have a language of their own.

In more recent times, the Csángós have been faced with a different problem. Since 1989 and the fall of the Iron Curtain, certain official Hungarian bodies have announced that they want to 'save the Csángós'. What this means is that they want, quite admirably, to save the language and the culture of this isolated people, and they are right to want to do so. The Council of Europe has expressed its concern for the plight of the Csángó minority, and has criticised the Romanian government for failing to provide education in anything other than Romanian in the Csángó-speaking areas.

Unfortunately, the Hungarians' efforts have been linguistically uninformed and misguided, as Hungarian academic linguists have tried pointing out to them. The official bodies have started out from the assumption that a Csángó is just a Hungarian speaker like any other, and that younger members of the community could benefit from scholarships and education in Hungary.

The problem is that the Csángós have been geographically separated from the main body of Hungarian speakers for very many centuries and their Hungarian is so very different from other varieties as to be initially incomprehensible to Hungarians. When I was fortunate enough to be taken by some Hungarian linguists on a fascinating trip to Csángó villages in Romania, they took the precaution of bringing an interpreter with us, a Hungarian anthropologist who had worked with Csángós for long enough to be able to understand them. So from a linguistic point of view, it would probably be more sensible to call their language *Csángó*, and regard it as a language closely related to Hungarian rather than Hungarian itself. But that would be to play into the hands of those Romanian nationalists who want to claim that Csángó is not a 'real language' and not worth preserving.

The policy of educating the Csángós in Hungary has not been a success, because they had too many linguistic difficulties there. It also does not help that Csángó is widely regarded by ordinary Hungarians as 'bad Hungarian' and a 'corrupt' version of their language – which is no less nonsensical than saying that Swedish is a corrupt version of Danish. Hearing Hungarians express such negative attitudes about their native language simply gives the Csángós one additional reason not to speak their own language and to switch to Romanian instead, as many of them have already done.

The European Union has done a lot of good work with its policies for promoting and maintaining minority languages. But these efforts need to be linguistically well informed if they are to succeed. We have to look at the languages and dialects involved themselves, rather than accept concepts like 'Hungarian' as unproblematical givens. Knowledge about the vowels and consonants and grammar and vocabulary of any language we are trying to save is important.

8.7 Turks in Europe

The Turkic language family consists of a large number of related tongues which are spoken over many different regions of Eurasia, ranging over 6,000 miles from the original Turkic homeland in Siberia to Eastern Europe. The Turkic languages which people may have heard of, apart from Turkish, are Kazakh, Kyrgyz, Turkmen, Uzbek and Azerbaijani (Azeri), all of them spoken in Asia: we are familiar with the names of the nation-states where they are spoken.

We are also familiar with the fact that Turkish itself, by far the largest member of the Turkic family in terms of numbers of native speakers, is spoken not only in Asia Minor but also in those parts of the Republic of Turkey which lie in Europe – the area known as Eastern Thrace, to the west of the Bosphorus and bordering on Bulgaria and Greece.

Turkish has also for centuries been spoken in Cyprus by maybe 20 per cent of the population of the island. But it is perhaps not so well known that Turkish has been spoken for hundreds of years in a number of other areas of mainland Europe – in North Macedonia, Kosovo, Romania and Serbia, with the largest group consisting of around 600,000 Turkish speakers in Bulgaria, about 9 per cent of its population.

There are also many tens of thousands of native Turkish speakers in Greece, particularly in Western Thrace, including especially the towns of Komotini and Xanthi. The exact number is difficult to determine since the Greek government refuses to cite or even collect statistics for the Turkish speakers of Western Thrace: it simply reports on the numbers of people who are Muslims, and many of the Muslims in northern Greece speak Slavic languages or Romany rather than Turkish.

The Turkic language family is also represented by several languages other than Turkish in different parts of our continent. There are over half a million speakers of Crimean Tatar in Crimea – they have been there much longer than the Ukrainians and Russians (see Section 6.3). Other parts of Russia also have millions of speakers of Turkic languages – for example Chuvash, which is spoken in the Russian republic of Chuvashia.

And by no means all of the European speakers of Turkic languages come from a Muslim background. Gagauz is a European language with over half a million mostly Orthodox Christian speakers in Moldova, Crimea, Bulgaria and Russia. And Urum is another Turkic variety spoken by several thousand people who are Orthodox Christians, including in Mariupol, Ukraine. The Urum people consider themselves to be ethnic Greeks, even though they are not Greek speaking: the origin of the name *Urum* is the same as the Greek word *Romiós*, 'Greek', which is derived from *Rome* – the Greeks were for centuries citizens of the eastern Roman Empire centred on Constantinople.

Intriguingly, another Turkic language, Karaim, is spoken by people whose religion is based on the Old Testament. The Karaim are found in small communities in Lithuania, notably in Vilnius and the town of Trakai. The language is severely endangered, but attempts are underway to revive it. The origins of these Turkic-speaking people are not fully understood. They could represent a diaspora of Jews in Anatolia who had become Turkic speaking after the arrival of the Turks from the east. Or they could have been Turkic-speaking people who converted to a form of Judaism at some stage. Another small Turkic-speaking group with the same kind of religion are the Krymchaks of the Crimea, whose language is closely related to Crimean Tatar.

It would be a mistake to suppose that the Turkic language family is a recent arrival in Europe. The original Bulgars were a Turkic-speaking group who had established themselves in what is now Ukraine as early as the 600s AD. And some of the greatly feared and rather mysterious Huns were probably Turkic-speaking; they first arrived in Europe, ranging as far afield as France and Greece, in the 300s AD.

8.8 Turks and Greeks

Many people in south-eastern Europe would agree that it is correct to say that Turks are a Muslim people who speak Turkish, and that Greeks are a Christian people who speak Greek. That is certainly the general stereotype and it is, broadly speaking, true.

Accurate, unbiased figures are not always too easy to come by, but the population of Greece consists of approximately 98 per cent Orthodox Christians, with some of the rest being Catholic; and Greek native speakers constitute about 95 per cent of the populace. As far as Turkey is concerned, probably 97 per cent of the population are Muslims, and very approximately 85 per cent of the inhabitants are native speakers of Turkish; the rest mainly have Kurdish or Arabic as their mother tongue.

But there are interesting exceptions, of both possible types, to this stereotyped picture. For example, in modern Turkey and Syria, as well as scattered elsewhere around the eastern Mediterranean, there are significant groups of people who are Muslims but are nevertheless native speakers of Greek.

Many of these are people of Cretan origin. About twenty years ago, I was fascinated to meet some young Muslim Syrian fishermen in Crete who were fluent native speakers of a Cretan dialect which the locals said was more Cretan than the one which they now spoke themselves. The nineteenth-century Cretan dialect had been preserved intact in their Syrian village after the emigration of their ancestors from Crete, without being influenced by Standard Greek – because in Syria the language of education and the media was Arabic.

Conversion to Islam after the Ottoman conquest of Greece and the Balkans was greater in Crete than elsewhere in the Greek world; almost half of all Cretans were Muslim in 1820. During the nineteenth century, however, many of these Turko-Cretans, as they were often – if inaccurately – called, left the island for other more predominantly Muslim areas of the Ottoman Empire. This exodus was driven by sectarian violence connected with the many Cretan insurrections against Ottoman rule, as well as by the eventual achievement of autonomy by Crete under the protection of the 'Great Powers' (Britain, France, Italy and Russia) in 1908.

Muslims still made up about 40 per cent of the Cretan population in 1832, decreasing to 20 per cent in 1858, and by 1911 there were only 28,000 left. Those who remained were then compelled to leave in 1923 as part of a compulsory exchange of populations mandated by the Lausanne Convention: hundreds of thousands of Muslims were forcibly transferred to Turkey from Greece, and well over a million Christians were removed from Turkey to Greece, regardless of their language background. The idea was that if people were Muslims they were 'Turks', and that if they were Christians they were 'Greeks': religion trumped language.

If we look at the reverse combination of language and religion, there are also groups in the region who are Christians but native speakers of Turkish; one such group are the Karamanlides ('karraman-LEETHE-ess'). Before they were expelled from Turkey in 1923, these Orthodox Christians lived in central Anatolia, geographically isolated from other Orthodox groups. Those who were literate wrote in Turkish but used the Greek alphabet. Our best guess is that they were originally Greek-speaking natives of the area who shifted language as a result of being surrounded by Turks, while holding on to their ancestral religion; but it is also theoretically possible that they were Turkish incomers who converted to Christianity.

The first book in *karamanlídika*, as this way of writing Turkish is called, dates from 1718, and the last one that we know of was printed in Thessaloniki in 1929. According to Professor Peter Mackridge of Oxford University in his 2009 book *Language and National Identity in Greece*, one of the first novels ever to be produced in Turkish was written using the Greek alphabet by a Christian teacher and journalist with a very Greek name, Evangelos Misailidis; it was published in Istanbul in 1871.

ORTHODOX

Dating from the 1400s, this English word has a first element derived from Ancient Greek *ortho*, 'straight, right', as in *orthography*, 'correct writing' and *orthodontics*, 'straight teeth'. The second part comes from Greek *doxa*, 'belief'. The meaning 'normal, conventional' is much more recent: in cricket, *left-arm orthodox spin* has nothing to do with believing anything.

9   Sounds

One of mankind's greatest ever intellectual achievements was the development of the Greek alphabet, the world's first truly alphabetic writing system, with a separate symbol for each of the speech sounds – the consonants and vowels – of the language. Prior to that, there had been pseudo-alphabetic writing systems using separate symbols for syllables, or for consonants only. But the Ancient Greeks brilliantly realised that for total efficiency in writing, you first had to work out what the different vowels and consonants of your spoken language were, and then assign a letter symbol to each one.

The Greek alphabet was first developed around 800 BC. The Latin alphabet, which was derived from the Greek, first appeared later, in the 600s BC. Today, while Greek is still written in the Greek alphabet, the majority of the languages of Europe are written in the Latin alphabet. There are also European languages which are written in the Cyrillic alphabet (see also Sections 4.8 and 7.12): the main ones are Russian, Ukrainian, Belarussian, Serbian, Montenegrin, Macedonian and Bulgarian. The Cyrillic alphabet came on the scene very much later – it was not developed until the late 800s AD – and was also derived from the Greek.

The Latin alphabet worked rather well for writing Latin because it was developed for that purpose, but it has caused several problems for those of us who now use it for writing our own tongues. Languages around the world differ quite considerably in the speech sounds they use, and European languages are no exception. The Latin alphabet had only five letters for vowels – *a, e, i, o, u* – making it most unsuitable for writing English, which has many more vowels than that. Exactly how many there are varies from accent to accent: in my speech I have 19 vowel sounds, and using 5 letters for 19 sounds is asking for trouble.

There are also problems with writing consonantal letters. Latin had no sound corresponding to English 'sh', so we use two letters – a digraph – to represent this single sound. This is a pity: the great intellectual breakthrough of the Ancient Greeks was to realise that the ideal alphabet should have one letter per sound, and one sound per letter.

Other European languages have resorted to the same tactic for the 'sh' sound, using two or even three letters: in German it is written *sch*, in Norwegian *sj* or *skj*, in Italian it may be *sci* and in Polish it is *sz*. Hungarian does write the 'sh' sound with a single letter, but that letter is *s*, so Hungarian speakers then have to write the 's' sound as *sz*. Happily, some European language communities, such as the Czechs, have done better than this at following the example of the Ancient Greeks and developed a new single-letter representation: š.

Latin, like many other European languages, also had no sound corresponding to the initial consonants of our words *thigh* and *thy*. We ended up writing *th* for both of them, which was rather foolish, as Old English did have two letters which we could have used: þ and ð. Or we could have followed Modern Greek and employed the letter theta, θ, for the consonant in *thigh* and delta, δ, for the one in *thy*.

Several other new letters have been invented for representing the sounds of certain European languages, including vowels. Norwegian and Danish both have ø, which corresponds to the ö vowel of Swedish, Finnish, Estonian, German, Hungarian and Turkish. The French, though, have stuck with the digraph *eu* for this vowel sound, as in *feu*, 'fire'.

Issues like this are all connected to the interlingual diversity of the systems of sounds which different languages employ. And it is these vowel and consonant sound systems which the following section now focusses on.

9.1 Vowels and Consonants

If you ask English-speaking people how many vowels there are in their language, many of them will tell you that there are five: *a, e, i, o* and *u*. If you ask Greek speakers the same question, many of them will reply that they have seven vowels, and that these are the vowels called *alpha, epsilon, eta, iota, omicron, omega* and *upsilon*: A, E, I, O, Ω, Y.

Both these answers are wrong. It is true that there are seven letters representing vowels in the Greek alphabet, but the Modern Greek language itself has only five vowel sounds: O and Ω represent the same sounds, and so do I and Y.

Some of us were told at school that English has five vowels, but our teachers were thinking of letters, not sounds. In fact, they were even wrong about the number of letters, because there are actually six of those: the letter *y* in words like *city* and *tryst* also stands for a vowel. And the number of vowel sounds English truly has is much higher than in Greek, but the actual number depends on which accent people speak with.

Most people with accents from the south-east of England have 19 different vowel sounds in their spoken English. These are the different vowels in words such as *pit, pet, pat, put, putt, pot, bee, bay, buy, boy, boot, boat, bout, peer, pair, purr, par* and *paw*, plus the vowel in the first syllable of *about*. In contrast, many Scottish speakers have only 14 vowels. But, regardless of accent, one of the great issues facing the English spelling system has been the problem of having to use a small number of vowel letters to represent a much larger inventory of vowel sounds.

Languages vary a great deal in terms of their inventories of vowels. Like English, the other Germanic languages also tend to utilise a large number of vowel sounds, something like 26 in the case of Faroese, 22 in Norwegian, 21 in Dutch and 18 in German. Polish uses only 8, and Spanish 5. Finnish has 8 vowels, but the Finns cleverly represent each vowel with a different letter: in addition to *a, e, i, o, u*, they also use *æ, ö* and *y*, where *y* denotes a sound close to German *ü* or French *u*. Vowel systems can also change a great deal over time: Ancient Greek used to have 22 vowels, while Modern Greek, as we saw above, has only 5.

Languages differ, too, in the number of consonant sounds their speakers use. Most varieties of English have 24 consonants, which we represent in our spelling system by means of the letters *p, t, ch, k, b, d, j, g, m, n, ng, f, v, th* (as in *thigh*), *th* (as in *thy*), *s, z, sh, si* (as in *vision*), *h, w, l, r* and *y* (as in *young*). Lithuanian has 29 consonants and Polish has as many as 31. Modern Greek has only 15 consonants.

The total number of speech sounds languages possess differs enormously around the world. Taking vowels and consonants together, the now-extinct Caucasian language Ubykh had about 86 different sounds. According to some linguists, Lithuanian has 57. Some forms of Scottish Gaelic have 52. In my accent of English, I have 43. Polish has 39 vowels and consonants; Spanish has a total of 22; Finnish 21; and Greek 20. Looking outside Europe, the Polynesian language Hawaiian uses only 13 sounds (8 consonants and 5 vowels), while one of the San languages of southern Africa has an amazing inventory of about 100 different sounds.

None of this seems to matter in terms of what languages can and can't do. But it does appear that languages with fewer speech sounds may tend to have longer words than languages with larger inventories. Modern Greek words are on average about 50 per cent longer than English words: the Greek word for 'use' is *chrisimopoió*.

BETA

The word *alphabet* comes from the first letters of the Greek alphabet, *alpha* and *beta*. In Britain we mostly pronounce *beta* 'beeta', but Americans and Canadians say 'bayta'; in the Republic of Ireland 'bayta' predominates. The American version is closer to how the name for this letter would have sounded in Ancient Greek, but in Modern Greek it is pronounced 'veeta'.

9.2 Aitch

The sound represented by our Latin-alphabet letter *H* has had a sorry history in the languages of Europe over the last 2,000 years or so.

Perhaps the decline started in Greek. The Ancient Greek words for 'six' and 'seven' were *heks* and *heptá*, respectively, as reflected in several Modern English words which were borrowed from Ancient Greek, such as *hexagonal*, 'six-sided' and *heptathlon*, 'an athletic contest featuring seven different events'. But in the Modern Greek words for these two numerals, *éksi* and *eftá*, the *h*'s have gone; probably starting around 200 BC, all Greek *h*'s were dropped.

About 500 years later the same process started happening in Latin, and as a result also in the languages which eventually developed out of it. The French word which descended from Latin *hominem*, 'man', is spelt *homme* but, unlike in Latin, the *h* is not sounded. The same is true of the Catalan, Spanish and Portuguese words for 'man', *home*, *hombre* and *homem*: they have no initial *h* sound. And the Romanian and Italian words for 'man', *om* and *uomo*, do not even have an *h* in the spelling.

Having lost Latin-based *h*, French then went on to lose *h* all over again. Starting in the fifth century, what is now northern France was invaded and became controlled by Germanic tribes from the other side of the Rhine, mostly Franks (which is why France is called France). These Germanic speakers eventually abandoned their own language and gradually adopted the Late Latin/Old French of the subjugated majority population of Romanised native Gaulish Celts. But a good number of Germanic words made their way into Old French in the process.

It is not a coincidence that many of these borrowed Germanic words had military connotations. Some contained the Germanic consonant *h*, and this sound therefore now reappeared in French in words such as *heaume*, 'helmet', *havre*, 'harbour', *haine*, 'hate' and *honte*, 'shame'. But then this *h* eventually disappeared too, although it left one trace behind. In Modern French, when the definite article *le*, 'the', is placed in front of Latin-derived *h*-initial nouns such as *homme*, it is reduced to *l'* – *l'homme* – as it is for words beginning with a vowel, such as *l'amour*; but for Germanic-origin *h*-initial words, *le* is not contracted – 'the helmet' is *le heaume*.

The *h*-dropping story then continued a few hundred years later across the Channel in England. In the late Old English of the end of the first millennium, the *h* at the beginning of words like *hring*, *hlaf* and *hnutu* was dropped, giving us Modern English *ring*, *loaf* and *nut*. During the 1300s and 1400s, *h* also started to disappear in words such as *dohtor*, *broht*, *niht*, *sih*, at least in the south of England, giving us modern *daughter*, *brought*, *night*, *sight*, where the consonant *h* is 'remembered' in the *gh* spellings but is lost from the pronunciation.

By the eighteenth century, *h* had also started to be dropped before *w*, so that *whales* (Old English *hwælas*) and *which* (Old English *hwilc*) came to be pronounced identically to *Wales* and *witch* in many parts of England. And then from the late 1700s onwards, in the local accents of many parts of England and Wales, initial *h* went missing from words like *hut*, *house*, *hammer*, with the result that pairs such as *ill* and *hill*, *edge* and *hedge* are now pronounced the same. Some speakers do this consistently, others are variable, and some speakers do not do it at all, particularly those on Tyneside and in rural East Anglia.

It is this last phenomenon – pronouncing *hedge* the same as *edge* – that is generally referred to these days as 'dropping your *h*'s'. But in actual fact, this is simply the final stage of a long process of *h* loss which has been going on for very many generations indeed.

FRANK

Our word *frank*, 'free, open' comes from mediaeval Latin *francus*, 'free'. This was originally from the name of the Germanic Frankish people who conquered northern France after the departure of the Romans. The point was that the only people who had total freedom in Frankish-dominated France were the Franks themselves.

9.3 Forth and Bargy

The English language came into being in Britain and spent its first 700 years on this island. When it did eventually start spreading beyond these shores, it was to the neighbouring island of Ireland. Ironically, this first expansion of the English language out of Britain occurred because of the activities of the French-speaking Norman conquerors of England.

In 1169 a group of Anglo-Normans arrived in County Wexford in south-eastern Ireland, supposedly at the invitation of a local Irish leader who had asked for military help. They came from the French/English-speaking area of Pembrokeshire, south-western Wales (see Section 4.5), which had been colonised around 1100. These people were aristocratic speakers of Norman French, but they brought their English-speaking soldiers and servants with them. According to Professor Michael Samuels, the available evidence suggests that the English incomers mostly spoke dialects from the West Midlands and the south-west of England.

The military adventures of the Anglo-Normans in Ireland soon gave them control of the Norse-Irish towns of Wexford, Waterford and Dublin. Large numbers of settlers then followed them, and much of the eastern and south-eastern coastal area of Ireland gradually became English speaking. There were further urban coastal settlements to the west in Galway, Limerick and Cork.

But, interestingly, in spite of the military and political power that the Anglo-Normans exercised in Ireland, a long process of assimilation then set in during which the English- and French-speaking colonial minorities gradually became culturally more and more Irish and shifted to speaking Irish Gaelic. By 1500, the English language had disappeared from nearly all of the island: English had obtained a good foothold in Ireland, and survived for a few centuries, but then died out.

Except that, in the far south-east of the country, on the Forth and Bargy peninsula to the south of the town of Wexford, mediaeval English did survive –

and continued to be used there until the nineteenth century. The dialect of the original twelfth-century English settlers was spoken in that area until the early 1800s and beyond. After the re-colonisation of Ireland by the English Crown in the seventeenth century, English gradually replaced Gaelic in much of Ireland, leading to the development of the Modern Irish English we are familiar with today. But people on that far south-eastern peninsula resisted the encroachment of this upstart modern form of English until the reign of Queen Victoria.

Their dialect was described by the philologist A. J. Ellis in his 1889 work *The Existing Phonology of English Dialects*. He was never able to hear this variety spoken but, using written sources and reports from people on the spot, he acquired enough information to be able to classify the dialect as grouping together with the dialects of the West Country and south coast of England.

One well-known characteristic of the dialect's pronunciation was the use of *v* rather than *f*, *z* instead of *s*, and *zh* instead of *sh* at the beginning of words. We are familiar with this feature from stereotypical West Country pronunciations such as 'Zummerzet' for Somerset, as well as forms like 'vrom' (from), 'zixpence' (sixpence) and 'zhilling' (shilling). Records from Forth and Bargy show the same kind of thing, with spellings such as *vear* (fear), *zich* (such) and *zeven* (seven).

The dialect also preserved archaic grammatical features: the mediaeval-style English past-participle forms using a prefix – *y-drow* ('thrown'), *y-spant* ('spent') and *y-go* ('gone') – are reminiscent of Chaucer's *y-clad* ('clad, clothed').

The dialect also retained the verbal form *cham* ('I am'). This appears in Shakespeare's plays in dialogues involving country-bumpkin characters; and it survived in the dialects of the English West Country until quite recently. The word was derived from the mediaeval English form of *I*, which was *ic*, pronounced 'itch': *ic am* thus gave *'ch am*, just as modern *I am* has become *I'm*.

VIXEN

Vixen is the female of *fox*, but we might wonder why it is not *fixen*. The answer is that *vixen* is a southern and western dialect form where the *f* of the original word *fyxen* has become a *v*, as also happened in *vat*, 'cask', which was originally *fatt*, and in *Vange* (in Essex), originally *Fen Ge* 'fen district'.

9.4 Jack and Jill

Many of us remember from our childhood the well-known nursery rhyme which goes: 'Jack and Jill/ Went up the hill/ To fetch a pail of water. Jack fell down/ And broke his crown/ And Jill came tumbling after.' *Jill* rhymes with *hill*, and *down* rhymes with *crown*. And because this is, after all, a nursery rhyme, we would expect *water* and *after* to rhyme too – but they do not exactly do that.

Rhymes from earlier periods in history can tell us quite a lot about how languages used to be pronounced and how they have changed over the centuries. At the time when *Jack and Jill* was composed – and in the place where it first came into being – the words *water* and *after* in the third and sixth lines of the piece did rhyme very well.

Water was originally – and for very many centuries – pronounced 'wahter', as it still is in some northern dialects of English. The vowel in the first syllable then gradually changed from 'ah' to 'aw' under the influence of the preceding *w*. The *w* sound has had this effect on words spelt with *a* throughout the English language. *Was* no longer rhymes with *as*, which it originally did; *watch* no longer has the same vowel as *catch*; and *warm* does not rhyme with *arm*, although it once did, as the spelling suggests.

This same sound change also affected the rhyming scheme of the first two lines of another nursery rhyme: 'Goosey goosey gander/ Whither shall I wander?' *Wander* was clearly intended to rhyme with *gander* – and originally it did. But then the influence of the consonant *w*, where the lips are involved in the articulation, changed the vowel sound from the short *a* vowel to short *o*, which is also pronounced with rounded lips. The rhymes of *wander* and *gander*, as well as of *water* and *after*, go back to a time before this sound change took place.

But, surely, even allowing for that, *after* would still not have rhymed with *water*, because of the *f*? Well, in the local dialects of the whole of the south of England, *after* is even today very often pronounced without the *f*. According to the *English Dialect Dictionary*, the word *afternoon* is pronounced *ahternoon* in Cornwall, Devon, Somerset, Dorset, Hampshire, Sussex, Kent, Middlesex, Essex, Suffolk, Norfolk, Cambridgeshire, Northamptonshire, Warwickshire, Staffordshire, Oxfordshire and Berkshire.

So originally, then, the end-of-line words in *Jack and Jill* did rhyme perfectly; and we can deduce that it must have been composed somewhere in the south of England, at a time after the *f* in *after* had disappeared but before the vowel in *water* had changed from *ah* to *aw*.

A similar clue to older pronunciations can be found in the words of another well-known nursery rhyme: 'Ride a cock-horse to Banbury Cross/ To see a fine lady on a white horse.' For Modern English speakers in most parts of the world, *horse* and *cross* do not rhyme, though they were clearly intended to do so by whoever it was who first came up with this nursery rhyme. But on both sides of the Atlantic there is an older and rather well-known dialectal pronunciation of the word *horse* as 'hoss', which would produce a rhyme with *cross*. Alternatively, there is also an older pronunciation of *cross* as 'crawss', which would then rhyme with *horse* for most English people except those in the West Country and northern Lancashire who still actually pronounce the *r* in words like this. This 'crawss' pronunciation is still preserved today by two very different groups of speakers in England: first, traditional dialect speakers in much of the south of England, who also pronounce *lost* as 'lawsst' and *frost* as 'frawsst'; and, secondly, elderly aristocrats. Jacob Rees-Mogg really rather spoils his image as 'the honourable member for the nineteenth century' by having abandoned this 'crawss' pronunciation in favour of the accents of a more modern age.

GANDER

Many animals have special English words for the female of the species. *Dog* and *pig* refer to either sex, but a *bitch* or a *sow* can only be female. With some animals, it is the other way round. *Gander* is a special word for a male goose, just as *drake* is a particular word for male duck.

9.5 Hamupeke

You might like to cast your eye over this list of twelve names, given here in the sequence which they usually occur in, and see what you make of it: Hanuere, Pepuere, Maehe, Aperira, Mei, Hune, Hurae, Akuhata, Hepetema, Oketopa, Noema, Tihema.

It probably did not take too long to work out that these are the names of the twelve months of the year as found in some language other than English. The language in question is actually Maori, indigenous to New Zealand. The Maori people do have their own traditional calendar, but this is the way the names of the English calendar are rendered in their language.

Like other Polynesian languages, Maori has relatively few consonants compared to European languages; in particular, it lacks the sounds which we write with the letters *b*, *ch*, *d*, *f*, *g*, *j*, *l*, *s* and *v*. The sound pattern of Maori also requires all syllables to contain no more than one consonant, hence Pepuere rather than February.

There are also six days of the week whose English names have Maori versions: Mane, Turei, Wenerei, Taite, Paraire, Hatarei; it takes quite an effort to figure out that Paraire is Friday. From these names, it can be deduced that Maori also lacks the consonants which we write using the letters *th* and *z* (the letter *s* in the English words *Tuesday* and *Thursday* is, of course, actually pronounced as a *z*).

All languages perform transformations like this when they borrow words from other languages which have different sound patterns. Many English-speaking people pronounce the name of the country now officially called Sri Lanka as 'Shri Lanka'. This is because, although English does have the sounds which we write with the letters *s* and *r*, the sound pattern of our language does not permit words to begin with those two sounds one after the other, even though it does permit words to begin with *shr*. (Linguistic scientists call these rules about permitted sound combinations *phonotactics*.)

Many English football commentators pronounce the surname of the Newcastle player Mbemba as 'Umbemba', and the Chelsea midfielder N'Golo Kante's first name as 'Ingolo', because English does not allow words to begin with *mb* or *ng* without a vowel being inserted before or between the two sounds – just as Maori inserts a vowel between the *p* and the *t* of September. The name of the Czech composer Dvorak is often pronounced with three syllables by English speakers, even though it has only two in Czech, because we tend to insert a vowel between the *d* and the *v* of his name since English does not allow a word-initial *dv* combination. Alternatively, other English speakers make the name fit in with the rules of English pronunciation by leaving out the *d* altogether. The Polish goal-keeper Szczęsny gives us the same problem. We have no difficulty with the *sz* (= *sh*) nor with the *cz* (= *ch*) sounds, but English does not permit these two to occur in sequence – so we insert a vowel in between.

This effect of sound patterns also explains why the Greek name for Hamburg is Amvourgo and the Italian name is Amburgo. Both languages prefer syllables to end in a vowel, and they both lack the sound we write with the letter *h* – Greek also lacks *b*. The Finnish version of the city's name is Hampuri – Finnish originally had no *b* sound either. Perhaps you might like to hazard a guess as to what the Maori version of this city's name might be?

The answer is Hamupeke. The Maori names of other major European cities include Hiniwa (Geneva, which is in the country known in Maori as Huiterangi), Pari (Paris, capital of Parani), Pearini (Berlin, capital of Tiamana), Whieni (Vienna, in Ateria) and Tapurini (Dublin, capital of Airangi).

And where do you suppose Ranana might be? Here's a clue: it is the largest city of the country which bears the Maori name Ingarangi.

MAORI

Maori was the first language to arrive in New Zealand – but when? A historian once said that as good a hypothetical date as any would be 1066. Maori's closest linguistic relative is the language (also called Maori) of the Cook Islands, which lie 2,000 miles to the east across the Pacific – a testament to the seafaring abilities of the early Polynesians (see Section 7.16).

9.6 Mbret

The Albanian word for 'king' is *mbret*. You might think that this has got nothing to do with any word in any language that you have ever come across before, but it would be surprising if you were right. Albanian is, after all, an Indo-European language, distantly related to English – and to most other European languages – although, like Greek and Armenian, it has no very close linguistic relatives. Also, it has been spoken in the Balkans for a very long time indeed – probably at least as long as Greek – and has come into contact in that southern European peninsula with many other languages which it has been influenced by and borrowed words from.

From about 200 BC, the Romans started becoming interested in the Balkans, partly because they were disturbed by acts of piracy carried out in the Adriatic from the western shores of the Balkan peninsula, and they invaded and gradually took control of most of the area. This eventually had interesting linguistic consequences. The Jireček line, named after the Czech historian Konstantin Jireček, divided the Balkan peninsula into a northern half where the Latin language and Roman culture came to achieve dominance, and a southern area where the Greek language and Greek culture remained dominant in spite of Roman military and political control.

In modern geographical terms, the Jireček line ran west to east across Albania, through the area of Skopje in North Macedonia, to Varna on the Black Sea coast of Bulgaria. The archaeological evidence which permitted Jireček to locate the whereabouts of the line included the fact that most of the classical inscriptions that we are aware of in the northern area are written in Latin, while those to the south of the line are mostly in Greek.

The local languages in the zone to the north of the line were gradually replaced by Latin, which survives there to this day in the form of Romanian. But Albanian lived on, perhaps because some of its speakers lived in more mountainous or otherwise inaccessible regions – just as it survived the much later incursions from the north by the South Slavs, the linguistic ancestors of the modern Serbs, Croats, Bosnians, Montenegrins, Bulgarians and Slavo-Macedonians.

Not surprisingly, however, Albanian was still very much influenced by the Latin language, and even though it is not directly historically derived from Latin like French, Portuguese and Romanian are, it now contains large numbers of words which were borrowed from the language of the Romans starting as early as about 100 BC. Some of these early loans have been altered so much in Albanian over the ensuing two millennia that they are difficult to recognise as such, and indeed were not widely recognised as Latin loans by linguistic scientists until the nineteenth century.

For example, the Latin word *amicus*, 'friend', has come down into Modern French as *ami*, into Spanish and Portuguese as *amigo*, into Catalan and Romanian as *amic* and into Italian as *amico*. We, too, have borrowed this word into English in forms such as *amicable*. But speakers of Old Albanian borrowed *amicus* very much earlier than we did, and it has subsequently been radically transformed by sound changes in Albanian, notably the loss of the first syllable. The Modern Albanian word for 'friend' is *mik*. When we have been alerted to what has happened here in terms of sound change, we can see the word's connection to, say, Romanian *amic*, but the link is not immediately obvious.

In the same kind of way, the Modern Albanian word *fqinj* means 'neighbour'. It was originally borrowed from Latin as *vicinus*, and so is related to the Romanian word *vecin* and to Spanish *vecino*, as well as less directly to English *vicinity*.

But what about *mbret*, 'king'? Well, that's easy once you know. *Mbret* is simply the Latin word *imperator*, 'general, emperor' as borrowed into Albanian 2,000 years ago and transformed by several natural processes of sound change in the language over the intervening centuries.

EMPEROR

In the 1200s AD, English borrowed the word *emperor* (from Latin *imperator*) from French. To the Romans, it had originally signified 'senior military commander'. In Modern English, it implies a particularly important kind of monarch. When Queen Victoria was declared 'Empress of India' in 1876, it was a kind of promotion.

10 Grammar

The Hungarian word ő can mean 'he', 'she' or 'it'. So can Estonian *ta* and Turkish *o*. There is no indication in any of these pronouns of what the gender of the person or entity being referred to is, or indeed even whether it is an animate being or not. Similarly, Finnish *hän* also means 'he' and 'she', and in Modern Finnish *se*, 'it', is often also colloquially used for 'he' and 'she' as well.

On the other hand, there are other languages which go further than English in marking natural gender in their pronoun systems. Icelandic not only indicates sex in its third-person singular pronouns, as English does with *he* and *she*, but also in the plural: it has feminine *thær*, 'they', masculine *their* and neuter *thau* for mixed groups.

A smaller number of languages distinguish between male and female human beings in their words for the second-person *you*. In polite Polish discourse, speakers address a man as *pan*, 'you', and a woman as *pani*. In Spanish, speakers address a group of female friends as *vosotras*, 'you (plural)', while a group of male friends would be *vosotros*.

Some languages even have a gender distinction in the first-person plural pronoun. Spanish *nosotras*, 'we (female)', is distinguished from *nosotros*, 'we (male)'. And there are languages outside Europe, including Japanese, where there are different male and female forms for *I/me*, even though in most circumstances it is generally rather clear whether a speaker is male or female.

This is just one of the fascinating socio-grammatical phenomena which are discussed in this section. Grammar is not the boring and scary subject which it was often made to seem by the way in which English was taught to earlier generations in schools.

Languages can differ from one another in their grammatical structures to a remarkable extent, as I have tried to illustrate in earlier discussions and in the pieces that now follow. And, in spite of being the most centrally linguistic and least sociological of all the facets of language, it can often be linked in all sorts of intriguing ways to aspects of particular societies and cultures. It is not a coincidence that the chapter that now follows is the longest in the book.

10.1 The

The word *the* is far and away the most common word in the English language. Every twentieth word or so produced by English speakers and writers is the definite article *the*. It is therefore rather difficult for English speakers to imagine how languages can manage without a definite article. But there are many which do. Latin was one such language; and in modern Europe, most of the Slavic languages do not have a definite article either.

Modern European languages can be divided up into three main types based on how definite articles are treated. First, in the east of the continent, there is a large area where the languages simply have no word corresponding to *the*. The Slavic languages Russian, Ukrainian, Belarusian, Polish, Czech and Slovak come into this category. For example, the Czech for *the boy ate the apple* is *chlapec jedl jablko*, 'boy ate apple'. You can often tell that these languages don't have a definite article by listening to their speakers using English: even if their English is very good, they may leave *the* out where we would expect it.

The neighbouring Baltic languages Lithuanian and Latvian also lack a definite article, and so do the Finnic languages Estonian and Finnish. The Sami (Lappish) languages of northern Scandinavia, too, manage without a word for *the*. So you can travel overland all the way from far northern Scandinavia to the shores of the Black Sea without ever encountering a single definite article.

There is also one other region which lacks a word corresponding to *the*. This lies in the northern part of the former Yugoslavia, where Slovenian, Serbian, Croatian and Bosnian, also Slavic languages, are spoken.

Secondly, there are the languages of southern and Western Europe which, like English, have a definite article which is placed before the noun. This includes the Celtic languages such as Gaelic (e.g. *an úll*, 'the apple'); the West Germanic languages like English, German (*der Apfel*) and Dutch (*de appel*); and the western Romance languages, including Spanish (*la manzana*), French (*la pomme*) and Italian (*la mela*). Hungarian (*az alma*) also comes into this category, as do Maltese (*it-tuffieħa*) and Greek (*to mílo*).

Languages can manage very well without definite articles, but when they do develop them – as Latin did in its transition to Italian and Romanian – articles can end up being placed either before or after the noun. So the third type of language has the distinguishing feature that the article is placed after the noun. Such languages can be found in two different regions. One lies in the part of the Balkans where Albanian, Bulgarian and Romanian are spoken (even though Bulgarian is a Slavic language). The other region with definite articles coming after the noun is Scandinavia, comprising Icelandic, Faroese, Norwegian, Swedish and Danish languages. In Icelandic, *epli* is 'apple' and *eplið* is 'the apple'.

It is a very intriguing fact that the geographical border between the Scandinavian zone, which has 'apple-the', and the major Western European zone, which has 'the-apple', does not run between Germany and Denmark, as you might suppose, but instead passes right through the middle of Denmark. The dialects of eastern Jutland go with their fellow Scandinavians and place the article after the noun, but the whole of western and southern Jutland follow Britain and Germany in placing the definite article first. The Scandinavian word for 'house' is *hus*. So in Norwegian, Swedish and eastern Danish, 'the house' is *huset*, but in a large area of Jutland it is *æ hus*. And likewise, 'the apple' is not *æblet* in western Jutland, as it is in eastern Danish, but *æ æble*.

Finally, in breaking news, reports are coming in from the north suggesting that both Finnish and Estonian, which currently do not have a word for 'the', are in the process of gradually transferring their allegiance from one language type to another by turning their demonstratives – their words for 'this' – into definite articles.

APPLE

In Old English, the word *apple* could refer to any kind of fruit: *finger-apple* meant 'date', and *earth-apple* meant 'cucumber'. Later, in mediaeval English, *apple* was applied to any kind of fruit or nut, except berries. *Apple of paradise* meant 'banana', and the original meaning of *pineapple* was 'pine-cone'.

10.2 Apostrophes

The English word *apostrophe* comes from a Greek term meaning 'turning away': in Modern Greek *apó* means 'from' and *strophí* is 'turn'. As used in English, *apostrophe* refers to the usage of the punctuation mark ' to indicate the omission of a letter from a word.

Often, letters are omitted in writing and replaced with an apostrophe to indicate that a sound has been left out in pronunciation, as in archaic and poetic *o'er* for *over*. But the exact meaning of 'omitted' here needs some thought. In English, omissions are generally optional. We can write both *she's* and *she is*, because both of these represent possible pronunciations. In other languages, this is not always the case – in French, 'the child' is *l'enfant*, with *le enfant* not being a possible spelling or pronunciation. And in Italian *l'amore*, 'love', is the only possibility.

Apostrophes are obviously not particularly important in any language, because we do not use them when we are speaking. It is true that they do play a role in the written language in distinguishing between pairs of English forms like *well* and *we'll*, *wed* and *we'd*, *were* and *we're*. But nothing very serious will happen if you write *Im* instead of *I'm*, *hes* instead of *he's*, *theyre* instead of *they're* or *dont* instead of *don't*. Perhaps someone might confuse *cant* with *can't*, or *ill* with *I'll*, but it's hard to think of a reasonable context where that might happen.

Past-tense verb forms such as *loved* and *moved* used to be pronounced with two syllables: *lov-ed*, *mov-ed*. When speakers began omitting the vowel of the final syllable in their pronunciation, this was then often indicated in writing by using an apostrophe: *lov'd*, *mov'd*. This could be useful for poets wanting to indicate the number of syllables they needed in a particular line of verse. But now that every-body speaking Modern English always pronounces *loved* and *moved* as one syllable, we no longer bother to do that with past-tense forms – although it really does seem better to write 'she ok'd the contract'.

The origin of the possessive apostrophe also lies in the omission of a letter. The plural of *fox* is written *foxes* but the possessive form is written *fox's* – even though the two forms are pronounced exactly the same – indicating that an original letter *e* has been omitted. This use of an apostrophe in the possessive where an *e* had been dropped later spread to instances where no letter had been omitted, as in *John's*, previously *Johns*.

An apostrophe was also commonly used in the plural forms of words bor-rowed from foreign languages, such as *folio's* (with the *e* of *folioes* being omitted), a practice which continues today in greengrocers' spellings like *tomato's* and *potato's*. 'Minding your p's and q's' also seems better with apostrophes.

Some commentators believe it is absolutely vital to use the possessive apostrophe correctly, because people will be confused if we do not distinguish between plural *cats*, singular possessive *cat's* and plural possessive *cats'*. But these rules were not established until the middle of the nineteenth century, and we managed perfectly well without them before that. In any case, when we are speaking, we pronounce all these words exactly the same: I do not ever remember wondering, in all my many decades as a native English speaker, whether someone was actually referring to more than one cat or not.

If we do not need apostrophes in speaking, why do we need them in writing? Can't we just get rid of them? German has made a move in that direction. *Wie geht es?* 'How's it going?' is usually abbreviated to *Wie gehts?* Before the spelling reform of 1996, this was most often written with an apostrophe: *Wie geht's*, but in the new reformed spelling system, the apos-trophe is no longer necessary.

Punctuation generally is a vitally important tool for indicating features of the spoken language, like intonation, which cannot otherwise be indicated in writing. But this is not true of English apostrophes.

CATASTROPHE

In Modern Greek, *katá* means 'down' and *strophí* is 'turn', so our Greek-origin word *catastrophe* originally meant something like 'a turn downwards'. English also has other rather rare Greek-origin words involving *strophí*, such as *epistrophe*, 'repetition' (*epí* = 'on'), *peristrophe*, 'revolution' (*perí* = 'around') and *metastrophe*, 'radical change' (*metá* = 'after').

10.3 He and She

I know from discussions that a number of people had the same experience as I did when I started reading Donna Tartt's 2013 novel *The Goldfinch*: it took me a couple of chapters before I realised that the narrator – the 'I' – was a man, not a woman. I was probably assuming a female narrator because of the sex of the author; perhaps the surprise I experienced was actually something which was intended by the author. If so, then it is interesting to note that it would have been impossible for her to engineer this kind of readership experience if she had been writing in certain other European languages.

If the book had been written in Polish, any reader would have cottoned on to the sex of the narrator from the very beginning, because the first phrase in the book is 'While I was . . . '. In Polish, a female narrator would have had to write 'I was' as *byłam*, versus *byłem* for a male narrator. In Polish, all past-tense verbs differ according to whether the subject of the verb is male or female.

In English, we do mark gender differences grammatically, but not on verbs. We mark them on pronouns – and then only in the third-person singular: *he* and *she*. How else could it possibly be? In fact, it could easily be otherwise. In Finnish, there is no distinction at all between 'he' and 'she' – *hän* means both. The same situation holds in Turkish, where the word for both 'he' and 'she' is *o*, as well as in Hungarian, where it is *ő*.

So how do people understand what a Finnish speaker means? Well, that is a very anglocentric question. French-speaking people would probably like to know how anyone manages to understand what English speakers mean when we use the word *they*. French has two different words for 'they': *ils* for males, *elles* for females. So does Spanish: *ellos* and *ellas*.

Polish has five different polite ways of saying 'you': *pan* is for a single male person; *pani* is for a single female person, *panowie* for two or more males; *panie* for two or more females; and *państwo* for a group of people of both sexes. It all makes the English word *you* seem really rather inadequate.

But there are advantages to speaking a language where gender has a low profile. We can say 'I'm just going out to see a friend' without anyone being any the wiser as to whether the friend is a man or a woman, a girl or a boy. But in many European languages you cannot do that. In Greek, *fílos* can only be a male friend; *fíli* is the feminine. Portuguese has *amigo* and *amiga*. Unsurprisingly, though, Finnish is like English and has only *ystävä* for both sexes.

There are currently linguistic changes going on in different parts of Europe with respect to the marking of gender. In French, *étudiant* tends to suggest a male student, so in most educational institutions today, people are careful to refer in writing to students not as *étudiants* but *étudiant(e)s*, using brackets and overtly covering both genders. In German, there is a relatively new practice of combining male *Studenten*, 'students', with female *Studentinnen* to give *StudentInnen*, with a capital *I*, meaning 'students (of both sexes)'.

In English on the other hand, we seem to be getting rid of even the gender distinctions which we do have. *Manageresses* are now most often *managers*; and *actresses* are now often called *actors*. Polish speakers might find this rather unsatisfactory. They would also certainly want to know, with reference to *The Goldfinch*, how English speakers can possibly tell from grammatical clues what sex a fictional first-person narrator is supposed to be. The answer is, obviously, that we can't.

10.4 They

Sam Smith has expressed the wish to be referred to as *they* rather than *he* or *she*. A number of younger people report that they already operate this pronoun system when requested to do so, and are happy to use it.

This is not without its problems, however. If somebody says *When Sam got home, they were very tired*, how is that going to be interpreted? The first response of some native English speakers might well be to ask 'Who – who were very tired?' This is because in normal everyday English, as spoken by many millions of mother-tongue speakers, *they* is plural, referring to two or more people. The natural reaction to hearing that sentence is therefore to try to identify which group of two or more people *they* refers to.

It is true, of course, that singular *they* does occur rather frequently in everyday English, and has done so for centuries. We use it as a singular when we make statements like *When the last person leaves, they should turn out the lights*. This is sometimes said to represent gender-neutral usage – *person* refers to both males and females. But *they* is only coincidentally gender-neutral here. The crucial thing about *they* in this context is that it is *indefinite*.

Normally, personal pronouns are definite, referring to people or things whose identity is known. In *When Mary got home, she was very tired*, the pronoun *she* refers to a particular – and in this case, named – person. We employ *they* of a singular person only when their identity is unknown. This has nothing to do with sex or gender, but with indefiniteness. When voting was taking place in 2013 to elect the new Pope, commentators proffered statements such as *When the new Pope is elected, they will have to . . . .* Everybody knew that the new pontiff would be male. What we did not know was exactly who it was going to be – which is why he was referred to as *they*.

There are other imaginable approaches to this issue. If we wanted to make it clear that *they* is being used a singular, we could use singular verb forms: *When Sam got home, they was very tired; Whenever Alex plays golf, they wins*. Most English speakers would probably find this difficult to do, however; and it would cause confusion in dialect areas where people normally say *they was* and *they goes* anyway.

English does also have a genuinely gender-neutral third-person singular pronoun, namely *it*, which is neither male nor female. But saying *When Sam got home, it was very tired* is not very felicitous either. The problem is that *it* is normally used for things or animals (though we do refer to pets as *he* and *she*). So, while referring to human beings as *it* really would be gender-neutral, most people would probably find it disagreeably dehumanising.

But whatever pronoun solution English speakers come up with, it will not work for many other European languages. It would be no good using the equivalent of *they* in Spanish because *ellos*, 'they', refers to males and *ellas* to females – and *ellos/ellas* does not have the same history of indefinite usage as English *they*. In many languages, gender also extends to forms associated with second-person 'you' and first-person 'I' and 'we'.

And if you are speaking French and want to say 'I'm happy', you have no choice but to choose one of two forms of the adjective 'happy': *je suis heureux* (masculine) or *je suis heureuse* (feminine) – there is no other possibility. In Polish, you have to choose between male and female verb forms: *przyjechałem* is 'I arrived' for a male speaker, *przyjechałam* for a female; no gender-neutral choice is available.

Some Swedish people now use a new pronoun, *hen*, '(s)he', rather than *hon*, 'she', or *han*, 'he', – we shall see how that works out. But it is not clear how this kind of solution could help French or Polish speakers seeking gender neutrality. And it is also not clear how the issue of nouns such as English *niece*, *nephew*, *aunt* and *uncle* might be handled.

FEMALE

Male and *female* do not have a common origin, even though they look related. *Male* derives from Latin *masculus*, 'male', via French *mâle*, while *female* comes from the very dissimilar Latin *femella*, 'woman', via French *femelle*. Our two modern words are alike because mediaeval speakers changed *femelle* to *female* under the influence of *male*.

10.5 Like

These days we hear the word *like*, meaning 'similar to', quite a lot. In fact, in the speech of many younger people today it seems to occur, like, all the time. But it is a word with an extraordinarily interesting and complex history, and one which is not completely understood.

One fascinating aspect of its story has to do with the fact that the Germanic sister languages of English all also have words which are related to our *like*.

German has *Leiche*; Dutch has *lijk*; the Afrikaans and Frisian words are both *lyk*; the word in Norwegian and Swedish, as well as in Icelandic and Faroese, is *lik*; and the Danish is *lig*. The similarities between all the words in these different languages is clear. And this is not surprising, since they all descend from the same ancient Common Germanic root *liko-*. But the rather remarkable thing about them is that all of these forms, apart from the English word *like*, mean 'corpse, body'.

This old meaning of the word is still around in English to an extent too. The word *lyke* means 'body' in the name of the famous Yorkshire 'Lyke Wake Dirge': 'When thoo frae hence away art passed, ivvery neet an' all, to Whinny-muir thou com'st at last, And Christ receive thy saule.' A *lyke wake* was a night-watch over the body of someone who had just died. *Lyke* is the northern dialect form of the word, with the corresponding southern form being *lych*. (This is the same correspondence that we see as between northern *dyke* and southern *ditch*). The southern form is mainly known from the word *lych-gate*, which refers to a covered churchyard gateway where the first part of funeral services used to be held.

The current meaning of *like*, having to do with similarity and resemblance, can be explained in terms of an original meaning of *liko-* having to do with 'shape' or 'form' – so *like* would originally have meant something like (!) 'having the same form as' or 'having the shape of'.

Like, then, was originally a noun meaning 'form, body' which became an adjective meaning 'similar to'. But from the thirteenth century it also became a preposition, as in *someone like me* and *like what I do*, and then in the sixteenth century it became a conjunction, as in *like I do*.

The ancient form *liko-* also has another descendant in Modern English. This, perhaps surprisingly, is the suffix *-ly* as it occurs in words like *manly* and *quickly*. What happened was that an ancient Germanic form such as *mann-liko*, meaning 'having the form or appearance of a man', came down into mediaeval English as southern *mannlich*, northern *mannlik*, 'manly'; the unstressed suffix *-lich/-lik* then became reduced in pronunciation to *-ly* during the fifteenth century.

From the sixteenth century onwards, we can also see the full form *like* becoming a noun again, meaning 'a similar thing/person' as in *the likes of*.

Surprisingly, the verb *to like* also has the same origin in the ancient Germanic word for 'form, shape, body', although how exactly this particular meaning of the verb developed is not entirely clear. *To like* originally meant 'to please', so *it liketh me* meant 'it is pleasing to me'. In Shakespeare's *The Two Gentlemen of Verona*, we find the line 'the music likes you not', which in Modern English would be 'you don't like the music'. The semantic change might have arisen via a meaning such as 'to be like', which could lead to an interpretation such as 'to be appropriate for'. So perhaps the original meaning of *it likes me* ('it is pleasing to me; I like it') was 'it is suitable for me'.

This is quite a likely solution to the problem. (*Likely* is a particularly interesting item, because the two halves of the word, *like* and *ly*, both have the same origin.) But it's, like, difficult to know.

DIKE

Old English *dic* has become both *dike* and *ditch* in Modern English. Confusingly, a dike can be a place which has been dug out, often in the form of a trench for channelling water, but it can also be a defensive bank formed by piling up the earth that came out of that same trench.

10.6 Logic

Over the years there have been plenty of people who have not hesitated to assert that French is a 'very logical language', the implication being that other languages are less so. But it is actually rather easy to point to aspects of French which do not, on the face of it, seem particularly 'logical' in our usual understanding of this word.

For example, why would 'I am going' be *je vais*, but 'we are going' *nous allons*, and 'we will go' *nous irons*? Is there anything logical about the fact that *la main*, 'the hand' is grammatically feminine but *le doigt*, 'the finger' is masculine – and is there in fact anything logical about grammatical gender anyway? Why, if you put the definite article *le*, 'the', before the noun *homme*, 'man', do you get *l'homme*, while if you put *le* before *hibou*, 'owl', you get *le hibou*, without the contraction?

French spelling is particularly difficult to regard as logical. This has nothing to do with the language itself, of course: spelling systems can be rationalised without the language itself being changed at all – Norwegian had a big spelling reform in 1907. But any supporter of the merits of the French language who wishes to argue that it is logical for the sequence of letters in *eaux*, 'waters', to represent the sound 'o' would be standing on rather tricky ground. English is no better, of course: it was perfectly sensible to spell our word *knight* like that in 1300 when the spelling was an accurate representation of the pronunciation (the *k* was sounded and the *gh* represented an 'h'), but today it makes no sense to use those six letters to stand for three sounds.

Languages which we could point to as being apparently rather more logical than French might well include Finnish. It is instructive to see how Finnish nouns behave grammatically.

For example, the word for 'car' is *auto*. *Autossa* means 'in the car', with the *ssa* ending representing a case known to grammarians as 'inessive', which signifies 'being inside'. Note, then, that *autoissa* means 'in the cars' – the marker of the plural is *i*, and here it is inserted between the noun and the case ending. Because of the regular way Finnish works, if we add the possessive marker *-si* to *auto*, this gives us *autosi*, 'your car'; and we can then easily guess that *autossasi* will mean 'in your car', with the structure of this word being *auto-ssa-si*, 'car-in-your'. The plural form 'in your cars' is *autoissasi* = *auto-i-ssa-si*, 'car-plural-in-your', again regular and transparent and – do we perhaps dare to say – logical?

Similarly, if we are told that *autosta* means 'from the car', and that *-sta* is the elative case ending meaning 'coming out from inside', then we can easily work out that *autoista* means 'from the cars', and we can also quickly figure out what *autostasi* and *autoistasi* mean.

Turkish is another European language which works in a similar way. The Turkish word for 'man' is *adam*. *Men*, the (scarcely logical) plural of English *man*, is *adamlar*. Similarly, the plural of *kitap*, 'book', is *kitaplar*, and the plural of *masa*, 'table' is *masalar*. 'Of the man' is *adamın*, employing the possessive marker *ın*, so *adamların* is transparently 'of the men'. And, if you know that *adama* is 'to the man', then you will be able to correctly predict that *adamlara* means 'to the men'.

The fact is, however, that languages are not based on logic. If they were, logicians would not have had to develop their own logical 'languages'. Human languages have to be systematic and regular to an extent, or small children would not be able to learn them as quickly as they do, but they are not necessarily particularly rational. Languages are not logical systems; they are linguistic systems, with rules and exceptions and irregularities.

BIL

The word *auto*, which means 'car' in French, German and many other languages, is an abbreviation of the original French *automobile* or the German equivalent *Automobil*, literally 'self-moving'. In the Scandinavian languages, a reverse kind of abbreviation is used. In Norwegian, Swedish and Danish, the word for 'car' is *bil*.

10.7 Nothing

If someone thanks you for something in Catalan, the standard response is *de res*, literally 'of nothing'. This may remind some people of Spanish and Portuguese, where the equivalent response would be *de nada*, with *nada* again meaning 'nothing'.

At first sight, the history of *res*, the Catalan word for 'nothing', seems very odd. Catalan, like the other Romance languages, is historically derived from the Late Spoken Latin of the Roman Empire, and Catalan *res* comes from Latin *res* which meant precisely the opposite of 'nothing', namely 'thing'.

But notice that exactly the same thing has also happened in Occitan, the language of southern France, where the word for 'nothing' is also *res*. And in French itself 'nothing' is *rien*, which too derives from Latin *res*, except in this case the word was derived from *rem*, the accusative or object case form of *res* in Latin. The same is true of the Arpitan (Franco-Provencal) language of western Switzerland, eastern France and north-western Italy, where 'nothing' is *ren*.

These are not the only known cases of a word changing its meaning from 'thing' to 'nothing'. In the Cretan variety of Modern Greek, 'nothing' is *prama*. This comes from *pragma*, which meant 'thing' in Ancient Greek and still has the same meaning in the modern language. *Pragma* was derived from the Ancient Greek verb *prattein* 'to do'. In Modern Greek, *pragmatika* means 'really', and this is obviously the origin of our English words *pragmatism* and *pragmatic*.

All of these forms meaning 'nothing' – *res, rien, ren, prama* – can also translate into English as 'anything' in certain grammatical contexts. The sentence 'Didn't you see anything?' in French can be *Tu n'as rien vu?*, and in Catalan *No has vist res?* In Crete, a conversation with someone standing on the shore with a fishing line in their hand might go *Prama? – Prama!* 'Anything? – Nothing!'

The intriguing question is: how did ancient words meaning 'thing' end up coming to mean 'nothing' in some modern languages? English *nothing* comes from Old English *nan*, 'not one', plus *thing*, which does make sense – there is no surprise about *not one thing* meaning 'nothing'. Norwegian *ingenting*, 'nothing', is also literally 'no-thing'. But why did *res* and *pragma* end up meaning 'nothing'?

The explanation is that forms like *rien* were so often used in negative contexts, in sentences of the type *Je ne veux rien*, 'I don't want (a) thing', that they gradually acquired negative meanings themselves: 'I don't want a thing' does mean the same as 'I want nothing'. Experts say that *rien* was so frequently used in combination with the negative word *ne*, 'not', that the negative meaning gradually transferred from the one form to the other, to the extent that the *ne* could be omitted. So while it is now still perfectly possible in modern French to say *Je ne veux rien*, you can also just say *Je veux rien*.

And there are several other cases of this kind of negative-meaning transfer. French *personne* means 'nobody': *Qui est venu? Personne!* translates as 'Who came? Nobody!' And *jamais*, 'never', used to mean 'always', from Latin *iam magis*, 'still more'. The Italian word *mai*, 'never', also comes from Latin *magis*, 'more' – so 'more' has turned into its opposite, 'no more'.

In Classical Latin, the word *res*, which modern *rien, ren* and *res* descend from, could also mean 'affair, matter': the Latin expression *in medias res*, sometimes used by people writing in English, means 'into the middle of things' and our word *republic* comes from the Latin *res publica*, 'public affair'. Latin *res* was related to the Sanskrit word *rayi*, 'property, goods'; these two words both came from the ancient Indo-European root *rehis*, signifying 'wealth'.

There is probably no moral to be drawn from this, but it is fascinating to observe that a word which 6,000 years ago meant 'wealth' now means 'nothing'.

PERSON

Person comes from the Latin word *persona*, which referred to a character in a drama and had originally meant 'mask' – Roman actors typically wore masks. It is possible that *persona* came from Latin *per-sonare*, 'to sound through', since the mask was something which the actors had to speak through.

10.8 Not

If you have learnt even a little bit of French, you will probably know that the word *pas* in that language means 'not'. *Pas mal!* is 'not bad'. *Pas encore* means 'not yet'. *Pas moi!* is the equivalent of 'not me!' *Pas devant les enfants*, 'not in front of the children', even has its own entry in the *Oxford English Dictionary*.

You may also know that *pas* in French has another totally different meaning: 'step', corresponding to the English word *pace*. A *faux pas* is literally a 'false step'. In ballet, a *pas de deux* is a dance for two people, and *pas de chat*, 'a cat's step', is a jumping step where each foot is alternately raised up to the knee of the opposite leg. The Spanish equivalent of French *pas* is *paso*, as in *paso doble*, literally 'double step'. *Pas*, *paso* and *pace* all descend from the Latin word *passum*, 'step'.

What is intriguing about the two senses of *pas* as 'not' and 'step' in French, however, is that they were originally one and the same word. On the face of it, this is something of a surprise. How could a word meaning 'step' end up meaning 'not'? – because that is what really did happen.

In Latin, the word for 'not' was *non*, and it was placed before the verb. *Vado* was a verb form meaning 'I go, I am going', so *non vado* signified 'I'm not going'. As time went by, however, it seems that people were increasingly inclined to say, instead or as well, *non vado passum*, meaning 'I'm not going (a) step'. This may initially have been for emphasis, and/or because the word *non* was increasingly being reduced in pronunciation, so that adding *passum* after the verb made it clearer what was being said.

Similarly, *non vedo*, 'I don't see' was increasingly expressed as *non vedo punctum*, 'I don't see (a single) point'; *non comedo*, 'I'm not eating' became *non comedo micam*, 'I'm not eating (a) crumb'; and *non bibo*, 'I'm not drinking' was expanded to *no bibo gutta*, 'I'm not drinking (a) drop'. We do the same kind of thing in English sometimes: *I'm not budging an inch; I'm not eating a thing; I'm not saying a word*.

As Latin gradually morphed into French, *passum* was reduced to *pas*, *punctum* became *point*, *micam* turned into *mie* and *gutta* changed to *goutte*. At the same time, *non* was gradually reduced to *ne*; so *non vado passum* gradually came to be expressed as *je ne vais pas*, and *no bibo gutta* became *je ne bois goutte*. Reinforcing the negativity of *non/ne* in this way eventually became the norm in French.

(One other development that occurred, as can be seen here, was that it became necessary in French to insert pronouns like *je* 'I', because Latin personal endings like *-o* 'first-person singular', as in *vad-o*, had been lost.)

Then, slowly, words such as *point* and *mie*, which had originally been employed to reinforce a negative statement, started acquiring negative meanings themselves, and their original more concrete meanings were gradually lost; so *mie*, 'crumb', ended up being extended as a marker of negation to verbs which had nothing to do with eating.

Similarly, *pas* lost all connection with walking and eventually became the most popular of all these negators, replacing most of the others. People started saying not only *je ne vais pas*, 'I'm not going', but also *je ne bois pas*, 'I'm not drinking' and *je ne mange pas*, 'I'm not eating'. In Modern French, this process has gone so far that *pas* has gradually taken over the main job of negating verbs, and the original negator *non*, now *ne*, is often simply omitted. You can say *je vais pas*, 'I'm not going', and *je bois pas*, 'I'm not drinking'; and *pas* can now operate entirely on its own – as in *pas moi*, 'not me'!

INITIAL

The word *initial* 'first' did not start being used in English until the sixteenth century; and the sense 'first letter of a word or name' dates no further back than the seventeenth century. It comes from Latin *initium* 'beginning', from *inire*, 'to go in', which we can also see in English words like *initiate*.

10.9 None

There are certain people in the English-speaking world who would like to prescribe how other people should speak. Many of these pedants think it is 'wrong' to say *None of them are very interesting*, and want us to use the singular verb *is* instead of the plural verb *are: None of them is very interesting*.

This is rather unfortunate, because nearly all native English speakers very frequently use *none* as a plural. It is entirely natural for mother-tongue speakers of English to respond to a question such as *Are any of them coming?* by replying *No, none of them are* – and this is a perfectly grammatical usage.

But the arguments which the prescriptivists use to back up their feeling that this is 'bad grammar' are interesting in themselves. Some people who think like this reckon, for example, that *none* should always be singular, not plural, because '*none* is short for *not one*'.

As it happens, none of them are right about that! In the earliest of all early Old English texts, our modern word *none* appears as *nan*. It was a word that was common to all the ancient Germanic languages, appearing in Old Frisian as *nān*, Old Icelandic as *neinn*, Old Saxon as *nēn* and Old High German as *nein*.

It is true that those forms themselves did come from an even more ancient Proto-Germanic form *ne ainaz*, where *ne* was a negative marker and *ainaz* was the numeral 'one'. But that early language was spoken in southern Scandinavia about 2,500 years ago, so it would not be easy to construct a persuasive argument about the correctness of different Modern English usages on the basis of what Proto-Germanic speakers said.

Another argument which prescriptivists have employed in favour of their argument that *none* should always be singular is based on an ingenious kind of pseudo-arithmetical reasoning. It goes like this: *none* refers to zero; zero is less than one; *none* therefore cannot refer to more than one; so *none* cannot possibly be plural, and so it must be singular.

But the issue here is not a matter of mathematics but of grammar. Everybody will agree that sometimes *none* has to be singular, as in *none of this beer is any good*, or *none of that bread was very fresh*. No one would ever say *none of this cheese are any good*. So what we can see at work here, then, is a rule of English grammar which all of us use automatically, without thinking about it: *beer*, *bread* and *cheese* in these sentences are singular, and so the negative word *none* agrees with them in being singular too. On the other hand, in cases where *none* is negating something which is plural, then in everyday English grammar it will also be plural regardless of any spurious mathematical arguments: *none of those cheeses are any good*.

A number of the other languages in the Germanic family agree with English about this. Corresponding to English *None of them are interesting*, many Dutch speakers would say *Geen van hen zijn interessant*, where *geen* is 'none' and *zijn* is plural 'are'. In the Norwegian sentence *Ingen av dem er veldig snille*, 'None of them are very nice', *ingen* means 'none' and, while *er* could translate as either 'is' or 'are', we can still tell that *ingen* is not being treated as a singular because the adjective *snille*, 'nice', has the *-e* ending which is a sign of the plural.

The people who compiled the *Oxford English Dictionary* understand all this. The *OED* says 'it is sometimes held that *none* can only take a singular verb, never a plural verb: *none of them is coming tonight* rather than *none of them are coming tonight*. There is little justification, historical or grammatical, for this view. *None* has been used for around a thousand years with both a singular and a plural verb.'

TO SCRIBE

We have a number of fairly frequently used verbs in English like *prescribe*, *circumscribe*, *ascribe*, *inscribe*, *describe*, *proscribe*, *subscribe* and *transcribe*, which all come from Latin *scrībere*, 'to write', with an added prefix. *Circumscribe* literally means 'write around'. Interestingly, though, the verb *to scribe* itself is not very often used in Modern English.

10.10 Causatives

Our ancestral Anglo-Saxon language performed many grammatical operations by alternations between the vowels of related words. In Modern English we do this less, but we have some traces such as *foot-feet, take-took, sing-sang-sung*. Also, if you *fell* a tree, it *falls*; if you *raise* something, it *rises*. Obviously *fall* and *fell, rise* and *raise*, are related words.

Verbs such as *fell* and *raise* are called causatives: *to fell* means 'cause to fall', *to raise* means 'cause to rise'. Old English had many pairs like this, but Modern English has only a few causatives left. One example is *sit* and *set*: if you *set* a child in a chair, you cause it to sit. Another pair is *lie* and *lay*: *to lay* means 'cause to lie down'. But we have lost the word *sench*, which meant 'cause to sink' – today, if you want to scupper a boat, you don't *sench* it, you just sink it. (German still has *sinken* and *senken*.) Similarly, *to stench* meant 'cause to stink' – John Donne wrote: 'after a horse that devours the grass, sheep will feed; but after a goose that stenches the grass, they will not'. The original meaning of *drench* was 'cause to drink'; as recently as the nineteenth century, one could drench a thirsty horse. And *bait* originally meant 'cause to bite'.

In contemporary English, even the causatives we do have are gradually going the way of *sench* and being lost. The distinction between *lay* and *lie* is disappearing in many forms of English. This process is helped along by the fact that *lay* is not just the present tense of the verb *to lay* but also the past tense of *lie*. Many of us these days tell the dog to lay down, and then perhaps go and have a nice 'lay-down' (rather than a lie-down) ourselves. It is rather likely that in a couple of hundred years' time the verb *to lie*, in the sense of being in a horizontal resting position, will have disappeared totally in favour of *lay*, just as *sench* has been replaced by *sink*.

German has retained this way of forming causatives through vowel alternations to a greater extent than English. German has *fahren*, 'to travel', and the causative *führen* 'to lead'; *(auf)wachen*, 'to awaken', *wecken*, 'to wake somebody up'; *schwimmen*, 'to swim', *schwemmen*, 'to be washed (e.g. ashore)'. Scandinavian languages also have some causatives which we do not: Norwegian *springe*, 'to jump' and the causative *sprenge*, 'to blow up'; *gråte*, 'to cry', *grøte*, 'to make (someone) cry'; Swedish *sova*, 'to sleep', *söva*, 'to send to sleep'.

Many of the world's languages have much more fully developed systems of grammatical causatives than the Germanic languages. Amongst European languages, Hungarian makes verbs into causatives not by changing their vowels but by inserting elements such as *-at-* or *-tat-*: *olvasnak* means 'they read' while *olvastatnak* is 'they make (somebody) read'; *mosok* is 'I wash' while *mosatok* means 'I get (somebody) to wash'. In Finnish *pesen* means 'I wash' and *pesetän* 'I get [something] washed'; *syön* means 'I eat', *syötän* 'I feed'.

We see the same phenomenon in Lithuanian: *degti*, 'to be burning', *deginti*, 'to burn something'; *sprogti*, 'to explode', *sprogdinti*, 'to make something explode'. Basque employs the causative suffix *-erazi*: 'to eat' is *jan* while 'to feed' is *janerazi*.

Turkish provides another good example of a European language with a fully developed system of grammatical causatives, which it forms by inserting *-dur-* or *-dür-* into a verb: *gülmek*, 'to laugh', *güldürmek*, 'to make someone laugh'; *durmak*, 'to stop' as in 'the car stopped', *durdurmak*, 'to cause to stop', as in 'the driver stopped the car'.

Some English speakers are fond of saying what a wonderful language English is. The fact is that all languages are wonderful, but I can't help thinking that our lack of a fully developed causative verb system means that English is missing out on something!

LAY OR LIE?

Using *lay* instead of *lie* is regarded by some as a 'mistake'. But it has been in common usage for many centuries. In the late 1500s, Francis Bacon wrote: 'nature will lay buried a great time and yet revive'. And no less a poet than Lord Byron wrote: 'thou dashest him again to earth: there let him lay'.

10.11 Suppletion

The most usual way to make past-tense verbs in English is to add *-ed* to the basic form of the verb: *want – wanted, love – loved; play – played*. So why is the past tense of *go* not *goed* but *went*? Even with irregular verbs which do not add *-ed*, like *sing – sang, run – ran, leave – left*, you can still see a clear link between the present-tense and the past-tense forms. But *go* and *went* do not seem to be even remotely connected.

This is a nice illustration of how languages are not necessarily entirely logical systems. Languages have to have large amounts of regularity or infants would not be able to learn them. But they do not have to be totally regular – they can tolerate a certain amount of irregularity, and most of them do.

It is not always possible to explain why a particular word behaves in a non-systematic way, but in the case of *go* we understand the process that produced this situation: the modern verb *go* was originally two separate words. *Went* used to be the past tense of *wend*, and only came to function as the past tense of *go* from about 1500 onwards. To compensate for this, *wend* then had to acquire the new past-tense form *wended*, as in 'he wended his way home'.

We can see the same kind of irregularity in the case of the adjective *good*. If we say *nice – nicer – nicest*, why don't we say *good – gooder – goodest*? The same question arises for all the Germanic languages: Norwegian has *god* – *bedre* – *best*, in Dutch it is *goed* – *beter* – *best*, and in German *gut* – *besser* – *best*; so this irregular pattern must have been present in our common parent Germanic language. It is obvious that we are again dealing with two originally different words here, one which gave us modern *good* and another which gave us *better* and *best*, but the peculiarity of the pattern is so ancient that we do not know what those words were.

In the case of the adjective *bad*, we know a bit more about the process (though we do not actually know where the word *bad* itself came from – it appears to be peculiar to English). Mediaeval English speakers said *bad* – *badder* – *baddest*, but gradually speakers started to use *worse* – *worst* instead, which was actually from an old Germanic root: in Danish *worst* is *værst*.

When unrelated forms are used for different versions of a single word like this, linguistic scientists call it 'suppletion'. You can see that the same process is currently beginning to happen with the noun *person*. We say *one person* but, while it is possible to say *two persons*, the normal plural of *person* is *people*, so we usually say *two people*. If you hear somebody trying to book a table in a restaurant for 'four persons', you can be almost certain that English is not their native language.

The most extreme form of suppletion in English is provided by the verb *to be*. This has numerous different forms, many of which look and sound nothing like one another: *be*, *been*, *being*; *is*; *are*; *was*, *were*. In older forms of English there was also *art* and *wast*.

Go and *went* came from two different original verbs about 500 years ago, but the different forms of English *be* descended from three or more different original word-forms in the ancient Indo-European language – and more like 5,000 years ago than 500. English *been*, German *bin* and Dutch *ben*, 'am', come from an Indo-European verb which meant 'to grow'. English *was*, German *(ge)wesen* and Dutch *(ge)weest*, 'been' come from an ancient root meaning 'to live'. We can see, too, that English *is*, German *ist* and Latin *est* have descended from a common root. And it is not a coincidence that English *am* corresponds to *jam* in Albanian and *eimai* in Greek.

COINCIDENCE

Originally, *coincidence* simply referred to a situation where two events co-incided – happened at the same time. But the most common modern meaning is probably 'a notable concurrence of events having no apparent causal connection'. This is relatively recent, though: until the 1800s, people seeking to convey the modern sense typically wrote of 'unexpected', 'strange' or 'singular coincidences'.

10.12 Dual

The grammatical distinction between singular and plural is straightforward enough: singular applies to one entity, and plural to more than one. But looking at different European languages shows us that things can be a bit more complex than that.

With English nouns, we generally show the difference between singular and plural through the absence versus the presence of the plural suffix -s: *one book, ten books*. With pronouns it is different: we have singular forms like *I, me, he, him, she* and *her*, versus very different plural forms like *we, us* and *they*.

But then we need to think about the word *both*: it is plural, in that it means 'more than one'; but it represents a particular kind of more-than-one, referring specifically to two, and only two. If you're enquiring about a family of five people, you can't say 'How are you both?' And you cannot ask a couple 'How are you all?' In English grammar, there is a distinction between *both* and *all* such that *all* means 'more than two'.

The word *both* is an example of the grammatical category which linguists refer to as 'dual'. English has several words which express dual rather than plural number. Just as dual *both* corresponds to plural *all*, so the word *either* is the dual equivalent of the plural form *any*, and the word *neither* is the dual form corresponding to plural *none*. If you were asked which one of two undesirable-looking apples you wanted, you would not reply 'I don't want any of them' − you would have to say 'I don't want either of them'. And you could not answer 'none of them' to that question − you would need to say 'neither of them'.

Some languages in Europe take the category of dual a good deal further than this and have a much more fully developed system than English, extending it to articles, pronouns and verb forms. In the South Slavic language Slovenian, the pronouns *tebe, vaju* and *vas* all mean 'you'; but *tebe* is singular, *vaju* is dual and *vas* refers to three or more people. The Slovenian verb forms *si, ste* and *sta* all translate as English 'you are', but they mean respectively 'you (singular) are', 'you two are' and 'you (plural = three or more) are'.

The dual number also plays a role in the Sami languages of northern Norway, Sweden and Finland and adjacent areas of Russia. In the Pite Sami language of northern Sweden, *dåj* means 'you (dual)' and *dij* 'you (plural)', while *såj* is 'they (dual)' and *sij* is 'they (plural)'. Pite Sami also has dual verb forms such as *viesson*, 'we two lived' and *viesojden*, 'you two lived', alongside plural verbs such as *viessop*, 'we lived' and *viessojde*, 'you lived' referring to any number of people above two. If you want to say 'thank you' to two people in Pite Sami, you have to say *Gijtov adnen*. To thank three or more people, one has to say *Gijtov ednet*.

It is an interesting fact that nearly all European languages used to have a fully fledged system of dual number but have now lost it. Ancient Greek had it, but

Modern Greek doesn't. Old English had the dual pronouns *wit*, 'we (dual)' and *git*, 'you (dual)', as opposed to *we*, 'we (plural)' and *ge* (later *ye*), 'you (plural)'. In Modern English we have abandoned this. Polish lost the dual number only in the last few hundred years. Maltese still has traces of the dual: *jum* means 'day (singular)', *jumejn* is 'days (dual)' and *ijiem* is 'days (plural)'.

Maltese has about 300,000 speakers; Pite Sami has no more than 50 speakers. Looking at languages around the world, it seems to be true that the bigger a language gets in terms of numbers of native speakers, the less likely it is to have dual verbs and pronouns.

It would be nice to say we understand why this is the case, but the truth is we do not.

DUEL AND DUAL

Duel and *dual* look like they are related words: a duel is a fight between two people; dual means 'pertaining to two'. But they do not actually come from a common source. *Duel* is from Archaic Latin *duellum*, 'war', which became *bellum* in Classical Latin. *Dual* comes from Latin *dualis*, 'containing two', which is derived from Latin *duo*, the number two.

10.13 Word Order

If you have grown up speaking English, it is very easy to suppose that English is normal, and that the way we do things in our language is the only way these things can be done. The order of words in English sentences would be a case in point.

In a sentence like *The cat scratched the dog*, it is obvious to us that it was the cat that was doing the scratching and the dog that was being scratched. It is hard for us to conceive of there being any other possible interpretation. But in fact there are languages in the world, such as the Hixkaryana language of northern Brazil, where putting *the cat* first in the sentence and *the dog* last would mean that the cat was the one that was being scratched and the dog the one that scratched it.

There are no languages like this in Europe, but languages on our continent do still show considerable differences in the way words are ordered in sentences. The two immediate neighbours which the English language shares this island with, Welsh and Scottish Gaelic, illustrate this very nicely.

English is a subject–verb–object language: we put the subject *(cat)* first in a sentence, then the verb *(scratched)*, and then the object *(dog)*. Welsh and Gaelic do it differently. In these Celtic languages, the verb comes at the beginning of the sentence: the typical order of elements in a sentence is verb–subject–object. In the Welsh sentence *Crafodd y gath y ci*, the verb *crafodd* means 'scratched'; *y gath* means 'the cat' and *y ci* means 'the dog', so the literal translation is 'Scratched the cat the dog'. This same word order is also found in Scottish Gaelic: *Ghluais an cat am ball* translates literally as 'Moved the cat the ball', corresponding to English *The cat moved the ball*. In the other Celtic languages, too – Manx, Cornish, Breton and Irish Gaelic – the verb comes first.

There are also many languages in the world in which it is usual for the verb to come, not first or second as in Welsh or English, but at the end: 'The cat the dog scratched' with the order subject–object–verb. European verb-last languages of this type include Turkish and Azerbaijani. In Turkish, the normal way of saying *Children like chocolate* is *Cocuklar cikolata sever*, 'children chocolate like'. In the South Sami language of north central Norway and Sweden, verb-final word order is also the norm: *Dah maanah utnieh* is literally 'they children have'.

Elsewhere, there are also languages where the normal word order is verb–object–subject, 'scratched the dog the cat'; Malagasy, the main language of Madagascar, is like this. There are no such languages in Europe, but some European languages do have a relatively free ordering of words in sentences. In Greek, *I gáta gratzoúnise to skylí*, 'The cat scratched the dog', could just as well be *Gratzoúnise i gáta to skylí*, or *Gratzoúnise to skylí i gáta*.

Germanic languages like German, Dutch, Norwegian, Swedish and Danish basically work like English, but they additionally have a 'verb-second rule' which means that the verb has to be the second main element of the sentence; so even if the first component in the sentence is not the subject, the verb still comes second. In Danish, *I maj kørte vi til kysten* is literally 'In May drove we to the coast', where English would have *In May we drove to the coast*. But English used to have this same rule, and even in the modern language we can still see traces of it, as in expressions such as *No sooner had he said that than it happened*, *Such was the situation that we couldn't stay*, *Then up the hill came the boy they were waiting for*, and *Especially attractive was her auburn hair*.

AUBURN

The Latin word *albus* meant 'white'. Our word *album* is a different form of the same word, which originally meant 'white or blank tablet'. *Alburnus* meant 'whitish', and in French it became *auborne*, meaning 'flaxen'. This was then borrowed into English as *abroun*, where the similarity with *brown* influenced the meaning, with the result that a word which originally meant 'off-white' now signifies 'reddish brown'.

10.14 *Je t'aime*

When young people were hitchhiking around Europe in the 1960s, one of the linguistic questions we used to ask was how to say 'I love you' in the different languages we encountered – you never knew when you might be lucky enough to be in a position where you might want to utter those words.

My friends and I had studied German and French at school, so we knew *Ich liebe dich* and *Je t'aime*. That in itself was linguistically rather interesting: in German you put *dich*, the word for 'you', after the verb *liebe*, 'love', as in English; but in French you did it the other way round and placed *te*, 'you', before *aime*, 'love'.

We discovered there were other languages where, like in French, you had to use what was to us a strange word order and say 'I you love', as in the Portuguese version *eu te amo*. Other Romance languages also put the object 'you' before the verb 'love' but dropped the subject pronoun 'I': in Spanish you can say *te amo* or *te quiero*, 'you I-love'; in Catalan it might be *t'estimo*, and Italian speakers say *ti amo*.

We didn't enquire about Albanian, because in those days there was no chance at all of getting into that country, and we had not been clever enough to find out that Albanian was also spoken in a large area of Yugoslavia (now Kosovo), as well as in smaller areas of Greece and Italy, which we actually could travel to. If we had taken the trouble, we would have found out that Albanian speakers use the same word order as Italian and Spanish speakers: *të dua* or *të dashuroj*, with the *të*, 'you', coming before the verb 'I-love'.

In Greek, too, the pronoun 'you' comes first: *s'agapó*, in which a contraction of *se* 'you' comes before the first-person verb *agapó*. And in other parts of the Balkans, the Slavic language Macedonian – which borders geographically on Greek- and Albanian-speaking areas – also places the verb after the pronoun *te*, 'you': *te sakam*, as does Turkish: *seni seviyorum*, where *seni* is 'you'.

There is, then, a general tendency for the languages of the whole of southern Europe, stretching from Portugal to Turkey, to favour the '(I) you love' word order.

On the other hand, there is a large area of north-western Europe, stretching from Iceland to Estonia and from Ireland to the former Yugoslavia, which goes with the 'I love you' order found in English and German. Norwegian has *eg elskar deg*, and Danish *jeg elsker dig*. In Welsh, we find *dwi'n caru ti*, where *caru* means 'love' and *ti* 'you'. The Slavic languages in this area leave out the 'I' because it is already marked on the verb (like in Spanish), so Russian has *ljublju tebja*, Polish *kocham cię*, Czech *miluji tě*, Slovenian *ljubim te* and Bosnian/Croatian/Montenegrin/Serbian *volim te*. Interestingly, Bulgarian, which is closely related to Macedonian, also tends to go with the north-western word order, putting the object pronoun after the verb: *obicham te*, 'I-love you'.

Of course the picture is much more complex than I have just painted it: in some Greek dialects, for instance, speakers say *agapó se* rather than *s'agapó*. And there are all sorts of grammatical complications which could be mentioned. But these facts make us realise that different languages have different grammatical structures and can perform the same grammatical operations in different ways. There is no reason why, in a sentence such as 'I love you', the words *love* and *you* should appear in one particular order, and it is therefore no surprise that different languages do it differently.

But it is an interesting fact that, in Europe, the differences are not distributed randomly: there is a rather clear geographical split between north-western Europe and the rest of the continent when it comes to word order.

And – a sad footnote – I don't think any of us ever did get to say *volim te*, or even *ti amo*, in earnest.

THEE

The widespread occurrence of *te* and *ti*, 'you', in languages as different as Welsh, Italian, Bulgarian and Albanian testifies to the fact that most European languages have descended from a common ancestor, Indo-European. English used to fit into this pattern too: as Elizabeth Barrett Browning famously asked, 'How do I love thee?'

10.15 Unseethroughableness

A German word made it into our news some while ago. The word was *Bundespräsidentenstichwahlwiederholungsverschiebung*. It was deemed to be newsworthy because of its extreme length, fifty-one letters. But the word only looks so amazingly long to English speakers because in our language we have adopted the practice of separating out the different components of our compound words when we write them. In German, as in many other languages, all the different elements of compounds are joined together to form a single written word.

This particular German example, which relates to an election of the Austrian president, can easily be rendered into English as 'federal presidential election-rerun postponement', a phrase which is not difficult to analyse or understand. The only difference between the Austrian word and the English-language version is that we place gaps or hyphens between the component parts so that it appears as five words instead of one.

We do not always agree in English about where and how to do this separation of words: I have just written 'English-language', but I could just as well have omitted the hyphen. In German, on the other hand, the equivalent word would have to be *englischsprachig*. Similarly, in Swedish it would be *engelskspråklig*, and in Polish *angielskojęzyczny*.

But there is another more serious point to be made here about compound words in German and other languages. I was once briefly ill with a condition called hyponatraemia. English friends enquired anxiously about what this rather scary-sounding term meant. Greek friends, on the other hand, understood immediately that it simply meant there was not enough sodium in my blood stream. In Greek, *aema* means 'blood', *natrio* is 'sodium' and *hypo* means 'under', so for them the meaning was totally transparent. The same would have been be true for speakers of Icelandic, where the condition is called *blóðnatríumlækkun*, literally 'blood-sodium-lowness'. The meaning of the English word is opaque, while the Greek and Icelandic words are completely transparent.

Ironically, the German word for opacity, *Undurchsichtigkeit*, is completely transparent to German speakers. The different elements of *un-durch-sicht-ig-keit* correspond to English 'un-through-sight-y-hood', so German speakers can immediately tell that it means 'unseethroughableness'. Our word *opacity*, on the other hand, really is opaque: English-speaking children hearing word for the first time cannot work out from its structure what it means, while a German child can do so easily with their version.

This aspect of English has been called 'the lexical bar'. Anglophone children are at a disadvantage because of the way English has expanded its vocabulary over the last few centuries by borrowing elements from Greek and Latin, rather than through creating compound words from our own resources so they are easy to understand and learn.

We can see how English compares with other languages in this respect by looking at a few more examples. The English word *omnivorous* corresponds to Norwegian *altetende*, 'all-eating'. Compare the opaque English term *ambidextrous* with the transparent German *beidhändig*, 'both-handed'. And we have the word *incoherent* while Dutch version is *onsamenhangend*, 'un-together-hanging'.

This problem of opacity and the lexical bar could have been avoided if we had followed the example of our European neighbours. Unlike their continental European counterparts, the English-speaking men who carried out the important work of expanding our vocabulary in the 1600s and 1700s, introducing new scientific, philosophical and cultural terms to the language, looked to Latin and Greek for help because they thought their own vernacular language was inadequate and inferior. They were wrong about that, which is a real pity.

It has been argued that this strategy of borrowing words from the prestigious languages of antiquity has kept important areas of English vocabulary out of the reach of large sectors of our population, and has led to the notion – very well known in the English-speaking world – of the difficult and feared elitist category of 'long words'. But, as the fifty-one-letter Austrian word shows, it is not the length of words which is the problem; it is their unseethroughableness.

10.16 *Igen*

On the train the other day, I was wondering why the people across the aisle from me kept saying 'again', until I realised that they were Hungarian and that they were in fact saying *igen*, the Hungarian word for 'yes'. To English speakers, it might seem rather surprising that a word as common as 'yes' should consist of more than one syllable: the vast majority of European languages use a single-syllable word to express the affirmative, such as German *ja*, Spanish *si*, Romanian *da* and Polish *tak*. But Hungarian, it turns out, is not alone in this: in both Czech and Slovak the word for 'yes' is *ano*, and in Turkish it is *evet*.

It is still generally true, however, that the words which are used most often in a language tend also to be amongst the shortest. The ten most frequent words in spoken English are *a, and, are, for, in, is, of, the, to, you*, all just one syllable in length. Moreover, these words are routinely reduced to an even shorter form in normal everyday speech: *is* is very often just *'s*, as in 'that's right'; the *f* of *of* is very often absent, as in 'a nice cuppa tea'; and *and* commonly gets shortened to a simple *n*, as in 'bread 'n' butter'.

If you think about it, this all makes sense. It is partly a matter of efficiency. If the word for *the* was five syllables long, all of us would take much longer to say or write anything than we do now – I have already used the word nine times in this piece. In addition, the more frequent a word is, the more predictable it is to listeners, and the fewer the clues they therefore need to recognise what the word is. Furthermore, all of these short lexical items as cited above are grammatical words which have very important jobs to do in the language but not much meaning as such: if someone asked you what 'the' means, you might not find it very easy to come up with an answer, even though you use it scores of times a day.

Many words of this type can be omitted in forms of written English where brevity is required, such as in newspaper headlines or pay-per-word telegrams or tweets. And there are languages around the world which lack independent words corresponding to some of these words altogether: *the* is absent from Chinese; *are* does not occur in Russian; and *yes* is not found in Gaelic.

The single-syllable English conjunction *but*, a typical grammatical word, predictably corresponds to equally short words in most other European languages: French *mais*, Dutch *maar*, Danish *men*, Italian *ma*. But some languages stand out as having two-syllable words in this function: German *aber*, Spanish *pero*.

The word for *and* similarly consists of only one syllable in nearly all European languages, as with German *und*, Norwegian *og* and Dutch *en*. In fact, in a number of European languages the word for 'and' consists of just a single vowel: *a, e, i* and *u* mean 'and' in respectively Czech, Portuguese, Catalan and Maltese. Gaelic, on the other hand, expresses 'and' by means of the surprisingly two-syllable word *agus*; in Scottish Gaelic, 'tea, sugar and milk' is *tì agus siùcar agus bainne*, which might seem to be a bit of a mouthful. But just as English *and* is frequently shortened to *'n'*, so Gaelic *agus* is very often shortened to *is* or *'s*. Similarly, Basque *eta*, 'and', very often occurs in the one-syllable form *ta*.

Interestingly, there is almost total pan-European agreement that the word for 'no' should have only one syllable: if we look around the continent, we find *ei, ez, le, ne, nee, nein, nej, nie, non, no, nu* . . . The only European language which refuses to conform to this pattern is Greek, which rather gloriously has a two-syllable word for 'no': *ochi*.

CUPPA

Cup of tea is normally pronounced 'cuppa tea' – which has led to *cuppa* being used as an abbreviated version of the phrase. *Cuppa* in the sense of 'a cup of tea' first appeared in print in the 1920s, and is now recognised as a word in its own right by the *Oxford English Dictionary*.

10.17 Thrice

In George Borrow's 1843 book *The Bible in Spain*, he reports one of his interlocutors, a servant, as saying to him: 'Though I have been turned out of so many families, I was never turned out of that one; and though I left it thrice, it was of my own free will.' Most readers of this column will be familiar with the word *thrice* – it occurs in the King James Bible: 'Before the cock crow twice, thou shalt deny me thrice.'

At earlier periods of history, all English speakers would have used this word quite naturally in their normal everyday speech. Nowadays, on the other hand, it is safe to say that most of us never use it. As early as 200 years ago, *thrice* had already become somewhat archaic. The most recent citation of the word in the *Oxford English Dictionary* comes from as long ago as 1859, from the decidedly uncolloquial verse of Alfred Lord Tennyson, whose *Idylls of the King* contains the line ' . . . with some surprise and thrice as much disdain'. George Borrow, too, wrote in a markedly archaic style.

What we would say in Modern English instead of *thrice*, of course, is *three times*. The change from *thrice* to *three times* appears to be part of a pattern. The forms *whence* and *thence* have also more or less disappeared from the language and been replaced by *from where* and *from there*. We no longer ask 'Whence have you come?' but 'Where have you come from?' Similarly, *whither, hither* and *thither* have been replaced by *to where, to here* and *to there*. 'Whither walkest thou?' is now expressed as 'Where are you walking to?'

Linguistic analysts would say that what is happening here is that *synthetic* structures are being replaced by *analytic* structures. To get an angle on what this means, we can consider the fact that the word *seldom* and the two-word phrase *not often* mean more or less exactly the same thing. 'I seldom go' and 'I don't often go' are no different from one another in terms of meaning in any significant way. In *seldom*, the negative element of the meaning and the frequency element are synthesised into one single word, while in the phrase *not often*, the two elements of meaning have been analysed out into two separate words which express these elements individually. The same thing is true of, for example, *neither* and *not either*, as with 'I like neither of them' and 'I do not like either of them'. Again, *not either* separates out the two different elements of meaning which are combined together in the single form *neither*.

For many speakers of Modern English, the analytical two-word forms feel more natural, and certainly less formal, than the synthetic equivalents. If I am right, *seldom* is now employed less often – or more seldom! – than *not often*. And most people are probably more likely to say 'I don't like either of them' than 'I like neither of them'. This is part of a very long-term trend in the evolution of the English language in which more analytical structures are winning out over synthetic ones.

Today we can see how this process is continuing by comparing the way younger people speak with that of older people. For example, plenty of younger people now seem to be quite happy to say *two times* rather than *twice*. To older people this can sound rather childish, but doubtless our own usage of *three times* would have sounded childish to older speakers in the eighteenth century when *thrice* was beginning to fall out of use. And possessive pronouns such as *mine* and *yours* and *theirs* also appear to be under threat today from potential analytical replacements: younger people these days are increasingly saying, not 'That's mine!', but 'That's my one!' That is my impression anyway – maybe your one is different.

HENCE

The word *hence* in the spatial sense of 'from here' has more or less died out in Modern English and been replaced by *from here*. But it still survives in the temporal sense, as in *ten years hence*, and in the sense of 'consequently': *I'm very sleepy, hence all the coffee.*

10.18 It Ordipends

An early linguistic experience which I still recall very clearly – I must have been about five years old – was the sudden realisation that English did not, as I had thought, have a verb *to ordipend*. It had seemed to me that people were always saying things like 'it ordipends on what happens'. My epiphany consisted, of course, in recognising that there were two words here, not one, and that what speakers were actually saying was 'it all depends'.

Another even earlier similar experience was when, having been instructed by my mother to fetch my mackintosh, I reported back to her that I had got my mack but I couldn't find my tosh. I possessed a matching mackintosh and sou'wester hat and, being familiar both with the word *mackintosh* and its abbreviated form *mack*, I had analysed the former as 'mack-and-tosh'.

This kind of reanalysis is very common in child language learning, but adults do it too, and this can have permanent consequences for a language. Quite a few English words show the effects of this kind of recutting. Old English *a nadder* was reanalysed as *an adder*, which is what the snake is now called in Modern English. No such reanalysis happened in German, and the equivalent Modern German word is still *Natter*.

Such 'rebracketing', as it is often called, can also be seen in *a newt*, which was originally *an ewt* or, more commonly, *an eft* – this is still the word for the amphibian in many English dialects. And *a nickname* was originally *an ekename*, where *eke* was a Mediaeval and Early Modern English word meaning 'also'; you can find it as *eke* or *eek* in Chaucer, and it is related to Modern German *auch* and Dutch *ook*, 'also'. In the same way, *an umpire* comes from *a noumpere*, which is derived from mediaeval French *nonper* meaning 'peerless, without equal, surpassing all others' – in other words, the umpire is the one who is in control.

Other English examples involve the reanalysis of the ends of words. The mediaeval singular noun *pease*, 'pea', was gradually reanalysed by English speakers as being a plural form, *peas*, and hence the new singular form *pea* came into being, though we still do have the term *pease-pudding*. Similarly, the singular noun *cheris* (compare this with French *cerise*) was reinterpreted as being plural because of the -*s* on the end, and so a new singular form *cherry* was created, probably in the fourteenth century.

This kind of reanalysis can occur in any language. Some French words had already received this same sort of treatment before they were borrowed into English. French *une orange* was a reanalysis of earlier *une norange*, which had come from Spanish *naranja* or Venetian *naranza* (see Section 1.7). English *notch* comes in the same way from Anglo-Norman *noche*, which was the result of a rebracketing of Middle French *une oche*, 'a nick, notch'.

Dutch has similar examples. The Late Latin word *nucarius*, '*nut* tree', was borrowed into mediaeval Dutch as *noker*, giving rise to the word *nokernoot*, 'walnut'. Eventually *een nokernoot* became reinterpreted as *een okernoot*, and in Modern Dutch the word is now *okkernoot*. And the Dutch word for 'adder' is also *adder*, the initial *n*- having been lost in exactly the same way as in English.

The Swedish pronoun *ni*, 'you (plural)', is also the outcome of this kind of recutting. This pronoun was originally just *I* (as it still is in Danish) but, starting in the 1600s, verb forms such as *haven I*, 'have you', began to be reanalysed by speakers as *have ni*.

This type of language change is bound to continue: since the late nineteenth century, many Americans have been using the amusing phrase 'if I had my druthers', with *druther* resulting from reanalysis of *I'd rather*. And since 1961 in the US (in the *Wall Street Journal*), and 1972 in the UK (the *Sunday Mirror*), *kudos* has sometimes been used as a plural, singular *kudo*.

APRON

A *napier* was the person in charge of the table linens of an aristocratic household. The name came from Old French *nape*, 'table cloth'. The diminutive form of *nape* – *naperon*, 'small cloth' – was borrowed into English in the 1300s, and by the late 1500s *a napron* had become reanalysed as *an apron*.

10.19 Betws-y-Coed

The name of the village of Betws-y-Coed in North Wales means 'prayer-house (in) the trees'. *Coed*, 'trees' is the plural of *coeden*, 'tree'.

This is an intriguing grammatical fact. In the languages of the world generally, plural forms of nouns are normally derived from, and more often than not longer than, singular forms. English *trees* is derived from *tree* by the addition of plural *-s*. German *Bäume*, 'trees', is obviously derived from *Baum*, 'tree', as is Dutch *bomen* from *boom*, and Spanish *árboles* from *árbol*.

But, in the same unusual way as *coed*, Welsh *pluen*, 'feather', is derived from the plural *plu*, 'feathers', *seren*, 'star', comes from *sêr*, 'stars' and *deilen*, 'leaf', is clearly based on *dail*, 'leaves'. Things seem to be the wrong way round: the singular forms are longer than the plural forms, and seemingly derived from them.

In fact Welsh is not really so very different from English, German, Dutch or Spanish. Most Welsh plurals are actually derived from singulars. *Llyfr*, 'book', has the plural form *llyfrau*, 'books', singular *pensil*, 'pencil', has the plural *pensiliau*; and the plural of *trên*, 'train', is *trenau*.

But Welsh does have the capacity to make a very interesting grammatical distinction which is not available in English. To call Welsh forms such as *coedon* and *coed* 'singular' and 'plural' is really not the correct analysis. *Coed*, 'trees', *plu*, 'feathers', *sêr*, 'stars' and *deil*, 'leaves', are better described as 'collective' nouns. *Coeden, pluen, seren* and *deilen*, the longer words which are derived from them, can be described as 'unitary' or 'singulative' forms. A *coeden*, 'tree', is an individual instance of the collective phenomenon signified by the term *coed* – which could just as well be translated into English as 'a wood' – which is, after all, a collection of trees. *Plu* could similarly be translated as 'plumage': a bird's plumage is made up of its feathers. And *deil* could very well be rendered as 'foliage', which consists of leaves. I can't, though, think of a satisfactory translation for the collective noun which corresponds to the singulative *mochyn* 'pig' other than to say that *moch* means 'pigs'.

English and Welsh are only very distantly related historically. And after 1,500 years of co-existence on the same rather small island, the two languages are still highly dissimilar in so many ways. A grammatical characteristic of Welsh which illustrates this point rather nicely is one which it shares with Gaelic and other Celtic languages such as Breton. In English, most grammatical transformations to words take place at the end of the word: *cat – cats, children – children's, walk – walked, sing – singing*. This is true of Welsh as well, as we just saw with *llyfr* and *llyfrau*. But Welsh can also carry out grammatical operations by alterations to the beginning of words. In Welsh, 'dog' is *ci*, but 'her dog' is *ei chi* and 'his dog' is *ei gi*. You have to understand how these initial 'mutations', as they are called, work before you can be confident about looking up a word in a dictionary. It's no use trying to find *nghar, gar* or *char* in most Welsh dictionaries because they are all mutated forms of the word *car*, 'car'.

PLUME

After the Roman invasion of AD 43, the Brittonic Celtic language borrowed many words from Latin which still survive in Modern Welsh. *Plu*, 'feathers', is from Latin *pluma*. English *plumage* also comes from Latin, but more indirectly, being a French form originally: Latin *pluma* became French *plume*, 'feather, quill, pen' – as in *la plume de ma tante*.

10.20 Schiphol

At Amsterdam's Schiphol Airport, passengers are often urged – in announcements made by Dutch people speaking English – to *keep* their boarding-passes ready. At British airports, passengers are generally asked to *have* their boarding-passes ready.

American English speakers typically *take* a shower, *take* a nap, and *take* a vacation, while British people are more likely to *have* a shower, a nap, or a holiday. In the USA, people might be admonished to *take* a guess or *take* a look at something, whereas on this side of the Atlantic people mostly *have* a guess, *have* a look.

Interestingly, Swedish speakers do the same as Americans when it comes to having a look – they too *ta en titt*, 'take a look'. The Portuguese *dar uma olhada*, '*give* a look', as do Italians, who *dare un'occhiata*. In Spanish you *echar un vistazo*, that is '*throw* a look'; and in Catalan you *fer un cop d'ull*, '*do* a look'.

We see the same pattern at work with British people normally *having* breakfast, whereas Italians might say *far colazione*, 'do breakfast'. Greeks can say *tróo proinó*, '*eat* breakfast'. And Americans, too, line up with the continental Europeans: instead of saying 'Shall we *have* lunch?', they are just as likely to come out with 'Should we *eat* lunch?'

The general picture is that speakers of British English seem much fonder of using *to have* than speakers of many other languages – and than speakers of American English – who prefer to use words like *take, give, throw, do* or *eat* instead.

British English was formerly more similar to the other languages in this respect. In the Old English of a thousand years ago, *have* simply meant 'to possess' and could not be used in phrases such as *have breakfast*. Even in mediaeval English, we have records of expressions such as *take bath,* which today would be 'have a bath'; *take ese,* rather than the modern 'have a rest'; *take nap,* rather than 'have a nap'; and *take reste,* now 'have a rest'.

What seems to have happened since the mediaeval period is that, in British English much more than in the American variety, *have* gradually acquired more and more active, dynamic meanings. From being a verb applying only to ongoing states such as 'owning' or 'possessing' – as in *having blue eyes*, or *having a new car* – it slowly also acquired the sense of something happening, so that it could be applied to actions or events, as in *having a coffee, having a good time* or *having a shower*.

How did this come about? There was a gradual process of change in English involving shifts in the meaning of *have* from the original 'possess', to 'come to possess' (i.e., 'receive'), then to 'take', and so on to the active usages we have today, where *have* can signify *eat, drink, perform, do* . . .

It is common for the meanings of words to change over time. Sometimes, words acquire narrower senses than they had previously: *deer* used to mean 'animal' but now has a much more specific meaning. Words can just as easily acquire broader meanings, however: *office* originally meant 'function, task, responsibility'.

Readers of this column may want to know why this broadening in the meaning of *have* occurred in English and not in other languages. While linguists are rather good at explaining why particular linguistic changes do or don't happen, we are unfortunately not always capable of figuring out why changes happen where and when they do, and not somewhere else or at some other time.

We can at least, though, make an intelligent guess about why American English *have* has not changed so much as it has in British English: large numbers of American are descended from immigrants who were not speakers of English but of continental European languages such as German, Yiddish, Italian and Spanish.

And New York was originally a Dutch colony called New Amsterdam.

COLUMN

Latin *columna* was an architectural term for an upright pillar. Newspaper columns were so called because they appeared on the page in the shape of vertical 'pillars'. Nowadays *column* refers to a section of a journal – of any shape – devoted to a particular topic which, like this one (I hope), appears on a regular basis.

10.21 Sempstress

The English word *seamstress* – as many people no longer seem to know – is most properly pronounced 'sem(p)stress'. *The Oxford English Dictionary* even offers *sempstress* as an alternative and historically earlier spelling. Pronouncing the word as 'seem-stress' is a recent spelling-pronunciation, resulting from the comparative rarity of the word these days, with people therefore encountering it in print before they have heard anybody say it.

Although the verb *to seam* meant 'to sew a seam', it could also be extended to mean 'to sew' in general. But the noun *seamstress* formed from this is, comparatively speaking, rather new in English. Until about 1600, the normal term for a woman who sewed for a living was *seamster* or *sempster*. The *-ster* suffix at the end of this version of the word was an old Germanic ending which had been used since Anglo-Saxon times to indicate a woman who carried out some kind of job or activity.

In older forms of English there were many words for women's professional activities which used this ending. A *backster* or *baxter* was a female baker, while a *brewster* was a woman who brewed beer. Female singers were *songsters* or *sangsters*. Babies' cradles were rocked by a *rockster*.

A *webster* was a woman who wove – a man doing the same work would have been called a *weaver* or *webber*. A *dexter* or *dyester* was a dyer, as was a *hewster* or *huester*; a *blaxter* bleached fabric; a *knitster* knitted; embroidery was carried out by a *browdster*; a *kempster* combed wool or flax for processing; and a *waulkster* or *walkster* was a female waulker or walker – the Scottish and Northern English label for a fuller of cloth.

Most of these words do not survive in Modern English, with the major exception of *spinster*. This originally meant a woman whose occupation was spinning thread. Later, because it was so common for unmarried women to do this, the term acquired the meaning of 'woman who is not married'. It then came to be added to women's names as an official indication that they were unmarried, the equivalent of *bachelor* for men on marriage certificates.

The ending *-ster* was eventually lost as a feminine suffix in English because terms like *baxter* and *webster* started being applied to men as well, probably as men started performing some of these jobs instead of, or as well as, women. Gradually the female meaning associated with *-ster* was forgotten. Terms such as *dempster*, 'a judge' (i.e. one who deemed) and *maltster*, 'a malt-maker', may never have referred to women.

Because the suffix was losing its feminine meaning, a new French-derived suffix *-eresse* started being used as a replacement. This is how English acquired words such as *actress* and *manageress*. *Seamstress* derived from the addition of this new French suffix to the original term *seamster* – which of course already had a feminine suffix!

Some of these female occupational words survive as surnames: Baxter, Webster, Dexter and Brewster are common enough family names in Britain. But in our sister language, Dutch, the suffix is still alive and well with its original feminine meaning intact. *Schrijver* means '(male) writer', but *schrijfster* is its female equivalent. A *speelster* is a female *speler*, 'player'. And there are many other Dutch male–female word pairs, such as *loper – loopster*, 'runner', *verkoper – verkoopster*, 'salesperson', *ontwerper – ontwerpster*, 'designer', *onderzoeker – onderzoekster*, 'researcher', *verzorger – verzorgster*, 'carer', and *begeleider – begeleidster*, 'guide'.

The fact that in English *-ster* is no longer associated with women can be seen from the modern development of words like *fraudster* and *hipster*. The same thing has happened in another sister language of ours, North Frisian, where the modern language has gender-neutral terms such as *schungster*, 'singer'. *Weewster* is their counterpart of *webster*, 'weaver'. Frisian *saister* corresponds to the obsolete English word *sewster*, which meant a person – originally a woman – who sewed. A *sempstress*, in other words.

YOUNGSTER

Youngster is a word meaning 'a young person', which first appeared in English in the sixteenth century. The apparently related, and most often dialectal, word *younker* actually comes from Dutch *jonkheer*, 'young master'. It is related to German *Junker*, 'a young nobleman', though the word became especially associated with Prussia.

11 Pedantry and Persecution

On 7 October 1992, something really rather tragic occurred: an elderly gentleman called Tecfik Esenc died in his sleep. This was very sad for his friends and family, of course, but it was actually a tragedy for all of us because Mr Esenc was the last mother-tongue speaker of an ancient European language called Ubykh, one of the languages of the Caucasus mountain range, which lies between the Caspian Sea and the Black Sea.

This was yet another nail in the coffin of linguistic diversity, adding to the growing list of dead and dying languages around the world. Of the 7,000 or so languages still spoken today, experts predict that 90 per cent will disappear over the next two centuries. We have sadly already used the adjective *extinct* of languages a number of times in this book.

Ubykh, which had been spoken for millennia in the north-western area of the Caucasus Mountains by the Black Sea, belongs to the Northwest Caucasian family. Other members of the family include Abkhaz and the Circassian languages Adyghe and Kabardian. A good hypothesis would be that the Caucasian languages are remnants of families of languages which were once spoken over a much wider area but which were swept away – except in the mountain fastness where they still remain, and to which some of them may have retreated – by the arrival of speakers of Iranian and other Indo-European languages who passed to the north and south of them on their journeys of expansion.

If so, then we can say that the Ubykh language, having survived for many millennia after the initial arrival of Indo-European, eventually died out because in the nineteenth century its homeland was attacked and invaded by the Indo-European-speaking Russians, under Czar Alexander II. In 1864, the Ubykh-speaking people decided to leave their homeland to avoid subjugation at the hands of the Russian army, and to escape massacres which were reported to have occurred elsewhere in the Caucasus as the Russians attempted to seize these lands for themselves. The Ubykhs headed for the neighbouring Ottoman Empire and settled in what is now Turkey. There, as a small minority in a foreign land, they gradually shifted, over a few generations, to speaking the majority language – Turkish – and Ubykh was slowly lost, with its last speaker dying 130 years after his people's first exodus from their native land.

Every language is a unique repository of a special human culture, and each language that dies out takes with it, for ever, a unique product of the human mind and of a particular human society.

It is a basic tenet of this chapter that all human languages are objects of wonder, and that all languages and dialects deserve respect, regardless of who they are spoken by. The sections that now follow are all, in their different ways, pleas for more linguistic tolerance and less linguistic prejudice.

11.1 Happiness

Norway is one of the most democratic, egalitarian countries in the world. It is also one of the happiest and most successful, and there is a very good case to be made for suggesting that this is not entirely a coincidence.

Amongst the approximately 200 nations of the world, Norway comes very near the top on all the important measures of well-being and quality of life. It is the leading country in the world on the United Nations Human Development Index. It is also first on the worldwide Happiness Index. It is the third richest country in the world in terms of Gross Domestic Product by head of population. It also comes third on the Quality of Life index. And it has the fifth lowest murder rate in the world. By contrast, the United Kingdom is ranked respectively 14th, 19th, 23rd, 27th and 30th on these measures.

Norway is also an enormously tolerant place. Its philosophy of egalitarian tolerance manifests itself in terms of attitudes to the way people speak. In the UK, and perhaps especially in England, speakers can be criticised for their 'bad English' or for 'speaking badly'. There is nothing like that in Norway: if you started talking about 'bad Norwegian', no one would understand what you meant – they would be baffled. Of course, foreigners trying to speak Norwegian might be considered to not be doing it very well. But as far as native Norwegian speakers are concerned, there are no dialects and accents of the language which are considered to be 'bad'.

Sadly, here, there is a long history of English children being told in school that their native dialects are 'incorrect'. They are told 'don't say *I ain't got none* – it's bad English'. In Norway, that would not happen. No Norwegian educator would want to say such a thing, and even if they did, they would not be allowed to, because it is against the law in Norway to try to 'correct' the way children speak in school.

In 1917, the Norwegian Parliament (the *Storting*) approved a passage in the school law which read: 'Pupils are to use their own spoken variety, and teachers shall as far as possible adapt their natural spoken variety to the dialect of their pupils'; so teachers were not allowed to try and make a schoolchild speak like them, and if anything it was to be the other way round. Today, Norwegians still accept that pupils should speak their local dialect in school. The current school law says: 'For spoken language in the classroom, pupils and teaching staff decide for themselves which variety they will use. Staff and school managers, in their own choice of vocabulary and expression, shall also take into consideration as much as possible the local dialect of the pupils.'

The other European countries which are most tolerant and welcoming towards local dialects are Luxembourg and Switzerland. Indigenous Luxembourgers are all native speakers of the Luxembourgish dialect, even though they also use French and German. And Swiss Germans are also all dialect speakers, using their dialects for nearly all purposes. They learn to read and write in Standard German, and speak Standard German in gatherings where French and Italian speakers are present, as well as to foreigners. You will also hear Standard German in broadcast news bulletins and other similar contexts in Switzerland, such as university lectures. But otherwise Swiss-German dialects rule supreme.

Is it then a coincidence that Switzerland is third on the United Nation's Human Development Index, or that it comes first on the Quality of Life index and third on the worldwide Happiness Index? Is it a coincidence that Luxembourg and Switzerland are the two richest countries in the world in terms of Gross Domestic Product by population?

Maybe it is. Achieving a more respectful and less hostile attitude to local accents and dialects in England might not make us as rich or successful as Norway, Switzerland or Luxembourg. But it would surely make this country a fairer and happier place.

11.2 Double Negatives

William Shakespeare was an educated man. His grammar-school education gave him a good knowledge of the grammar of Ancient Greek and Latin, and he was familiar with the works of Ovid, Virgil, Seneca, Plutarch, Cicero and Horace. He is also rather well known for writing wonderful English – including lines such as: 'You know my father hath no child but I, nor none is like to have' (*As You Like It*); 'Nor go neither; but you'll lie like dogs and yet say nothing neither' (*The Tempest*); and 'No woman has, nor never none shall be, mistress of it' (*Twelfth Night*). The fact is that the very erudite Shakespeare was perfectly happy to use the grammatical construction which pedants these days in the English-speaking world disparagingly call the 'double negative'.

These disparagers believe that double negatives are wrong and constitute bad grammar. If asked to justify this belief, they often respond that if someone says they DON'T want NONE, they must mean they DO want SOME. This is obviously not true: if you ask for something in a shop and get the reply *We ain't got none*, you don't hang around waiting for it – you leave the shop.

The pedants' argument is that two negatives make a positive, as if English was the same as mathematics. But they have got their maths wrong. 'Double negative' is not an accurate term, because the grammar of most English dialects allows for three or more negatives; and in maths, three negatives can make a negative, so there should be nothing to object to in the case of triple negatives like *I couldn't find none nowhere*. But of course the pedants do not like triple negatives either.

The Polish sentence *Nigdy nie moglem nigdzie zadnego znalezc* literally means 'never not I-could nowhere none find', or as many English speakers would say, *I couldn't never find none nowhere*. In Polish you have to express it that way: in a negative sentence, everything that can be negated must be. This is a form of grammatical agreement, just like what we see in the Spanish phrase *las hermosas casas rojas grandes*, 'the beautiful large red houses'. The noun *casa* is feminine and, in this sentence it has the plural form *casas*, so everything in this sentence which can be marked as plural and feminine has to be so marked – the definite article takes the feminine plural form *las*, and the adjectives are marked as feminine plural by the endings -*as*/-*es*.

Linguists call the kind of grammatical agreement we see in *I couldn't find none nowhere* multiple negation. It is very common in the world's languages, and is actually more widespread than the single negation we find in Standard English. In Europe, formal Standard French has *je ne sais rien*, 'I don't know nothing', though in colloquial styles French speakers will say *je sais rien*.

British schoolchildren who say *I don't want none* are likely to be told this is wrong. But that makes little sense in the wider European context. The Romance languages all have the equivalent of 'I don't want nothing': in Spanish it is *no quiero nada*, in Portuguese *não quero nada*, in Italian *non voglio niente* and in Romanian *nu vreau nimic*.

In the Slavic languages, such as Croatian, Russian and Bulgarian, multiple negation is also the norm. The Slovak equivalent of English *she didn't eat anything* is *ona nič nejedla*, 'she didn't eat nothing'.

The Greek word for 'nothing' is *tipota*, and the translation of the English sentence *I didn't find anything* is *Dhen vrika tipota*, 'I didn't find nothing'. Albanian has the same structure: *Nuk gjeta asgjë*, with *asgjë* meaning 'nothing'; so does Hungarian: *Nem találtam semmit*, where *semmit* is 'nothing'. Likewise in Lithuanian and Maltese.

The moral is that there is nothing wrong with saying *I don't want none*. King Alfred said it, Chaucer said it, Shakespeare said it. And it is extremely European.

11.3 Best

After a football match, it is often said by those talking about the event that 'the best team won' – or in the case of a losing team managed by Jose Mourinho, that the best team did not win.

Everybody who speaks English as their native language knows exactly what the word *best* means. If someone is best at something, then there is nobody who is better than them. If you are able to run 100 metres in 13 seconds and your brother can only do it in 15 seconds, then you are the best at running 100 metres. If one football team has beaten another one, then the evidence points towards them being the best team – though it is perfectly true, of course, that one team can play more skilfully and attractively than another and still fail to win.

There are some people, however, who believe that it is not correct to use the word *best* like this. They argue that if there are only two of you – you and your brother, for instance – then you are not the *best* but the *better* performer. *Best*, they argue, should be reserved for referring to one of three or more people or entities. So after a football match, they believe we should say that the *better* team won (or in the case of Mourinho, not).

This argument has absolutely no foundation in the grammar of the English language. There is no reason why English speakers should not say that something or somebody is the best or fastest or nicest of two. If you are the top, the leader, the superior one, then you are the best, regardless of how many are being evaluated.

Adjectives like *better* and *faster* are technically known as comparatives, while forms such as *best* and *fastest* are called superlatives. If a good athlete compares herself as a runner with everyone else in her family, she might be able to say that she is faster and better than all the other family members – and that she is therefore the fastest and the best. In the same way, if she compares herself just with her brother, then she would still be the fastest and the best – superlative – even if there are only two siblings who are being compared.

It is quite true that people of my age were taught at school that there is a rule which states that a phrase using *better* has to indicate the better of two. But the reason we were taught this rule is that there is no such rule. The real rules of English grammar do not have to be taught to native speakers. By the time we are three or four years old – so before we arrive at school – we have acquired most of the genuine rules of English grammar already.

We all figured out the very important English-language rule that adjectives come before nouns without any formal instruction. Nobody ever told us that it was wrong to say *a car black* – even very young children quite naturally say *a black car*. Speakers of other languages such as French, Welsh and Gaelic learn a different rule about the order of nouns and adjectives, once again without anybody telling them. Young speakers of these languages rather early on quite spontaneously say *voiture noire, car du, càr dubh* – literally 'car black'.

Similarly, English speakers know that it is entirely normal, if you have to choose between the old red car and the new blue car, to say that the blue one would be 'the best choice'. But notice that there actually is a rule here: no one would say 'the blue one would be *a* best choice'. If the indefinite article *a* is used, then the comparative *better* occurs, not the superlative. But it is the use of *a* rather than *the* which determines which is used, not how many items are being compared. That is something else we all learnt without anybody telling us.

> **CLUMSY**
>
> Just as *drowsy* comes from *to drowse*, so *clumsy* seems to have come from the now vanished verb *to clumse*, which meant something like 'to become stiff with cold'. The adjective *clumsy*, with its modern meaning of 'lacking in agility or dexterity', did not come into use in English until about 1600.

11.4 Decimate

The word *decimate* was originally borrowed into English from Latin, with the first record of this word being used in our language dating from 1591. It was employed at that time as a technical term, with a very specific meaning, by writers treating aspects of Roman military history: they used *decimate* to refer to a particular punishment meted out by the Roman army.

If a large number of soldiers deserted, it would not have been a good idea to sentence all of them to death, because then there might not have been enough soldiers left to continue fighting. Instead, as the price for desertion, cowardice or mutiny, the Romans developed the practice of executing every tenth soldier, chosen at random, from a recalcitrant squadron. Soldiers were divided up into groups of ten. Then everyone drew lots – and this was a lottery you really did not want to win, since the unfortunate man who got the short straw was bludgeoned to death by the other nine.

The Latin word for this practice was *decimare*, 'to take one in ten', which was derived from the Latin word for 'ten', *decem*.

By 1626, *decimate* was being used by people writing in English in a more general sense of removing or destroying one in every ten of anything, not just mutinous soldiers. And rather soon after that, from 1660 onwards, we find the word being used in a much broader sense which was not connected to the number ten at all. The meaning had now become something like 'to reduce or destroy drastically', or simply 'to devastate or ruin'. This mid-seventeenth-century usage is, as the *Oxford English Dictionary* states, now 'the most usual sense' of the word in Modern English as well.

This 'most usual' meaning of *decimate* is not very popular with certain critics who claim that since *decimate* is derived from Latin *decem*, 'ten', it should not be used in a more general way which is unconnected with the number ten. These critics are claiming, in effect, that it is wrong to talk of, say, fishing stocks in the North Sea being 'decimated' unless a scientific study has been carried out which shows that precisely 10 per cent of the fish in that sea have been lost, no more and no less.

Clearly, however, the English word *decimate* has not meant 'decreased by a tenth' for over 300 years. The fact is that a word means what it currently means – and you cannot change that fact by appealing to what a word used to mean, especially not in the Latin of 2,000 years ago.

Advocates of this erroneous point of view are suffering from what is known technically as the 'etymological fallacy': the mistaken belief that words ought always to keep their original meaning. But acting on that belief would get us into serious difficulties. We would have to reserve the adjective *fantastic* for things which were imaginary. We would need to restrict the adjective *dilapidated* to buildings made of stone (Latin *lapidem* meant 'stone'). We would feel obliged to confine the usage of the adjectives *awful* and *terrible* to things which inspire awe and terror. And we would be obliged to use the words *September*, *October*, *November* and *December* to refer to July, August, September and October, because the names of these months are derived from the Latin words for seven, eight, nine and ten respectively.

We would, of course, be very ill-advised to do any of these things. English speakers know very well what *decimate* really means in our contemporary language. If we read reports on the sport pages that the Manchester City squad have been decimated, we are very much more likely to suppose that several of the players have been struck down by the flu or injury rather than that one-tenth of the squad have been chosen by lot and executed after losing 3–2 away to Norwich City.

APODEKATÍZO

In some languages, words corresponding to *decimate* are more transparently connected to the concept of 'ten' than our English word, and are therefore probably less likely to be used in the same broad 'devastate, ruin' way as English *decimate*. The Greek term is *apodekatízo*, which incorporates *deka*, 'ten'. The Polish is *zdziesiątkować*, which also contains the element *dziesi-* 'ten'.

11.5 You and Me and the Gatepost

There seem to be quite lot of self-appointed experts on the English language around who like to invent grammatical rules. One of these 'rules', which Americans in particular seem to be very worried about, concerns *among* and *between*, and states that writers should only use *between* to refer to two people or entities, and that for three or more the correct preposition to use is *among*.

This is complete nonsense; but if we are charitable and look into the history of these words a little bit more deeply, we can just about see where this misguided idea came from. The word *between* contains the element *-tw-*, which is historically related to *two*. In Old English, the feminine and neuter form of the numeral was *twa*. We no longer pronounce the *w* in the word *two* itself, although it is still retained in words for *two* in most of the languages which are closely related to English. In Scots, it is *twa*. The German word is *zwei*, Dutch and Afrikaans have *twee* and in Frisian it is *twa*. The Swedes have *två*, in Icelandic it is *tvö* and in Faroese *tvey*.

The original *tw-* also survives in English in related words such as *twelve*, which was originally 'two left' (i.e. if you subtract ten from twelve). *Twenty* means 'two tens' and *twice* is 'two times', while *twins* refers to two children born together. *Twain*, an archaic word which still survives in the phrases 'never the twain shall meet' and splitting something 'in twain', comes from the Old English masculine form *twegen*, 'two'.

The word *twine* goes back to an Old English form meaning 'double thread', where the threads have been *twisted* – another related word – together. *Twill* was originally a type of cloth woven from such double thread. And a *twig* first meant a forked branch – one which had divided into two. *Between* (and its cousin *betwixt*) are derived from Old English forms related to the number *two* and preceded by *be-* (which was a reduced form of *bi*, modern *by*).

The word *among*, on the other hand, derives from medieval English *on mang*, from earlier *on gemange*, where *gemang* meant 'a crowd' or 'an assembly of people'. The Old English verb *gemengan* meant 'to combine, to mingle'. So the *ming-* part of *mingle* and the *-mong* part of *among* are historically related; and the original meaning of *among* was 'in the company of'. It is not at all surprising, then, that in Modern English *among(st)* and *between* mean different things, and are not just automatic variants which have to be used mechanically according to whether or not three or more entities are involved.

Consider the following sentence: 'There are several differences between these four different population-groups.' There is absolutely nothing wrong with this sentence. If, however, we were to listen to the coterie of self-appointed English grammar 'experts' who claim that this sentence is incorrect, and substitute *among* for *between* because there are more than two groups involved, we would utterly change the meaning of the sentence. Differences *between* groups and differences *among* groups obviously refer to very separate concepts – to intergroup and intragroup differences respectively.

It is normal in English to choose *between* entities, however many there are, and to see connections or relationships *between* people, regardless of the number. We also distinguish and differentiate *between* entities, even if there are three or more.

So don't worry – it is not and never has been wrong to use *between* for more than two objects or individuals. The *Oxford English Dictionary* offers many examples of such usages going back to the 900s AD, including this one from 1400: 'I shalle telle yow why in youre ears privily between us three.'

It is rather certain, I think, that no native speaker of English would ever think of saying 'among you and me and the gatepost'.

COTERIE

Coterie means a set or a circle of people or a clique who regard themselves as exclusive in some way and, often, as superior to outsiders. Ironically, the word is related to *cottar*, and in its original French meaning referred to a group of impoverished peasants who rented land from the same landlord.

11.6 #I Too

In normal native English, the personal pronouns *I*, *he*, *she*, *we*, *they* are only used when they appear as the subject of a verb: *I am leaving now; He likes coffee; She would like some too; We are coming; They would prefer tea*. Otherwise, *me*, *him*, *her*, *us*, *them* – forms which are technically known as oblique pronouns – are employed: *It's me; It was them that did it; Who wanted coffee? Him!* In this respect English behaves like French, where the correct grammatical reply to the question *Qui est là?*, 'Who is there?' is not *C'est je*, 'It's I', but *C'est moi*, 'It's me'. Similarly, in Norwegian one says *Det er meg!*, 'It's me'.

Oblique pronouns are also used when there are two subjects joined together by *and*: the majority of native English speakers say *I went to London yesterday*, but *Mary and me went to London yesterday*. It is also quite normal to say *John and them are leaving now*, while *John and they are leaving now* sounds rather odd. English speakers also say *Them and us are travelling together*, not *They and we are travelling together*.

A centuries-long inferiority complex in the English-speaking world with respect to Latin has led to attempts by self-appointed authorities to get rid of the use of these oblique pronouns everywhere except where they occur as objects. This is on the mistaken assumption that they are 'accusative-case' forms, as in Latin. It is argued that *Me and him are coming* 'should be' *He and I are coming* (also involved in this particular example is the view that 'it is not polite to put yourself first'). This particular attempt has been partly successful, and the *He and I* structure is the one which is now most often used in formal speech and writing.

Similarly, pedants claim that *It was her that did it* 'should be' *It was she that did it*. This seems to have had some success in written American English – with certain contemporary novelists, for instance – but is still normally absent from the speech of the overwhelming majority of English speakers. It is much less frequently argued that the answer to *Who wanted coffee?* should be *He!*, presumably because this sounds just too absurd.

But no doubt there are some pedants who believe that the *#Me Too* movement should be *#I Too*. Some Americans really can be heard to reply *This is he/she* on the phone to someone who has asked to speak to them by name, though this is widely felt to be weird by most English speakers elsewhere.

There are a number of cases, however, where the 'accusative-case' hypothesis has had consequences for the English language which were not those intended. First, it has produced 'hypercorrect' forms, for example the incorrect use of subject pronouns joined by *and* after prepositions instead of oblique pronouns, in sentences such as *There was a great rapport between he and his mother.*

But the most notable unintended consequence undoubtedly lies in the phenomenon of *me*-avoidance. There is a long history of pronouncements by English-speaking pedants along the lines that it is 'wrong' to say *Mary and me are coming*, and that *I* should be used rather than *me*. The propagation of this view has produced great insecurity on the part of many native speakers about using *me*, and they now often therefore use constructions such as *He brought it for Mary and I*, as well as the very common *between you and I*.

When speakers are also told that these are wrong, too, this causes further insecurity. All this is now leading to the increased use of *myself* instead of *I* or *me* – as in *There is a great rapport between John and myself*, and *Mary and myself are coming* – as a way of avoiding the problem. Unofficial language planners have tried to make English more like Latin, but the result has been the exact opposite.

WEIRD

The way in which we use the adjective *weird* today is historically particularly associated with Scots, but it was originally an Old English noun meaning 'power, fate, destiny'. Later it also came to be applied to persons with mystical powers – witches or wizards – as in Shakespeare's 'weird sisters' in *Macbeth*.

11.7 Don Kichot

In all European languages, there is a tradition of using names for famous countries, towns, and geographical features which differ from their native-language names (see also Section 5.1). We call *Deutschland* Germany, *Magyarország* Hungary, *Suomi* Finland, *Norge* Norway and *Österreich* Austria. The rivers *Donau*, *Rhein*, *Tevere* and *Wisła* appear in English as the Danube, Rhine, Tiber and Vistula. The *Bodensee* is what we call Lake Constance, and we know *Lac Léman* as Lake Geneva.

This practice also extends to famous historical figures. We refer to the Greek philosopher and scientist *Aristotelis* as Aristotle; we know *Omiros* as Homer, and we call Ploutarchos Plutarch. The ancient Roman writers *Vergilius*, *Ovidius* and *Titus Livius* go by the English-language names of Virgil, Ovid and Livy. The Roman Emperor we call Trajan was called *Traianus* in Latin; and Hadrian was *Hadrianus* to the Romans. It is true that we do spell Julius Caesar as they did in Latin, but we pronounce it very differently: ancient Romans would have called him, approximately, Kie-sar.

We also have our own names for a number of more modern historical figures. Spinoza was actually called *Espinosa*, Titian's Venetian name was *Tiziano* and Petrarch was called *Petrarca* in his native Italian. The Russian Emperor Peter the Great's name was *Pyotr*, and Empress Catherine the Great's subjects knew her as *Yekaterina*. It works the other way round too: Shakespeare is known as *Szekspir* in Polish, *Šekspirs* in Latvian and *Šekspyras* in Lithuanian.

Last year [2016], Jeremy Paxman was sneered at in the electronic media for his pronunciation on the TV programme University Challenge of the names of the Spanish fictional characters Don Quixote and Don Juan, which he pronounced 'Don Kwiks-ot' and 'Don Jew-an'. The Twittersphere was immediately full of comments from smug know-alls who laughed at what they claimed was his ignorance of Spanish; and some of the national press quickly followed suit.

In fact, it was the scornful tweeters, and those journalists who followed them, who were showing their lack of knowledge. The smart alecs who were disdainful about Paxman were demonstrating rather clearly their own ignorance: they did not even seem to know that in Spanish the character's name is not Quixote but *Quijote*; and they were obviously ignorant of the fact that in the English-speaking world we have a centuries-long tradition of spelling the name of Cervantes' character with an *x* and pronouncing it 'kwiksot' or 'kwiksoat'. This is simply what the character's name is in English – something which is rather obvious from the fact that we pronounce the adjective derived from it, *quixotic*, as 'kwiksotic'. One would only use the pronunciation 'Ki-ho-te' if one were speaking Spanish (which, of course, Jeremy Paxman was not).

And this is not just an English custom: Cervantes' main character's name is rendered differently in a variety of languages. No one claims that French speakers are ignorant because they call him *Quichotte*; in Italian his name is *Chisciotte*; and in Polish *Kichot*. There are similar traditions for the names of other fictional characters. Cinderella is known as *Cendrillon* in French, *Aschenputtel* in German, *Popelyushka* in Ukrainian and *Kopciuszek* in Polish. Hamlet is called *Amleto* in Italian, and *Amlet* in Greek.

The same goes for the fictional character Don Juan, which Jeremy Paxman also pronounced correctly as 'Jew-an'. The Italian version is *Don Giovanni*, and in Catalan it's *Don Joan*. You can tell what the long-established English tradition for the name is by looking at Byron's epic poem *Don Juan*, which he began writing in

1818. It contains rhymes which depend on the pronunciation of the name as 'Jew-an', such as: 'It is not clear that Adeline and Juan / Will fall; but if they do, 'twill be their ruin'.

I think we can be rather sure, too, that no one is going to tweet complaints about calling Jesus by the well-known English-language version of his name rather than by the one he probably used himself, *Yeshua*.

CAESAR

The first Roman Emperor, Augustus, was the adopted son of Julius Caesar, and he took the Caesar family name. Successive emperors were then called *Caesar* in Byzantium as well as Rome, and it became the general label for imperial rulers in eastern and northern Europe. The German form *Kaiser*, and the Russian variant *tsar*, are very well known, but there are many others, including Polish *cesarz*, Finnish *keisari* and Norwegian *keiser*.

11.8 Banned Languages

The freedom to use your native language is a fundamental human right, so one of the most shameful blots on the history of our continent is the disgraceful tale of European governments attempting to make it illegal to speak certain languages. This has included the governments of Britain, France, Germany, Spain, Italy and even Norway and Sweden.

Banning the use of a language might seem to be a highly bizarre and difficult thing to attempt to do: how can you stop someone from speaking their own language, especially if they are monolingual? But this has not prevented governments of many different European nations from trying to do exactly that, sometimes in extremely punitive and unpleasant ways. Such actions have undoubtedly contributed to the death of some of Europe's smaller languages.

A well-known example of a language which has suffered in this way is Kurdish in Turkey. Since the inept carving-up of the Ottoman Empire by the European powers after World War I, it has been the fate of Kurdish speakers to find themselves linguistic minorities in Iran, Syria, Iraq and Turkey. Kurdish is a member of the Iranian sub-family of Indo-European languages, while Turkish is in origin a Central Asian language which is related to Kazakh, Azerbaijani and Uzbek, but not to any major European language.

Kurdish was banned in Turkey in 1938, meaning among other things that it could no longer be used in print or education, leading to considerable loss of literacy in the language. In 1961, a new Turkish constitution allowed Kurdish publications to appear once again, but after the 1980 military coup, Kurdish was officially prohibited not just in public but also in private: there were cases of people being imprisoned for speaking, writing or even singing in Kurdish.

In 1991, the Turkish government again legalised the use of Kurdish, and from 2006 private TV channels began to broadcast a limited amount of Kurdish-language output, although cartoons and educational programmes were specifically forbidden. It is still not legal to use Kurdish as a language of instruction, even in private schools, in spite of the fact that there are around 14 million Kurds in Turkey, some 18 per cent of the population. Unsurprisingly in view of this linguistic oppression, by no means all of them still speak Kurdish, though at the most conservative estimate the language has at least 8 million speakers in Turkey, with many in rural areas being monolingual. Since 2012 it has been possible to study Kurdish as a subject in some places, and a few unofficial schools have been opened with Kurdish as the main language of instruction, but they have no state recognition, and at least one was forced to close in 2015.

The fall of the Ottoman Empire also had another unfortunate linguistic consequence: the boundaries of northern Greece were redrawn after World War I in such a way that large numbers of native speakers of the Slavic languages Bulgarian and Macedonian were left on the Greek side of the border. Since then, there has been a history of Greek governments denying that these Greek Slavic speakers even exist. When the Greek fascist dictator Metaxas took power in 1938, Slavic speakers were forced to take on Greek-language surnames, and the speaking of Slavic was declared illegal even in their own homes – policemen were sent around villages to listen outside windows and arrest anyone speaking Slavic.

Unsurprisingly, large numbers of Slavic speakers left Greece altogether. However, today there are still many tens of thousands of native Slavic speakers in Greece, with some estimates going as high as 250,000. There are radio stations in northern Greece which broadcast in Macedonian Slavic, but even now these are reported to be facing official opposition – something for which there can be no justification in a modern European nation which respects human rights.

TURKEY

Certain gallinaceous birds of African origin acquired the name *guinea fowl* when they were imported into Europe by the Portuguese from West Africa. The same birds were referred to as *turkeys* when they arrived via Turkish possessions in North Africa. When the American birds we now know as *turkeys* first came to the attention of English speakers, these were wrongly identified as the same bird and the latter name was transferred to them.

11.9 Anti-Semitic

One of the most anti-Jewish words in the English language is *anti-Semitic*. In terms of the history of our language, it is a rather new word – no one used it until about

140 years ago. The term, as is well known, is used to apply to people who demonstrate prejudice against or hostility towards Jews as an ethnic or religious group (a phenomenon much older than 140 years).

But why do we call this form of racism *anti-Semitic* rather than using the more obvious phrase *anti-Jewish*? Hostility to Catholics is called anti-Catholicism. Those who demonstrate hatred or fear of Irish people as an ethnic group are labelled anti-Irish. Anti-Americanism is another well-known label for a form of prejudice and hostility. So what is the point of using *anti-Semitism* as a label? If certain narrow-mindedly bigoted people are anti-Jewish, then why don't we just say so?

What seems to have happened is that in racist Victorian England, Jewish people were discriminated against and looked down upon as being inferior, in much the same way that people of sub-Saharan African origin were also discriminated against. Indeed, sadly, this disgraceful anti-Jewish prejudice did not disappear with the demise of Her Majesty Queen Victoria. Within rather recent living memory there were golf clubs in Britain which refused to accept Jewish people as members, and Jews have suffered many other forms of exclusion. They were not allowed to become MPs until 1858; and the career of Benjamin Disraeli, Prime Minister in 1868 and again from 1874 to 1880, benefited from the fact that he was baptised at the age of twelve.

This discrimination and prejudice had linguistic consequences: in the racist climate of Victorian times, the word *Jew* acquired negative connotations, and people became uncomfortable about using the term – as if it was not very polite to draw attention to the fact that some people had the misfortune to be Jewish. Some English-speaking people today still avoid saying 's/he's a Jew', preferring instead to say 's/he's Jewish'.

The same thing was true of the word *Black* as applied to people of sub-Saharan African origin. This term, too, came to be avoided, and it was only rather recently that we stopped using the words *Negro* and *Coloured* as euphemisms for referring to black people.

In the nineteenth century, English speakers similarly developed euphemisms for *Jew*, notably *Israelite* and *Semite*. But in our modern age of diversity and equality, we should no longer have any need for embarrassing, twisted pseudo-euphemisms based on 'Semite' such as *Semitic* and *anti-Semitic*.

There is also another good reason to get rid of the term *anti-Semitic*: used in this way, *Semitic* is a highly inaccurate term. The Semitic peoples of the Middle East historically spoke languages which descended from the Proto-Semitic language. These included, yes, Hebrew, the ancient language of the Jews; but also Aramaic, Akkadian, Assyrian, Syriac, Phoenician, Moabite and Ugaritic, with the Semitic language of Carthage – Punic – being a variety derived from Phoenician. Most of the Semitic peoples, in other words, were not Jews.

Modern Semitic languages (see also Section 7.14) include: the Ethiopian language Amharic, which has about 17 million speakers, most of them Christians; Tigrinya, a language with about 6 million (again mainly Christian) speakers in Ethiopia and Eritrea; and Tigre, which has a million speakers, mostly in Eritrea. There are also a number of South Arabian languages which are related to the Ethiopian languages and are spoken along the southern edge of the Arabian peninsula in Yemen and Oman, such as Mehri, Harsusi, Hobyot, Jibbali and Socotri.

But the largest Semitic language is Arabic, which has well over 300 million speakers, with perhaps around 20 million of them being Christians, including many Palestinians. Maltese, an indigenous European Semitic language, is also historically a variety of Arabic, but now constitutes a separate language.

The fact is that the Tigrinyan and Tigre people of Ethiopia are just as much Semites as the Jews. And so too are the Arabs.

ERITREA

The Republic of Eritrea takes its name from the Latin name for the Red Sea, which forms its eastern boundary. The Latin form was *Mare Erythraeum*, which came from Ancient Greek *Erythraikos Pontos*, where *póntos* meant 'sea' and *erythrós* was 'red'. *Erythrism* is a Modern English biological term for 'reddening', akin to *albinism*, 'whitening'.

12 Communication

At the university in Norway where I used to work, there is a regulation stating that teaching shall normally be carried out in Norwegian. Of course, people lecturing on English literature are allowed – encouraged – to do this in English, and a class put on for a group of international postgraduate students might also be conducted in English. But the norm is, very reasonably at a Norwegian university, that Norwegian should be the language of the classroom.

There is also, however, a very interesting footnote that goes along with this rule: it reads 'for the purposes of this regulation, Swedish and Danish count as Norwegian'.

The point is that, although we think of Norwegian, Swedish and Danish as being different languages, they are all mutually intelligible. When Norwegians travel to Sweden, they carry on speaking Norwegian, though they may slow down a little and reduce their usage of colloquial idioms somewhat in order to improve communication. Currently, at Oslo airport many of the young people working in the bars and cafes are Swedish, and will reply to you in Swedish even if you speak to them in Norwegian. Several times already in this book I have referred to the languages collectively, for example in noting pan-Scandinavian words such as *bil*, 'car', and *hus*, 'house'.

It is not the case, then, that if two dialects are mutually comprehensible, they are necessarily dialects of the same language. But mutual intelligibility is a difficult thing to measure, and it is not always totally mutual: communication may be easier in one direction than in the other. Scandinavians claim that Danes find it easier to understand Norwegian than vice versa. The same is true on the Iberian peninsula: Portuguese people will tell you that they find it easier to understand Spanish than Spanish speakers do trying to understand them; and Spaniards may even tell you they find it easier to understand Italian than Portuguese, even though Italian is not nearly so closely related to Spanish.

At a particular hotel in a small village in Crete, the Bulgarian workers always used to speak Greek to their Serbian co-workers, until one day they realised that they could communicate rather well with each speaking their own languages, if they spoke slowly. And then, after a week or so had gone by, they did not even have to speak slowly any more. Dialect geography mattered here too. Those Serbians who spoke dialects from the eastern part of their country, which is closer to Bulgaria, were quicker at learning to understand Bulgarian than people from further west.

Every year, Finnish and Estonian phoneticians have an academic meeting in Helsinki or Tallinn where they present scientific papers, each in their own language. The meetings are very enjoyable and fruitful occasions. But sometimes the differences between the two languages get to be too much for everybody to communicate easily, and they give up and switch to English.

Reading a closely related language may be easier than processing its spoken form. At Schiphol Airport in Amsterdam, a German man boarding a plane for Berlin complained to his wife that there were no German newspapers. She picked up a copy of the Dutch paper *De Volkskrant* and said: 'I'm going to read this – it's the same language, you know!'

Language is by no means only, or even mainly, for communication. But communication is certainly one of its functions, and a very complex one too. In this coming section, I hope I will be able to unravel some of these complexities by presenting some interesting examples and analyses.

12.1 *Faux amis*

Teachers of foreign languages sometimes use the French term *faux amis*, or the English equivalent *false friends*, to alert learners to the dangers of assuming that words have the same meaning across languages just because they look or sound similar.

The French word *table* does indeed mean 'table', and French *six* really does mean 'six'. But a French *demande* is something much more polite than an English *demand* – it means 'request'. It is easy to see how this could cause confusion and misunderstanding on the part of beginning learners. The two words have a common source: the English word was borrowed from French in the 1300s, its ultimate origin lying in Latin *demandare*, 'to entrust'. And they have closely related meanings which differ in a small but very significant way: the French form signifies 'to ask', while the English word, as per the *Oxford English Dictionary*, means 'to ask in such a way as to command obedience or compliance'.

Contrast this with the fact that English and German both have a word *die*. These do not qualify as true false friends because the meanings of the two words are so very different, and they typically occur in very different contexts. In German, *die* is the definite article corresponding to English 'the'. The resemblance between the two forms is a total coincidence; no learner is going to confuse the one with the other, especially as the pronunciations are also different – the German word sounds like 'dee'. The same is true of English and Polish *lot* (it means 'flight' in Polish), and of English and Czech *pole* (meaning 'field' in Czech).

Confusion is much more likely to occur where a common origin has led to a similarity of meaning as well as of form. Catalan *embarassada* means 'pregnant', not 'embarrassed'. *Limone* is the German for 'lime', not 'lemon'. Greek *empathia* does not signal 'empathy' but, on the contrary, 'hostility'. Italian *gusto* means 'taste', not 'enthusiasm'. And Norwegian *full* is 'drunk'.

Even amongst varieties of English there are false friends. Australian *crook* denotes that someone is 'unwell', and South African *robot* means 'a traffic light'. Most of us probably think we are quite good at recognising and understanding American vocabulary. We know that the *boot* of a car is the *trunk* in the USA, that a *freeway* is the same kind of entity as a *motorway*, and that their *sidewalk* is what we would call a *pavement*. But how many people on this side of the Atlantic know what Americans mean by *pavement*? The first time I saw a sign in a small American town saying 'No cycling on pavement', I was not at all surprised – you are not allowed to cycle on the pavement in this country either. But then I was told that it in fact meant that you *must* cycle on what we would call the pavement, because in the USA the *pavement* is the 'roadway'. In this small town, they wanted cyclists to keep to the sidewalks.

Other American false friends include the words *nervy* and *scrappy*, particularly in a sporting context. In this country, a *nervy* player would be one who is rather on the timid and nervous side – full of nerves – and you wouldn't want such a person taking your penalties in a football match. But in America, such a team member is one who is not full of nerves but full of nerve – that is, very brave or impudent!

And in this country, if you said of a football match that it was a *scrappy* game, you would mean that it was not very good: neither side really produced any coherent play that was enjoyable to watch. In the USA, on the other hand, a scrappy football game is one which is a 'good scrap': a keenly fought contest in which the teams are well matched and are trying their hardest.

ROBOT

Robot is a rare example of an artificially invented word becoming established in the general vocabulary. It was introduced in the 1920 science-fiction play *Rossum's Universal Robots* by the Czech writer Karel Čapek, a friend of the founding President of Czechoslovakia, Thomas Masaryk. Čapek derived the word from Czech *robota*, 'forced labour, serfdom'.

12.2 Aunts

A few years ago, the Greek translator of a book I had written got in touch to ask if a 'cousin' I had referred to in the text was a man or a woman. I didn't know, which was inconvenient because in Greek, as in many other languages, you do need this information: a Greek cousin can be either a *ksadérphi* (female) or *ksáderphos* (male), but there is no gender-neutral term which covers both possibilities.

We might have the same problem with translating from Turkish into English: while we distinguish between male *nephew* and female *niece*, Turkish has a single term for both sexes: *yeğen*. Finnish translators encounter the same issue the other way round with our English words: a *niece* can be either a 'sister's daughter' or a 'brother's daughter' — and Finnish makes a linguistic distinction between the two: *veljentytär* is your 'brother's daughter' and *sisarentytär* is your 'sister's daughter'.

There are many difficulties like this when translating kinship terms from one language to another. For English speakers, the word *aunt* is a perfectly simple, everyday word which we are all entirely familiar with. But if we look at it more closely, we can see that the concept behind this word is actually complex. *Aunt* can apply to no fewer than four different types of biological-social relationship: your father's sister, your mother's sister, your father's brother's wife, or your mother's brother's wife. Occasionally that can be confusing, and speakers do sometimes find themselves having to use explanatory phrases such as *my Mum's sister* or *an aunt by marriage*.

It is no surprise, then, that there are languages in the world which have four different words for 'aunt', labelling each of these relationships in an unambiguous way. Many European languages draw a three-way distinction. In Danish, your *moster* is your 'mother's sister', your *faster* is your 'father's sister' and your *tante* is either your 'father's brother's wife' or your 'mother's brother's wife'. Turkish makes the same distinction: your mother's sister is your *teyze*, your father's sister is your *hala* and an aunt by marriage is a *yenge*.

In older forms of Polish, there was also a system with a three-way contrast, but it worked the other way round from Danish and Turkish. Older Polish made a difference between the two different types of aunt by marriage: *stryjenka* was 'father's brother wife' and *wujenka* was 'mother's brother's wife'. The third word, *ciocia*, meant 'parent's sister', regardless of whether the parent was the mother or the father. So between them, Polish and Danish pick out each of the four different relationship possibilities, even though neither of them recognises all four.

But that is not the end of such complexities. Many languages have different words for siblings depending on whether or not they are older or younger than the speaker. In Turkish, *ağabey* is 'brother older than me', while in Hungarian *öccs* means specifically 'younger brother' and *húg* is 'younger sister'. In the North Sami language of northern Scandinavia, this older–younger dimension extends across generations into words for 'aunt' and 'uncle': *siessá* means 'father's sister', but *goaski* and *muotta* mean respectively 'mother's older sister' and 'mother's younger sister'. Some languages — the Turkic language Uighur, for instance — extend the Sami-style system by also distinguishing between 'father's older sister' and 'father's younger sister'. So there are not simply four possible relationships inherent in the English word *aunt*, but six.

Individuals in any group of human beings anywhere in the world can have the same range of biological relationships with one another: everybody has, or has had, a father and a mother; and anybody could in principle have a son, or a daughter or a brother, or a sister. But the way in which these relationships are differentiated from one another, or grouped together and labelled using single words, can vary very considerably, and fascinatingly, from one language to another.

KITH

Most people probably know the phrase *kith and kin*. But do they know what *kith* actually means? It comes from Old English *cyth*, 'known' – so 'people one knows'. *Cyth* was related to Old English *couth*, 'familiar'. Today people who are 'not familiar (with how to behave properly)' are *uncouth*.

12.3 'The Flipper of an Elderly Seal'

My German–English dictionary says that the German word *keltern* is to be translated into English as 'to press (of grapes, for the purpose of making wine)'. The word comes originally from Latin *calcatura*, 'stamping', which is derived from *calcare*, 'to trample underfoot', which is ultimately derived from *calx*, 'heel'.

It was from the Latin-speaking Romans that the Germanic-speaking peoples first learnt how to make wine, which is why English *wine*, German *Wein*, Ditch *wijn* and Scandinavian *vin* all are derived from the Latin word *vinum*, 'wine'.

In English, sadly, we do not have a single word for 'to press grapes for the purpose of making wine'. But it is not too difficult to work out why we lack such a lexical item from our language. The climate and topography of most of the island of Britain, for much of its history, has not been particularly conducive to the production of Riesling or Gewürztraminer or Grüner Veltliner, so we have not traditionally had a great deal of use for a word with this meaning.

For the same type of reason, the English language also lacks words such as *goahpalat*, 'the kind of snowstorm in which the snow falls thickly and sticks to things', *luotkku*, 'loose snow', *moarri*, 'frozen surface of snow' and *ruoknga*, 'thin hard crust of ice on snow'. These are all words which are found in the North Sami language which is spoken in the far north of Norway. Most British people will be somewhat familiar with the phenomenon of 'loose snow', but most of us do not have much cause to talk about it very often; and if and when, from time to time, we do, we have the words 'loose' and 'snow' available to us to put together to convey this particular meaning. We would, of course, be at much more of a disadvantage if we wanted to express the concept of *guoldu*: 'a cloud of snow which blows up from the ground when there is a hard frost without very much wind'.

The point is that when speakers need to talk about particular phenomena on a day-to-day basis, their language will tend to have evolved in such a way as to provide single words to indicate those phenomena in a quick and efficient way.

We do not necessarily even have to look at languages spoken in far-off places to illustrate this point. British sheep-farmers have a number of words for different types of sheep which are mostly unknown to those of us who are not involved in that business, including *ewe-hogg*, 'ewe lamb after mating', *gimmer*, 'ewe between first and second shearing', *freemartin*, 'twin female rendered infertile by the effect of the male twin's dominant hormones during pregnancy', and *shearling*, 'a sheep shorn once'.

But it is still true that the more different cultures are from one another, the more likely there are to be differences in types of vocabulary. The Alaskan Eskimo language Yupik has a number of words which illustrate this rather nicely. The *Yupik Eskimo Dictionary* contains several forms which reflect a very distinct culture that was formed in a very specific milieu. It is safe to say that most of the inhabitants of the British Isles have never needed words such as *araq*, 'ash made from birch tree fungus and mixed with chewing tobacco', *caginraq*, 'pelt of a caribou taken just after the long winter hair has been shed in spring', *partak*, 'spruce root stretched above water from which to hang a line of snares just above the water's surface to catch waterfowl', *qamigartuq*, 'he goes seal-hunting with a small sled and kayak during the spring', or *puguq*, 'it (a fish or seal) came to the surface, emerging halfway'. Perhaps especially unlikely to be needed in the context of modern British society is the very fine Yupik word *qellukaq*, 'the flipper of an elderly seal'.

CARIBOU

The caribou is the North American reindeer. We borrowed the word *caribou* from the French, who had acquired it from the Algonquian Micmac language of the Canadian Maritime provinces and neighbouring areas of Quebec and Maine. Micmac *qaripu* derives from a verb meaning 'to scrape away snow', which is of course what reindeer do to reach edible vegetation in winter.

12.4 The Day After Tomorrow

There is nothing that can be said in one language that cannot be said in another. The current interest in 'untranslatable words' is a little misplaced. Recently there has been a lot of discussion about the Norwegian and Danish word *hygge* which, it is claimed, cannot be translated. But that is not true. Here is a translation: 'comfort; cosiness; friendly, homely, cheerful atmosphere'.

What is true is that in order to translate a single word from one language to another, you might need to use several words. The French for 'anticlockwise' is *dans le sens inverse des aiguilles d'une montre*. Languages do not differ in what they can say, but they do differ in terms of what they can say in a single word.

In English we have the words *yesterday*, *today* and *tomorrow*, but we do not have any single words that refer backwards or forwards in time beyond one day. If today is Friday and we want to talk about Sunday, we have to use four words and say 'the day after tomorrow', which is rather a mouthful compared to the single German word *übermorgen* or Norwegian *overmorgen*; similarly, Greek has *methavrio*, and in Hungarian it is *holnaputån*. These words are all derived from words meaning tomorrow – *morgen* in German and Norwegian, *avrio* in Greek, *holnap* in Hungarian – but in some varieties of Sardinian, 'the day after tomorrow' is expressed with a single word, *barrigadu*, which does not contain the word 'tomorrow'.

The same is true going backwards in time. Where we, rather long-windedly, have to say 'the day before yesterday', German has the single word *vorgestern*, Greek has *proxthés* and Hungarian has *tegnapelőt* (the elements *gestern*, *exthés* and *tegnap* in these words all mean 'yesterday'). These terms are translatable into English, but only at greater length.

Other examples of single-word time references which are absent from English can be found in several European languages. *Mañana*, 'tomorrow', is stereotypically supposed to be a favourite word used by Spanish speakers to postpone something, but Greek has not only *methavrio*, 'the day after tomorrow', but also *metamethavrio*, 'the day after the day after tomorrow': one Greek word to seven in English.

Some languages have single words which are lacking in English to refer to specific parts of days. Dutch has *vanmiddag*, 'this afternoon' and *vanavond*, 'this evening'. The Welsh word *heno* also means 'this evening, tonight', and so does the Greek word *apopse*. In Cretan Greek 'last night, yesterday evening' is expressed by a single word, *opsargas*. The North Frisian language of northern Germany has the rather special term *marling*, 'this morning'. And, unusually amongst European languages, North Frisian also has a word for 'this week': *waaling*.

This same lexical mismatch across languages can also be observed when it comes to terms for years. In the German of Austria, Switzerland and Bavaria, speakers use a single word corresponding to English 'this year': *heuer*. Lovers of Austrian wine will be familiar with places called *Heuriger*, which is short for *heuriger Wein*, 'this year's wine' and refers to an open-air inn where the new wine can be sampled along with food.

The Welsh, Hungarians and Greeks likewise have a single word for 'this year': respectively *eleni*, *idén* and *fétos* (*fétino krasí* is Greek for 'this year's wine'). These languages also have a single word which means 'last year': *llynedd* in Welsh, *tavaly* in Hungarian and *perisis* in Greek (with *perisinós* signifying 'last year's, from last year').

Some varieties of English do a little better than others on this single-word score. In earlier forms of English, in addition to *to-day* and *to-morrow*, there was the word *to-year*, 'this year'. Chaucer wrote: 'Yet hadde I levere [rather] wedde no wyf to-yeere'. This word has sadly long since disappeared from mainstream English, but I do remember very clearly from my childhood hearing older Norfolk dialect speakers, born in the last years of the nineteenth century, saying things like 'That's a lot warmer to-year than that was twelve month ago'.

12.5 Base 20

For a while in the 1960s, an innovation called 'the new maths' was introduced into British schools. Pupils became acquainted, amongst other things, with the fascinating new mathematical concept of bases other than 10. This was considered revolutionary – which was very odd when you consider that for centuries British schoolchildren had already been working with many different arithmetical bases.

When I went to school, we had to learn to do arithmetic using base 12 for inches and feet, and for pence and shillings – there were twelve pence in a shilling. We also counted eggs in base 12: half a dozen, two dozen, and so on. With weights, we used base 16 for ounces and pounds, and base 14 for pounds and stones. And we needed to be able to work with base 20 for shillings and pounds, as well as for hundredweights and tons: there were twenty hundredweight in a ton. We also all knew that a *score* was twenty: three score years and ten was seventy years.

Even so, we normally used base 10 for most purposes: English counting numbers are organised decimally, in tens (twenty to twenty-nine, thirty to thirty-nine, and so on).

We can tell that base 10 has been the norm for very many centuries in our culture from the forms we use in the language itself. *Thirteen, fourteen, fifteen* etc. are clearly originally derived from *three, four, five* etc. plus *ten. Twenty, thirty, forty* etc. obviously have to do with *two, three, four* etc. as multiples of ten. *Eleven* is probably derived from a root which meant 'one left (after counting to ten)' – the Old English form was *endleofan* – and *twelve* was similarly derived from 'two left (after ten)'.

But there are also a number of European languages where there are strong linguistic traces showing that base 20 has had a history of being the standard way of doing arithmetic in their communities. In the French of France, the word for eighty is *quatre-vingt*, 'four twenties'; ninety is *quatre-vingt-dix*, 'four twenties (plus) ten'; ninety-one is *quatre-vingt-onze*, 'four twenties (plus) eleven'; and ninety-six is *quatre-vingt-seize*, 'four twenties plus sixteen'; seventy-six is *soixante-seize*, 'sixty (plus) sixteen'.

In Danish, twenty is also used as a base in a rather complicated way. The number sixty is *tre-sinds-tyve*, 'three times twenty'; the full form is *tresindstyve* but it is much more usually shortened to *tres*. And fifty is *halvtreds*, which is short for *halvtredjesindstyve*, which means 'half (of twenty) (less than) three times twenty'.

The Danes still use the older Germanic word-order pattern for double-digit numbers – 'five-and-twenty' rather than our 'twenty-five' – so that fifty-five is *fem-og-halvtredjesindstyve*, or *femoghalvtreds* for short, where *fem* is 'five' and *og* is 'and'. The corresponding Norwegian word for fifty-five, *femti fem*, is very much more transparent and easier to process; and in fact Danes often use Norwegian-like forms when talking in Danish to Norwegians and Swedes, in order to be more readily understood.

This vigesimal – base 20 – system has also traditionally been used in the Celtic languages of the British Isles and Brittany. In Scottish Gaelic, 20 is *fichead*, 40 is *dà fhichead*, 'two twenties', 60 is *trì fichead*, 'three twenties' and so on right up to 199, with 180 being *naoidh fichead*, 'nine twenties'. As in French, seventy is 'three twenties and ten' – *trì fichead 's deich*.

Basque and Georgian, both pre-Indo-European languages of Europe, also use the vigesimal system. In Basque, forty is *berrogei*, which is 'two twenties'; sixty is *hirurogei*, 'three twenties'; and eighty, *laurogei*, is 'four twenties'. Again, as in French, seventy-six is *hirurogeita sei*, 'three twenties (plus) sixteen'.

Some people have suggested that the Basque system provided the model for the system now found in the Celtic languages, which were probably the first Indo-European languages to come into contact with Basque. That could be true. But, sadly, I have no space left to discuss this any further as this column is already six-hundred-and-four-and-half-of-twenty-less-than-four-times-twenty words long.

12.6 Five-and-Twenty Past

When telling the time, for the first twenty years of my life or so I always said *five-and-twenty past two* rather than *twenty-five past two*, and I continued to use that type of formulation on at least some occasions for many years after that. My grandparents, all born in the 1880s, almost certainly never said anything else, and this was also the normal, everyday way of telling the time for my parents. It is a pity, I now feel, that I was part of the first generation to abandon this centuries-old usage, though it is pleasing to know that there are still some people around who maintain it.

The reason I used to say *five-and-twenty past two* was, of course, that everybody else said it too. That was the way of telling the time which I learnt as a child, as I was acquiring the sort of English spoken around me by everybody who I normally came into contact with on a day-to-day basis in my Norfolk home. But there was nothing particularly East Anglian about it: this was what many people used to say over more or less the whole of England.

One interesting thing about my earlier usage was that it was entirely confined to telling the time. No one ever said *It's five-and-twenty miles from here to Cromer*. That seems to be because this usage was a relic left over from a bygone age. For many hundreds of years, English speakers always used to put all units (not just *five*) before the tens when using numerals: *four-and-thirty*, *seven-and-fifty*, *six-and-ninety* – and not just when telling the time. In the Old English language, twenty-four was *feower-and-twentig*. Shakespeare wrote of 'five-and-thirty leagues'. Many people are aware of lines in folk songs like 'When I was one-and-twenty', and most of us know the nursery rhyme with 'four-and-twenty blackbirds baked in a pie'.

This type of structure gradually died out, however, with the loss spreading slowly from one sphere of usage to another until in the end time-telling was the last context where it survived, although in some areas it also lasted almost as long in expressions of age: *she's four-and-twenty years old*.

This units-tens order which has now almost disappeared from English, apart from the time-telling vestiges, was formerly the norm in all Germanic languages. The Modern German for twenty-four is still *vierundzwanzig*, 'four-and-twenty'; in Dutch it is *vierentwintig*; the West Frisian is *fjouwerentweintich*; and the Danish is *fire-og-tyve*. Swedish, however, has the tens-unit order, like Modern English: *tjugo-fyra*.

The 'four-and-twenty' way of counting is rather unusual in the languages of the world, and it is not so surprising that it died out in English. It is perhaps significant that when we write numbers using numerals, we put the tens before the units. People working in German report that when writing down numerals – for example an address given over the phone – there is a split-second delay: if a number in the 'four-and-twenty' form is to be written down, you can't start writing when you hear the 'four' but have to wait until the 'and twenty' comes along.

The Norwegian situation for numbers is more complicated: there, both orders occur. In 1951, the Norwegian government introduced an official plan to change the numerals over from the 'four-and-twenty' system to the 'twenty-four' type. Their expectation was that, once it had been introduced in the schools and promoted elsewhere, the change would take only a few years to come into effect in the speech of the Norwegian people. But the older system, even if it is now much less used by younger people, is still alive and reasonably well, especially in informal speech, nine-and-sixty years later.

12.7 Exclusion

Anybody who has lived in Britain for any length of time will know that the way people speak English in Aberdeen sounds very different from the way in which it is spoken in Abingdon. The accents of people from Newcastle-upon-Tyne in the English north-east are very different from those of Newcastle-under-Lyme in Staffordshire. Speakers of Carlisle English have very different-sounding consonants and, especially, vowels from those of Cardiff English. And, on the basis of the way they speak, no one would mistake a Scouser for a Cockney.

This raises a very interesting question: why is this the case? Why do people pronounce English – or any other language – differently in different places? Why is it that the English of Southampton has a different ring to it from the English of Southport? Why is the German of Berlin different from the German of Berne, and the Spanish of Madrid different from that of Murcia?

There are, of course, two different ways of answering 'why' questions of this sort. If the question means 'how did it come about that people from different places have distinct accents – what is the reason?', then we can come up with something of an answer. All languages are constantly changing, and they change in different ways in different places and amongst different social groupings. Even if you start off with a situation where everybody speaks in the same way, regional variation will start to set in after some generations – although exactly why this happens is not easy to explain: linguistic scientists are sometimes driven to say things like 'that's just how languages are'.

But if the question means 'what is the point of different accents – what is the function of this variation?', then we have to provide a different kind of answer. Dr Emma Cohen, a cognitive anthropologist at the University of Oxford, has argued that there was an evolutionary advantage to the development of different accents. When early human beings lived in relatively small groups, it was always possible to tell whether someone was a member of your group because you knew everybody personally and could recognise them by sight, so outsiders were easily identifiable as such. But when groups became bigger, that could no longer be done so readily.

However, once different Palaeolithic communities began to develop different accents, then it was possible to recognise outsiders simply by listening to them speak. If someone had an even slightly different accent from you, you would instantly know that they were not a member of your group and might therefore be hostile, so you should perhaps be careful in dealing with them. Accents, in other words, functioned as badges of membership.

Crucially, they were badges of membership which were rather secure against being used fraudulently. For early humans, there was an evolutionary advantage inherent in the fact that, after childhood, it is very difficult to acquire a new accent perfectly. Nearly everybody has a foreign accent when speaking any language or dialect which they have learnt as an adolescent or adult, because only young children are genetically programmed to master the millimetre- and millisecond-accurate coordination of the different speech organs which is necessary for reproducing particular speech sounds perfectly in rapid speech. Anyone attempting to imitate your group's accent and getting it even slightly wrong might be a person to be particularly wary of.

Sadly, in Modern England, accents as badges of membership are often misused to make sure that outsiders stay outside – for example, by denying them access to certain jobs. A report which was published in 2015 found that elite firms in Britain are still heavily dominated by people from privileged social backgrounds, because companies systematically exclude bright young working-class applicants from their staff by including a candidate's accent amongst their selection criteria. Firms like this may be elite, but they are also dismayingly Palaeolithic.

PALAEOLITHIC

The term *Palaeolithic* refers to the earliest of the three sub-divisions of the Stone Age (the others being the Mesolithic and Neolithic), which lasted around 2.5 million years. *Paleo* comes from the Ancient Greek for 'old', and *lith* derives from Greek *lithos* 'stone', an element we also see in *monolith*, originally a 'single block of stone'.

12.8 Demography vs Prestige

After the Norman conquest of England in 1066, a variety of Old French became the language of power and prestige in the country, because it was the language of the ruling class. Anglo-Norman French was rather different from the French of Paris, and can usefully be regarded as a different language. We still have traces of it in modern Britain. The phrase *La Reine le vault*, 'the Queen desires it', continues to be used at Westminster to show Her Majesty's assent to parliamentary bills. And we still use occasional French-style noun-adjective phrases like *heir apparent* and *court martial*.

But in spite of the power and prestige attached to the Norman ruling class, the Anglo-Norman tongue was dead and gone as a spoken language after 300 years. When it comes to competition between languages, demography usually wins out over prestige. Although the Normans were in charge, there were many more of us than them, and so the English language prevailed.

When the Normans abandoned French for English, they were doing something they had already done once before. Their ancestors were originally Scandinavians who had arrived in northern France speaking Old Danish, but only a few generations after taking control of Normandy and having the area itself named after them, they switched to French, the language of the majority.

We see this pattern repeated many times. During the Germanic diaspora, the Visigoths invaded Iberia in the early 400s AD, bringing their East Germanic language with them. They took control of most of Spain and Portugal, as well as parts of south-western France, and founded a kingdom which lasted until the early 700s, when it succumbed to the Moorish invasion from North Africa. But well before that, the Visigoths had succumbed linguistically to the power of numbers and abandoned their language in favour of the variety of Late Spoken Latin which later became Spanish.

Some of the West Germanic-speaking Franks underwent the same fate. Originally inhabiting the east bank of the Rhine, they started expanding west across the river in the fifth century and gradually took control of the Rhineland, the Low Countries and northern France – which bears that name because it was the Kingdom of the Franks. In those regions where the ruling Franks remained a demographic minority – the areas which are now France and southern Belgium – they eventually switched from speaking Germanic Franconian to the Latin-derived language of the Romano-Celtic population, which later became Old French. Some of the linguistic characteristics which distinguish French from the Occitan of southern France are thought by many scholars to be due to Frankish influence.

Later on, the same kind of process occurred in Ireland – and once again the Normans were involved. A number of Anglo-Norman forces, including an army led by King Henry II, invaded Ireland from Wales and England in the 1160s and 1170s. The troops were led by Anglo-Norman nobles but consisted mainly of English speakers (see also Section 9.3). Eventually much of Ireland came under Anglo-Norman/English control, but a couple of centuries later most of the descendants of these original overlords and their followers had forgotten their native tongues and were speaking the Gaelic of the native Irish.

The Bulgars were a semi-nomadic Turkic-speaking group of peoples who lived on the Eurasian steppe, north of the Caspian and Black Seas. Some of them migrated south, arriving in the eastern Balkans in the late 600s AD, where they conquered the local population and became the ruling elite. However, by the mid-800s they were all speaking local South Slavic dialects. These days, when we talk about Bulgarian, we are referring to a Slavic, not a Turkic, language.

The moral is that human beings speak like those people around them they have most contact with, not like the posh and the powerful. In fact, it is rather normal for powerful alien elites to end up speaking the language of the common people.

12.9 If We All Spoke the Same Language

There are people who believe that languages are divisive. The world would be a much better place, they reckon, if we all spoke the same language. Surely it would be much easier to achieve worldwide cooperation and peace if there was one single world language?

In fact, nothing could be further from the truth. A very large number of the most bitter and bloody conflicts in human history have been fought out between peoples who spoke the same language and had no trouble at all in understanding one another's speech.

Somewhere between 600,000 and 850,000 soldiers died in the American Civil War – that's as many Americans as died in both world wars plus all the other wars the USA has ever been involved in all added together. It was no help at all to those unfortunate Union and Confederate Civil War fighters that both sides spoke the same language.

The history of Europe is full of similar cases. The English Civil War of 1642–1651 brought about appalling levels of death and destruction – something which many of us remember hearing absolutely nothing at all about in our school history lessons. Over 80,000 people – 'people' meaning men of course – were killed in the actual fighting; and an additional 100,000 women, children and men died from disease brought on by the war. Approximately 4 per cent of the entire population of England perished because of a war which was being fought between two sides who both spoke, most of them, only English and nothing but English.

The 1917–1923 Russian Civil War which followed the Revolution was one of the greatest catastrophes there has ever been: some estimates reckon that there were as many as 12 million military and civilian casualties. Most of those, though by no means all, were native Russian speakers; and Russian was the single language of wider communication used from one end of the country to the other.

The Spanish Civil War of 1936–1939 did involve speakers of Basque, Catalan, Galician and Spanish, but everyone involved could also speak the national language, Spanish, which was in any case the mother tongue of the vast majority of the combatants and non-combatants. Over 600,000 people died, and many more were imprisoned or displaced.

The Greek Civil War was another disastrous conflict in which nearly everyone involved was a native speaker of the same language, and where even the Slavic, Albanian and Romanian speakers who were involved were able to speak Greek. The fighting between leftist and rightist Greek forces, which lasted from 1946 to 1949, led to 150,000 deaths and to over 1 million people – out of a total population of around 7 million – having to leave their homes.

Within living memory, the carnage that occurred in Yugoslavia between 1991 and 2001 was yet another tragic example of people who spoke the same language slaughtering each other. About 150,000 people lost their lives, including 14,000 in Sarajevo alone. Not everyone in Yugoslavia spoke the same language: in Kosovo they spoke Albanian. But everywhere else they spoke Serbo-Croat, except in Slovenia and Macedonia, where closely related South Slavic languages were spoken. Nowadays Serbia, Croatia, Bosnia and Montenegro all claim that they speak different languages, but they are all perfectly mutually intelligible (see Section 7.12).

Contrast this with Switzerland, which has four indigenous languages – Swiss-German, French, Italian and Romansch – but which has not been involved in any fighting since 1847.

SLAV

Slovene, Slovak, Slavic – these words have the same root. Slavs are peoples who speak Slavic languages like Russian, Ukrainian, Polish, Czech, Croatian, Bulgarian. The name Slav has no connection with slave, and probably none with Slavic *slovo*, 'word'. Most likely it is derived from a river anciently called Slova; we are not sure where that river was, but it may well have been the Dnieper.

---

13 Sport

Britain seems to have played a more influential role than most other countries in the development of what are now the internationally most popular sports. With only a little exaggeration it could be said that, of all the major internationally played sports, the Scots invented golf and the English invented all the rest. Some Americans will probably want to lay claim to baseball, but not even that is theirs: Jane Austen famously wrote in her 1798 novel *Northanger Abbey* that the heroine preferred 'cricket, base ball, riding on horseback' and running about to reading books. And the earliest written reference to baseball in England comes from the 1740s.

Of course, we do have to accept that ice hockey and lacrosse were developed in Canada. But, even allowing for the fact that lacrosse was originally played by the indigenous peoples of Canada and the United States and not the colonists, we can certainly still say that English-speaking peoples have played a vital role in the development of world sports.

There are numerous linguistically interesting phenomena associated with these sports. Even if we restrict ourselves to English, we can note differences of usage between different anglophone societies. American English speakers, for instance, generally avoid the singular form *sport* and are more likely to say 'My daughter is very good at sports'. Americans most often talk about the *offense* in different sports, whereas British people are probably more likely to say *attack*. Cricket has *bowlers* while baseball has *pitchers*. And as is well known, the word *football* has many different meanings according to what is the most popular of all the many games involving feet and a ball in a particular place, such as Association Football or soccer in England, American Football in the USA and Canadian football in Canada. In different parts of Australia, *football* can refer variously to Australian Rules football, Rugby League or Rugby Union.

In this chapter, I examine a number of similarly interesting linguistic phenomena – words, names and usages – which are linked to, or can be exemplified through, sporting activities, institutions, and sports people.

13.1 Manchester United's Sun-Skerry

As is well known to most English football fans – and to the entire population of Norway over the age of three – the manager of Manchester United is called Ole

Gunnar Solskjær. Like very many Norwegians, he has two given names which he actually uses – Ole and Gunnar – so it is just the very poetic Solskjær which is his family or surname: *sol* is the Norwegian word for 'sun', and *skjær* corresponds to English *skerry*, 'rock covered by the sea at high tide'. Somehow, Sunskerry seems a much more appropriately romantic name for a high-flying football manager than Atkinson, Ferguson or perhaps especially – let's be honest – Klopp.

Like most Norwegians, Ole Gunnar is not only a proud and unashamed speaker of his native dialect, in his case the urban dialect of Kristiansund, but also a brilliant speaker of Mancunian English. But Jürgen Klopp, too, is also a very good English speaker. And his surname also has a story to tell. Although the Liverpool manager grew up in southern Germany, his family name is very obviously (to any German dialectologist) a north German or Netherlandic name: the Dutch and North German word *appel*, 'apple', corresponds to south German *Apfel*, so the south German equivalent of Klopp would be *Klopf*. There is a place in the Rhineland Palatinate in Germany where there is a Klopp Castle; but it is more likely that the surname comes from the Dutch and Low German verb *kloppen*, 'to knock, beat, pound'– the south German form would be *klopfen* – which is related to the English word *clap*. This would signify that a forebear worked in a manual occupation of the same type as indicated by the English surname Leadbeater.

Josep 'Pep' Guardiola Sala, the manager of Manchester City, is also linguistically very interesting. He was born and grew up in Catalonia, and his native language is Catalan. Josep is the Catalan equivalent of English Joseph, Italian Giuseppe and Portuguese and Spanish José. But like the members of all the linguistic minorities living in Spain – albeit, in the case of Catalan, a minority with many millions of speakers – Pep has of necessity had to learn Spanish as well (see also Section 7.9).

Unai Emery Etxegoien, who manages Arsenal, is another Spanish citizen whose mother tongue is not Spanish, though like Guardiola he does speak it fluently. Emery grew up in Hondarribia, a strongly Basque-speaking town which is called Fuenterrabía in Spanish and Fontarrabie in French. Hondarribia lies just across the French border from the French-Basque town of Hendaia (Hendaye in French). But his native language is the oldest of all the European languages, Euskara or Basque (see Section 7.6).

The manager of Tottenham Hotspur is Mauricio Roberto Pochettino Trossero. He, too, is from a predominantly Spanish-speaking country, Argentina, but – like Lionel Messi – he comes from an Italian-speaking background and bears an Italian-language surname. His great-grandfather emigrated to South American from the Piedmont area of north-western Italy and settled in the surprisingly named town of Murphy, which is called after a nineteenth-century immigrant from Ireland, John James Murphy. (The surname Murphy is derived from the Irish Gaelic name Ó Murchadh, 'fighter at sea', from *muir*, 'sea', and *cath*, 'fight'.) As far as I know, Pochettino does not speak Irish. But his name does signify something to Italian speakers: *poco* means 'a little', and the surname Pocchetino translates as 'a tiny little bit'.

Obviously, a degree of multilingualism is most helpful if you are planning a career as a top-level football manager.

But I have to come clean now before I finish this piece and admit that, according to Norwegian onomasticians (linguistic experts on names) – even if this is not known to the average Norwegian – the surname Solskjær actually derives historically from a farm in the Kristiansund area that was originally called Solskjela, which meant, rather unromantically, 'soggy bottom'. And in a prequel to Ole Gunnar's soccer conquests in England, the Norwegian King Harald Fairhair defeated local chieftains in battles at Solskjela in AD 862 and 863.

SOGGY

Rather surprisingly, *soggy*, 'saturated with moisture, soppy, soaked', is a rather new word in the English language. We have no record of it before about 1800, though the noun *sog*, 'swamp, bog, quagmire', does put in an appearance in the 1500s. We are not at all certain whether the word originally comes from 'soaken', that is, *soaked*, but that is a possibility.

13.2 De Bruyne

Football fans will know that Kevin De Bruyne is the brilliant Belgian midfielder who plays for Manchester City, as well as for the Belgian national team. They may not all be quite so familiar with other foreign soccer stars such as the Spanish international left back Alberto Moreno, the German full back Christopher Braun, the French defender Arnaud Lebrun, or the American midfielder Carli Lloyd – she has played for the USA international team nearly 300 times. But, interestingly, all of these players bear essentially the same surname as the former Manchester United and England defender, Wes Brown.

The words *bruin*, *moreno*, *braun*, *brun* and *llwyd* mean 'brown' in, respectively, Dutch, Spanish, German, French and Welsh. De Bruyne literally means 'the brown one'. Like the other names meaning 'brown', it was originally a nickname given to people because of the colour of their hair or because of their darker-than-usual complexion. In mediaeval times, when family names began to be established and passed on from generation to generation, the nickname turned into a surname. According to the *Oxford Dictionary of Family Names in Britain and Ireland*, almost 400,000 people in Great Britain were recorded in the 2011 census as having the family name Brown or Browne.

Our English-language surname Black (including Blake, Blaik and Blaikie) is also in origin a byname referring to a person's complexion. In predominantly pale-skinned northern Europe, the nickname – later a family name – signified that a person had skin of a somewhat darker hue than most other people. The surname of Tom Dezwarte, the Belgian road-racing cyclist, means 'the black one' in Dutch. And from the world of cricket, the Australian international fast-bowler Andrew Fekete's family name means 'black' in Hungarian.

Another cricketer with a colour-based family name is the former England fast-bowler Darren Gough, whose surname comes from Welsh word for 'red', *coch*. Like Gough, the English-language surname Read or Reade also indicates that the original bearers of the nickname had red hair or a ruddy complexion; the family names Rudd and Ruddy imply the same thing. The Dutch surnames Rood, De Rood(e), Roode and Roodt also all derive from the word for the colour red. Le Rouge or Lerouge have the same origin in French, and Rosso is the equivalent name in Italian.

Words for the colour white are also frequently employed as surnames, having originally been used as a nickname for people who had a pale complexion or fair hair, or perhaps who were prematurely grey. In Great Britain, the surname White or Whyte is not as common as Brown, but it is common enough, with about 140,000 bearers in the 2011 census. Equivalent family names in other languages include Leblanc in French and De Wit in Dutch, both meaning 'the white one', as well as German Weiss, Italian Bianco, Welsh Gwyn and Polish Biały, which simply mean 'white'.

There are also a handful of people in Britain with the name Yellow, a nickname also based on hair colour. More common is the surname Bowie or Bowey, which comes from the Scottish Gaelic word *buidhe*, 'yellow', which was also used as a nickname.

Happily, however, the family name Green or Greene did not come about because early bearers of the name had green hair or a sickly complexion – it was because they lived near the village green.

HANDFUL

Handful was obviously originally two words, *hand full*. This can be seen from the fact that the plural used to be *handsful*. But in the 1500s some people started writing *handfuls*, and since the nineteenth century this has been normal usage, showing that *handful* is now very definitely just a single word.

13.3 Borussia and Albion

Those of us who follow Champions League football have become familiar over the years with the names of many European football clubs. More often than not, we do not give these names much thought – and indeed some names, like FC Basel and Sevilla, do not require much thought. But there are other team names which are opaque to us unless we take the trouble to find out what they mean.

Take Borussia Dortmund, for instance: what exactly does it mean? Unlike other titles used by teams across Europe – *Sporting, Athletic, Olympic, Real* ('royal') – *Borussia* offers few obvious clues as to why it should have been adopted by the club's founders, though it is a name the club shares with other German sides, such as Borussia Fulda, Borussia Mönchengladbach and Borussia Neunkirchen.

All these clubs are located in the west or centre of Germany, but their shared name derives from much further east, from beyond the current border of Germany with Poland, from a long-lost ancient Baltic people. These people spoke a language related to Latvian and Lithuanian, and inhabited an area along the Baltic Sea coast which today lies in Poland, Russia and Lithuania. They were called *Prussi* in Mediaeval Latin – nobody is sure where that name came from – and the area they lived in was known as Prussia (see Sections 4.7, and 6.2). At some point, the alternative Latin names *Borussi* and *Borussia* also emerged, because some people developed the mistaken idea that Prussia derived from Slavic *po Russia* meaning 'next to Russia'.

So: the name *Borussia* was a mistake. And the people who lived in Borussia were not even Germans. So why on earth is this name now given to western German football teams in towns like Dortmund which are very much nearer to the Netherlands than to Lithuania?

The answer is reasonably clear. In the 1200s, the Prussians – who had never been Christianised – were conquered by the German Teutonic Knights (see Section 4.7); and their language gradually gave way to German, just as the people themselves were absorbed and replaced by the German incomers. But the name *Prussia* survived after the Teutonic Knights' takeover; and the German incomers eventually came to be known as 'Prussians' themselves. The new Germanised Prussia then gradually became a significant military and political power, with its capital in Königsberg (now Russian Kaliningrad), though as the kingdom expanded, its capital moved to Berlin. Prussia eventually became the dominant state in Germany, and its borders eventually came to extend right across northern Germany as far west as the Dutch frontier.

The people of Dortmund, then, were not Borussians, nor Baltic Prussians, nor even German Prussians. But for many decades after 1813, they lived in an area which was officially part of the Kingdom of Prussia – a fact which still lives on in the name of their football club.

There is another, even longer historical story to tell about another set of opaque football-club names – all those British clubs with *Albion* in their name. These are found not just in England (Plymouth, Burton and West Bromwich, amongst others), but also Scotland (Stirling, and Albion Rovers from Coatbridge) and Wales (Albion Rovers again, this time from Newport). And it is fitting that we should find them in each of the three home countries, because *Albion* is the oldest known name for Britain.

A search for the origins of this name involves us in travelling back very many centuries. *Albion* was used in an Ancient Greek sailing manual dating from as long ago as c. 550 BC, and it occurs in the Latin writings of Pliny the Elder in about AD 50. It was probably originally a Greek version of a Celtic word for Britain. The Romans must have acquired it from the Greeks, and then it would subsequently have been borrowed into English from Latin.

Albion appears to be related to the Latin word *albus*, which meant 'white'; one possibility is that the Celtic Gauls of northern France called Britain 'white' because of the chalk cliffs along the coastline of southern England which were visible to them across the English Channel.

Today, Celtic-speaking people are themselves commemorated in the name of the Spanish football team Celta Vigo, who play in the originally Celtic-speaking Galician area of north-western Spain, and also in the name of the Scottish club, Glasgow Celtic.

The name Albion also lives on outside football in the Welsh word for Scotland – *Alban* –and its Gaelic counterpart *Alba*. Within the sphere of football, it is particularly well represented in the name of the club whose home is right by that white southern English coastline which perhaps gave rise to the name in the first place: Brighton and Hove Albion.

13.4 Champions League

Since the game of football originated in Britain, it is no surprise that many languages have simply borrowed our English word for the game: Spanish has *futbol*, Hungarian *futball*, Serbian *fudbal*. But other languages have come up with a local form of the term by combining their own word for 'foot' with their own word for 'ball' – so we have Dutch *voetbal*, Danish *fodbold*, Finnish *jalka-pallo* and Greek *podó-sphero*.

This knowledge can sometimes help us to work out what the names of certain European football clubs signify. The Finnish word for 'football' explains the name of the club HJK Helsinki, which in full is Helsingin Jalkapalloklubi. The Greek term accounts for the name of the Cypriot team APOEL Nicosia, whose full Greek form is Athletikós Podospherikós Ómilos Ellínon Lefkosías, 'Athletic Football Club of Greeks of Nicosia' (the city we know as Nicosia is called Lefkosía in Greek).

Yet other languages have invented their own words for football. The AC in AC Milano stands for Associazione Calcio, where *calcio* is the Italian word for 'football' – it originally meant 'kick'. The NK in NK Maribor is the acronym for Nogometni Klub. *Nogomet*, the Slovenian word for 'football', was borrowed from

Croatian, where *noga* means 'foot' and *met* comes from the verb *metnuti*, 'to put (something where you want it to go)'.

A classical education may also help in working out where football-club names come from. The name of the Greek team Panathinaikós means 'all-Athenian'. And the Turin-based club Juventus takes its name from Latin *iuventus*, 'youth' (the same concept is honoured in the name of the Swiss team, Berne Young Boys who, however, helpfully use an English appellation).

But sometimes an ordinary British education of any kind is no help. Most people will have no idea that the name of the Turkish club Galatasary means 'Galata Palace'. Turkish *saray*, 'palace' was originally borrowed from Persian, and also appears in the name of the Bosnian city Sarajevo.

Equally opaque to most of us is the team name Shakhtar Donetsk. We know that Donetsk is a city in south-eastern Ukraine – although the unstable military situation in that country means the team are now playing in Kharkhiv – but what about *Shakhtar*? We might guess that the name means something like 'Donetsk United', but in fact the Ukrainian word *shakhtár* means 'miner'. The original base from which these football-club players were drawn was the coal-miners' trade union.

Eintracht Frankfurt more or less corresponds to 'Frankfurt United'. *Eintracht* means 'harmony, concord, unity', and is composed of *ein*, 'one', and *tracht*, from the German verb *tragen*, which is historically the same as our English verb *to draw*, so the word's initial sense was something like 'drawing together into one'.

The name of the north German club Werder Bremen also has an interesting history dating from its foundation. *Werder* is a Low German topographical term meaning an 'island in a river, an elevation in a wetland'. Old English had the same word in the form of *waroth*, 'bank' or 'shore', which survived into later forms of English as *warth*: Warwick in Cumbria, on the River Eden, was originally Warthwic, 'village on a bank'. English has now lost this word altogether, and it is not very common in German nowadays either; but in the name of the Bremen team, *Werder* refers specifically to the floodplain by the river where the club played their matches in their very earliest days at the turn of the twentieth century.

Europeans might equally welcome foundation-story explanations for certain puzzling British club names: we could start by telling them that Arsenal was founded by munitions workers at the Royal Arsenal in Woolwich.

BASLE

The name of the Swiss city which is called Basel in German descends from its Roman name, Basilia. The French name – France is just down the road – is Bâle. In Italian it's Basilea, and in Greek Vasilía. The English-language name is Basle.

13.5 Tennis

The British are sometimes said, no doubt somewhat inaccurately, to have invented most of the world's most important sports: football, tennis, golf, cricket, rugby union, rugby league, baseball, croquet, snooker, hockey, curling, darts ... So it is interesting to notice that we have not been quite so good at coming up with English-origin names for these sports. Often, it seems, we have relied on the languages of our European neighbours for the names we refer to our games by.

Tennis is not an English word. In the early 1400s, the game was known as *tenetz*, pronounced with the stress on the second syllable, which suggests a French origin. And, indeed, *tennis* does appear to have come from a form of the French verb *tenir*, 'to hold, keep, receive'. The immediate source was the Anglo-Norman exclamation *Tenetz!* meaning '(get ready to) receive!' This would have been what a player who was about to serve the ball called out to their opponent. In Modern French, *Tenez!* can still mean 'here you are', as when giving somebody something.

The ancient sport of golf was invented by the Scots. But as far as we can determine, the word *golf* is not Scots or Gaelic or even English. Though experts are not entirely sure about this, it appears rather likely that the name is Dutch in origin: *kolf* meant 'bat' or 'club' in Dutch, and in the mediaeval period some Dutch-speaking peoples in what is now Belgium and the Netherlands did play a number of different games which involved hitting a ball with a stick.

Cricket is also a game which involves hitting a ball with a stick – and what could possibly be more English than cricket? But the word *cricket* is probably not English either. It may well derive from Old French *criquet*, which meant 'post' or 'stick', though some authorities think it is more likely to have come from the mediaeval Dutch dialect word *krik*, 'stick'.

Yet another sport requiring players to hit a round object with a piece of wood is hockey, and once again the name is probably not English. The word *hockey* is thought to have come from Mediaeval French *hoquet*, meaning 'shepherd's staff, crook'; hockey sticks are in fact shaped rather like a crook, with a curve at the bottom. And it is then no surprise to find that the word *croquet* is also French. It is essentially the same as the word *crochet*. *Crochet* is the diminutive form of *croche*, meaning 'hook', with *croquet* being the northern French dialect form of the same word.

Surely *rugby* must be an English word? Isn't it named after the English school in the Warwickshire town of Rugby where the game was first played? Yes, but it is interesting to note that the name of the town is itself not entirely English. Originally it was: its Old English name was Hrocasburg, which over the centuries became Rockburh, where the ending *-burh* meant 'fortified place'. The modern form of this name should have ended up being something like Rockbury or

Rugbury. But as a result of the Viking invasions, which were followed by Danish settlement in much of northern, central and eastern England, including Warwickshire, the name of the town eventually changed to Rugby, with the English -*bury* ending being replaced by the Scandinavian -*by*, 'village, homestead', which still means 'town' in Danish and Norwegian and 'village' in Swedish. So it could be argued that the town name Rugby is only half English.

Even the word *sport* itself was not originally English. It is an abbreviation of the earlier word *disport*, which meant 'diversion, relaxation, recreation, entertainment, amusement', and which came into English from Norman French.

English can always, however, lay claim to the name of the world's most popular sport, football. This word is totally English in its linguistic origins, being composed of two venerable and incontrovertibly English words: *foot* and *ball*.

13.6 Foul

On 22 June 1986, in a World Cup quarter-final football match played between England and Argentina in Mexico City, the Argentinian player Diego Maradona knocked the ball into the England net with his hand and claimed a goal – which was incorrectly awarded by the match officials. Argentina won the match 2–1, and England were eliminated from the tournament.

Many England football supporters might agree that what Maradona did that day constituted an act which was 'grossly offensive, physically loathsome, and indicative of putridity and corruption' – which is part of the dictionary definition of the word *foul*. Technically speaking, of course, a *foul* in football is something rather less than grossly offensive. Handling the ball in soccer is simply an *offence* against the rules of the game. But that so-called 'hand of God' goal is still capable of arousing strong feelings on the part of aggrieved England supporters: synonyms for the adjective *foul* which they might agree with include *tainted, filthy, noxious, gross, rank, polluted, abominable, wicked, obscene, defiled, ugly, shameful* and *disgraceful*.

The word *foul* goes back to the Old English *fúl*, 'dirty, offensive, morally polluted'. In Modern Dutch, *vuil* means 'dirty, filthy', while in Danish *ful* means 'nasty, ugly'. German *faul* denotes 'rotten, decayed, putrid' but also 'lazy, indolent, slothful'. These words all stem from an Ancient Germanic root *fulo-*, derived from an earlier form *fu-* which was related to the Latin words *pus*, 'purulent matter', *putere*, 'to stink' and *puter*, 'rotten'. *Pus* and *putrid* have now also become English words. Very fittingly, as some football supporters might think in the context of that football match in Mexico City, English *putrid* and *foul* have the same origin.

However, over the centuries, the meaning of *foul* has weakened in many situations, including in sporting contexts, where the word generally now simply means 'against the rules' – *foul* is the opposite of *fair*. A *foul ball* in baseball is one that a batter hits beyond the foul line, which is drawn from the home plate through the first and third bases. In snooker, a *foul stroke* occurs when a player hits the wrong ball or does not hit a ball at all. In football, *foul* was originally an abbreviation of *foul play* – the phrase *foul throw* is still used for a throw-in which is illegally executed.

Our English-language football term has been borrowed into a number of other languages, with various spellings. Turkish and Polish both have *faul*, while in Maltese it appears as *fawl*. In Greek it is *phaoul*, which also translates as 'free kick'. Swedish has *foul*, and the German form *Foul* can also, as in English, be a verb: *Shilton wurde gefoult* 'Shilton was fouled'. The two German words, *faul* and *Foul*, have the same ultimate origin, but today they have two quite different meanings.

In Maradona's native Spanish, the word for a foul is the much more innocent sounding *falta*, which has the same root as *fault* – these two words both come from Latin *fallita*, 'failing, falling short', from the verb *fallere*, 'to fail'.

If committed by a defender in the penalty area, a *foul, phaoul, faul, fawl* or *falta* should lead to the award of a *penalty*, a term which came into English via French from Latin *penalitas*, 'punishment'. *Penalitas* is derived from classical Latin *poena*, 'revenge, unpleasant consequence, suffering', which was borrowed from Ancient Greek *poiné*, 'blood money'. In the case of football, the unpleasant consequence simply takes the form of an attacking player being allowed to take a free shot, from a distance of twelve yards, at the goal, defended only by the goalkeeper. In most cases no blood is involved – but of course it is genuinely a form of vengeance, and if a goal is scored, as is the case somewhat more often than 80 per cent of the time in the English Premier League, a certain amount of pain and suffering may ensue for the defending team.

ARGENTINA

Appropriately enough for a country which, although mainly Spanish speaking, has a majority of its population with at least some Italian ancestry, the name Argentina comes from the Italian word *argentine*, 'silvery, made of silver', from *argento*, 'silver'. The normal Spanish word for 'silver' is *plata*.

14 Names

The scientific linguistic study of names and their origins is known as *onomastics* or *onomatology*, from Ancient – and indeed Modern – Greek *ónoma*, 'name'. This can include the study of surnames, personal names, place-names and river names. In this chapter we look at all of these, as well as names of countries, seas and peoples.

Names are very interesting in themselves simply in their capacity as words with an origin and a history; but as has been seen in earlier chapters, they can also be highly controversial. Macedonian, as we have already noted several times in this book, is the name of the South Slavic language which is spoken in North Macedonia – except there are many Bulgarians who will tell you that, actually, Macedonian is not a language at all but just a dialect of Bulgaria.

And what is the language which is found in the northern part of Belgium to be called? Is the name of the language spoken in Antwerp *Flemish* – or is it *Dutch*? If the latter, then it is clearly a variety of the same Dutch language which is also spoken in Amsterdam in the Netherlands. But perhaps it should rather be regarded as a separate, Belgian language? The balance of opinion at the moment seems to be that they are different varieties of the same language, but this has not always been so, and still not everyone agrees.

And what name should the language of the Sami people of northern Scandinavia bear? Lappish, Lappic, Sami, Saami, Sámi? None of these names is entirely free of political loading.

And it is by no means only the names of languages which can be controversial in this way. As we saw earlier, whether the current capital of Slovakia goes by the name of Pressburg, Pozsony or Bratislava is by no means an innocent choice. And the decision as to whether to call the largest city in Turkey Istanbul or Constantinople is one fraught with all sorts of political, ethnic and historical implications.

In Ireland, whether you choose to use the name Pádraig rather than Patrick, or Ó Murchadh rather than Murphy, is a highly significant choice. And so is the preference of the name Myanmar or Burma for that South East Asian country.

In the chapter which now follows, we shall be looking further at a range of names, not from the point of view of controversies associated with them as we did earlier in this book, but at the fascinating stories they can tell us about history, origins and cultural associations.

14.1 Patronymics

Gaelic names like MacDonald and McAdam are patronymics – surnames derived from a boy's father's given name: *mac* is the Scottish and Irish Gaelic word for 'son'. It also means 'son' in the Gaelic of the Isle of Man, but in typical Manx names, *mac* has been abbreviated to *'c*, so Clague is derived from MacLiaigh, and Kermode from MacDermod. The corresponding Welsh patronymic is *mab*, and this too has been abbreviated to *ab* or *ap*: Bevan was originally ab-Evan, and Pritchard ap-Richard.

Surnames are a relatively new phenomenon in many parts of Europe, and the practice of passing family names down through the generations has still not been adopted in Iceland. Icelanders have a second name derived from the name of one of their parents, traditionally the father. A man whose name is Jón Sigurdsson is so called because his father's name is Sigurdur. His sisters have the second name Sigurdsdóttir, while any children he has himself will be called Jónsson or Jónssdóttir.

This system was traditionally used elsewhere in Scandinavia. Hereditary family names only became compulsory in Denmark in the 1850s, in Sweden around 1900 and in Norway in the 1920s. Often Norwegians took their new surname from the place where they lived, so that many people in a particular village might now share the same name even though they are unrelated. But patronymics such as Danish Hansen and Swedish Andersson also continued to be used in Scandinavia, with the innovation that they became hereditary, so the first element no longer changed from one generation to the next. Crucially, women now also had surnames ending in *-son* rather than *-dottir*.

In England, patronymic names stopped being genuinely patronymic many centuries earlier than that. Someone called Mary Johnson is obviously not anyone's son; and Fred Johnson is named, not after his father, but after some distant ancestor's father. All surnames had become fossilised in this way in most parts of England by the 1400s; from then on, it was understood that someone called Taylor was not necessarily a tailor but the son, grandson, great-grandson and so on of a tailor; and that someone called Short might actually be quite tall.

Patronymics are found in many other European languages. German surnames like Jakobsohn and Friedrichsohn are cases in point. Slovenian, Croatian, Bosnian and Serbian surnames are very often patronymics derived from a male given name plus the suffix *-ic*, such as Petrovic, Pavlovic and Tomic. The surnames of twenty-one out of the twenty-six players in the current Serbian men's football squad end in *-ic*. This ending is a diminutive, so the original meaning of Petrovic was 'little one of Peter'.

The same method of forming patronymic family names can be found in Greece. Cretan family names typically end in the diminutive *-akis*, so Theodorakis originally meant 'the little one (i.e. the child) of Theodore'. Some Greek families who originally came to Greece as refugees from Asia Minor have surnames derived from the Turkish word *ogul* meaning 'son', like Kostoglou, 'son of Kostas'. In Cyprus, surnames are frequently grammatically possessive forms: Pavlou is the genitive of Pavlos, so '(child) of Paul'.

Spanish names such as Sanchez and Rodriguez – and the Portuguese equivalents Sanches and Rodrigues – are also possessive patronymics, meaning 'of Sancho' and 'of Rodrigo' – with the possessive *-ez/-es* endings derived from the Germanic language of the Visigoths who were the overlords of Iberia from the fifth to the eighth centuries.

British and Irish surnames starting with *Fitz* – like Fitzgerald and Fitzwilliam – are also patronymics. They derive from the Anglo-Norman word *fiz*, 'son', which is the same word as French *fils*: Anglo-Norman French was the language of the aristocracy of England, and parts of Scotland and Ireland, from the eleventh to the fourteenth centuries.

Fitzhugh, McHugh, Kew, Pugh and Hewson – originally from different parts of the British Isles – are all versions of the same patronymic family name, 'son of Hugh'.

MATRONYMICS

English has scores of patronymics like Wilson and Richardson, but we have matronymics as well. Margetson and Megson come from Margaret and its pet form Meg. Ibbotson is from a nickname for Isabelle; Marrison and Merrison are from Mary, Annison from Annie and Allison from Alice. There was once also a Sheriff of London called Simon Fitzmary.

14.2 Tomkinson

There are quite a lot of people in Great Britain, and in other English-speaking parts of the world, who have surnames ending in *-kins* or *-kinson*: Atkins, Dickinson, Jenkins, Parkinson, Simkins, Tomkinson, Watkins, Wilkinson – and plenty more. If we think about the composition of these names, it is rather obvious what the *-son* part means. The *-s* in Tomkins and Atkins similarly means 'of Tomkin', with the 'child (of)' meaning being understood. But what exactly does the *-kin* part mean? Where did that come from?

We might suppose that this element has something to do with *kin* in the sense of 'group of people descended from a common ancestor, and so connected by blood-relationship; a family, stock, clan' – after all, surnames are very much linked to family membership. But there is actually no connection there at all: *kin* in the sense of 'family' is a totally different word, coming from Old English *cynn*, which has the same origin as Latin *genus*.

It is not easy for Modern English speakers to work out what the *-kin* in Watkins and Watkinson might denote because in Modern English this *-kin* does not really mean anything at all. But it used to signify something – not least during the fourteenth and fifteenth centuries, when the practice of giving people surnames was beginning to become established. And it turns out that we can get help in interpreting what this element used to mean by looking at other languages which are closely related to English.

For example, the equivalent form to *-kin* in Modern German is *-chen*, as in the word *Brötchen*, 'bread roll', which comes from *Brot*, 'bread' plus *-chen*, a diminutive suffix signifying 'small'– a *Brötchen* is literally 'a small bread'. *Mädchen*, 'girl', originally meant 'little maid', and *Häuschen* is the diminutive of *Haus*, 'a small house' – or 'housekin' in English, if we had such a word.

In older forms of Dutch, the equivalent of 'little house' would have been *huisken*, though in the modern language *-ken* tends to have become *-ke* or *-eke*. The West Frisian language of the northern Netherlands also has the diminutive suffix *-ke*, from an earlier *-ken*, as in *famke*, '(little) girl', from *faam*, 'maiden'. In the North Frisian language of northern Schleswig-Holstein, the same suffix occurs, as in *köpke*, 'little cup', from *kop*, 'cup'.

According to the *Oxford English Dictionary*, in those cases where *-kin* does occur in English, it is mostly found in words borrowed from or influenced by Dutch. *Firkin*, 'small beer cask', is from older Dutch *ferdekyn* = *vierdekijn*, a diminutive of *vierde*, 'a fourth, quarter'. *Catkin* probably comes from Dutch *katteken*, 'little cat'. *Manikin* is from the Dutch for 'little man', while *mannequin* is the same word, as it has come into English from Dutch via French. *Jerkin* and *bumpkin* may also be Dutch-origin words. And in East Anglia, people know the word *hudkin*, 'finger stall [a medical covering]', which quite possibly comes from an older Dutch or Flemish word *hoedekin*, 'little hat'.

There are some English-origin *-kin* words such as *lambkin*, 'little lamb', and *napkin*, 'little nape (tablecloth)'. However, it is in the English-language family names already mentioned that the *-kin* suffix survives most strongly. For many of these names, it is easy to work out what they would have meant: Wilkin was 'little Will', and Tomkin meant 'little Tom'. Dickens and Dickinson were originally '(son) of little Dick'.

Other such names may take a little more thought: Atkins was 'little Adam', Watkin meant 'little Walt', Larkin was 'little Lawrence' and Jenkins meant 'of little John'. Rankin was from Ranolff or Randoph. Hoskin(s) came from a diminutive form of Osbert, with an added *h*, while Hopkin(s) was a diminutive of Hobb, a rhyming nickname from Rob(ert) or Robin. Dawkins was originally '(of) little David'. And – my favourite – Parkins(on) and Perkins came from Pierre, or Peter.

PETITE

In French, the word *petite* is simply the grammatically feminine form of the adjective meaning 'little': a table can be *petite*. As the word has been borrowed into English, however, it means something much more specific. It is used of a woman or a girl to indicate that she is diminutive in an attractive way.

14.3 Shakespeare

Some family names, in spite of having been passed down across the generations for the last 500 years or more, still retain a form which makes it easy to see what they originally meant. We have already noted colour-based names like Brown and White. Particularly interesting, though, are names which read like mini-sentences.

One such name consists of a verb plus an adverb: Golightly. This is not just an invention of Truman Capote's for his character Holly Golightly in *Breakfast at Tiffany's*, the part played by Audrey Hepburn in the film derived from the book. It is also a perfectly real family name that would originally have meant something like 'walk nimbly'. The *Oxford Dictionary of Family Names in Britain and Ireland* shows that there were over 900 people bearing that surname in the most recent UK census.

We also find quite a number of sentence-like surnames which are formed from a verb plus a noun. Hornblower is another real name, not just a fictional one thought up by C. S. Forester for his Napoleonic Wars naval captain Horatio Hornblower. The name was applied to someone who blew a horn – that is, the town or village watchman who was charged with signalling an emergency or the beginning and end of a curfew.

Another surname with this kind of structure is Drinkwater, which would probably have been given as a nickname to a person who preferred to drink water rather than small beer, the weak ale that was the beverage of preference for many people in the Middle Ages when water was often contaminated; fermented drinks also provided some degree of protection against infection. It could perhaps also have been used ironically of a drunkard. There is a similar French-language name, presumably awarded to individuals for the same reason, Boileau.

An English-language name of the same type is Gotobed. It is perhaps hard to believe, but true, that this originally meant exactly what it says – it was a nickname given to someone who, one supposes, went to bed frequently or perhaps very early, though there is no indication as to what reason or purpose sent them to their bed so often. There is nothing mysterious, either, about the surname Dolittle or Doolittle, which appears to have genuinely been a label given as a nickname to lazy people who were not actually inclined to do very much. And Makepeace really was the name for an arbitrator or peacemaker; though it could also very likely have been used ironically of someone who raised hell and created disturbances.

Quite a large number of occupational nicknames are equally transparent. A Mr Leadbetter or Leadbeater would have been someone who worked with lead and would, from time to time, have had to pound it into shape. My own surname is an East Anglian dialect form of Threadgold, which was a nickname for someone who 'threaded gold' – in other words, an embroiderer who sewed fine robes and surplices for the clergy.

The name Wagstaff also looks as if it ought to refer to someone who wagged a staff, and it probably was used initially for a beadle. Wagstaff is not totally dissimilar in form and meaning to the name Shakespeare. And Shakespeare did also certainly mean what it said. It was possibly first used for a man who was a military spear carrier, but it is equally possible that it was a nickname for someone who was belligerent or quick to arm himself. It is also conceivable that, like Wagstaff, it had some kind of obscene significance. This is not the place to enter into an extended discussion of that possibility, but the fact is that the name of our revered Bard might well have had a bawdy meaning applied, not of course to the good William himself, but to some licentious male ancestor.

SURNAME

The word *surname* originally meant 'additional name', signifying a name which was bestowed on someone over and above their personal name. The prefix *sur-* comes from French *sur*, 'over', from Latin *super*. The prefix appears with the same meaning in other English words like *surcharge, surpass, surcoat, surface, surfeit, surmount, survive* – and *surplice*.

14.4 Tedesco

People with the surname Inglis are usually Scottish. That might seem rather strange, because the name is the Scots-language word for 'English' – and why would Scottish people have been called Inglis? But actually, of course, there would be no point in calling someone from England 'English' unless they lived in another country, such as Scotland, where being English was unusual and therefore something which distinguished them from everybody else. People called Inglis are typically Scots who have a distant ancestor who came from England.

This same type of pattern can be seen across Europe. Domenico Tedesco is the Italian manager of the Spartak Moscow football team. Since *tedesco* is the Italian word for 'German', we can assume he had an ancestor who moved to an Italian-speaking area from some German-speaking location.

The same process would have come into play with an ancestor of the Czech politician Boguslaw Niemiec, who is ethnically Polish but whose surname is the Polish word for 'German'. The last name of the Hungarian international football star Krisztián Németh also means 'German' in his mother tongue. And the French word for 'German' – *allemand* – is the family name of the former French Olympic fencer, Jean-Pierre Allemand.

People with German-language surnames denoting different countries of origin include the great East German human-rights activist Paul Oestreicher, whose family name means 'Austrian'; and the Nobel Peace Prize winner Albert Schweitzer (= 'Swiss'), who was born in Alsace, Germany (now part of France).

The Italian-language surname Greco most often derives from the Italian word for 'Greek'. And we can also find family names in the Greek language which signify origins in other countries: the surname of the internationally known Greek professor of linguistics Amalia Arvaniti means 'Albanian'; and the Greek-Canadian professional gambler Bob Voulgaris's name is Greek for 'Bulgarian'.

But some names, like Inglis, are rather more complicated to explain. A fairly common German-language surname is Deutsch, which means 'German'. Why would German people be called 'German'? One possibility is that the name was used to refer to German speakers living on the eastern edge of the German-speaking area, where the population consisted of a mixture of Germans and Slavs.

And why would the famous goalkeeper Petr Čech, who is Czech, have a surname that means 'Czech' in Czech? Maybe because Čech is also the Slovak word for 'Czech'; or because the name was used by Moravians, people from what is now the eastern part of Czechia, to refer to people from Bohemia, the western part of the country.

The surname Scott also has a history which needs some explanation. It is predominantly a Scottish name, which again seems contradictory: if Inglis is a Scottish name, we would expect Scott to be English – which it isn't. The clue to this puzzle lies in the fact that, in Scotland, Scott is a name which is particularly associated with the Borders and other parts of the Scottish south. The people who were first labelled 'Scots' were the Gaelic-speaking people from Ireland who crossed the Irish Sea and settled in Argyll, in the west of Scotland, and who then spread into the rest of the Scottish Highlands and the Western Isles. Scott was a name which the Scots-speaking Lowlanders used for these Gaelic-speaking Highlanders.

The surnames Welch and Welsh also have a rather complex story to tell, because it is not necessarily the case that those who bear this family name are English people descended from some Welsh ancestor. The original Old English meaning of *Welsh* was simply 'foreigner', so if you are a Welch, you probably had a forebear who came to England from some other country – but that may or may not have been Wales.

And as to the mystery of why some British people are named Britain, the answer seems be that one of their ancestors was a Breton – from Brittany in France.

14.5 Coromandel

The first Europeans to arrive in Aotearoa/New Zealand were the Dutch seaman Abel Tasman and the crews of his two ships, who turned up there in 1642. New Zealand had at that time already been inhabited by the Polynesian Maori people for at least 300 years, and maybe several centuries longer than that. The Maori had traversed 2,000 miles of the Pacific Ocean to get to New Zealand.

Not surprisingly, then, the East Polynesian Maori language is the source of hundreds of modern New Zealand place-names, like Hokitika, 'correct return', Mangonui, 'big shark', Tauranga, 'landing place', Waipu, 'reddish water', Whangaroa, 'long harbour', Whitianga, 'crossing' ... . Many names are not Maori as such but are derived from the language: Timaru is probably from *Te Tihi-o-Maru*, 'the peak of Maru', and Oamaru is from Maori *Te Oha-a-Maru*, 'the place of Maru'.

The non-Maori place-names of New Zealand are almost entirely of European origin. Zealand itself is from Dutch *Zeeland*. Dannevirke, a town in the North Island, has a Danish name; and Haast was called after Julius von Haast, a German geologist. But, as might be expected in this former British colony, most of the European place-names are of British origin.

Gaelic provided the source for some of these. Dunedin is from *Dùn Èideann*, the Scottish Gaelic name for Edinburgh. Invercargill is made up of Gaelic *inbhir*, anglicised as Inver, meaning 'confluence', plus the surname of William Cargill, the founder of the Otago settlement in the South Island.

But the majority of the non-Maori names in New Zealand are of English origin, mostly deriving from place-names or surnames, though all of these places have Maori names, too: Auckland is Tāmaki; Christchurch is Ōtautahi; Dunedin is Ōtepoti; and Wellington is Te Whanga-nui-a-Tara.

There is at least one New Zealand place-name, however, which is neither Maori nor European in origin. This is Coromandel, a small town on the west coast of the beautiful Coromandel Peninsula of the North Island – and its origin is quite a complex story. The town was named after a Royal Navy ship, the *HMS Coromandel*, which was built in 1798 and was used to transported convicts to Australia in 1820 before sailing on to New Zealand to collect timber and undertake coastal survey work, including survey-ing the peninsula which also came to bear its name.

But where did the name of the Royal Navy vessel itself come from? The ship was made for the East India Company (and originally called the *Cuvera*, then the *Malabar*). It was eventually renamed after the Coromandel Coast, which is what European traders – mostly Dutch, Portuguese and English – called the coastlines of the south-eastern Indian states of Andhra Pradesh and Tamil Nadu.

In this area of southern India, the two closely related Dravidian languages Telugu and Tamil are dominant (they belong to a totally different language family from Hindi, Bengali and the other languages of northern India). *Coromandel* seems to be a European – most likely Dutch – rendering of a Telugu and/or Tamil name. The *Encyclopaedia Britannica* believes that this name was Chola Mandalam, where *Chola, Cola* or *Coda* was a very early dynasty of Tamil rulers, and *mandalam* is a Dravidian word meaning 'circle, area, realm'. Another suggestion is that it comes from the Dutch pronunciation of Karimanal, a place on the Indian Coromandel Coast. *Kari manal* is Tamil for 'dark sand', and there are indeed spectacular black sand beaches on that part of the Indian coast.

The beautiful beaches of the Coromandel Peninsula in the North Island of New Zealand, on the other hand, are very much of the golden sand variety. Still, that South Indian-language name, whatever its exact origin, is surely now in Aotearoa/ New Zealand to stay.

AOTEAROA

Aotearoa is the Maori name for New Zealand, but it seems to have been used originally just for the North Island. *Ao* can mean 'cloud, dawn, daytime, world' in Maori; *tea* is 'white, bright'; and *roa* is 'length, long'. The name is usually translated as '(Land of the) long white cloud', but there is no total agreement about this.

14.6 Devon and Kent

It makes perfectly good sense that the names of many of the counties of England should have their origins in the dominant language of the country, English. Rather obviously, *Norfolk* was originally two English words, North Folk; similarly, Suffolk was South Folk. Essex was the country of the East Saxons, with Middlesex and Sussex being the homelands of the Middle and South Saxons. And Northumberland means exactly what it says – the land north of the Humber.

In contrast, on the other side of the Atlantic, there are very few names of American states of English-language origin, in spite of the fact that the USA is also a predominantly English-speaking country. It is true that Washington was named after George Washington, whose surname derives from an English place-name: there is a Washington in County Durham and another in Sussex.

New Hampshire and Maryland are also basically English-language names.

But, while the *New* in New York is obviously English, *York* is the anglicised version of the Old Norse form of the English city's name, *Jorvik*. And the *Jersey* in New Jersey is not English at all: the French name for this British Channel Island came from the Old Norse language of the Viking Normans. The *-ey* ending meant 'island', as it does also in Guernsey and Alderney (and Orkney): the Modern Icelandic word for 'island' is *eyja*, and the Norwegian is *øy*.

Most other American state names are not even slightly English in origin. Some come from other European languages. Rhode Island was probably originally Dutch *Rood Eiland*, 'red island'. Vermont is from seventeenth-century French *vert mont*, 'green mountain'. Nevada comes from the Spanish verb *nevar*, 'to snow': *nevado* is its past participle, literally 'snowed' – or as we would say in English 'snowy' – with *nevada* being the feminine form, as in *tierra Nevada*, 'snowy land'. *Colorado* is similarly the masculine past participle of the verb *colorar*, 'to colour', so literally 'coloured'. In Spanish it often also means 'red, rosy': *ponerse colorado* signifies 'to blush', and *rio colorado* would mean 'red river'. *Florida* is the feminine form of the Spanish word for 'flowered, i.e. full of flowers'. And Montana was originally Spanish *montaña*, 'mountain'. California was also a Spanish-origin name, although it is not certain exactly what it actually meant.

Appropriately, more than half of the names of US states are not European at all but are derived from indigenous Native American languages which were spoken in the Americas many thousands of years before the arrival of any European language. Several different indigenous languages are represented amongst these names. Connecticut, perhaps meaning 'long river', is from Mohican, a member of the Algonquian language family. Michigan comes from another Algonquian language, Ojibwe, also known as Ojibwa and Chippewa. Missouri's name is derived from yet another Algonquian language, Miami-Illinois, as is Illinois itself. Kentucky probably comes from an Iroquoian language, and perhaps means 'prairie'. Alabama was originally from Choctaw, a Muskogean language; so was Oklahoma. And the Dakota in North and South Dakota comes from Sioux.

This predominance of indigenous state names in the USA raises the interesting question of whether there are any equivalent pre-English county names in England. The English language arrived in this country only about 1,500 years ago, while the Brittonic Celtic language, the ancestor of Welsh, had been spoken here well before the Anglo-Saxons arrived, maybe as much as 4,000 years earlier, so we might expect to find some such names.

There are in fact at least two pre-English county names which parallel the indigenous American names. Kent is derived from the name of the Celtic tribe, the *Cantiaci*, whose name also appears in the name of Canterbury. And *Devon* is derived from *Dumnonia*, the name of the Celtic kingdom of the Dumnonii people which used to cover what is now Cornwall, Devon and part of western Somerset.

The name of originally Welsh-speaking Cumberland, too, was based on Welsh *Cymry*, 'Welsh people'. In AD 945, the area was ceded to the Gaelic-speaking King Malcolm of Scotland by the anglophone English King Edmund, and was regained for England by the French-speaking King Henry II in 1157.

14.7 -ton

Travellers crossing from England to France via the Channel Tunnel emerge into French daylight in the vicinity of a place called Fréthun, south-west of Calais. In the Pas-de-Calais and the neighbouring Nord *départements*, there are many place-names with the same basic ending, including Offretun, Hardenthun, Connincthun, Autun, Landrethun and Warneton (which is on the France–Belgium border).

Within ten miles or so of where I am sitting right now in Norfolk, England, there are places called Easton, Weston, Norton, Sutton, Newton, Oulton, Upton, Melton, Claxton, Dunston, Carleton, Stratton – and very many more. England as a whole is full of place-names which end in -ton: Northampton, Southampton, Luton, Taunton, Brighton, Darlington, Preston . . .

The resemblance between the endings of these French and English names is not a coincidence. Like Fréthun, the English -ton names are due to settlement by Angles and Saxons who migrated out of northern Germany near the beginning of the fifth century AD. Many of these place-names are well over 1,500 years old – though we might suppose that Newton could be a little more recent. The final element of all these names was originally the West Germanic word tūn. The macron line over the letter u indicates that the vowel in this word was long – it would have sounded rather like 'toon'. But in Old English place-names, the vowel eventually got shortened, and the form was also later generally respelt as -ton to make for greater legibility when using cursive handwriting.

In Modern English, the full form of tūn with an original long vowel has become the word town. In the Old English of 1,500 years ago, tūn meant 'enclosure'. Rather soon, however, it acquired the meaning of 'enclosure around a house' and then 'homestead' – this meaning still survives in Modern Scots toun, 'farmhouse'. From there, the meaning of Old English tūn gradually became modified until it came to mean 'settlement' or 'village'.

Our sister languages in the Germanic family have retained the word to this day, but English is the only one in which the meaning of 'town' has developed from it. In Modern Dutch, the corresponding word tuin most often means 'garden', as does West Frisian tún and North Frisian tün – so there the word has come to refer to a very particular type of enclosure. In German, on the other hand, the related word Zaun actually means 'fence' – probably the oldest meaning of the word – while Low German Tuun means 'hedge', so in these languages tūn applies to the feature which does the enclosing rather than to the enclosure itself.

In Sweden, there are many place-names ending in -tuna, such as Eskilstuna. And Norway also has place-names ending in -tun/-ton: Nordtun provides an exact parallel to English Norton; Optun is equivalent to Upton. Hilton, a farmstead in southern Norway, is where the famous hotelier Conrad Hilton's family originally came from. These names all go back to the Viking age, but it is likely they originally referred to an individual farm; Scandinavian tun never underwent the change of meaning from 'homestead' to 'village' which occurred in English.

In Old Norse, tún meant 'a hedged plot, enclosure, court-yard, homestead, home field, home meadow'. In Modern Norwegian, tun means 'a yard or farmyard, usually surrounded by a cluster of buildings', while in Faroese tún denotes a 'yard, courtyard, cobbled (court)yard between houses', with the Swedish meaning being very similar to the Faroese. Icelandic *tún*, on the other hand, signifies 'field, hayfield'. As a testament to the Nordic heritage of our Northern Isles, in the Scots spoken in Shetland, *toon* also means 'a field adjacent to a farmhouse or croft, a home field'.

So this ancient Germanic word, which in its full version has come to mean variously 'town', 'farmyard', 'garden' and 'fence', has for a millennium and a half also survived as the second element of place-names in the form of *-tun(a)*, *-ton* and *-t(h)un* on the western edge of Europe, from Norway across to Norfolk and down to northern France.

STRATA

The Romans were famous for their construction of long, straight paved roads. English place-names such as Stratton, Stradsett, Stradbroke, Stradishall and Stratford all go back to Latin *strata*, 'highway, paved road'. So do other names like Stretham, Strethall and Stretton. These towns and villages were all originally settlements on or alongside a Roman road.

14.8 Place-Name Stories

On the east coast of the North Island of New Zealand, there is a place called Buffalo Beach. New Zealand is well known to have no indigenous terrestrial mammals, and it very definitely has no buffalo.

Rather surprisingly, it turns out that in order to understand the origins of this somewhat unexpected place-name, we need to know a little bit about historical events which took place more than 9,000 miles away from New Zealand – in Canada. Most Europeans are probably not aware that, between 1837 and 1839, serious anti-government rebellions flared up in (mostly English-speaking) Upper Canada, now Ontario, and (mostly French-speaking) Lower Canada, now Quebec. The uprisings were forcefully put down; some participants were executed for treason, and many more were transported to Australia. Amongst these were fifty-eight French Canadians, plus eighty-two Americans who had been captured during the so-called 'Patriot War' which followed the rebellions. (This 'war' consisted of little more than a few skirmishes fought by unofficial American raiders crossing the border and attacking British forces.)

These convicted men were transported from Canada via Liverpool to Australia on a ship called the *HMS Buffalo*. (Most of them were eventually released and allowed to return home.) After the *Buffalo* had discharged its unfortunate cargo in Australia, it was sent off to New Zealand to pick up a shipment of timber. Once there, however, it was driven onto the shore and wrecked by a violent storm; the remains of the *Buffalo* still lie at the bottom of the bay off the New Zealand beach which now bears its name.

Unlike Buffalo Beach, some place-names have an origin which is more or less instantly transparent. Southend in Essex was indeed situated at the southern end of the original settlement of Prittlewell. Yarmouth in Norfolk actually is located at the mouth of the River Yare. And there genuinely was a new castle on the banks of the River Tyne in Newcastle upon Tyne.

There are similarly transparent place-names in other British languages. Aberystwyth means 'mouth of the Ystwyth' in Welsh. Inverness is Scottish Gaelic *Inbhir Nis*, 'mouth of the Ness'. And many European names have equally straightforward meanings: Oostende (Ostend) is Flemish for 'east end', Le Havre means 'the harbour' in French and Beograd (Belgrade) is Serbian for 'white city'.

But the origins of most place-names are not nearly so clear. You need to be well-versed in etymology and philology to be able to work out how lots of different English-language names originated. There is no way of knowing that Brightlingsea in Essex meant 'the island of [a man called] Brihtric' in Old English without researching it. Or that Nottingham was formerly Snotingaham, signifying the homestead (*ham*) of the people (*inga*) of an Anglo-Saxon chieftain called *Snot*.

For other place-names, however, it helps to have some historical background information to fully understand the origin, just as it does with Buffalo Beach. The town of Battle in Sussex is a case in point. After the Battle of Hastings in 1066, the Pope ordered the Normans to do penance for the terrible slaughter which had occurred during their conquest of England. King William began the construction of an abbey on the site of the battle; and work on the abbey church was completed during the reign of William the Conqueror's son, William Rufus. A settlement gradually grew up around the abbey, and today Battle is a normal small English town, albeit with an unusual and memorable name.

Similarly, Wallsend in North Tyneside is so called because it is situated at the end of a wall. However, this was not just any wall, but Hadrian's Wall, the nearly eighty-mile-long defensive barrier built by the Romans in the second century AD across Britain from the Solway Firth to the North Sea. What exactly the purpose of the wall was is a matter of some dispute, but it certainly marked the northern limit of the Roman Empire.

FIRTH

Firth is a Scots word meaning 'coastal inlet, arm of the sea, estuary of a river'. Its origin lies in the Old Norse word *fiorðr*, which has come down into Modern Norwegian as *fjord* and into Modern Faroese as *fjørður*. The word *firth* was not employed by people writing in English until the seventeenth century.

14.9 The Broads

Broad and *wide* mean pretty much the same thing – they are very close to being synonyms. The *Oxford English Dictionary* defines *broad* as 'extended in the direction measured from side to side; wide'; the word *wide* is also defined as 'having great extent from side to side'. Both *broad* and *wide* are also said by the *OED* to be the opposite of *narrow*.

Typically, though, when two words with very similar meanings are available in a language, they end up being used in rather different ways. Cricket fans may not be surprised to learn that the surname Broad, shared by the England fast-bowler Stuart and his batsman father Chris, was originally a nickname applied to people of significant girth; *a wide* in cricket, on the other hand, is a ball which is illegally bowled out of the batsman's reach, with a run being awarded to the batting side in compensation.

For the linguist, the two words *broad* and *wide* are both a little bit mysterious in origin. *Broad* corresponds to Scots *braid*, Dutch *breed*, German *breit* and Norwegian *breid*; it is clearly, therefore, a word which we have inherited from our linguistic ancestor, Common Germanic. But there are no obviously related words which correspond to *broad* in any other European language family, and we know little about the ultimate origin of the word. There is a theory that *broad* and the corresponding noun *breadth* are in some way related to *spread*, German *spreizen*, Dutch *spreiden*. But this does not really help us very much because it is not easy to understand what might have happened to the initial *s-*; and in any case, the original source of the Common Germanic form of *spread* is not known either.

Similarly, the word *wide* is also Common Germanic in origin: the German is *weit*, the Dutch *wijd*, and the Danish *vid*. But once again, there do not seem to be any related forms in other European languages, and we do not know where the word originally came from.

The name of the region we call the Norfolk Broads shows a rather specialised usage of the term *broad*. The Broads are an area of rivers and shallow reedy lakes in the English county of Norfolk; the region is very well known as a destination for people enjoying boating and walking holidays. These lakes, as was only discovered in the 1950s, are actually mediaeval peat workings which were flooded as water levels rose. The network of waterways contains over sixty Broads, sixteen of which are open to navigation by holidaymakers, with one of these being located in the neighbouring county of Suffolk – hence the more pedantically accurate, if clumsier, alternative name, the Norfolk and Suffolk Broads. The largest of these lakes is Hickling Broad, which at 1.4 square kilometres is rather bigger than Grasmere in the Lake District.

The origin of *broad* as used to refer to these Norfolk waterways is no mystery. It is a Norfolk dialect form which dates from at least the mid-seventeenth century, signifying a place where one of the six main rivers of the region widens out into more extensive lake-like waterways – so 'broad waters', as opposed to 'narrow waters' or rivers. In 1651, the Norwich-based polymath Sir Thomas Browne wrote of 'lakes and broades'.

Americans are often amused on first encountering the term 'Norfolk Broads' because of the American use of the slang term *broad* to mean 'woman'. This seems to have become current in US English only at the beginning of the twentieth century. But where did that usage come from? It has been suggested that it might be a reference to the fact that women on average have proportionally broader hips than men. It has also been proposed that the usage may come from an American term 'abroadwife', meaning a 'woman away from her husband'. But I think the honest truth is that we haven't actually got the faintest idea – it is yet another linguistic mystery.

14.10 The Names of Seas

An earlier, alternative English-language name for the North Sea was 'the German Ocean'. Because of conflicts between Britain and Germany, this name totally disappeared from use in the years leading up to World War I. These days, this sea has an equivalent name involving the label 'north' in all of the languages around its edges: *Nordsjø* in Norwegian, *Nordsø* in Danish, *Nuurdsia* in North Frisian, *Noordsee* in Low German, *Nordsee* in German, *Noardsee* in West Frisian and *Noordzee* in Dutch. But there was an earlier German name for this sea which makes perfectly good sense if you think about the geography: the earlier German name was *Westsee*. In some of the dialects of the North Frisian language which is spoken just south of the Danish border on the North Sea coast in northern Germany, this name still survives today as *Weestsiie*.

But that is not the only European body of water which has in its time been called the 'West Sea'. In some of the languages spoken in the countries around the Baltic Sea – Polish, Russian, Lithuanian and Latvian – words related to this body of water's English name are also used to refer to it. In Polish it is called *Morze Baltyckie*. The etymology of the term *Baltic* is not known with any degree of confidence, but one possibility is that it comes from the Lithuanian word for 'white', *baltas*. In other languages around the Baltic Sea, it is called the 'East Sea': in Danish it's *Østersøen* – it does after all lie to the east of Denmark; in Swedish it is *Östersjön*, in Low German *Oostsee*; and in German *Ostsee*. But, interestingly, the Estonian name is Läänemeri: *läänes* means 'west' and *meri* means 'sea': 'West Sea' is a very reasonable Estonian name for it when you consider that the Baltic Sea does indeed lie to the west of Estonia.

Extraordinarily, however, the corresponding Finnish-language name for the Baltic, *Itämeri*, does not mean 'West Sea', but 'East Sea'. This is in spite of the fact that Finland is just to the north of Estonia, and that the Baltic Sea lies mostly to the south-west of Finland. The explanation for this strange fact is that, from the 1200s until 1809, Finland was governed as a part of Sweden, and the Finnish name *Itämeri* is simply a translation of the Swedish *Östersjön*.

These different names for the same sea – Baltic Sea, East Sea and West Sea – live together very peacefully in Northern Europe. But sometimes the names of seas can become ideologically very charged. The part of the Mediterranean which lies between Crete and North Africa is usually known as the Libyan Sea – *Liviko Pelagos* in Greek. But there are some Cretan Greek nationalists who think that the Libyan Sea ought to be called the Cretan Sea.

They are probably forgetting that it is not unusual for a sea to be named after what lies on the other side. The German Ocean was one such English name. The Irish Sea is another: the English and Welsh call the sea between Britain and Ireland after the name of the place you get to if you cross it: the Welsh is *Môr Iwerddon*, where *môr* is 'sea' and *Iwerddon* 'Ireland'. However, the Irish do not refer to it as the British Sea! They generally call it the Irish Sea, too, though one possible Irish Gaelic name is *An Mhuir Mheann*, 'the Manx Sea'.

Another perhaps sensitive sea name is 'the English Channel'. In other languages, the English are not necessarily considered to have anything to do with this stretch of seawater. The Dutch name is most often simply *Het Kanaal*, 'the Channel'. The French name for it is *La Manche*, which means 'the sleeve', an allusion to its shape, which contains no reference to England. On the other hand, one of the French names for the Channel Islands does include a reference to England which the English-language name does not: *Les îles Anglo-Normandes*.

14.11 The Minch

The sea between the northern Outer Hebrides and the Scottish mainland is called the Minch, while the more southerly strait between the Outer Hebrides and the Isle of Skye is known as the Little Minch.

The word *minch* is not known as such to English speakers – it is not an English word – but since the areas of Scotland on either side of the Minch have historically been Scots Gaelic-speaking rather than anglophone, it would seem sensible to suppose that the word is Gaelic in origin. But it isn't. The Minch has a number of Gaelic names, including *An Cuan Leòdhasach*, 'The Sea of Lewis', but none of them resembles *minch*.

Another good guess would be that the name has an Old Norse origin. The Outer Hebrides were under the control of the Norwegian Vikings for several centuries, until the mid-1200s, and there are many Nordic place-names in the Hebrides, as well as on the other side of the Minch. Stornoway, the capital of Lewis and Harris and the largest urban centre in the Outer Hebrides, is *Steòrnabhagh* in Gaelic but was originally Norse *Stjórnavágr*. The name of Lewis itself may be from Norse *Ljoðahús*, 'song house'; and Brue in the north-west of Lewis is unmistakably from Old Norse *brú*, 'bridge'. In the Old Norse sagas, Skye was known as *Skíð*. Cape Wrath, which was a place where sailors had to change course, takes its name from Norse *hvarfa*, 'turn round'; and Durness is from Old Norse *dyr-nes*, 'animal headland'.

But Minch is not Old Norse either – it is far too recent for that; Minch did not appear on maps at all until 1745.

So where did this name come from? One interesting clue as to its origins lies in the fact that, on early maps, the name appears with a number of different spellings, including *Mynch*, *Minsh*, *Mensh* and – note especially – *Mansh*. Dr Domhnall Uilleam Stiùbhart from the University of the Highlands and Islands suggests that the word was in fact originally a colloquial name used by foreign sailors and fishermen travelling to and around the Hebrides, and that the ultimate origin of the term was the French name *La Manche*.

Today, *La Manche* is the name French speakers use to refer to what we know as the English Channel (see Section 14.10). But it was originally used, starting in the early 1600s, to refer to any long narrow sea strait. Definitions of the word *manche* – literally 'sleeve' – which were given by seventeenth-century French lexicographers include *un bras de mer*, 'an arm of the sea', and *une longueur de mer entre deux terres* – 'a stretch of sea between two areas of land'. There are maps from that time where the Bristol Channel is shown as *La Manche de Bristol*. In the colloquial parlance of French sailors, the southern North Sea between East Anglia and Holland was called *La Manche de l'Est*, and the Irish Sea was *La Manche de l'Ouest*.

French sailors were very numerous and influential along the coasts of Britain and in British ports, so this usage would gradually have become very familiar to English-speaking fishermen and passed into their nautical slang. During the second half of the eighteenth century, Scots-speaking fishermen from the Clyde and the Scottish east coast, as well as from Orkney and Shetland, increasingly voyaged to north-western Scotland in search of herring and cod, and they would also have helped to popularise this nautical word in and along the shores of the Minch itself and beyond.

Also influential in the transfer of the term from French to English may have been the French privateers who lurked off the coasts of Britain when there were hostilities between England and France during the long years of the War of Spanish Succession, attacking merchant ships returning from lucrative overseas trading expeditions. In 1704, a John Mackenzie of Assynt in north-western Scotland wrote that 'we ar plagued wt a little pirratc or priveteer in ye Lews manche'.

HEBRIDES

The Hebrides – sometimes known as the Western Isles – were called the Southern Isles by the Vikings. The name *Hebrides* itself seems to have begun life as a mistake: the original form of the name is thought to have been Latin *Hebudes* (from Ancient Greek *Heboudai*), with *Hebrides* being an accidental misprint which subsequently became established as the norm.

14.12 River River

There are several waterways in England and Scotland called the River Avon. This is a rather odd name, because Avon comes from the word *abona*, which meant 'river' in the original language of our island, Brittonic Celtic. The Modern Welsh word for 'river' is *afon*, while in the other Brittonic languages, Cornish and Breton, it is *avon*. The related Goidelic Celtic languages also have similar forms: in Irish and Scottish Gaelic 'river' is *abhainn*, and in Manx it is *awin*.

In one way, then, it is not surprising that there are so many rivers in England and Scotland called Avon – at least eight of them. But the name 'River Avon' is still rather peculiar because it literally means 'River River' – why would anyone want to call a river that?

The answer is that the name arose in bilingual situations where speakers of an incoming language (Old English) were in contact with an indigenous language (Brittonic or Old Welsh). Hearing a Briton referring to a river as *avon*, Angles and Saxons mistakenly believed that this was the name of a particular river and called it that.

Of course very many Celtic river names, such as Thames, Derwent and Stour, did not succumb to bilingual confusion and have survived. But the fact that there are so many River Avons in locations as far apart as Devon and Stirlingshire shows that this was a frequent enough occurrence.

There are many other examples of the repetition of elements in names for topographical features resulting from contact between languages. In the UK, there are at least four rivers called the Ouse, which probably comes from the Brittonic word *udso* meaning 'water' – so the literal etymological meaning of *River Ouse* is 'River Water'. Given that British rivers do tend to have water in them, this redundancy can only have been due to confusion arising out of language contact.

Another Welsh–English bilingual misunderstanding resulted in the name of Penhill in Yorkshire: Welsh *pen* is 'head, top, summit, hill'. Knockhill in Scotland derives from exactly the same confusion, but in this case between Gaelic and English: in Gaelic, *cnoc* means 'hill'.

Other Scottish examples of bilingual tautological naming involve the language of the Vikings, Old Norse. In the name of Wig Bay, near Stranraer, *wig* comes from Scandinavian *vik*, 'bay'. And we often talk of the Orkney Islands, although the *-ey* element is from Old Norse and actually means 'island'. We can see a similar repetition further north in the name of the Faroe Islands, where the *-oe* also corresponds to Norse for 'island', thus giving us 'Sheep-island Islands'.

This kind of reduplicative naming process has happened all over Europe. The Spanish river El Rio Guadalquivir was originally Arabic *Al-wadi al-kabir*, where *wadi* means 'river-bed' and *kabir* 'big'. *Góra Chełm* is a small mountain in southern Poland: *góra* means 'mountain' and *chełm* comes from an ancient Germanic root which survives in Modern Low German as *holm*, 'small hill'. The name of the *Val d'Aran* in Catalonia consists of two words both meaning 'valley' – Occitan *val* and Basque *haran* – which reflects contact between indigenous Basque speakers and incoming speakers of Vulgar Latin as the Roman Empire expanded.

Confusion can also occur across generations. The Anglo-Saxons did not actually use the name River Avon themselves, because *river* was not an Old English word – it was borrowed into English from Anglo-Norman only in the 1300s. So the first part of the name River Avon was originally French, and the second part Welsh! The word the Anglo-Saxons did use for 'river' was Old English *ea*. The *ey* at the end of river names such as the Welney, Waveney and Wissey was originally *ea*, so the River Wissey is in origin 'the River Wiss-river'. The bilingual confusion here was between Old English and later forms of English, as English speakers gradually forgot what *ea* had meant.

VULGAR LATIN

Vulgar Latin was the everyday language spoken by the ordinary people of the Roman Empire from around AD 200 onwards. It was this variety of Latin, rather than the written classical Latin of Cicero and Virgil, which gradually morphed over the centuries into the modern Romance languages French, Catalan, Spanish, Portuguese, Italian, Romanian, Sardinian and the Romansch language of south-eastern Switzerland.

14.13 Jacinda

One of the placards that was being carried at the massive anti-Brexit demonstration in London in March 2019 read 'Please Can We Have New Zealand's Prime Minister Instead?' Some Australians have had the same idea: 'Lets make a deal – we send you our prime beef, you send us your Prime Minister!' The *New York Times*, too, believes that 'America deserves a leader as good as Jacinda Ardern'.

Jacinda Ardern compares so brilliantly favourably with certain other Prime Ministers and Presidents who we can all think of that we can only envy the Kiwis their wise choice of leader. Her compassion, intelligence, sensitivity, empathy, all-inclusiveness – the sheer humanity and common sense of the woman – have provided many people all round the world with optimism and hope, in spite of everything dispiriting that is happening right now. And it would not be too surprising if one happy consequence of her popularity would be the arrival around the world in the next few years of large numbers of small girls who will also be called Jacinda.

The name Jacinda is generally reckoned to be derived from *Jacinta*, which is the feminine form of the Spanish and Portuguese word *jacinto*, which means 'hyacinth'. Other Romance languages have similar words: Catalan *jacint*, Italian *giacinto* and French *jacinthe*. Older forms of English also had the word *jacinth* for this plant, and Hungarian has *jácint*.

The name itself comes from the Ancient Greek word for the flower, *iakinthos*, from even earlier Archaic Greek (the word is found in Homer) *wakinthos*. We possess written records of the Greek language dating back 3,500 years to about 1450 BC, but the word *hyacinth* must be even older than that because – as academic Greek etymologists agree – the word is of pre-Greek origin.

The ancestors of the Greeks traversed the Balkan peninsula from the north and first arrived in what is now Greece in, very approximately, 2000 BC. When they arrived, there were of course already people inhabiting the area, and the Greek language then proceeded to borrow many words from the languages of these people. We do not know what those languages were, but at least one of them certainly contained the element *-inth-*, which has subsequently passed, not only into Ancient Greek, but also via Greek and then Latin into many modern languages, including English.

The words that the Greek arrivals from the north borrowed from the people who were already living there naturally included terms for phenomena that were unfamiliar to them. These unfamiliar items seem to have included plants and trees – presumably those that did not grow further north. In addition to *hyacinth*, for example, some Modern English speakers also know the pre-Greek words *absinthe* and *terebinth* (the tree which is the source of turpentine) and – my gardening friends tell me – *colocynth* and *calamintha*. Our word *mint* (French *menthe*) also comes from Ancient Greek *minthi*.

Words connected with various kinds of technology also seem to have been borrowed into Greek from the unknown language or languages of these original inhabitants. One such term containing *-inth* which has survived for maybe 4,000 years and entered into Modern English came to us from Ancient Greek *plinthos*, 'brick', and is now Modern English *plinth*. The pre-Greek name of the city of Corinth, in Greek *Kórinthos*, has also given us our word *currant*, 'raisins of Corinth'.

To return to hyacinths: in Greek mythology, Hyacinthos was a young man who was accidentally killed by the god Apollo. The story goes that, from the blood of Hyacinthos which was spilt onto the ground, Apollo created a flower, the hyacinth, whose reappearance every spring symbolises the rebirth of his accidentally slain friend. Since Ancient Greek times, the hyacinth has been linked to the arrival of spring; it is also associated with the celebration of the Persian New Year.

The hyacinth flower is connected with hope and renewal. So too is Jacinda Ardern. May she be with us for many more springs.

Further Reading

Aitchison, Jean. 2012. *Language Change: Progress or Decay?* 4th ed. Cambridge: Cambridge University Press.

Alkire, Ti, & Carol Rosen. 2010. *Romance Languages: a Historical Introduction*. Cambridge: Cambridge University Press.

Anthony, David 2007. *The Horse, the Wheel, and Language*. Princeton: Princeton University Press.

Bauer, Lawrie, & Peter Trudgill (eds). 2005. *Language Myths*. London: Penguin.

Britain, David (ed.). 2007. *Language in the British Isles*. Cambridge: Cambridge University Press.

Clackson, James. 2007. *Indo-European Linguistics: an Introduction*. Cambridge: Cambridge University Press.

Clackson, James, & Geoffrey Horrocks. 2007. *The Blackwell History of the Latin Language*. Oxford: Blackwell

Corbett, John, J., Derrick McClure & Jane Stuart-Smith (eds.). 2003. *The Edinburgh Companion to Scots*. Edinburgh: Edinburgh University Press.

Coulmas, Florian. 2002. *Writing Systems: an Introduction to Their Linguistic Analysis*. Cambridge: Cambridge University Press.

Crystal, David. 2012. *English as a Global Language*. Cambridge: Cambridge University Press.

Crystal, David. 2012. *Spell It Out: the Singular Story of English Spelling*. London: Profile Books.

Crystal, David. 2014. *Language Death*. Cambridge: Cambridge University Press.

Crystal, David. 2017. *The Story of Be: a Verb's-Eye View of the English Language*. Oxford: Oxford University Press.

Crystal, David, & Hilary Crystal. 2013. *Wordsmiths and Warriors: the English-Language Tourist's Guide to Britain*. Oxford: Oxford University Press.

Dixon, R. M. W. 1997. *The Rise and Fall of Languages*. Cambridge: Cambridge University Press.

Durkin, Philip. 2011. *The Oxford Guide to Etymology*. Oxford: Oxford University Press.

Ekwall, Eilert. 1960. *The Concise Oxford Dictionary of Place-Names*, 4th ed. Oxford: Oxford University Press.

Evans, Nicholas. 2010. *Dying Words: Endangered Languages and What They Have to Tell Us*. Oxford: Wiley-Blackwell.

Fortson, Benjamin. 2010. *Indo-European Language and Culture*. Oxford: Blackwell.

Hanks, Patrick, Richard Coates & Peter McClure (eds.). 2016. *The Oxford Dictionary of Family Names in Britain and Ireland*. Oxford: Oxford University Press.

Harbert, Wayne. 2006. *The Germanic Languages*. Cambridge: Cambridge University Press.

Heine, Bernd, & Tania Kuteva. 2006. *The Changing Languages of Europe*. Oxford: Oxford University Press.

Higham, Nick (ed.). 2007. *The Britons in Anglo-Saxon England*. Woodbridge: Boydell.

Hogg, Richard. 2012. *An Introduction to Old English*. Edinburgh: Edinburgh University Press.

Hogg, Richard, & David Denison (eds.). 2006. *A History of the English Language*. Cambridge: Cambridge University Press.

Holman, Katherine. 2007. *The Northern Conquest: Vikings in Britain and Ireland*. Oxford: Signal Books.

Horrocks, Geoffrey. 1997. *Greek: a History of the Language and Its Speakers*. London: Longman.

Hughes, Arthur, Peter Trudgill & Dominic Watt. 2012. *English Accents and Dialects: an Introduction to Social and Regional Varieties of English in the British Isles*, 5th ed. London: Edward Arnold.

Hughes, Geoffrey. 2000. *A History of English Words*. Oxford: Blackwell.

Kontra, Miklos, Robert Phillipson, Tove Skutnabb-Kangas & Tibor Varday. 1999. *Language – a Right and a Resource: Approaching Linguistic Human Rights*. Budapest: Akadémiai Nyomda.

Labov, William. 2009. *Dialect Diversity in America: the Politics of Language Change*. Charlottesville: University of Virginia Press.

Liberman, Anatoly. 2005. *Word Origins and How We Know Them: Etymology for Everyone*. Oxford: Oxford University Press, 2005.

Lust, Barbara. 2006. *Child Language: Acquisition and Growth*. Cambridge: Cambridge University Press.

Mallory, J. P. 2005. *In Search of the Indo-Europeans*. London: Thames & Hudson.

Matras, Yaron. 2002. *Romani: a Linguistic Introduction*. Cambridge: Cambridge University Press.

May, Stephen. 2012. *Language and Minority Rights: Ethnicity, Nationalism and the politics of language*. New York: Routledge.

Miller, D. Gary. 2012. *External Influences on English: From Its Beginnings to the Renaissance*. Oxford: Oxford University Press.

Mitchell, Bruce, & Fred Robinson. 2001. *A Guide to Old English*. Oxford: Blackwell.

Stockwell, Robert, & Donka Minkova. 2001. *English Words: History and Structure*. Cambridge: Cambridge University Press.

Townend, Matthew. 2002. *Language and History in Viking Age England: Linguistic Relations between Speakers of Old Norse and Old English*. Turnhout: Brepols.

Trudgill, Peter. 1999. *The Dialects of England*. Oxford: Blackwell,

Trudgill, Peter. 2004. *Dialects*, 2nd ed. London: Routledge.

Trudgill, Peter. 2016. *Dialect Matters: Respecting Vernacular Language*. Cambridge: Cambridge University Press.

Trudgill, Peter, & Jean Hannah. 2017. *International English: a Guide to Varieties of Standard English*, 6th ed. London: Edward Arnold.

Watson, Moray, & Michelle Macleod. 2010. *The Edinburgh Companion to the Gaelic Language*. Edinburgh: Edinburgh University Press.

Woodard, Roger (ed.). 2008. *The Ancient Languages of Europe*. Cambridge: Cambridge University Press.

Index

2 1982 03151 1060

CPSIA information can be obtained
at www.ICGtesting.com
Printed in the USA
LVHW050253080322
712833LV00015B/2323

9 781108 965927